BLADE OF THE IMMORTAL

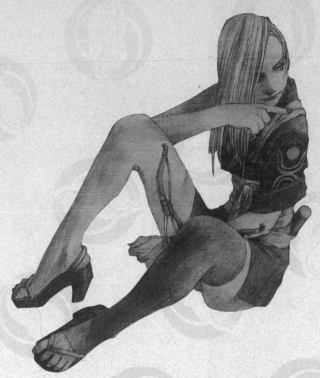

Beasts

publisher
Mike Richardson

series editor
Tim Ervin-Gore

collection editor
Chris Warner

collection designer
Debra Bailey

art director
Mark Cox

**English-language version produced by Studio
Proteus for Dark Horse Comics, Inc.**

BLADE OF THE IMMORTAL VOL. 11: BEASTS

This volume collects issues sixty-six through
seventy-two of the Dark Horse comic-book series,
Blade of the Immortal.

Published by
Dark Horse Comics, Inc.
10956 SE Main Street
Milwaukie, OR 97222

www.darkhorse.com

To find a comics shop in your area, call the
Comic Shop Locator Service toll-free at 1-888-266-4226.

First edition: December 2002
ISBN: 1-56971-741-9

1 3 5 7 9 10 8 6 4 2

Printed in Canada

art and story
HIROAKI SAMURA

translation
Dana Lewis & Toren Smith

lettering and retouch
Tomoko Saito

Beasts

DARK HORSE COMICS®

ABOUT THE TRANSLATION

The Swastika

The main character in *Blade of the Immortal*, Manji, has taken the "crux gammata" as both his name and his personal symbol. This symbol is also known as the *swastika*, a name derived from the Sanskrit *svastika* (meaning "welfare," from *su* — "well" + *asti* "he is"). As a symbol of prosperity and good fortune, the swastika was widely used throughout the ancient world (for example, appearing often on Mesopotamian coinage), including North and South America and has been used in Japan as a symbol of Buddhism since ancient times. To be precise, the symbol generally used by Japanese Buddhists is the *sauvastika*, which moves in a counterclockwise direction and is called the *manji* in Japanese. The arms of the *swastika*, which point in a clockwise direction, are generally considered a solar symbol. It was this version (the *hakenkreuz*) that was perverted by the Nazis. The *sauvastika* generally stands for night, and often for magical practices. It is important that readers understand that the swastika has ancient and honorable origins, and it is those that apply to this story, which takes place in the 18th century [ca. 1782–3]. *There is no anti-Semitic or pro-Nazi meaning behind the use of the symbol in this story. Those meanings did not exist until after 1910.*

The Artwork

The creator of *Blade of the Immortal* requested that we make an effort to avoid mirror-imaging his artwork. Normally, Westernized manga are first copied in a mirror-image in order to facilitate the left-to-right reading of the pages. However, Mr. Samura decided that he would rather see his pages reversed via the technique of cutting up the panels and re-pasting them in reverse order. While we feel that this often leads to problems in panel-to-panel continuity, we place primary importance on the wishes of the creator. Therefore, most of *Blade of the Immortal* has been produced using the "cut and paste" technique. There are, of course, some sequences where it was impossible to do this, and mirror-imaged panels or pages were used.

The Sound Effects & Dialogue

Since some of Mr. Samura's sound effects are integral parts of the illustrations, we decided to leave those in their original Japanese. We hope readers will view the unretouched sound effects as essential portions of Mr. Samura's extraordinary artwork. In addition, Mr. Samura's treatment of dialogue is quite different from that featured in typical samurai manga and is considered to be one of the features that has made *Blade* such a hit in Japan. Mr. Samura has mixed a variety of linguistic styles in this fantasy story, with some characters speaking in the mannered style of old Japan while others speak as if they were street-corner punks from a bad area of modern-day Tokyo. The anachronistic slang used by some of the characters in the English translation reflects the unusual mix of speech patterns from the original Japanese text.

GLOSSARY

Ittō-ryū: the radical sword school of Anotsu Kagehisa

kawara-ban: an early form of news tabloid. Roughly printed on wood blocks, these cheap scandal sheets were popular among Edo's working class.

kenshi: a swordsman (or swordswoman), not necessarily born into the samurai caste

mon: a small coin

Mugai-ryū: sword school of the Akagi assassins; literally, "without form"

Nakasendō: one of the five main thoroughfares connecting Edo to the provinces. The Nakasendo was the inland route to Kyoto, while the more famous Tokkaido followed the coast.

rashamen: a Japanese woman who slept with foreign men, a contemptuous term from the first days of contact between Japan and the West. By the time of this story, almost all such contact was limited to the port town of Nagasaki in southern Japan.

ryō: a gold piece

sekisho: checkpoint regulating travel from Edo to other *han* (feudal domains). All travelers had to submit papers at official checkpoints along the main highways in and out of Edo.

tegata (tsuko tegata): official travel pass for transiting *sekisho*

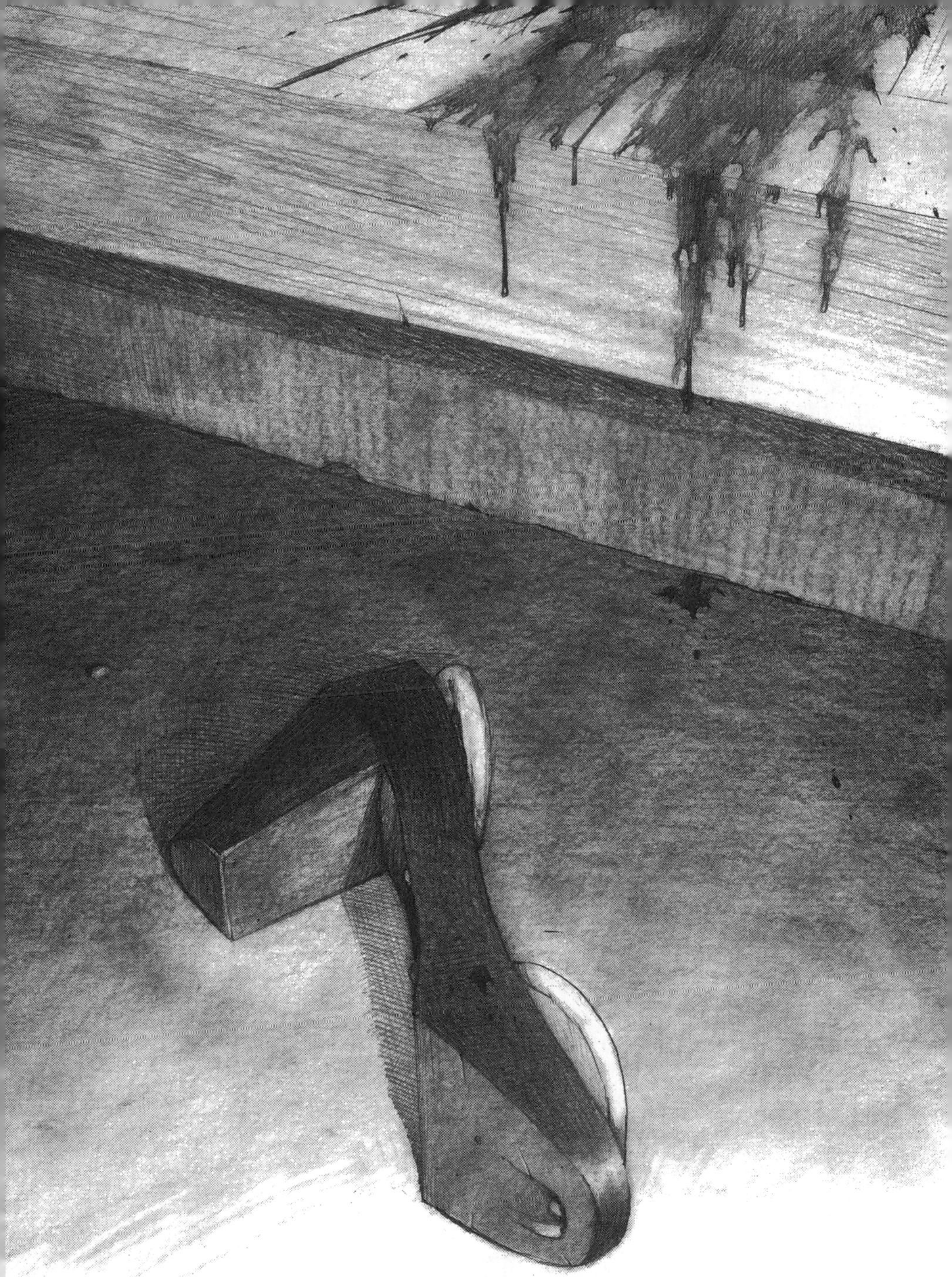

BEASTS
Part 1

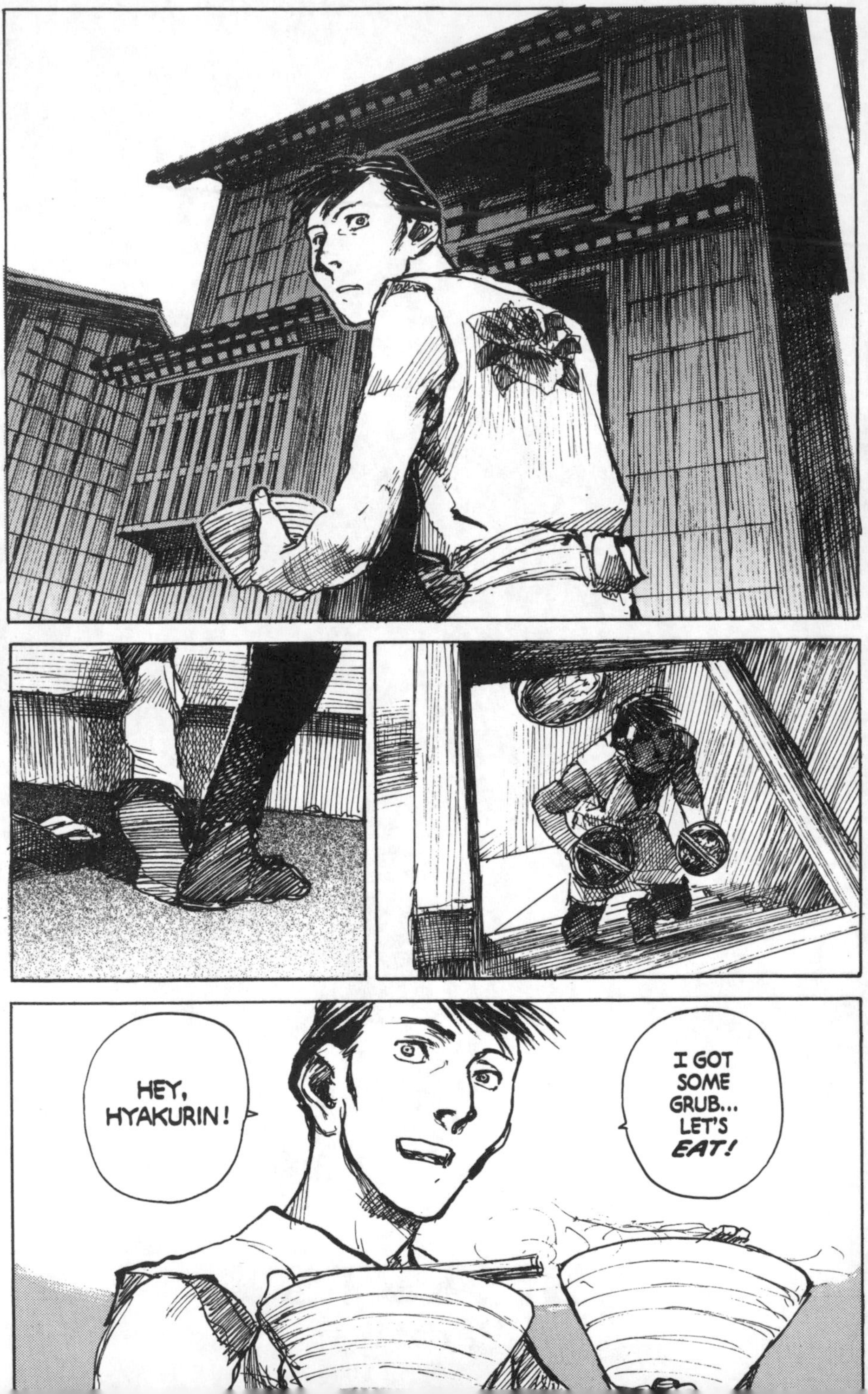
I GOT SOME GRUB... LET'S *EAT!*
HEY, HYAKURIN!

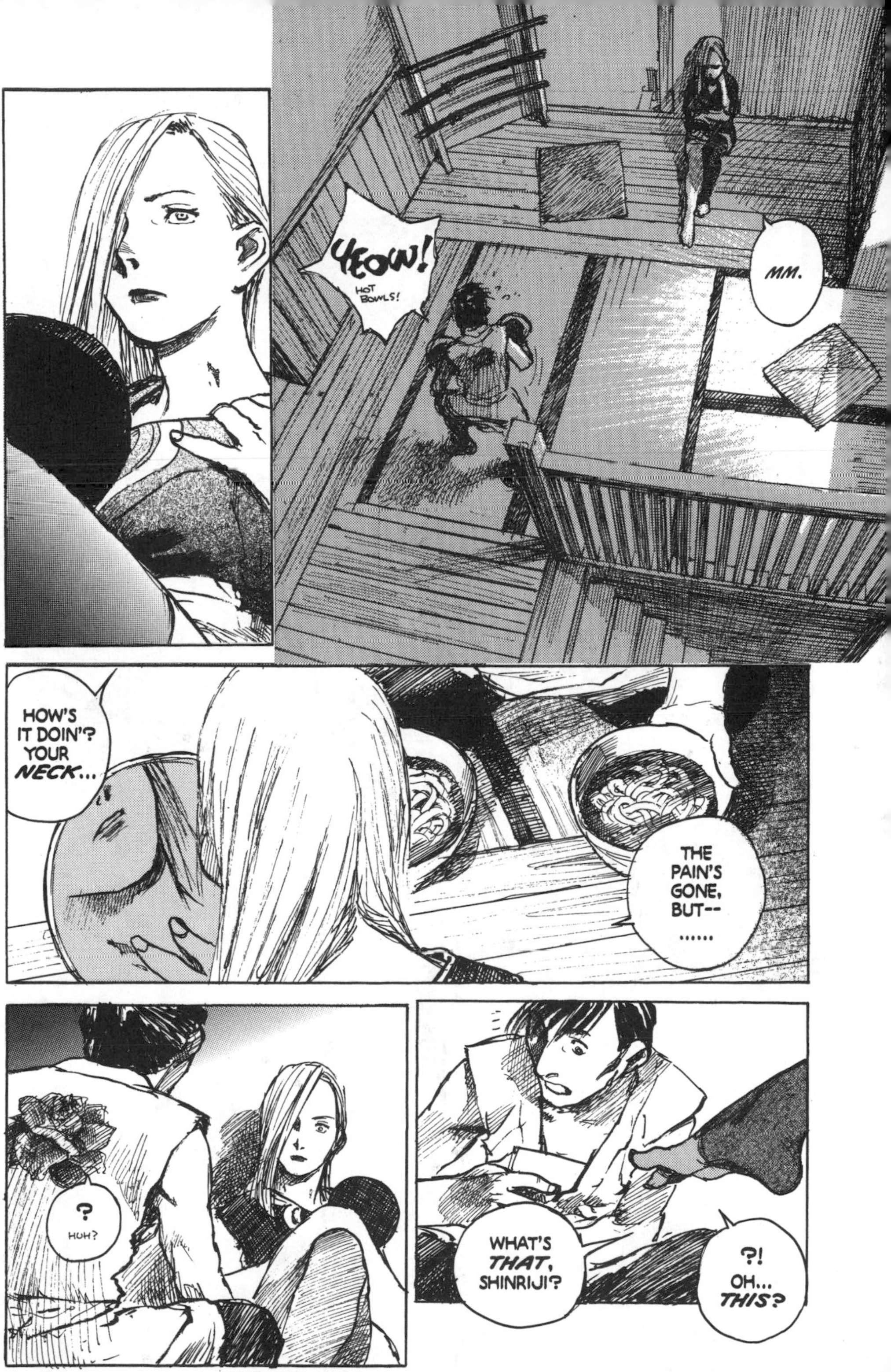
MM.
YEOW!
HOT BOWLS!
HOW'S IT DOIN'? YOUR NECK...
THE PAIN'S GONE, BUT-- ......
WHAT'S THAT, SHINRIJI?
?! OH... THIS?
?
HUH?

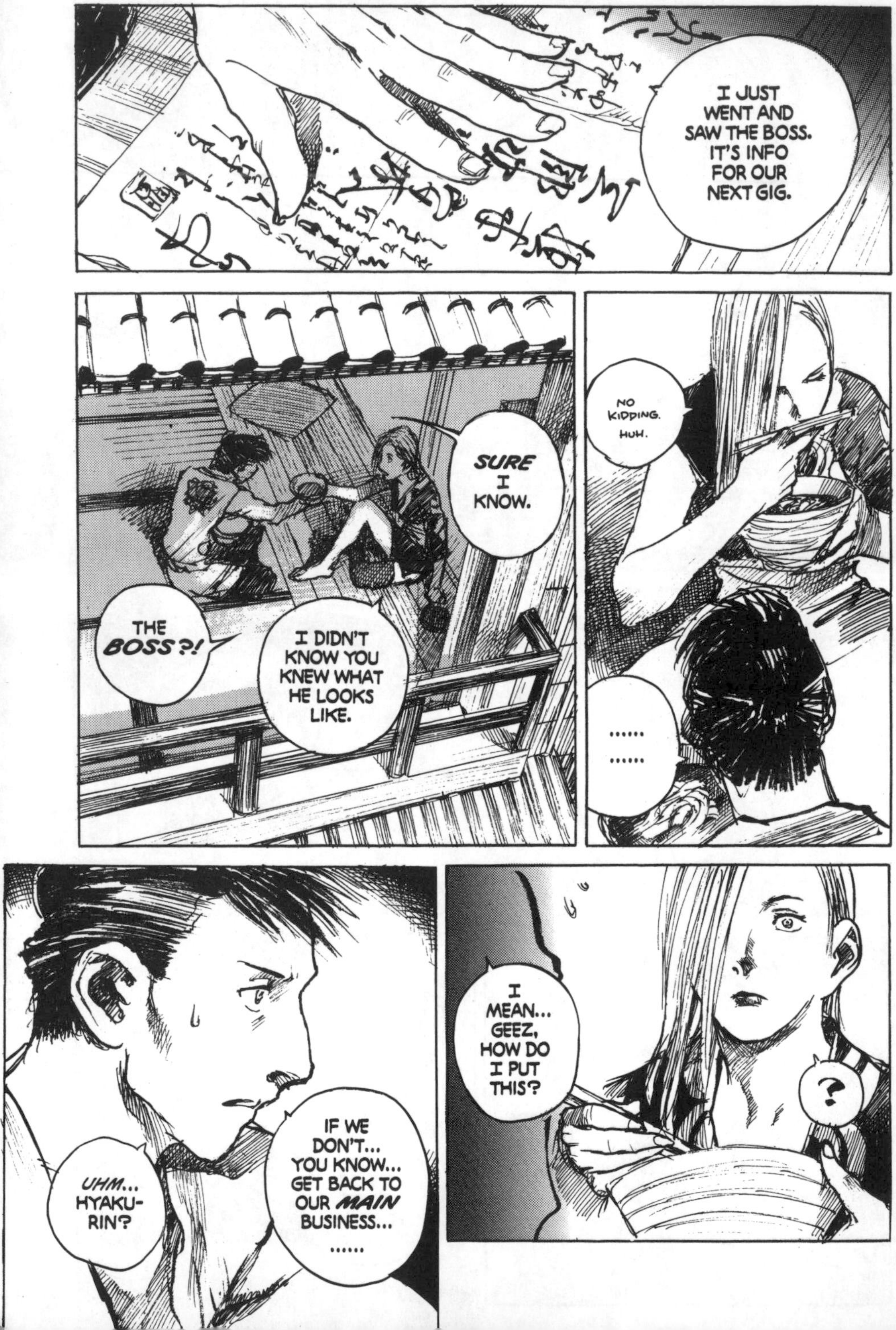
I JUST WENT AND SAW THE BOSS. IT'S INFO FOR OUR NEXT GIG.
NO KIDDING. HUH.
....
THE *BOSS*?!
I DIDN'T KNOW YOU KNEW WHAT HE LOOKS LIKE.
SURE I KNOW.
I MEAN... GEEZ, HOW DO I PUT THIS?
?
UHM... HYAKU-RIN?
IF WE DON'T... YOU KNOW... GET BACK TO OUR *MAIN* BUSINESS... ......

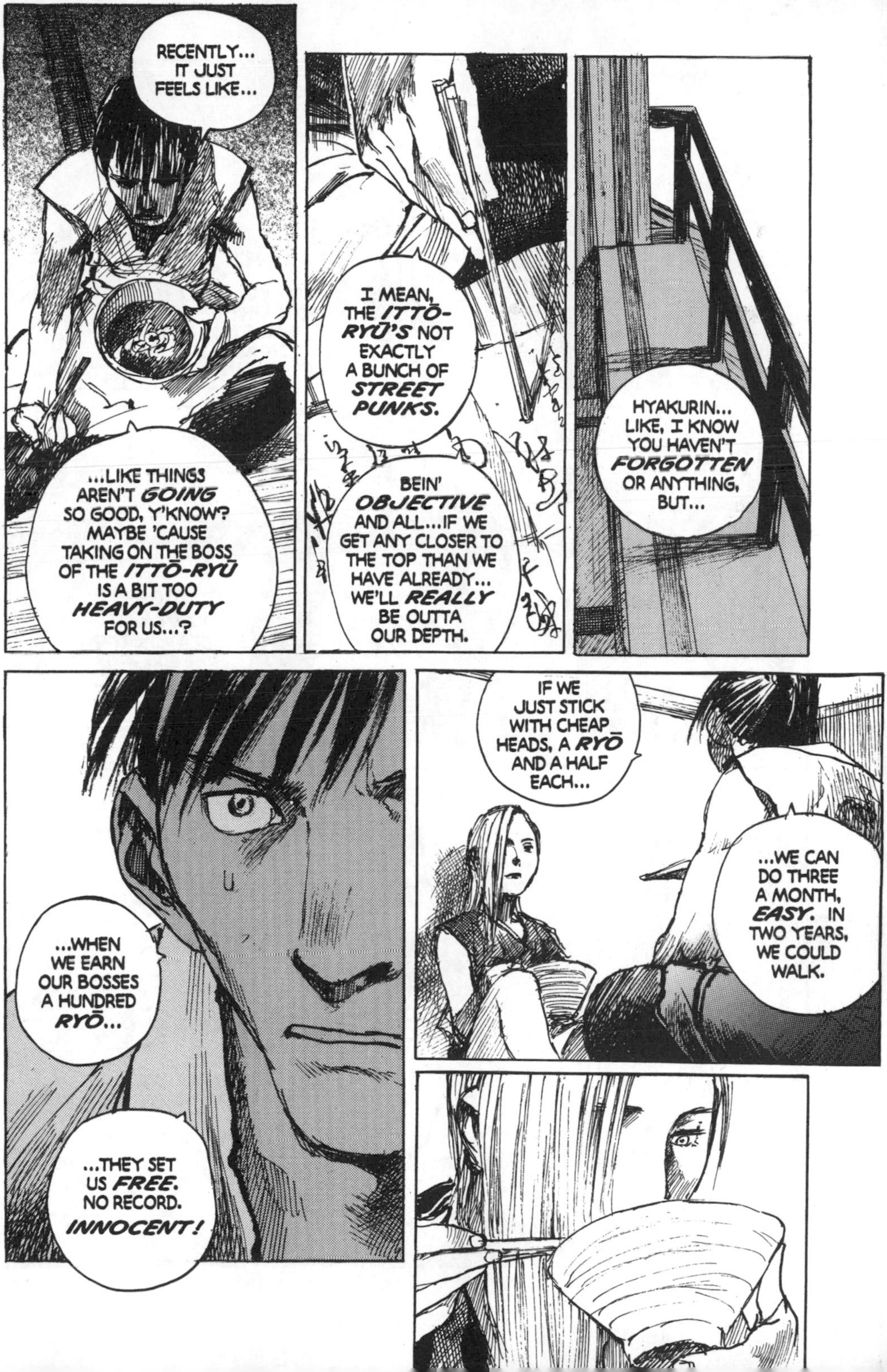
RECENTLY... IT JUST FEELS LIKE...
...LIKE THINGS AREN'T GOING SO GOOD, Y'KNOW? MAYBE 'CAUSE TAKING ON THE BOSS OF THE ITTŌ-RYŪ IS A BIT TOO HEAVY-DUTY FOR US...?
I MEAN, THE ITTŌ-RYŪ'S NOT EXACTLY A BUNCH OF STREET PUNKS.
BEIN' OBJECTIVE AND ALL...IF WE GET ANY CLOSER TO THE TOP THAN WE HAVE ALREADY... WE'LL REALLY BE OUTTA OUR DEPTH.
HYAKURIN... LIKE, I KNOW YOU HAVEN'T FORGOTTEN OR ANYTHING, BUT...
...WHEN WE EARN OUR BOSSES A HUNDRED RYŌ...
...THEY SET US FREE. NO RECORD. INNOCENT!
IF WE JUST STICK WITH CHEAP HEADS, A RYŌ AND A HALF EACH...
...WE CAN DO THREE A MONTH, EASY. IN TWO YEARS, WE COULD WALK.

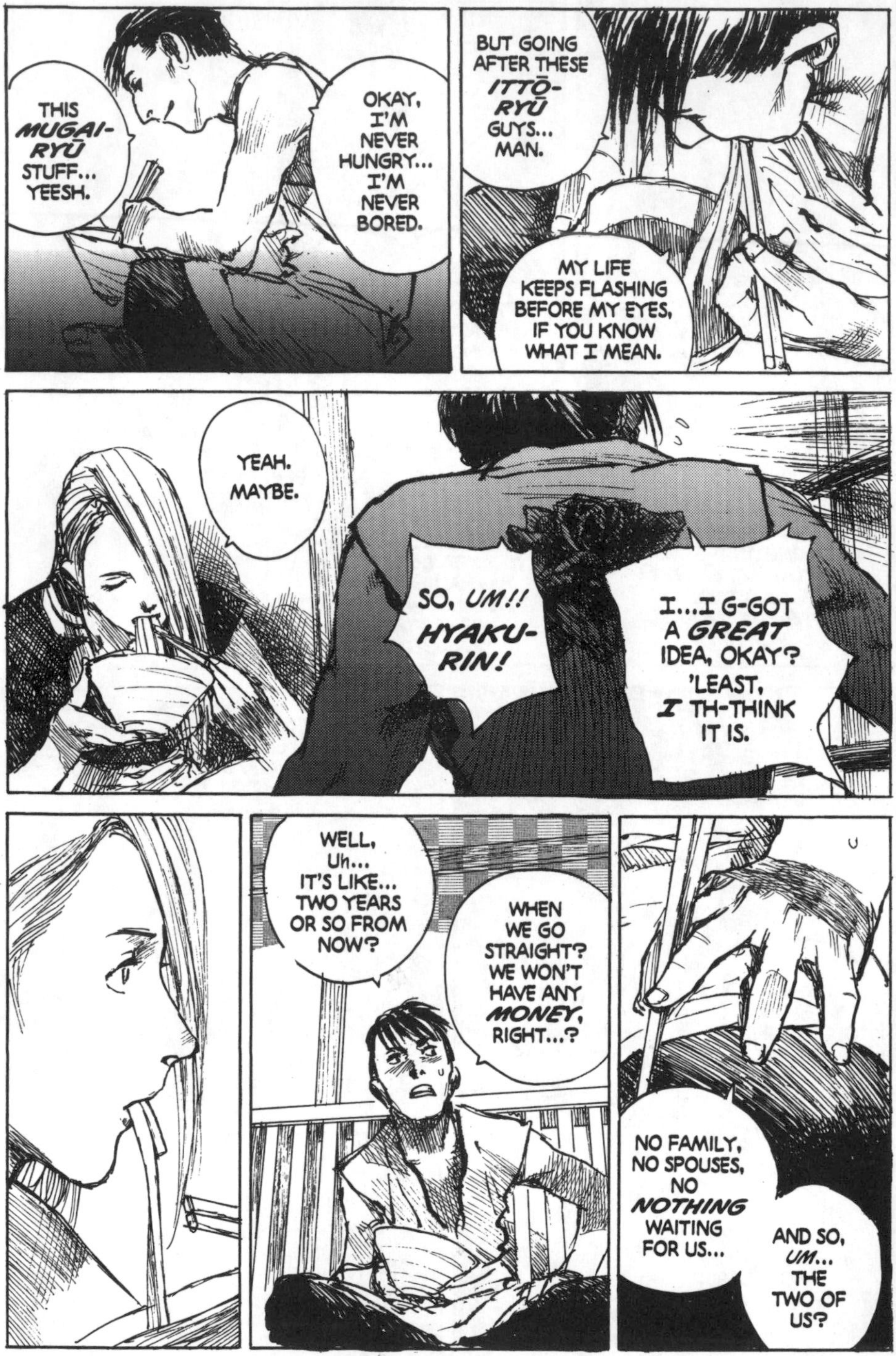
THIS MUGAI-RYŪ STUFF... YEESH.
OKAY, I'M NEVER HUNGRY... I'M NEVER BORED.
BUT GOING AFTER THESE ITTŌ-RYŪ GUYS... MAN.
MY LIFE KEEPS FLASHING BEFORE MY EYES, IF YOU KNOW WHAT I MEAN.
YEAH. MAYBE.
SO, UM!! HYAKU-RIN!
I...I G-GOT A GREAT IDEA, OKAY? 'LEAST, I TH-THINK IT IS.
WELL, Uh... IT'S LIKE... TWO YEARS OR SO FROM NOW?
WHEN WE GO STRAIGHT? WE WON'T HAVE ANY MONEY, RIGHT...?
NO FAMILY, NO SPOUSES, NO NOTHING WAITING FOR US...
AND SO, UM... THE TWO OF US?

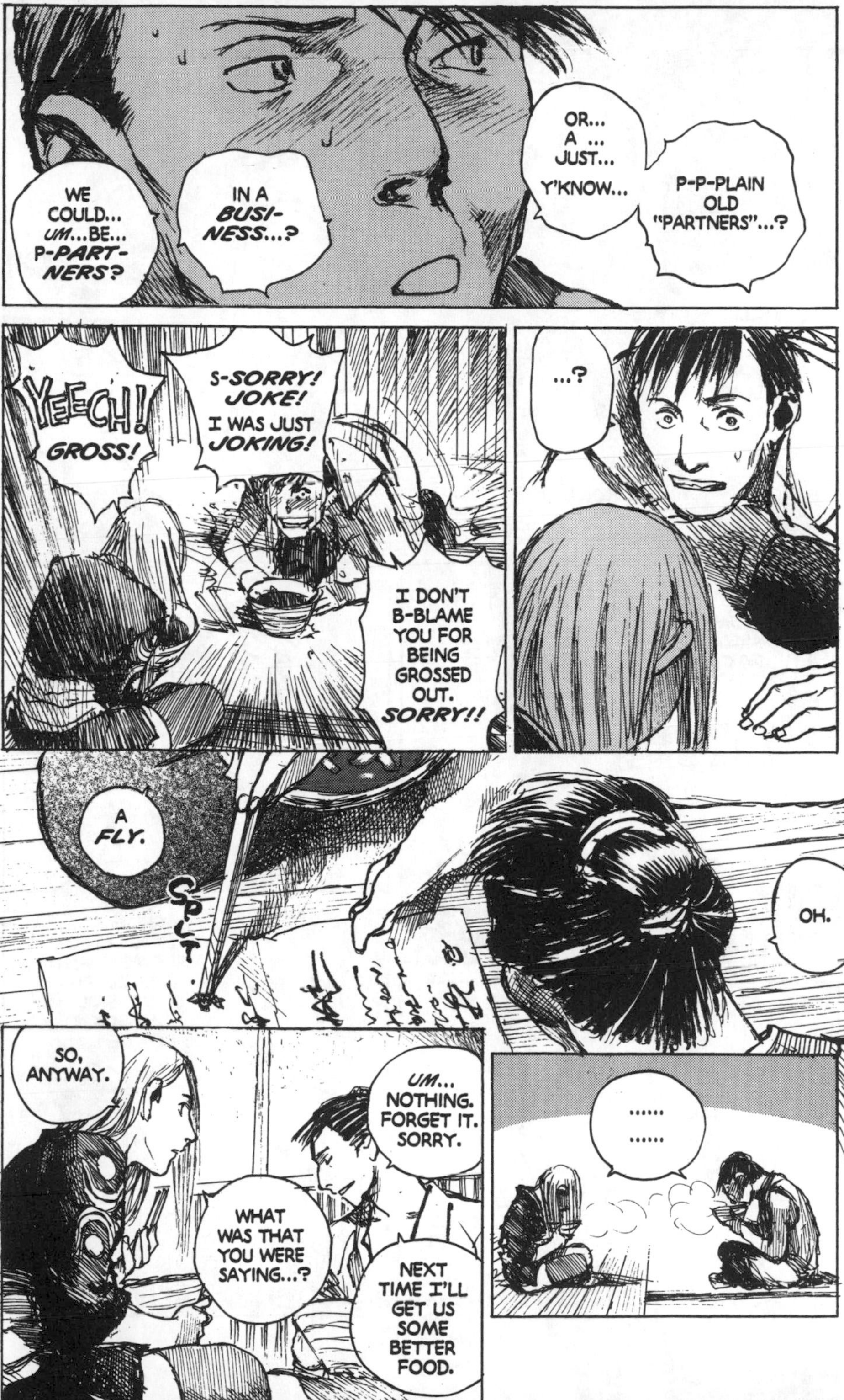
WE COULD... UM...BE... P-PARTNERS?
IN A BUSINESS...?
OR... A ... JUST... Y'KNOW...
P-P-PLAIN OLD "PARTNERS"...?
YEECH! GROSS!
S-SORRY! JOKE! I WAS JUST JOKING!
I DON'T B-BLAME YOU FOR BEING GROSSED OUT. SORRY!!
...?
A FLY.
SPLT
OH.
SO, ANYWAY.
WHAT WAS THAT YOU WERE SAYING...?
UM... NOTHING. FORGET IT. SORRY.
NEXT TIME I'LL GET US SOME BETTER FOOD.
......
......

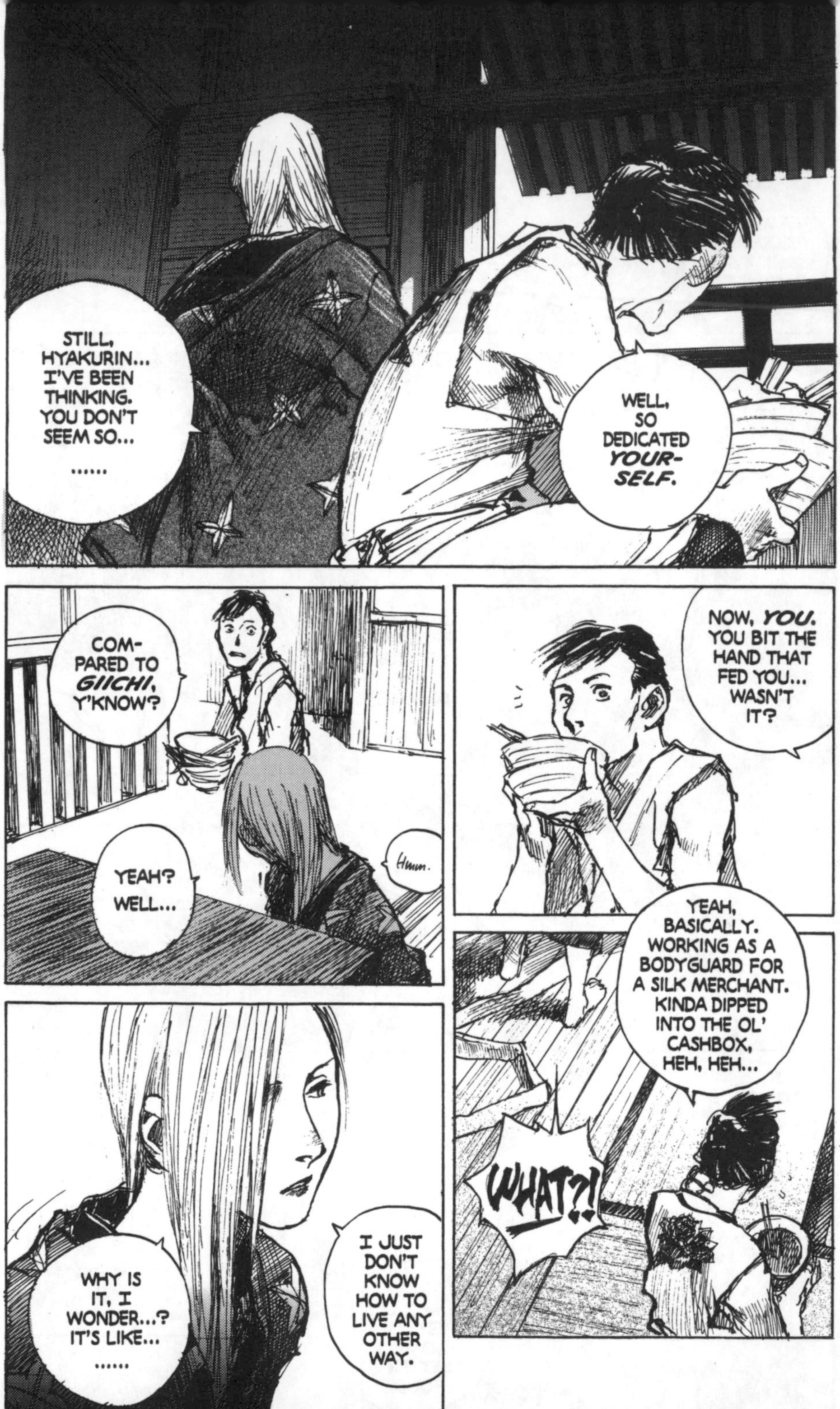
STILL, HYAKURIN... I'VE BEEN THINKING. YOU DON'T SEEM SO... ......
WELL, SO DEDICATED *YOURSELF*.
COMPARED TO *GIICHI*, Y'KNOW?
YEAH? WELL...
Hmm.
WHY IS IT, I WONDER...? IT'S LIKE... ......
I JUST DON'T KNOW HOW TO LIVE ANY OTHER WAY.
NOW, *YOU*. YOU BIT THE HAND THAT FED YOU... WASN'T IT?
YEAH, BASICALLY. WORKING AS A BODYGUARD FOR A SILK MERCHANT. KINDA DIPPED INTO THE OL' CASHBOX, HEH, HEH...
WHAT?!

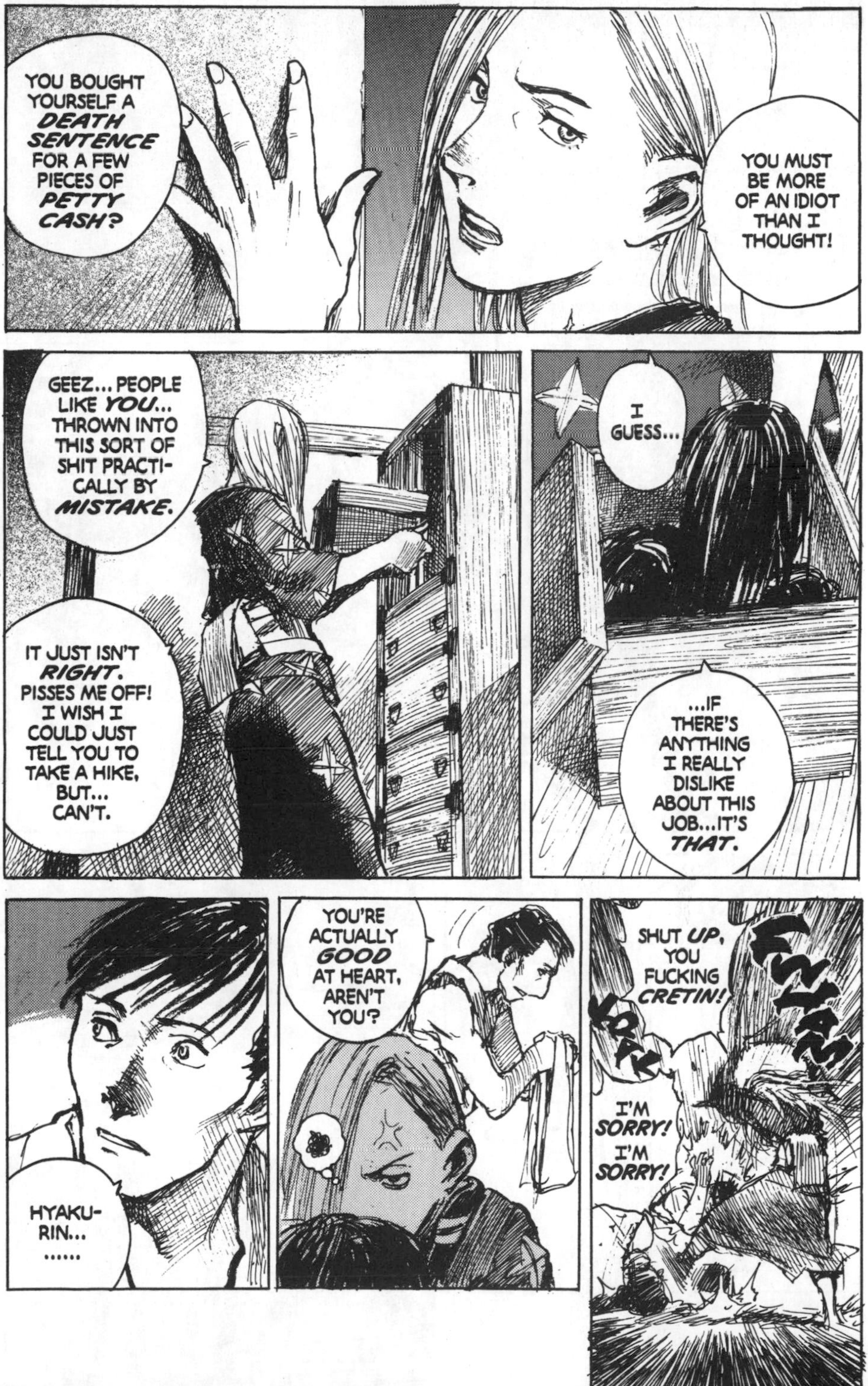

YOU BOUGHT YOURSELF A *DEATH SENTENCE* FOR A FEW PIECES OF *PETTY CASH?*
YOU MUST BE MORE OF AN IDIOT THAN I THOUGHT!
GEEZ... PEOPLE LIKE *YOU*... THROWN INTO THIS SORT OF SHIT PRACTI-CALLY BY *MISTAKE*.
IT JUST ISN'T *RIGHT*. PISSES ME OFF! I WISH I COULD JUST TELL YOU TO TAKE A HIKE, BUT... CAN'T.
I GUESS...
...IF THERE'S ANYTHING I REALLY DISLIKE ABOUT THIS JOB...IT'S *THAT*.
HYAKU-RIN... ......
YOU'RE ACTUALLY *GOOD* AT HEART, AREN'T YOU?
SHUT *UP*, YOU FUCKING *CRETIN!*
I'M *SORRY!* I'M *SORRY!*

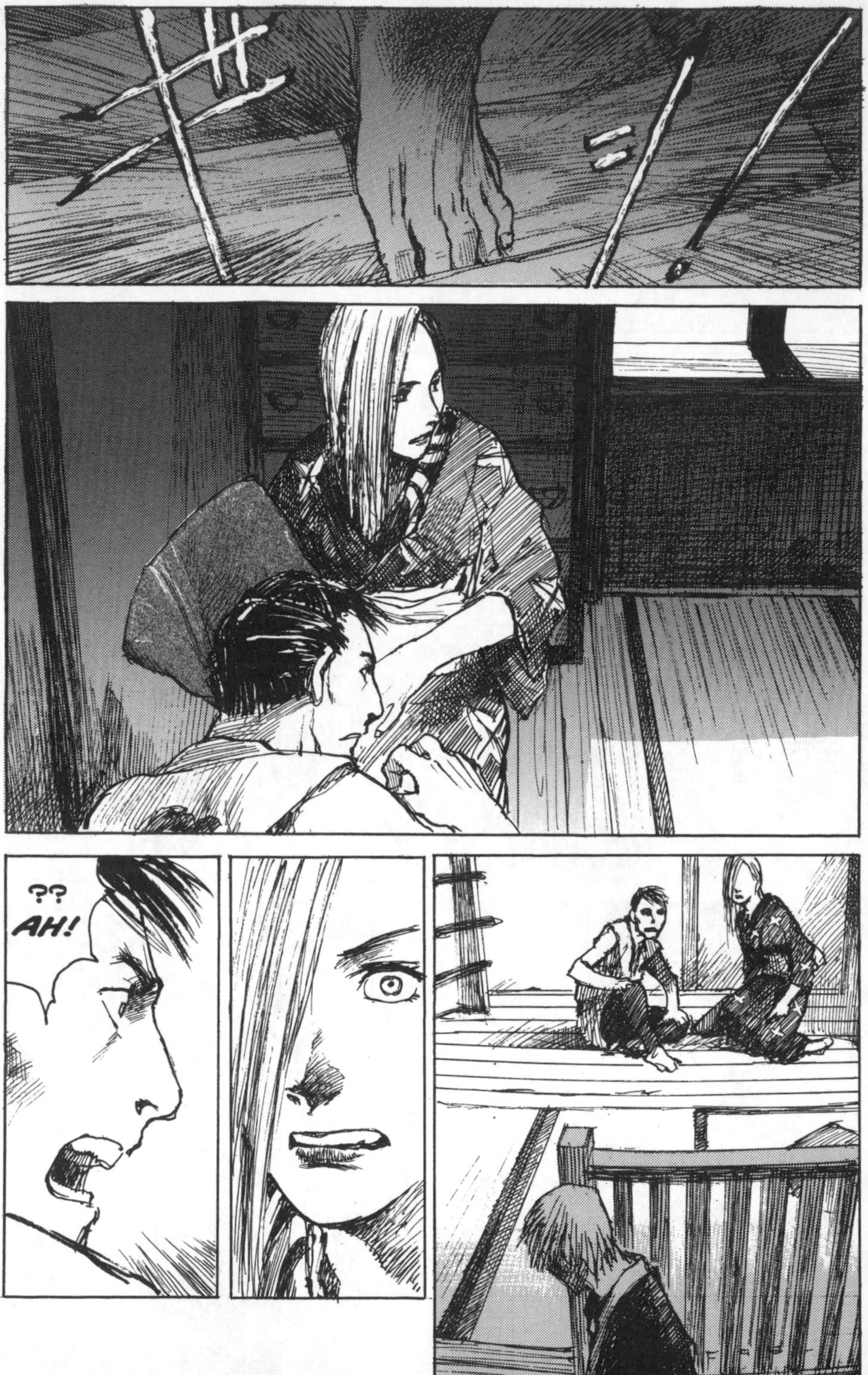
??
AH!

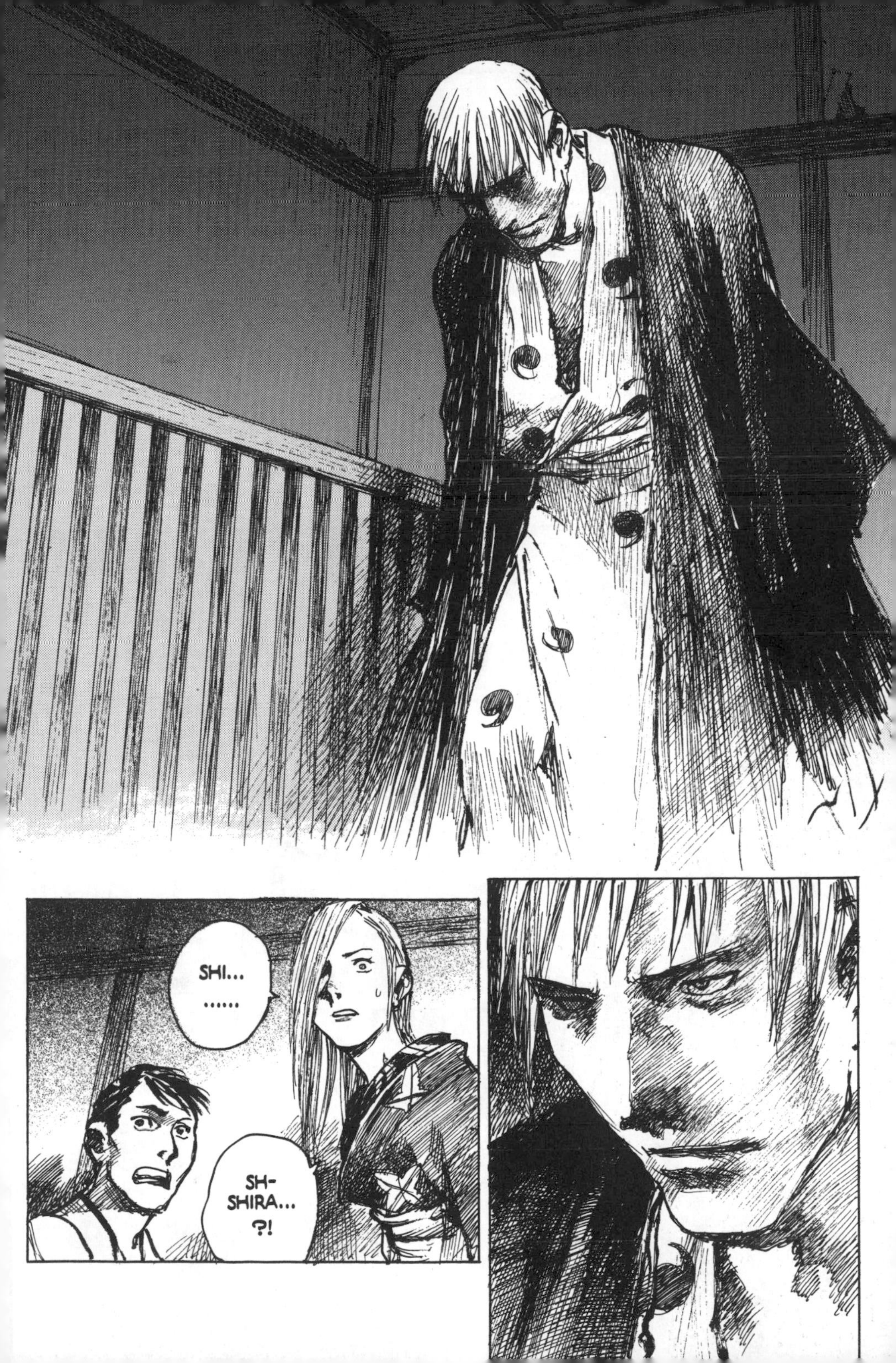
SHI...
......
SH-
SHIRA...
?!

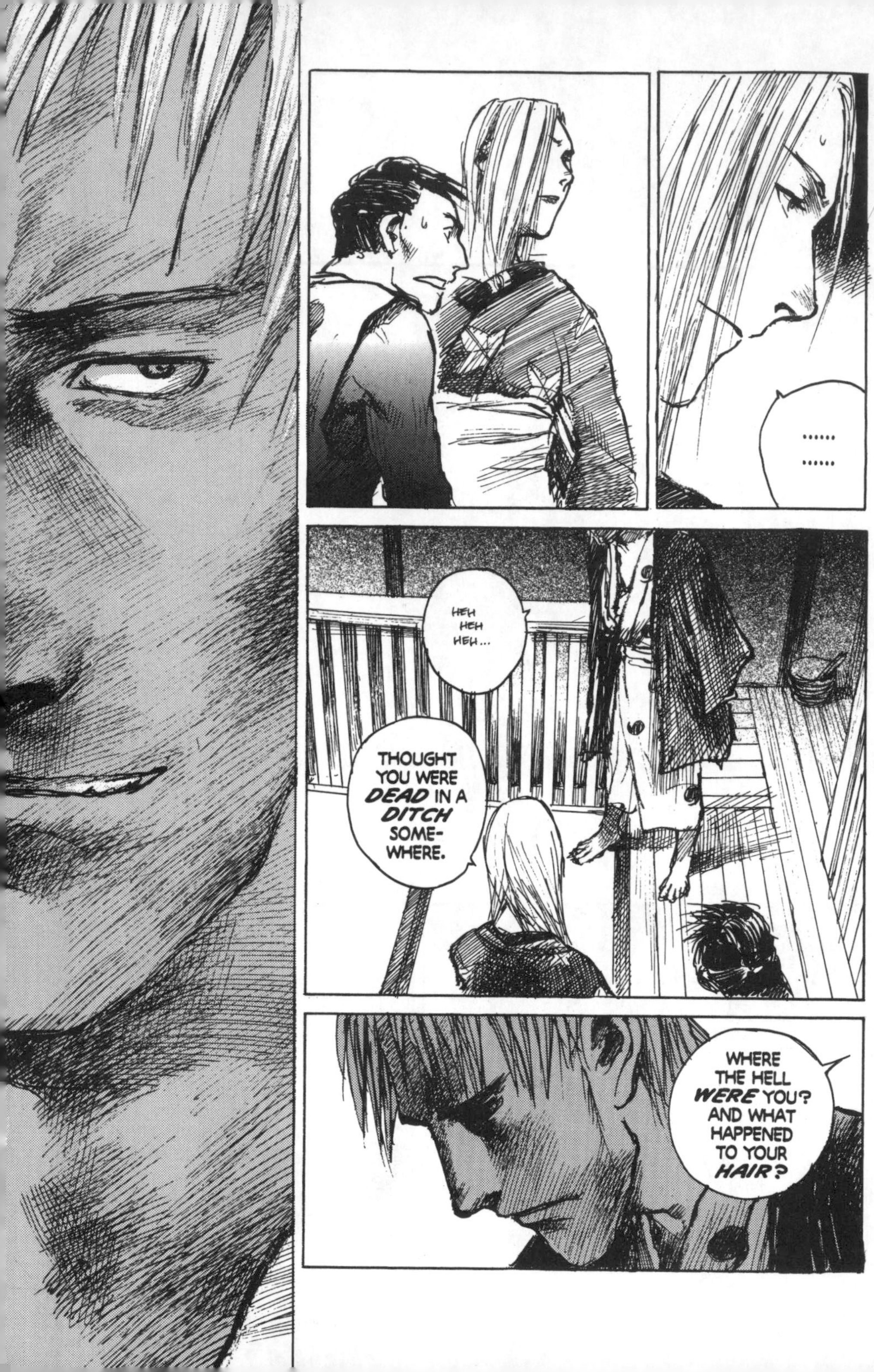

......
......
HEH HEH HEH...
THOUGHT YOU WERE DEAD IN A DITCH SOME-WHERE.
WHERE THE HELL WERE YOU? AND WHAT HAPPENED TO YOUR HAIR?

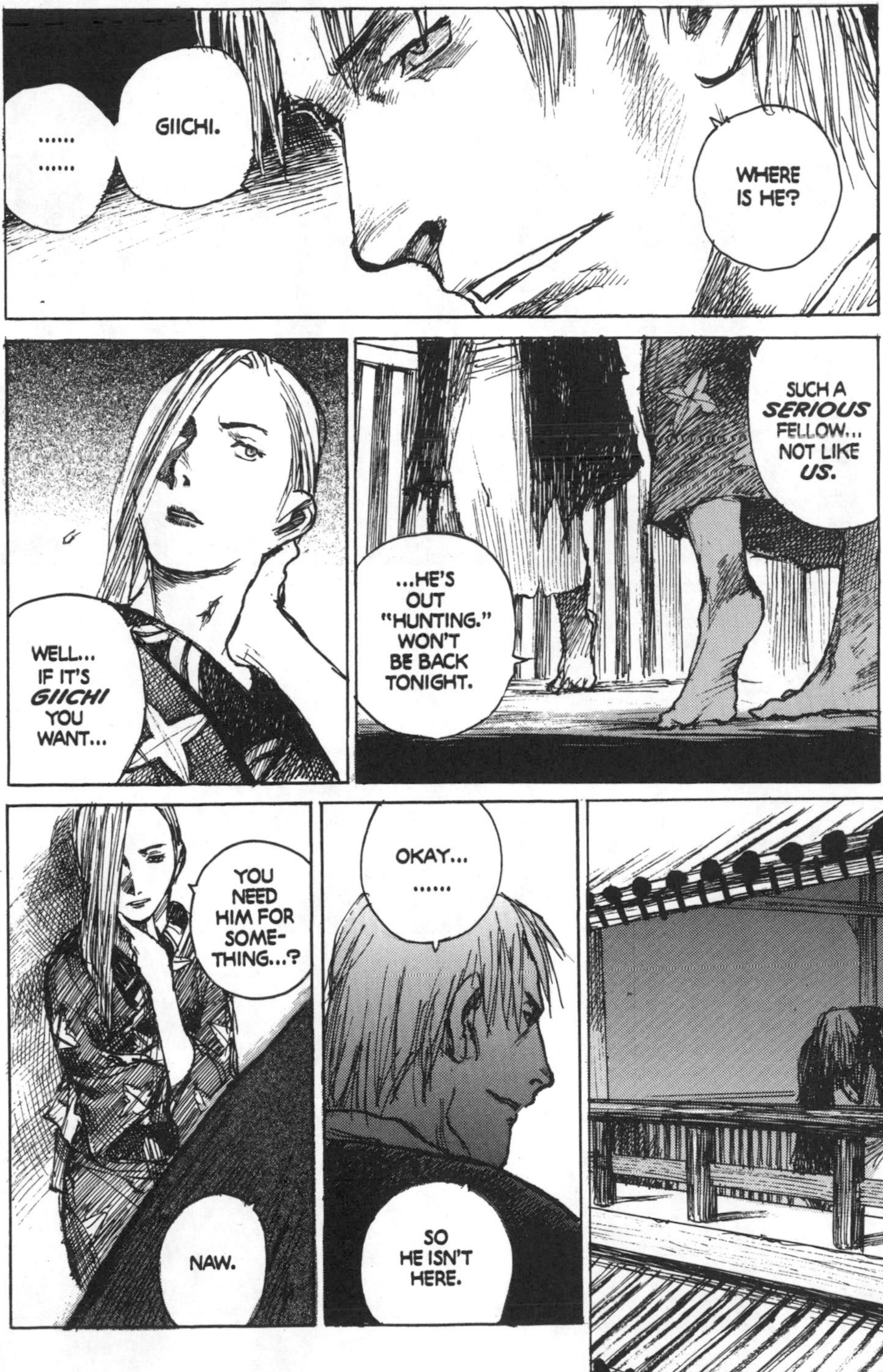

....
GIICHI.
WHERE IS HE?
WELL... IF IT'S GIICHI YOU WANT...
...HE'S OUT "HUNTING." WON'T BE BACK TONIGHT.
SUCH A SERIOUS FELLOW... NOT LIKE US.
YOU NEED HIM FOR SOME-THING...?
NAW.
OKAY... ......
SO HE ISN'T HERE.

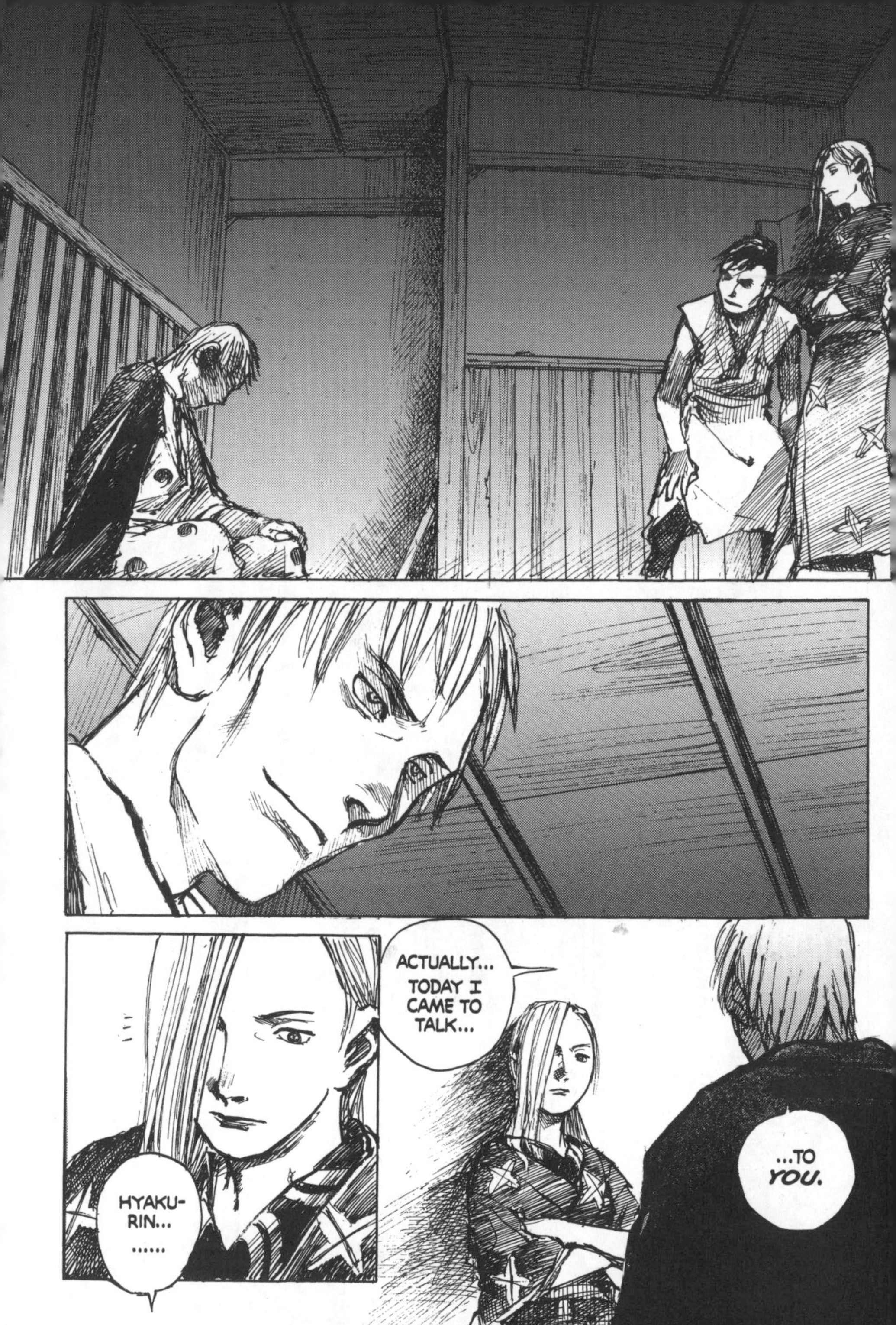
ACTUALLY... TODAY I CAME TO TALK...
...TO YOU.
HYAKU-RIN... ......

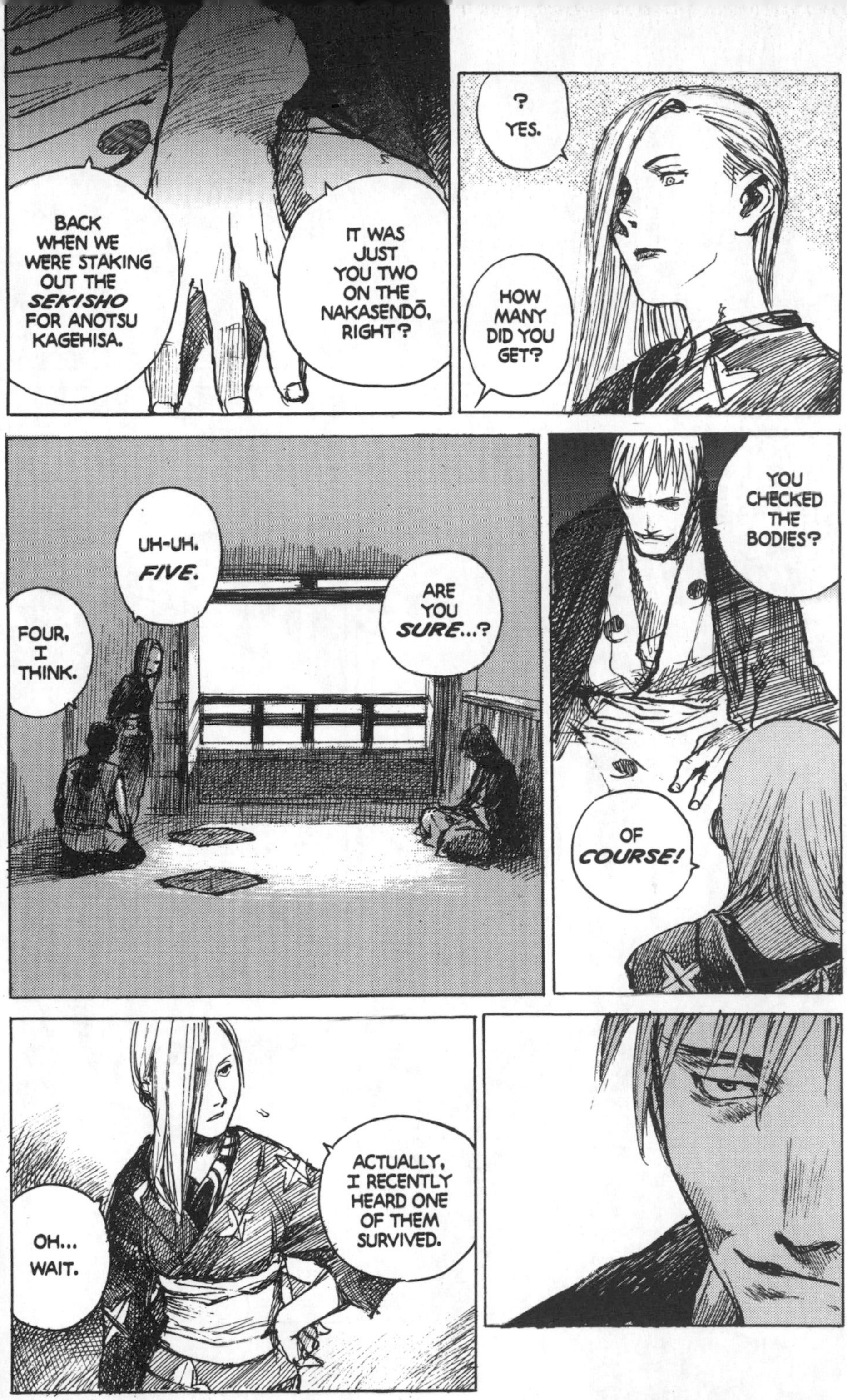
BACK WHEN WE WERE STAKING OUT THE *SEKISHO* FOR ANOTSU KAGEHISA.
IT WAS JUST YOU TWO ON THE NAKASENDŌ, RIGHT?
? YES.
HOW MANY DID YOU GET?
FOUR, I THINK.
UH-UH. *FIVE.*
ARE YOU *SURE*...?
YOU CHECKED THE BODIES?
OF *COURSE!*
OH... WAIT.
ACTUALLY, I RECENTLY HEARD ONE OF THEM SURVIVED.

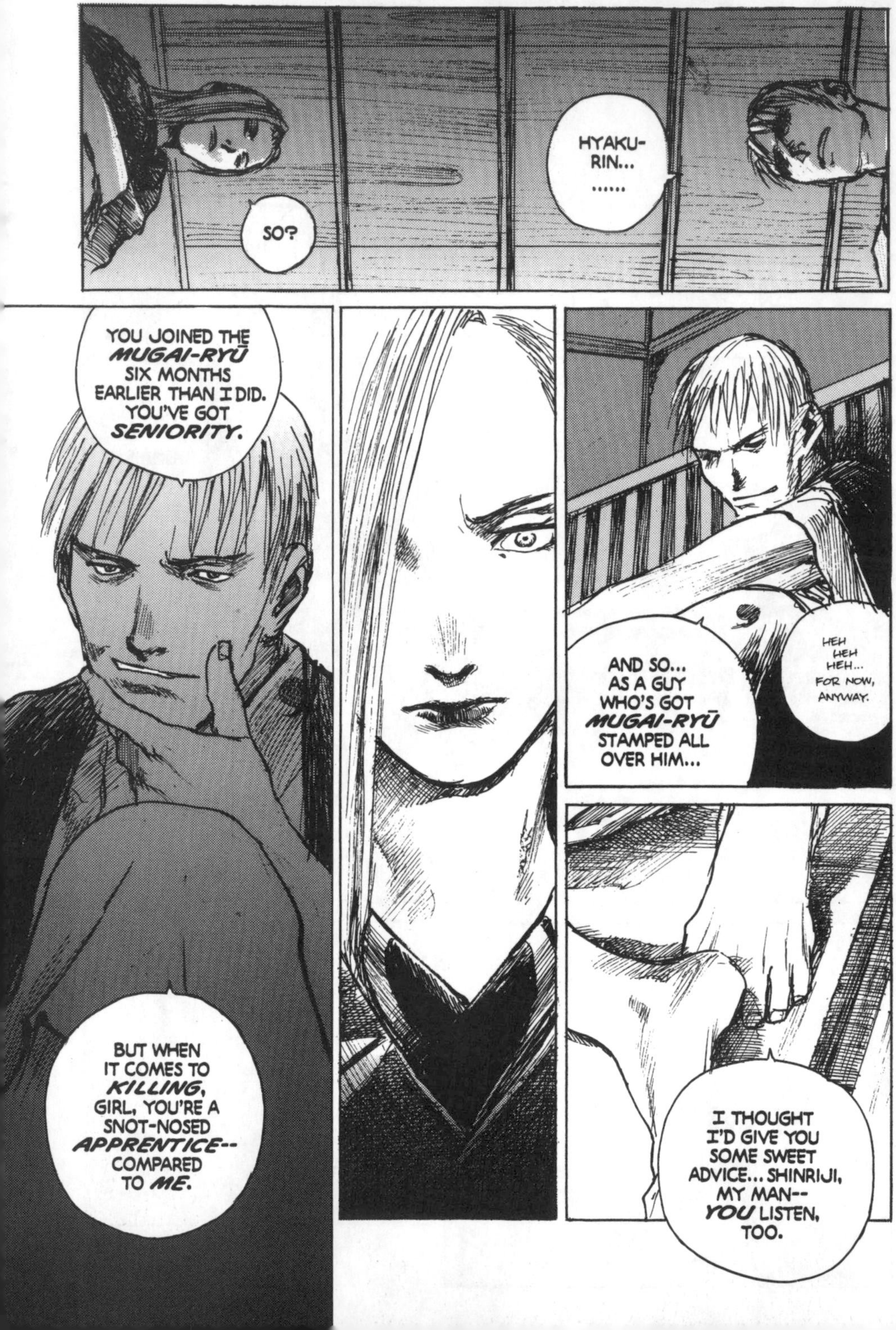
HYAKU-RIN... ......
SO?
HEH HEH HEH... FOR NOW, ANYWAY.
AND SO... AS A GUY WHO'S GOT MUGAI-RYŪ STAMPED ALL OVER HIM...
I THOUGHT I'D GIVE YOU SOME SWEET ADVICE... SHINRIJI, MY MAN-- YOU LISTEN, TOO.
YOU JOINED THE MUGAI-RYŪ SIX MONTHS EARLIER THAN I DID. YOU'VE GOT SENIORITY.
BUT WHEN IT COMES TO KILLING, GIRL, YOU'RE A SNOT-NOSED APPRENTICE-- COMPARED TO ME.

LETTING SOMEONE WHO'S SEEN YOUR FACE ESCAPE *ALIVE*...

...EVEN BY A *FLUKE*... WELL, *PROS* DON'T DO THAT.

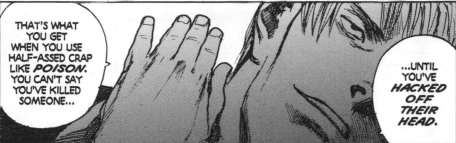

THAT'S WHAT YOU GET WHEN YOU USE HALF-ASSED CRAP LIKE *POISON*. YOU CAN'T SAY YOU'VE KILLED SOMEONE...

...UNTIL YOU'VE *HACKED OFF THEIR HEAD*.

WOUND A WILD *BEAST*, AND YOU'LL PAY FOR IT *LATER*.

IN *SPADES*, BLONDIE. *SPADES!*

THAT'S A LAUGH.

HAH...!

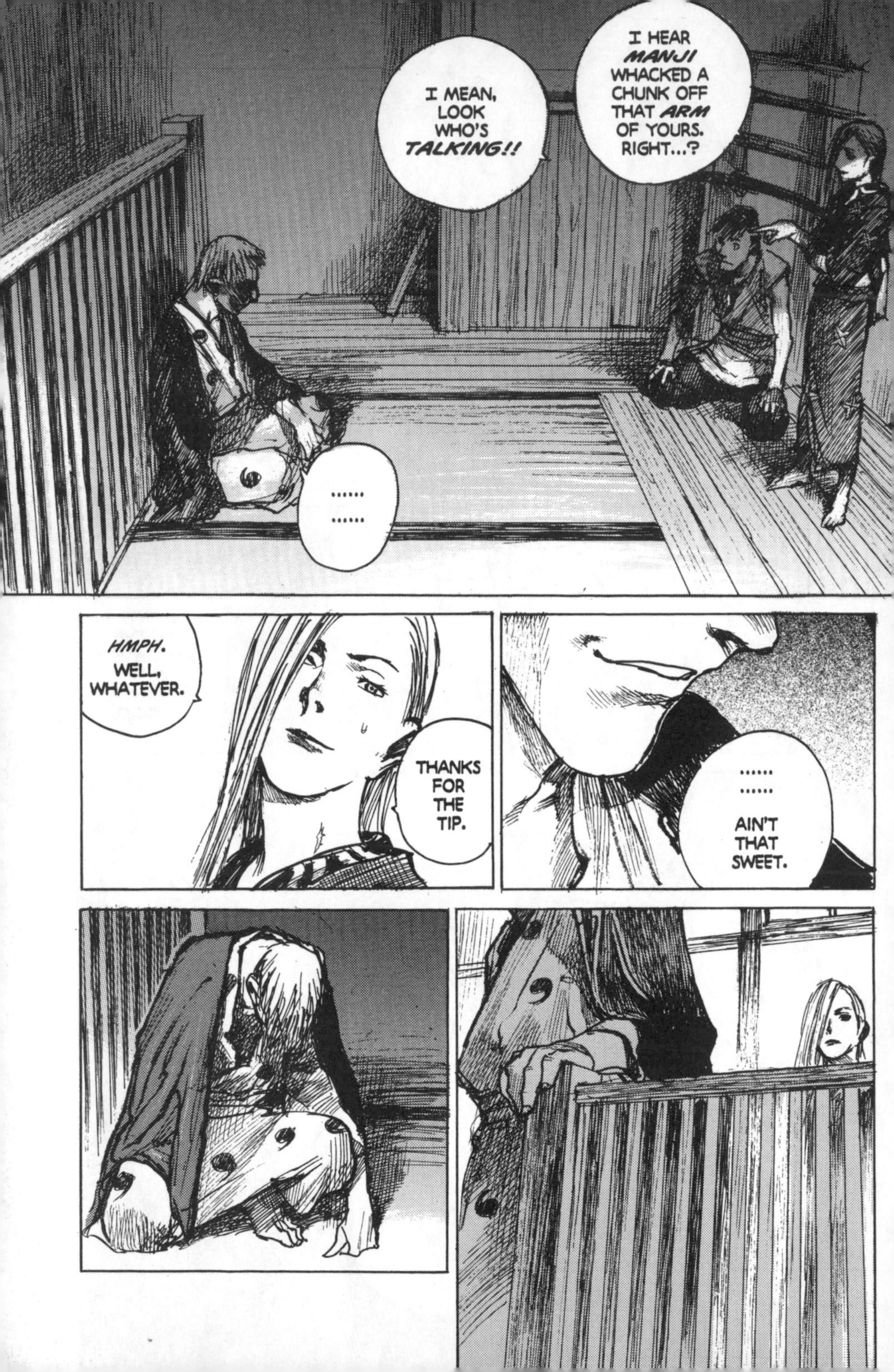
I HEAR MANJI WHACKED A CHUNK OFF THAT ARM OF YOURS. RIGHT...?
I MEAN, LOOK WHO'S TALKING!!
....
.... AIN'T THAT SWEET.
HMPH. WELL, WHATEVER.
THANKS FOR THE TIP.

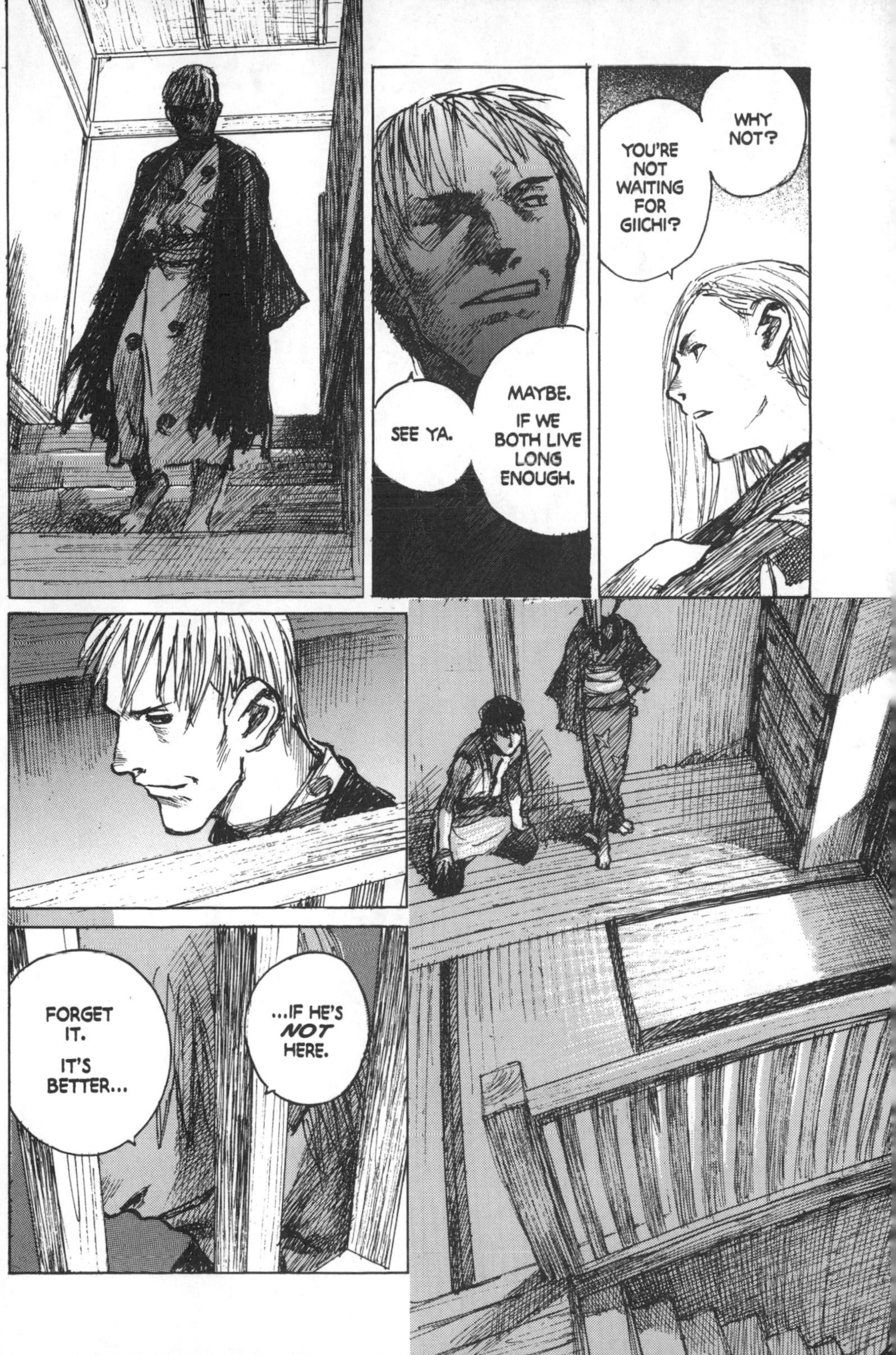
SEE YA.
MAYBE. IF WE BOTH LIVE LONG ENOUGH.
YOU'RE NOT WAITING FOR GIICHI?
WHY NOT?
FORGET IT. IT'S BETTER...
...IF HE'S *NOT* HERE.

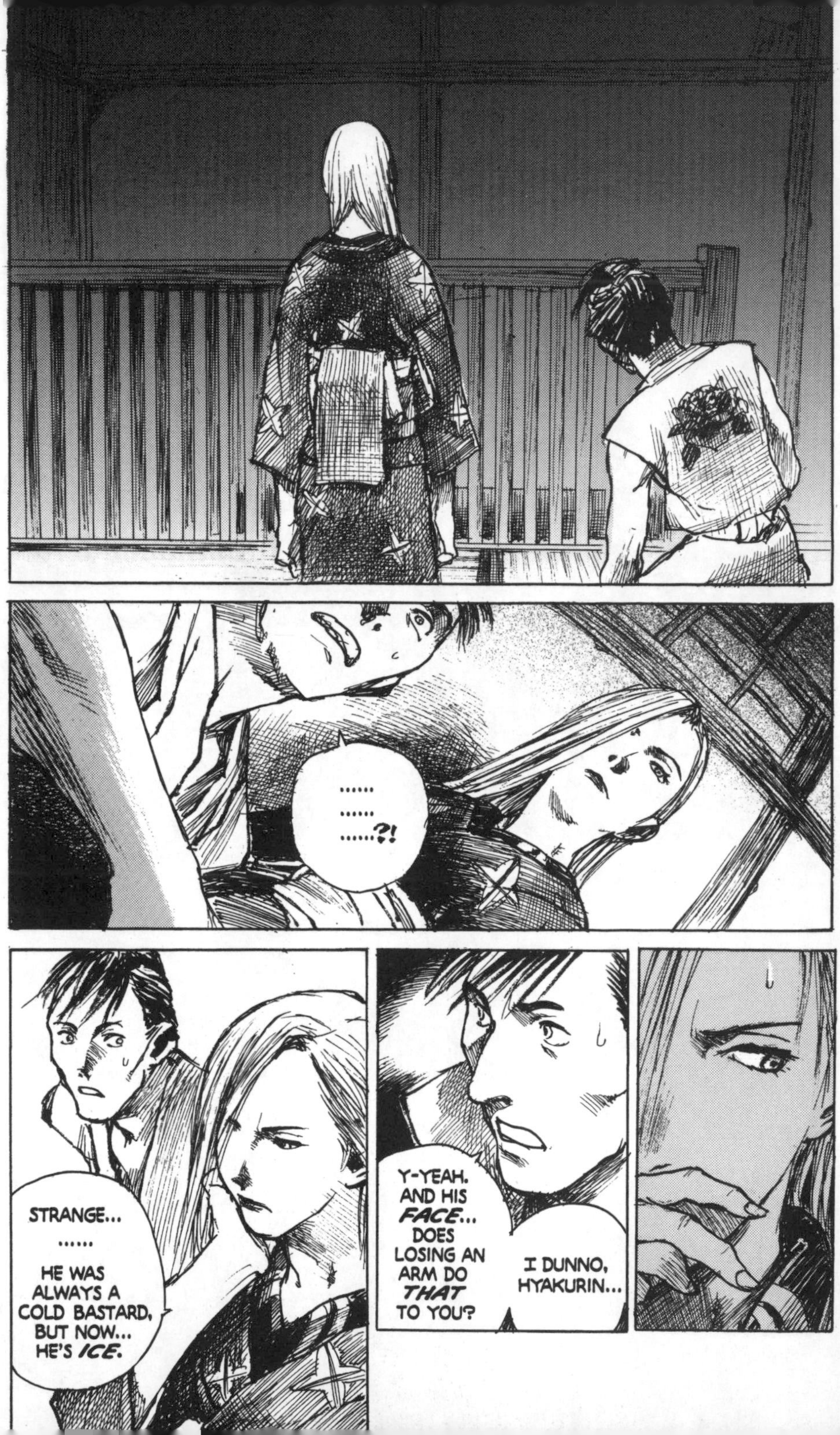
......
......
......?!
STRANGE...
......
HE WAS ALWAYS A COLD BASTARD, BUT NOW... HE'S *ICE*.
Y-YEAH. AND HIS *FACE*... DOES LOSING AN ARM DO *THAT* TO YOU?
I DUNNO, HYAKURIN...

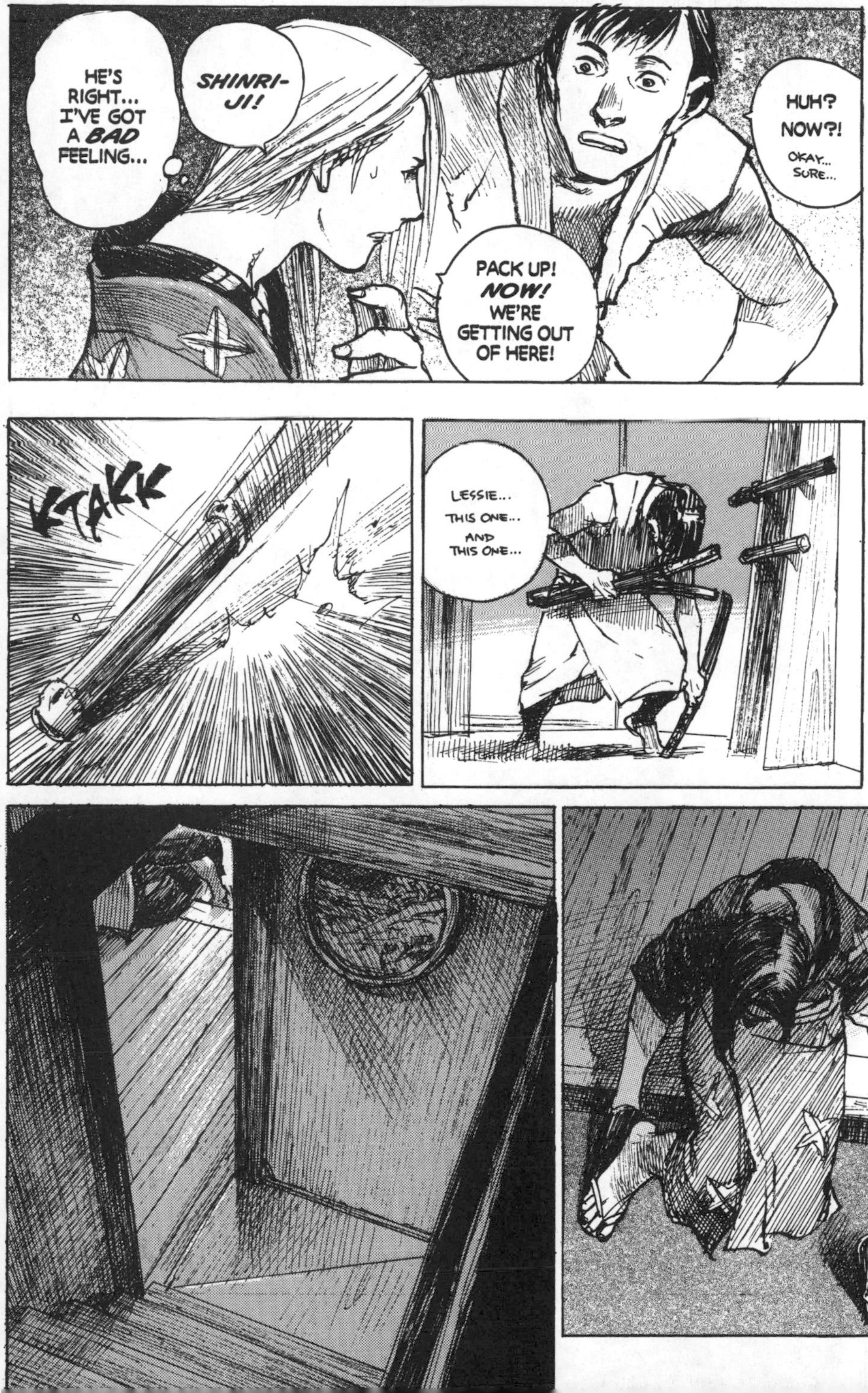
HE'S RIGHT... I'VE GOT A *BAD* FEELING...
SHINRI-JI!
PACK UP! *NOW!* WE'RE GETTING OUT OF HERE!
HUH? NOW?! OKAY... SURE...
KTAKK
LESSIE... THIS ONE... AND THIS ONE...

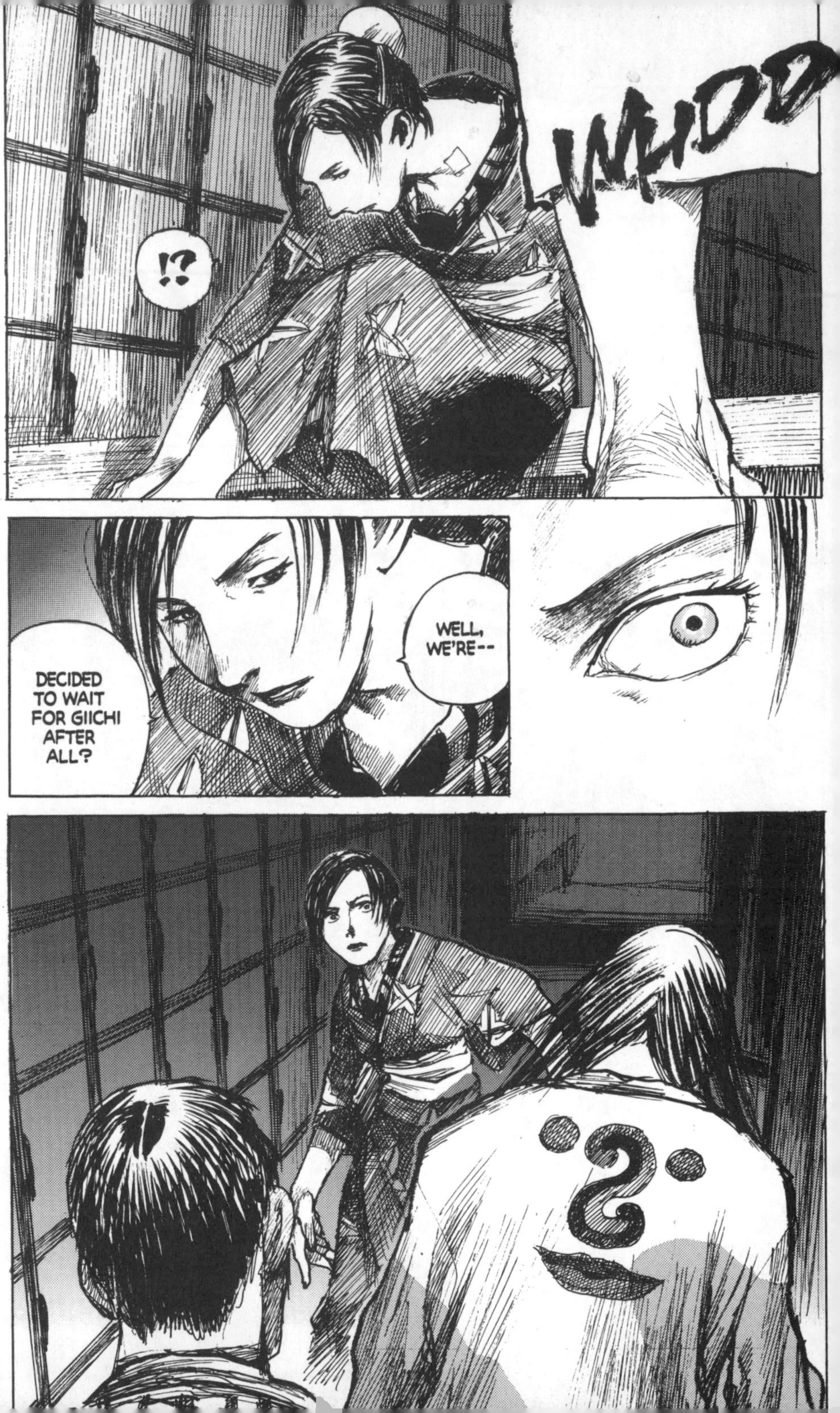
!?
WELL, WE'RE--
DECIDED TO WAIT FOR GIICHI AFTER ALL?

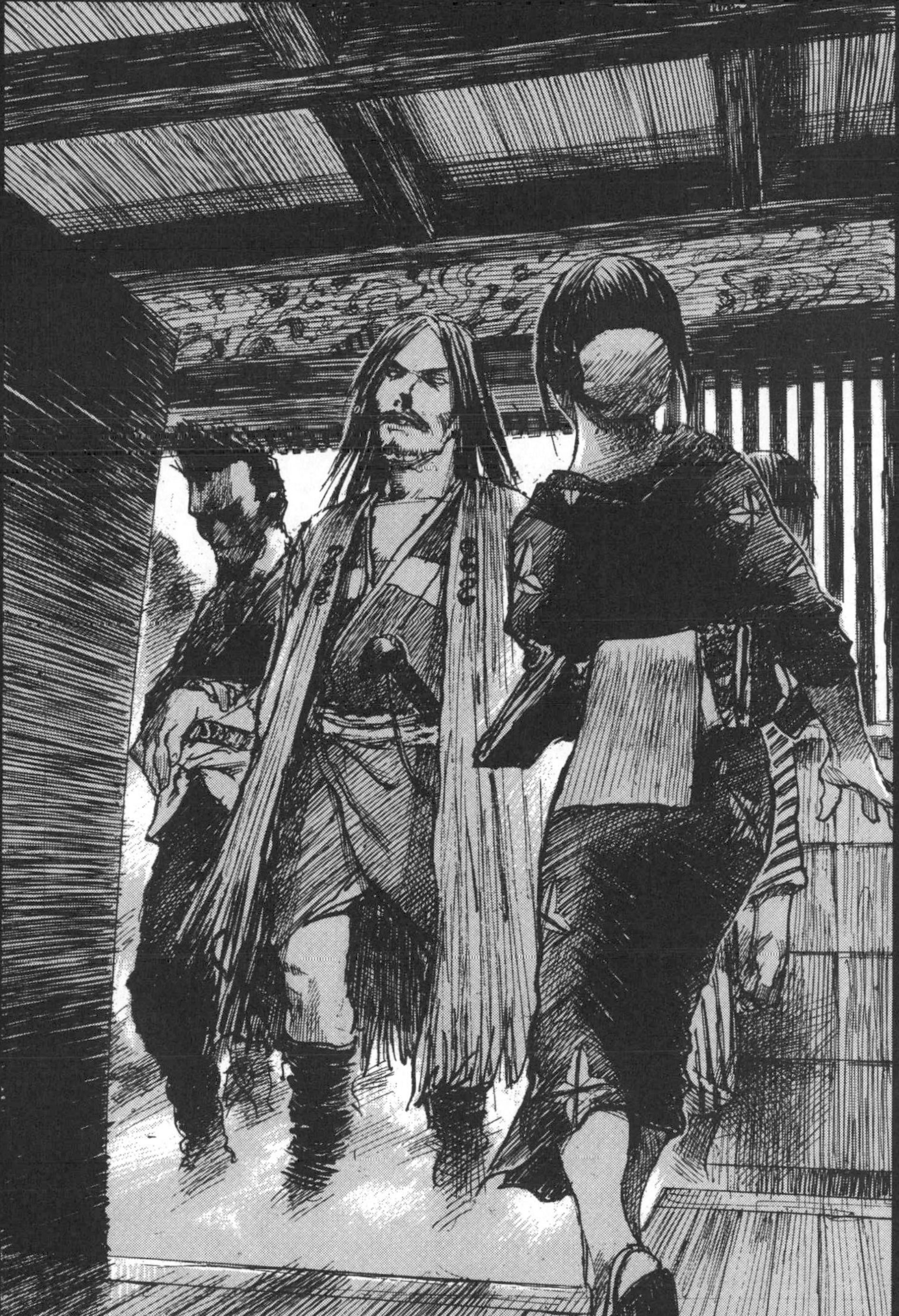

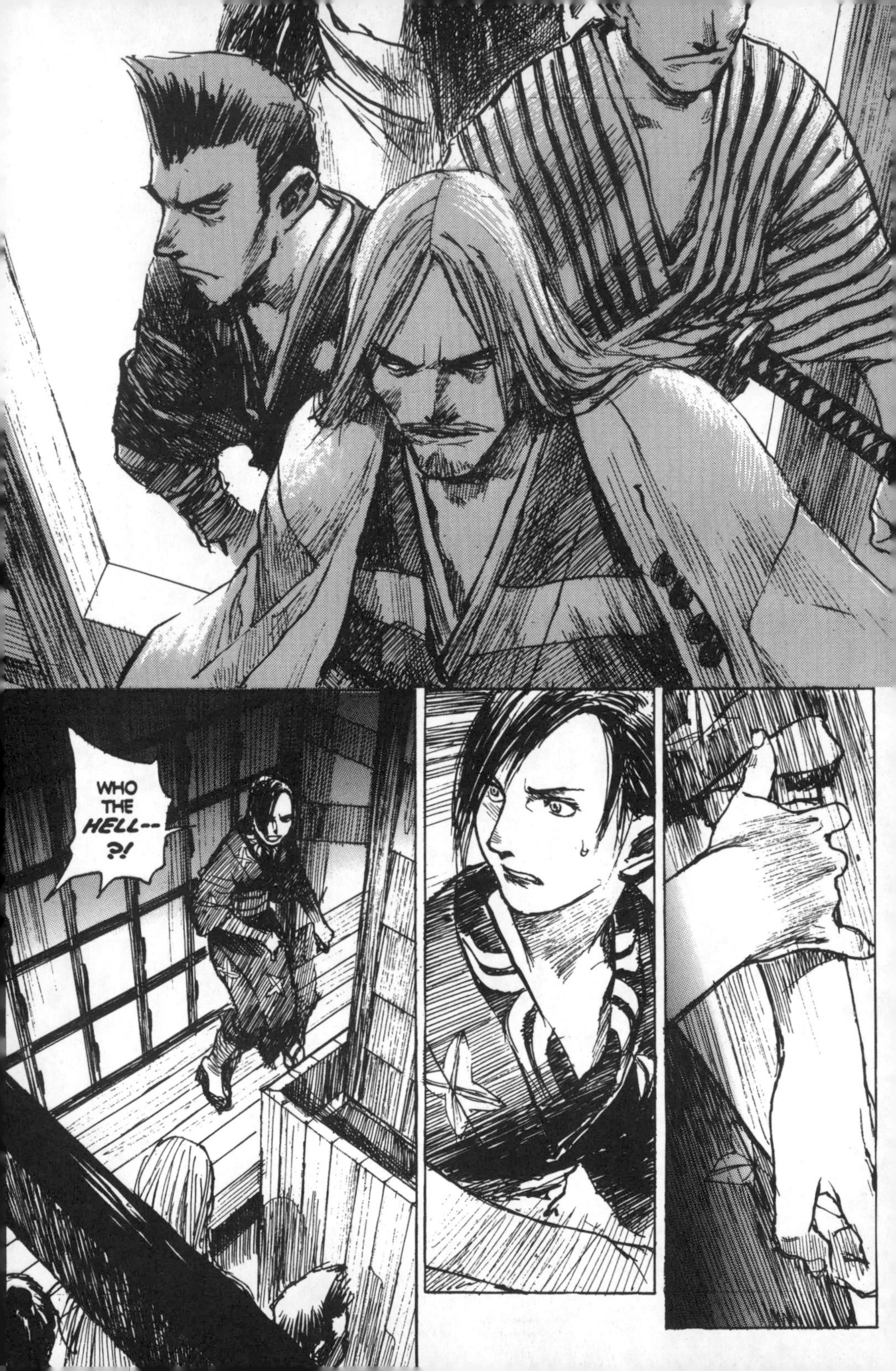
WHO THE HELL-- ?!

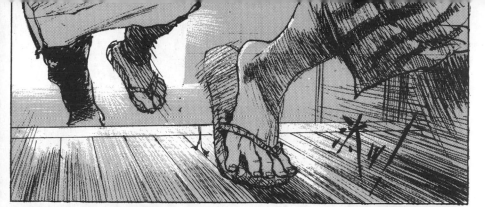

LET *GO*,
YOU
*ASS-
HOLES!*

OW...!

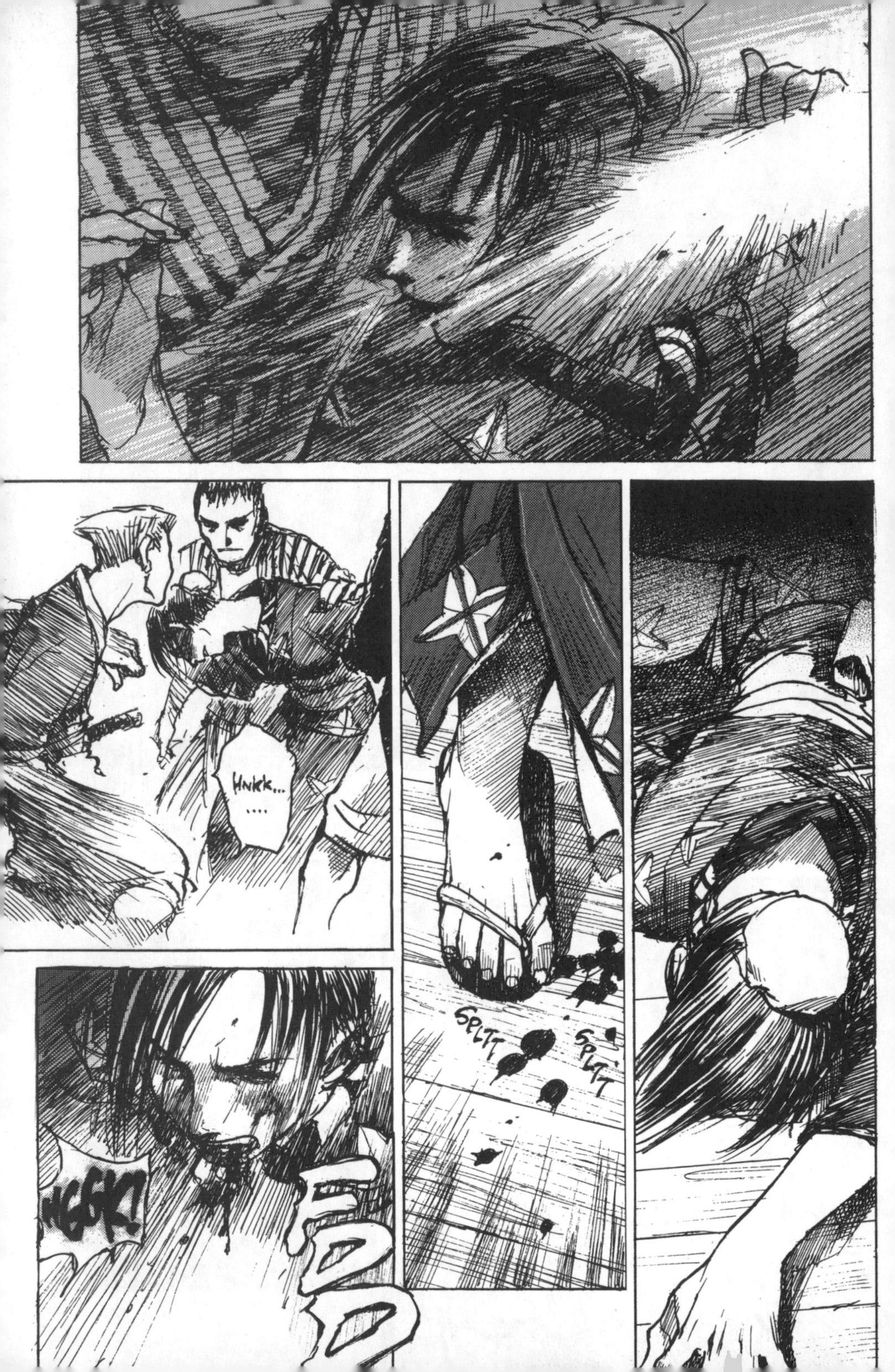

HNKK...
....
SPLTT
SPLTT
HGGK!

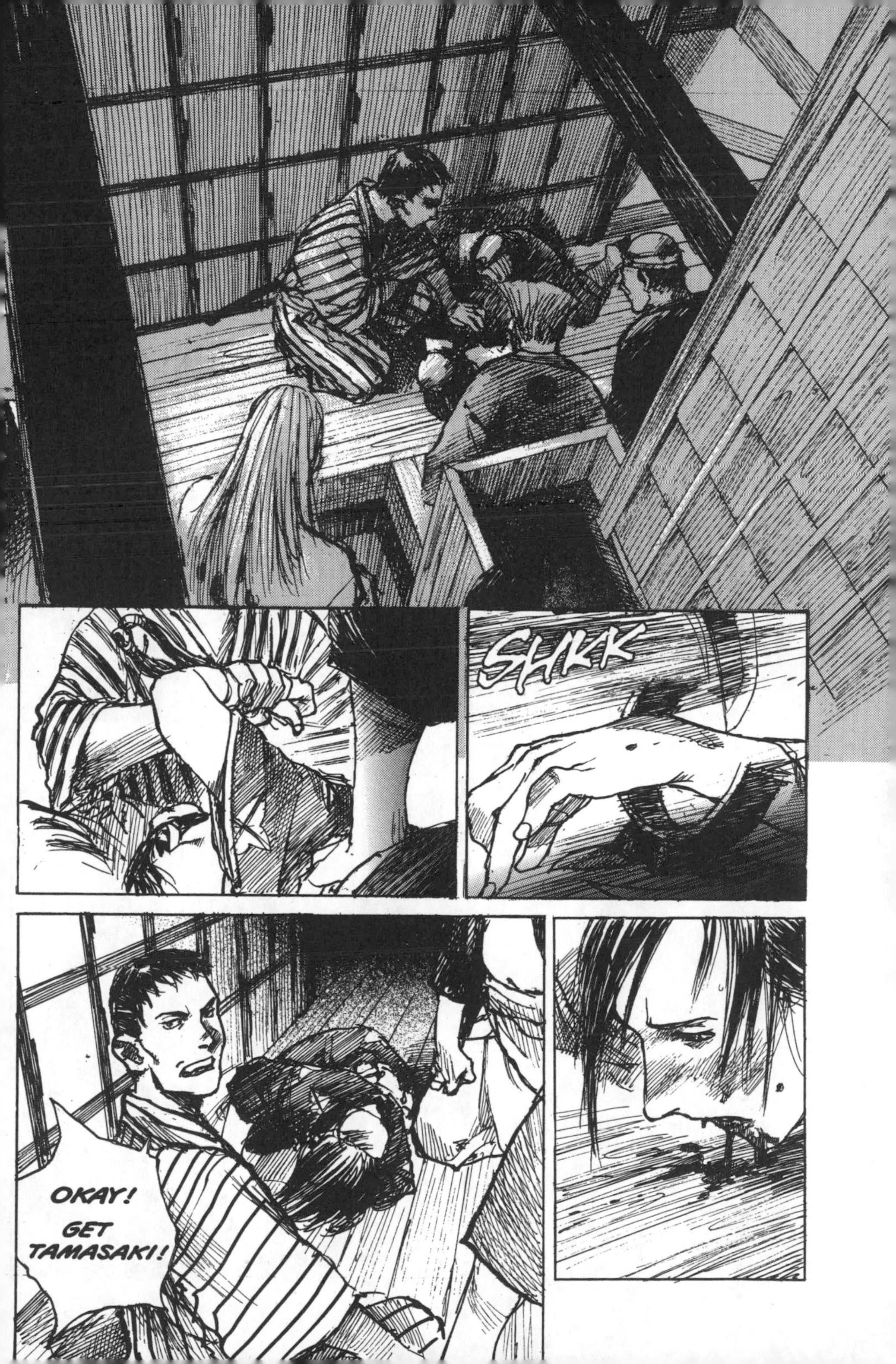
SHKK
OKAY!
GET TAMASAKI!

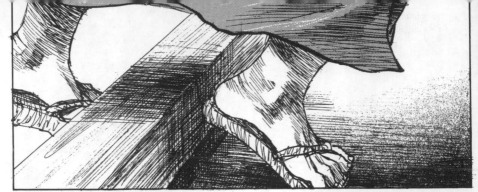

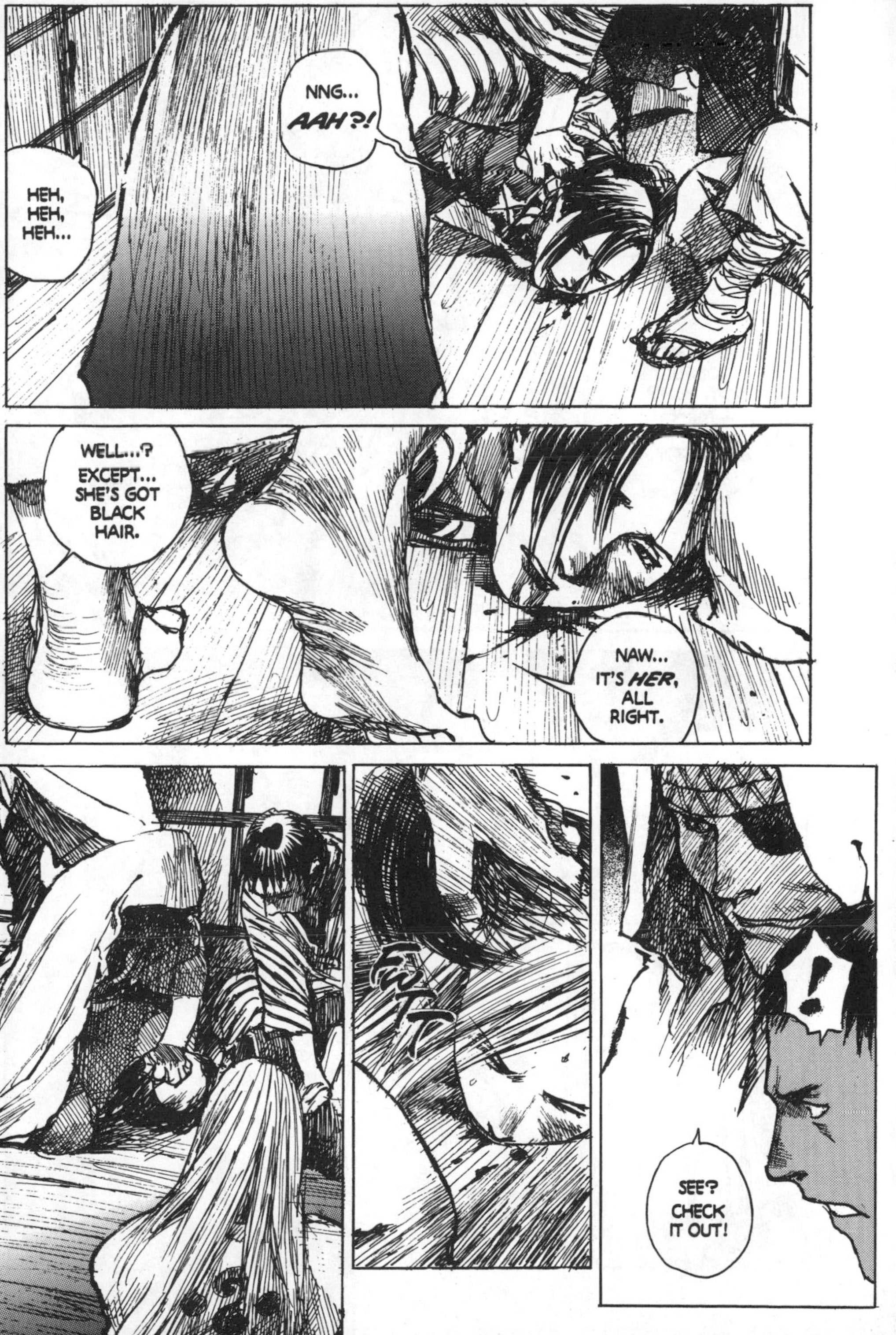
NNG... AAH?!
HEH, HEH, HEH...
WELL...? EXCEPT... SHE'S GOT BLACK HAIR.
NAW... IT'S HER, ALL RIGHT.
!
SEE? CHECK IT OUT!
FWTT

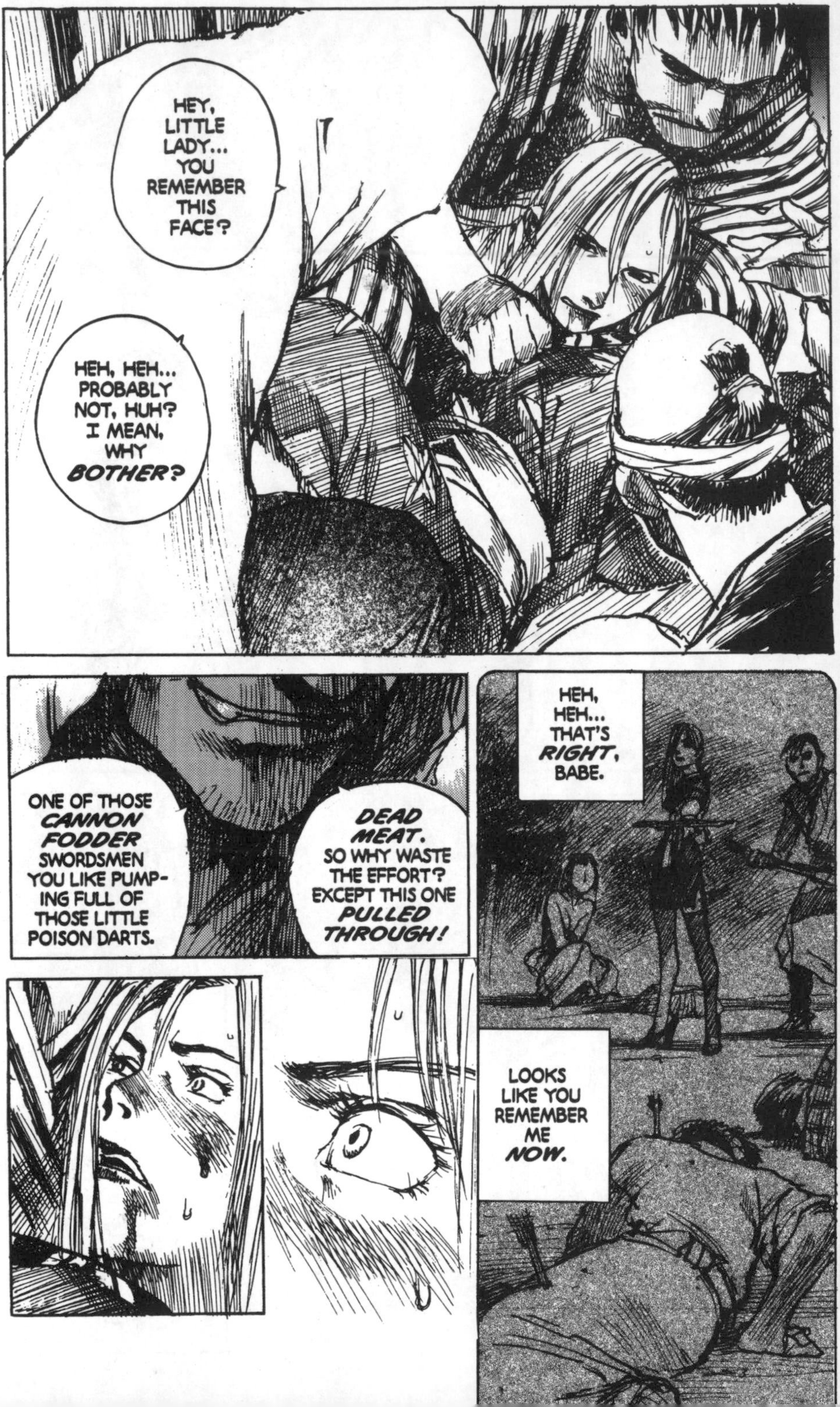
HEY, LITTLE LADY... YOU REMEMBER THIS FACE?
HEH, HEH... PROBABLY NOT, HUH? I MEAN, WHY BOTHER?
ONE OF THOSE CANNON FODDER SWORDSMEN YOU LIKE PUMPING FULL OF THOSE LITTLE POISON DARTS.
DEAD MEAT. SO WHY WASTE THE EFFORT? EXCEPT THIS ONE PULLED THROUGH!
HEH, HEH... THAT'S RIGHT, BABE.
LOOKS LIKE YOU REMEMBER ME NOW.

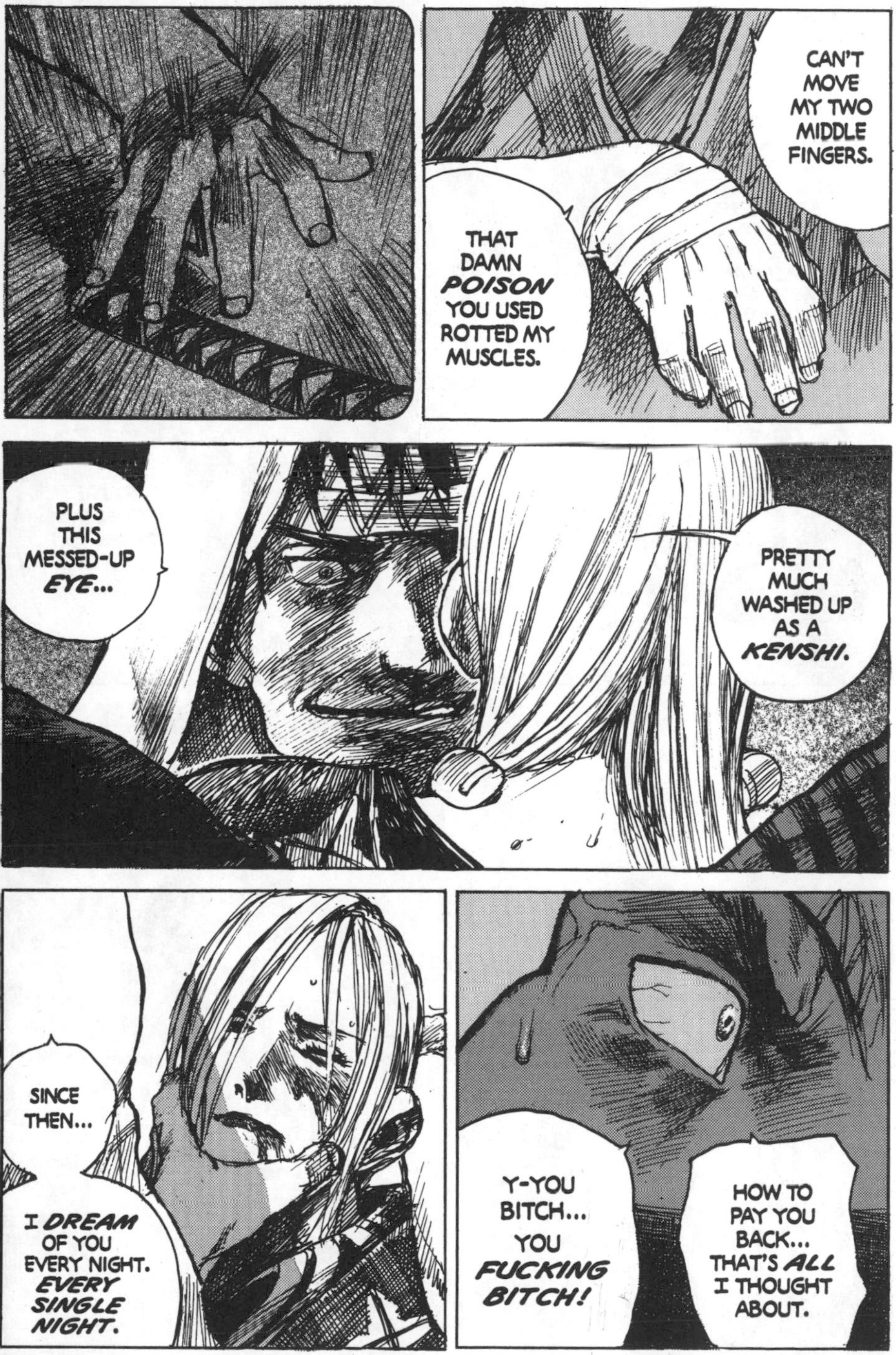
CAN'T MOVE MY TWO MIDDLE FINGERS.
THAT DAMN *POISON* YOU USED ROTTED MY MUSCLES.
PLUS THIS MESSED-UP *EYE*...
PRETTY MUCH WASHED UP AS A *KENSHI*.
SINCE THEN...
I *DREAM* OF YOU EVERY NIGHT. *EVERY SINGLE NIGHT*.
HOW TO PAY YOU BACK... THAT'S *ALL* I THOUGHT ABOUT.
Y-YOU BITCH... YOU *FUCKING BITCH!*

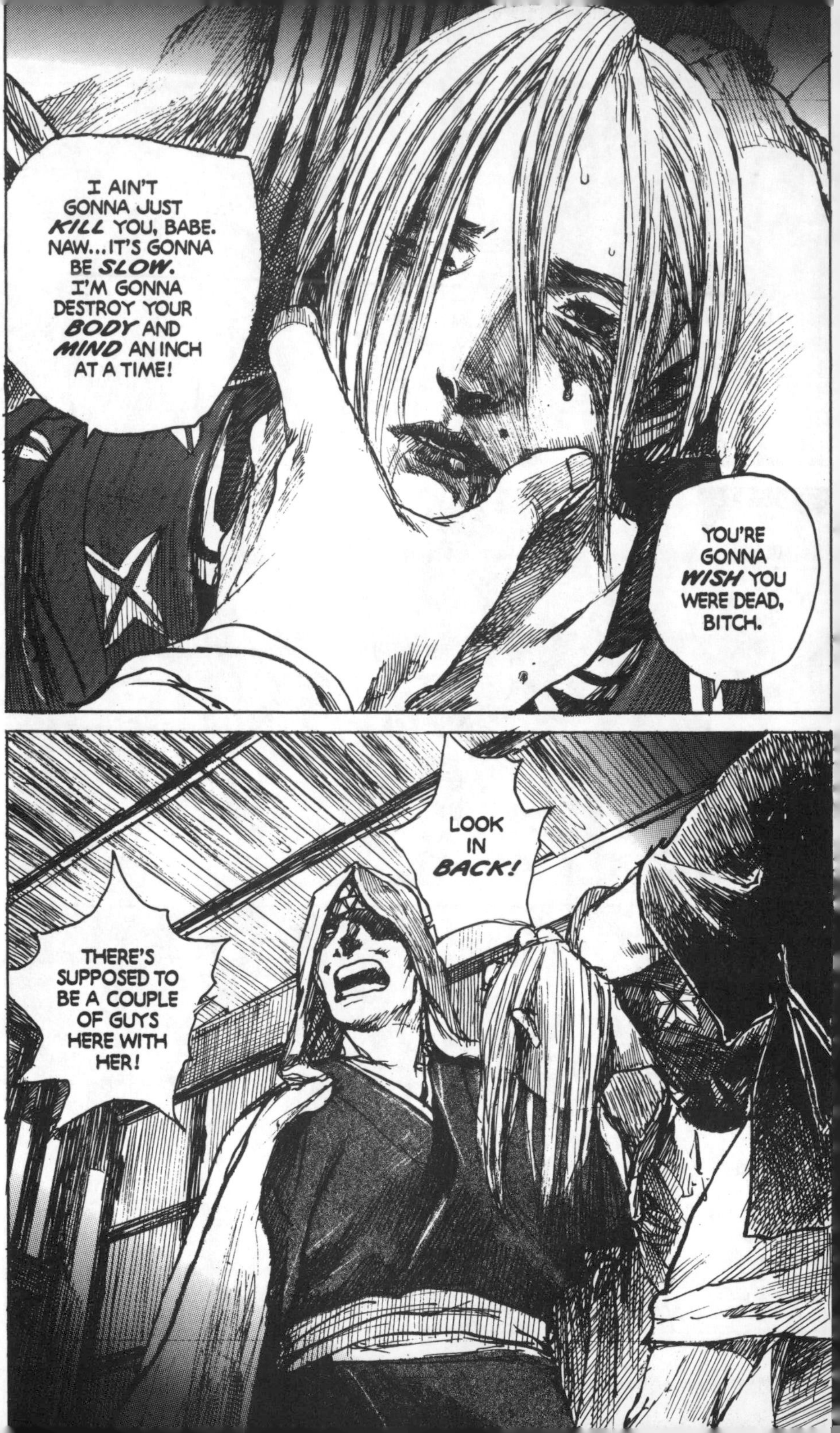
I AIN'T GONNA JUST KILL YOU, BABE. NAW...IT'S GONNA BE SLOW. I'M GONNA DESTROY YOUR BODY AND MIND AN INCH AT A TIME!
YOU'RE GONNA WISH YOU WERE DEAD, BITCH.
LOOK IN BACK!
THERE'S SUPPOSED TO BE A COUPLE OF GUYS HERE WITH HER!

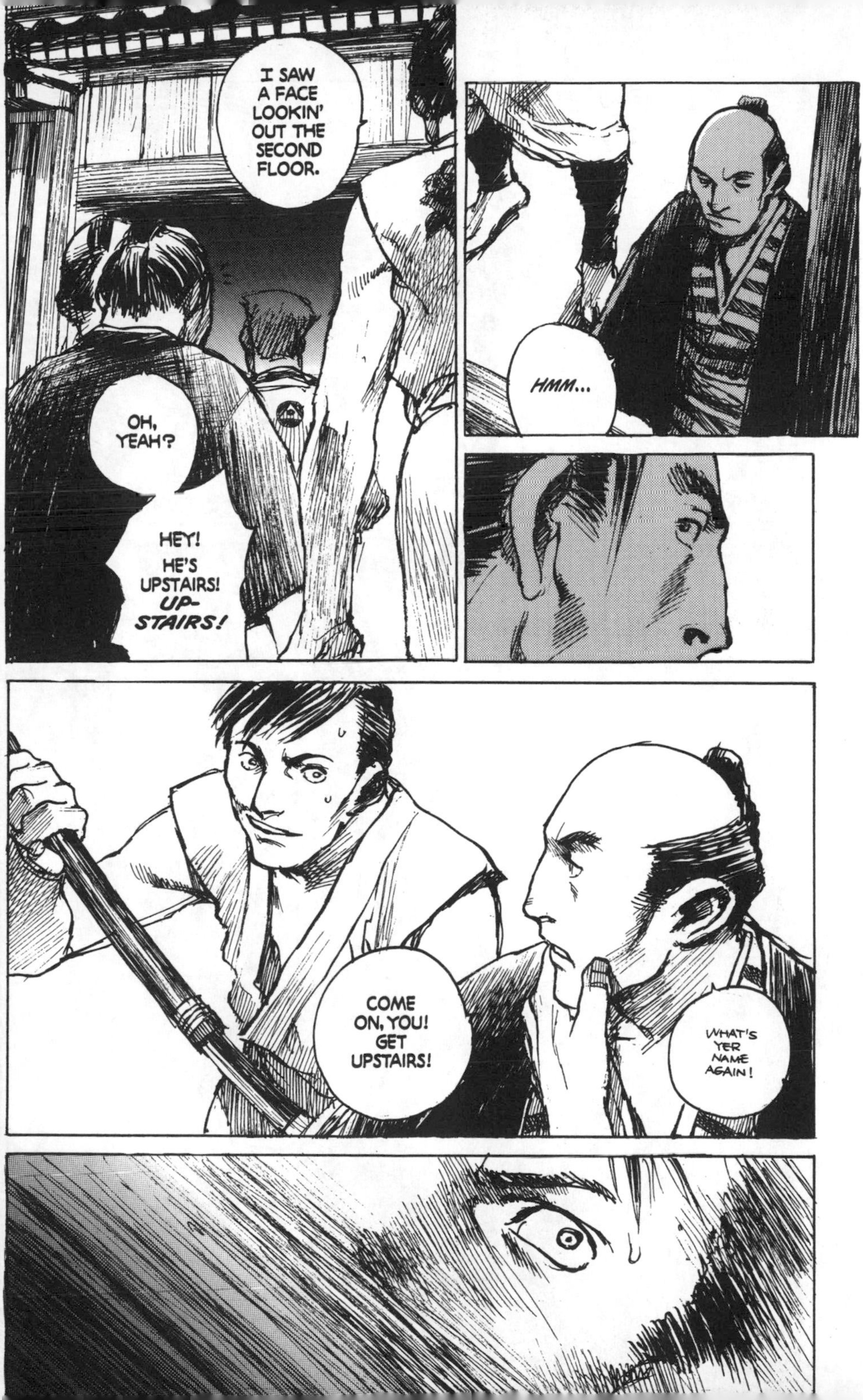
I SAW A FACE LOOKIN' OUT THE SECOND FLOOR.
OH, YEAH?
HEY! HE'S UPSTAIRS! UP-STAIRS!
HMM...
COME ON, YOU! GET UPSTAIRS!
WHAT'S YER NAME AGAIN!

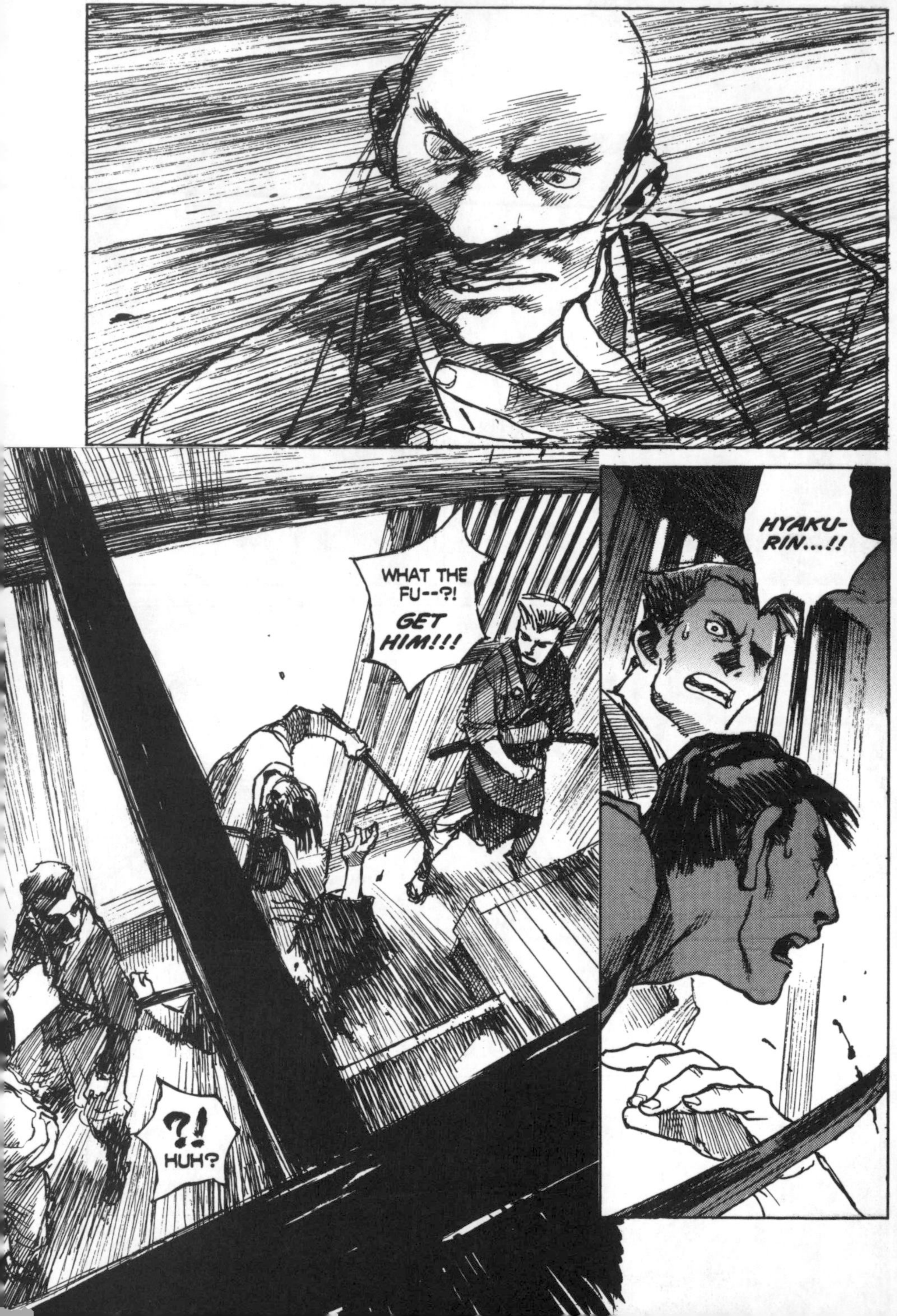
HYAKU-RIN...!!
WHAT THE FU--?! GET HIM!!!
?! HUH?

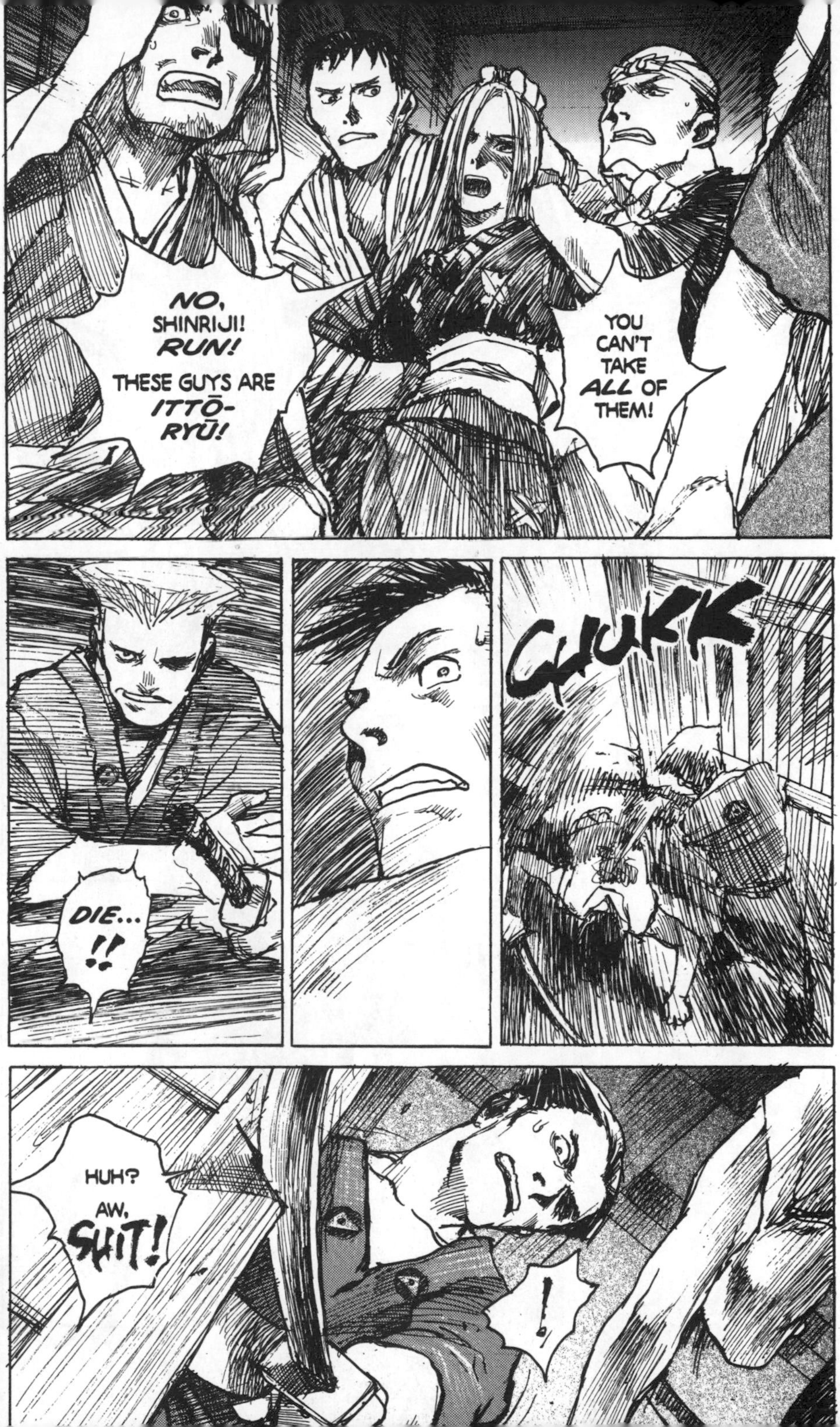
NO, SHINRIJI! RUN!
THESE GUYS ARE ITTŌ-RYŪ!
YOU CAN'T TAKE ALL OF THEM!
DIE...!!
GUKK
HUH? AW, SHIT!
!

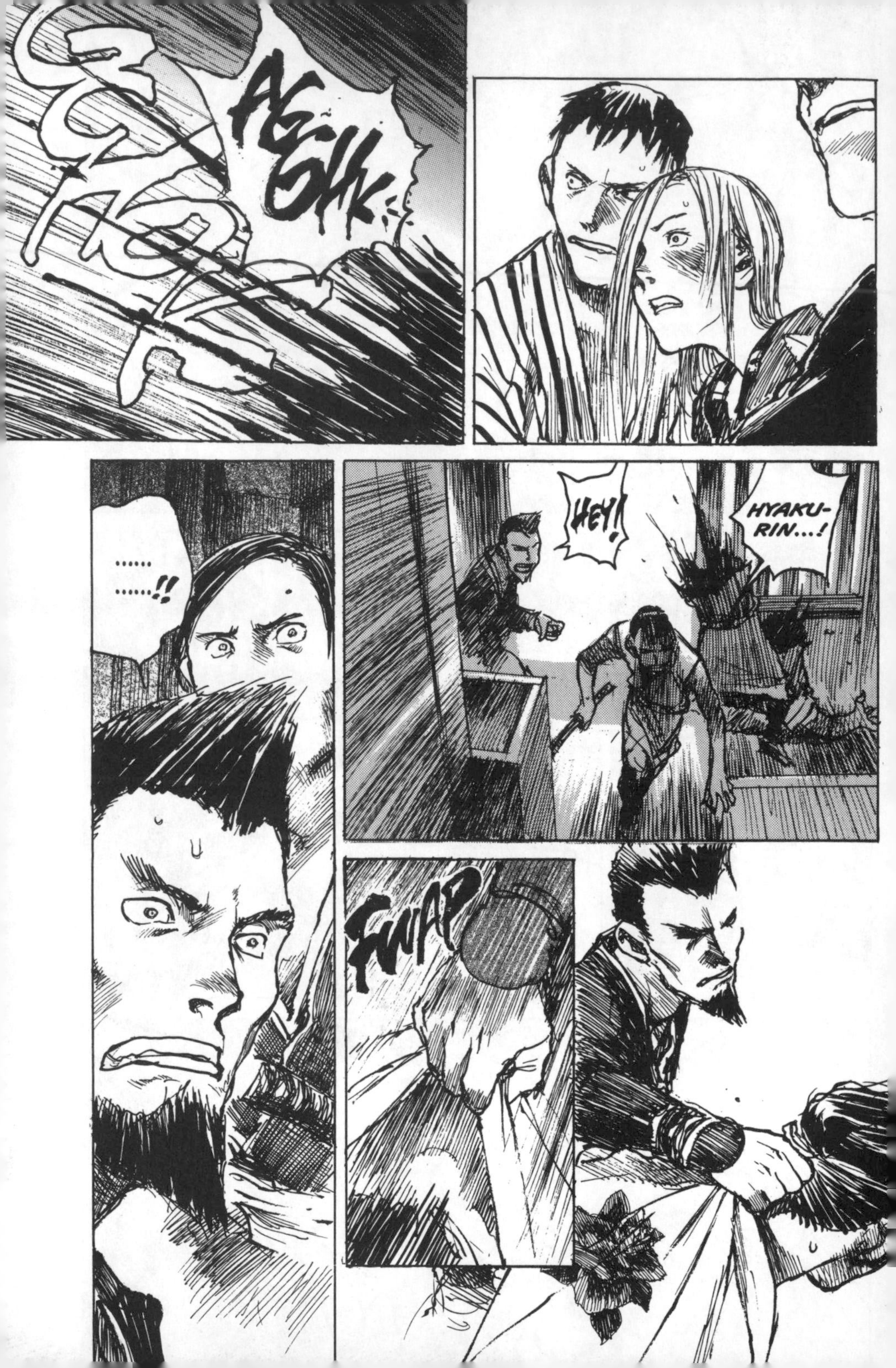
AG-GHK
HYAKU-RIN...!
HEY!!
......
......!!
FWAP

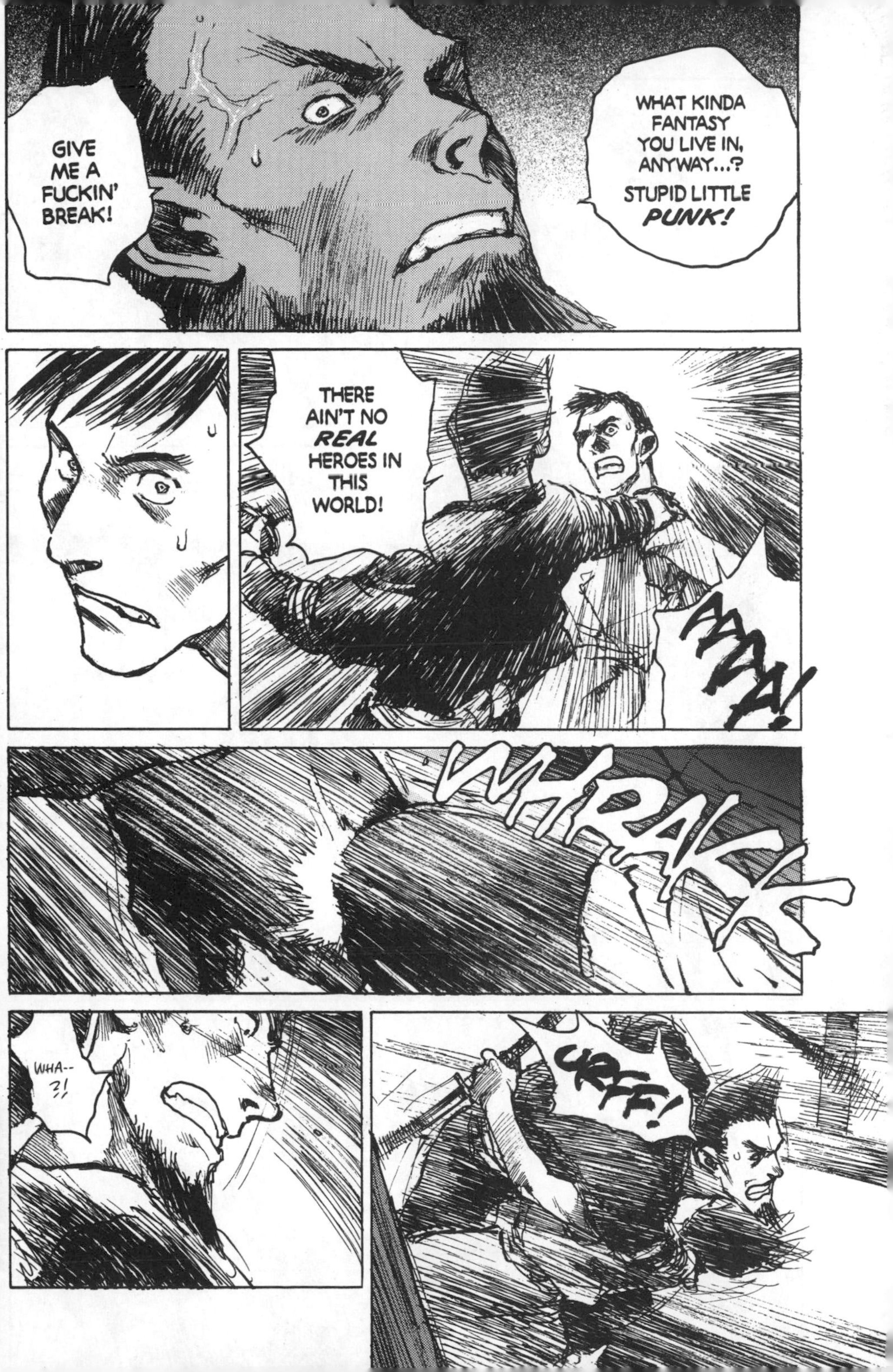
WHAT KINDA FANTASY YOU LIVE IN, ANYWAY...? STUPID LITTLE *PUNK!*
GIVE ME A FUCKIN' BREAK!
THERE AIN'T NO *REAL* HEROES IN THIS WORLD!
AAAA!
WHPAKK
URFF!
WHA-- ?!

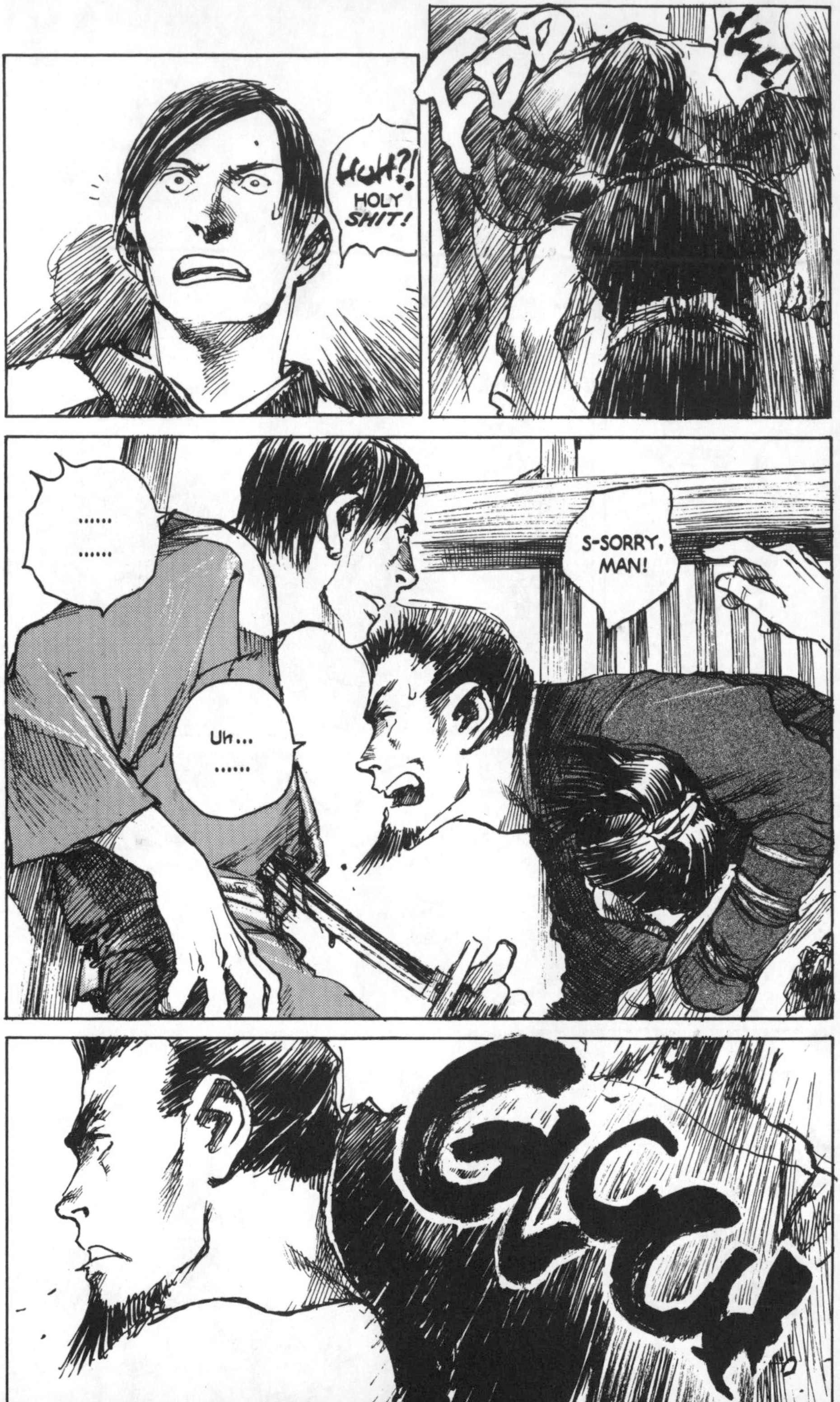
FDD
HUH?! HOLY SHIT!
S-SORRY, MAN!
....
Uh... ......
GLCH!

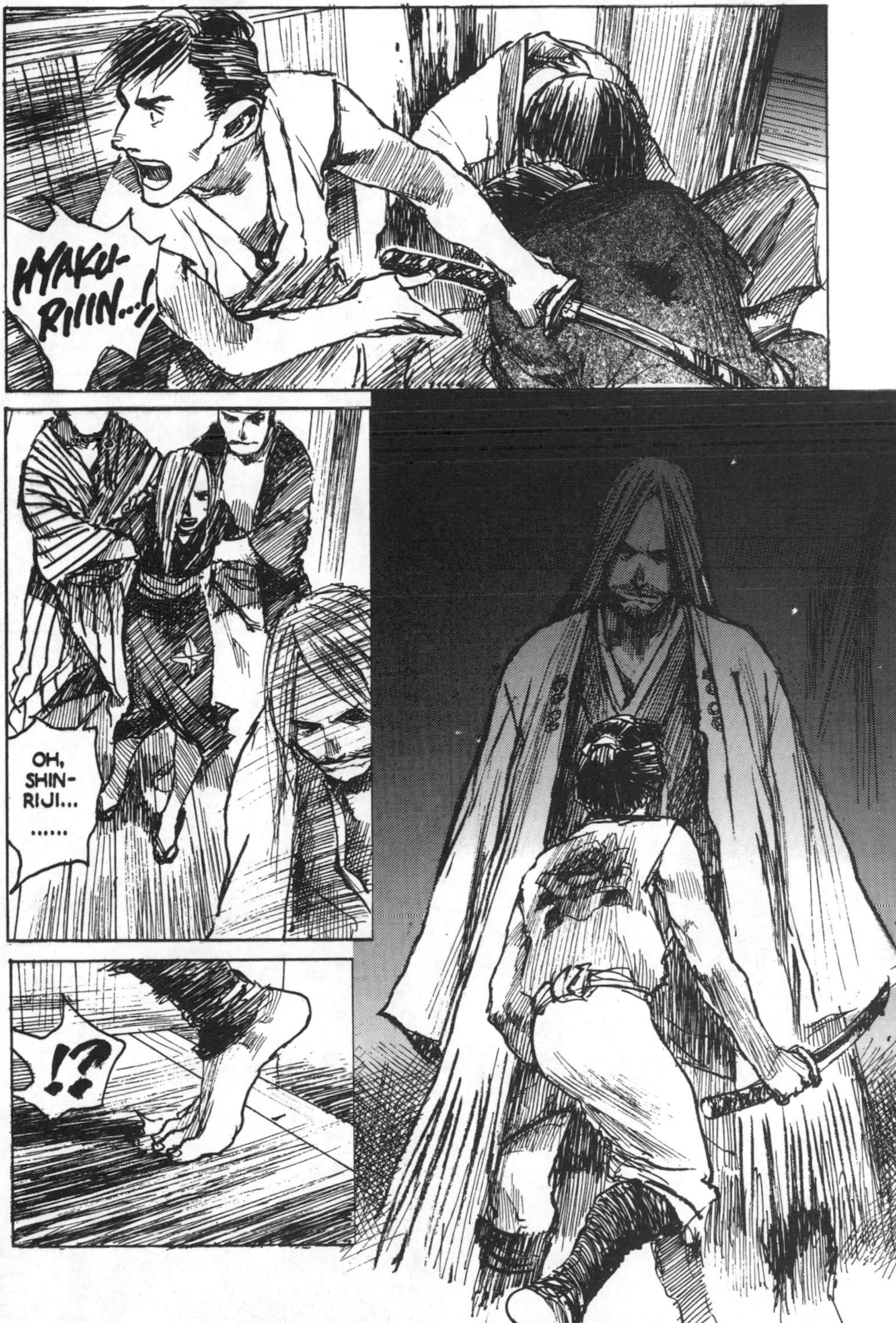
HYAKU-RIIIN...!
OH, SHIN-RIJI...
......
!?

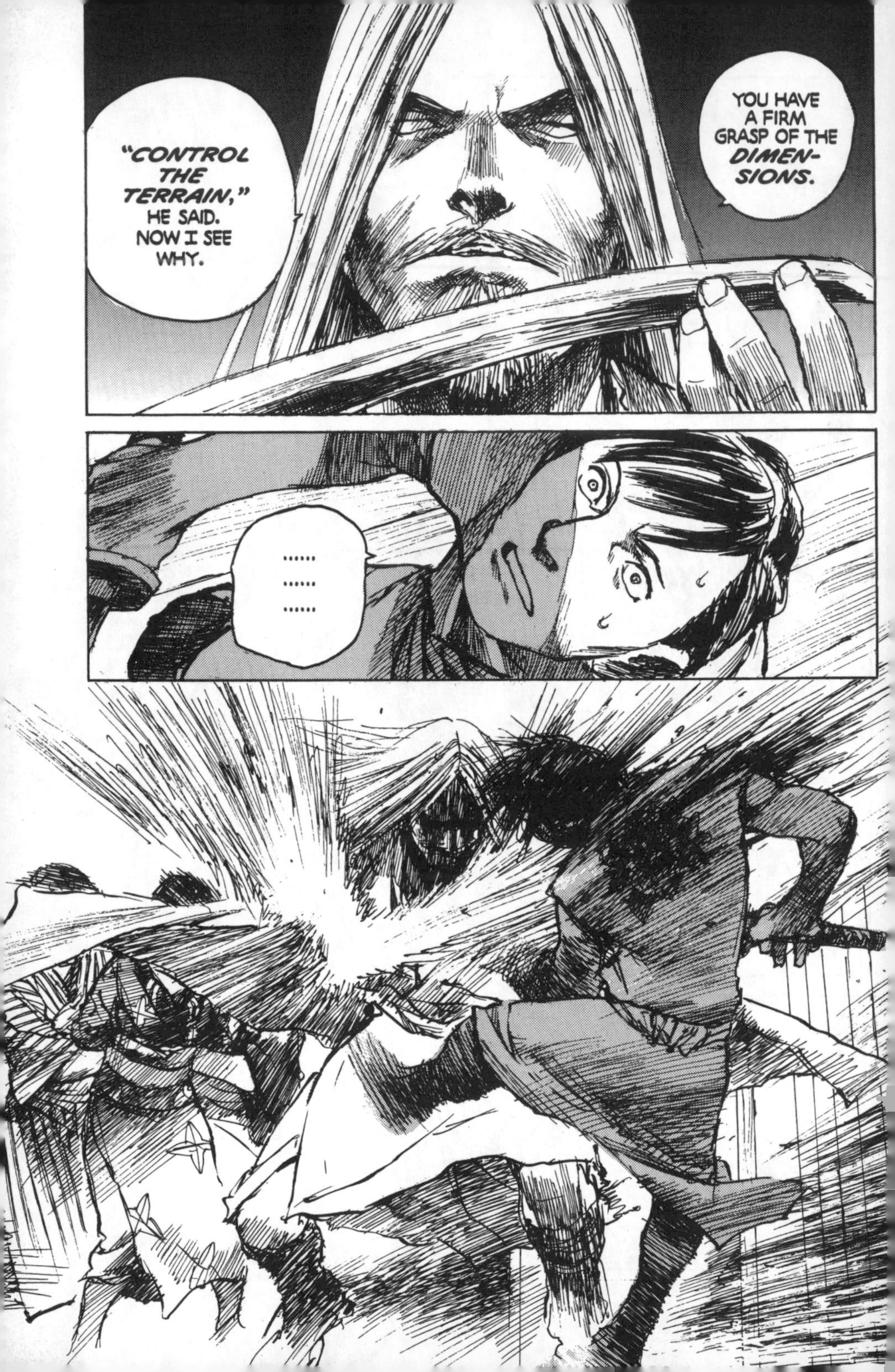
YOU HAVE A FIRM GRASP OF THE *DIMEN-SIONS.*
"CONTROL THE TERRAIN," HE SAID. NOW I SEE WHY.
......
......
......

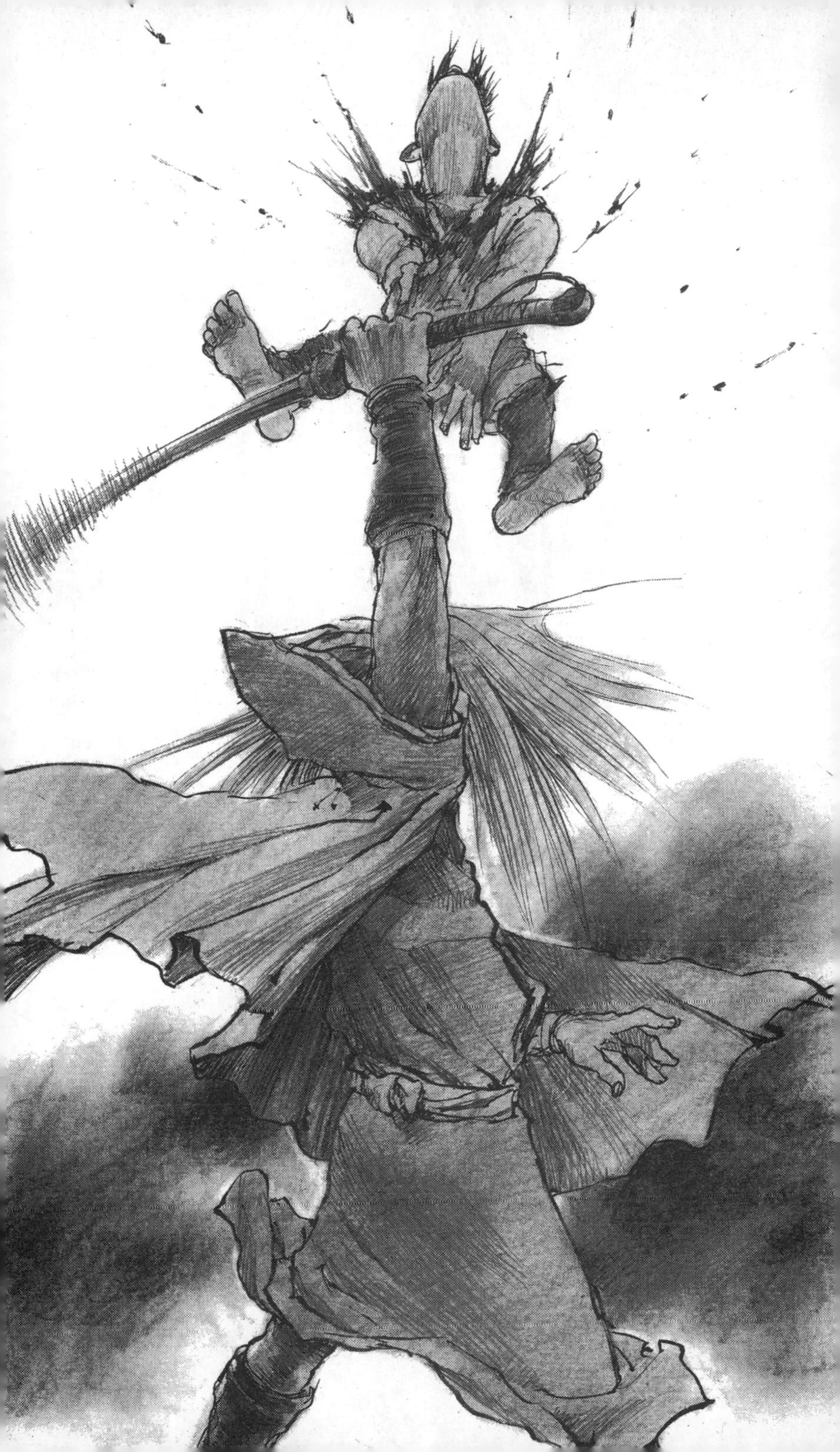

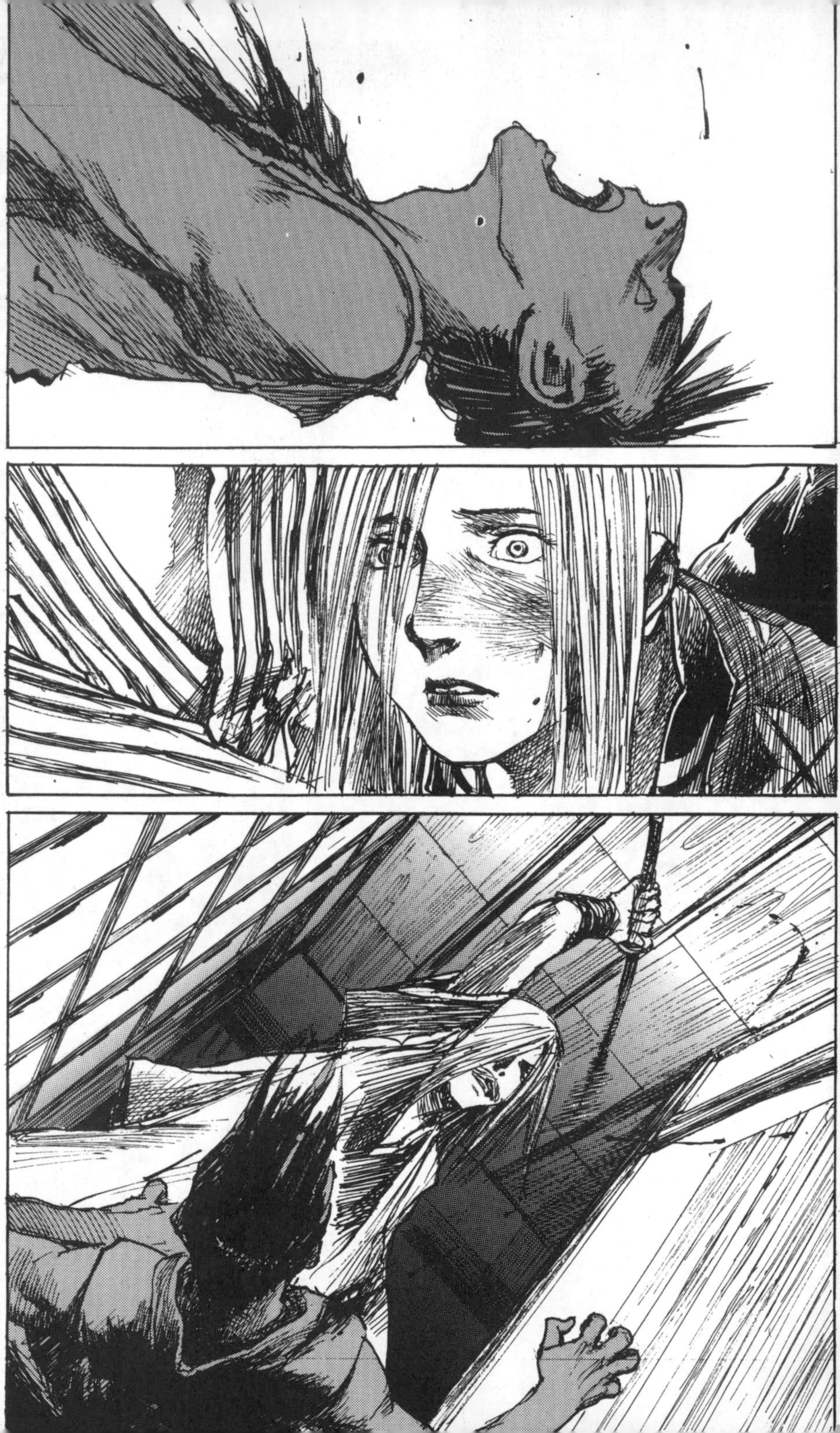

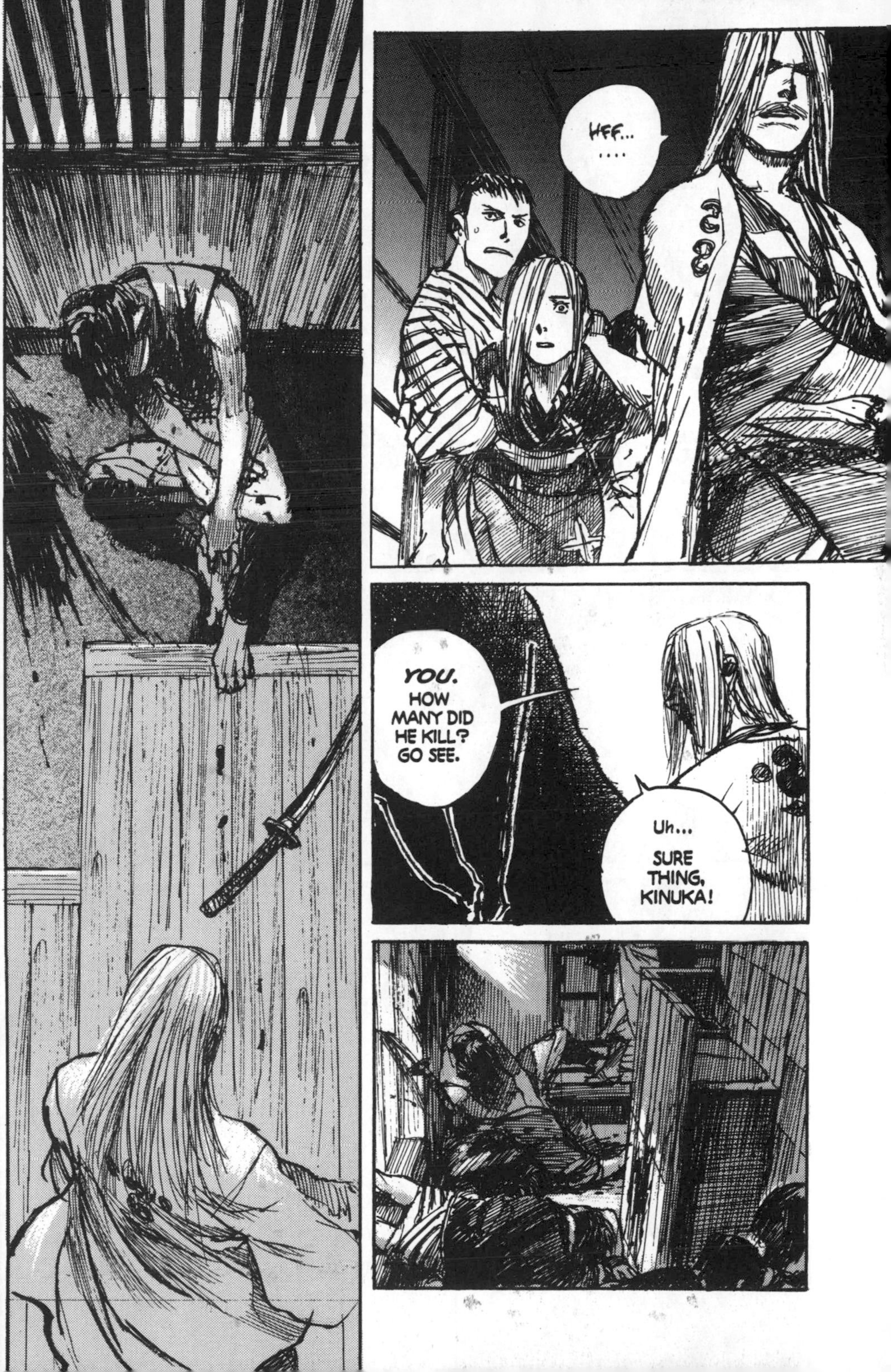
HFF... ....
YOU. HOW MANY DID HE KILL? GO SEE.
Uh... SURE THING, KINUKA!

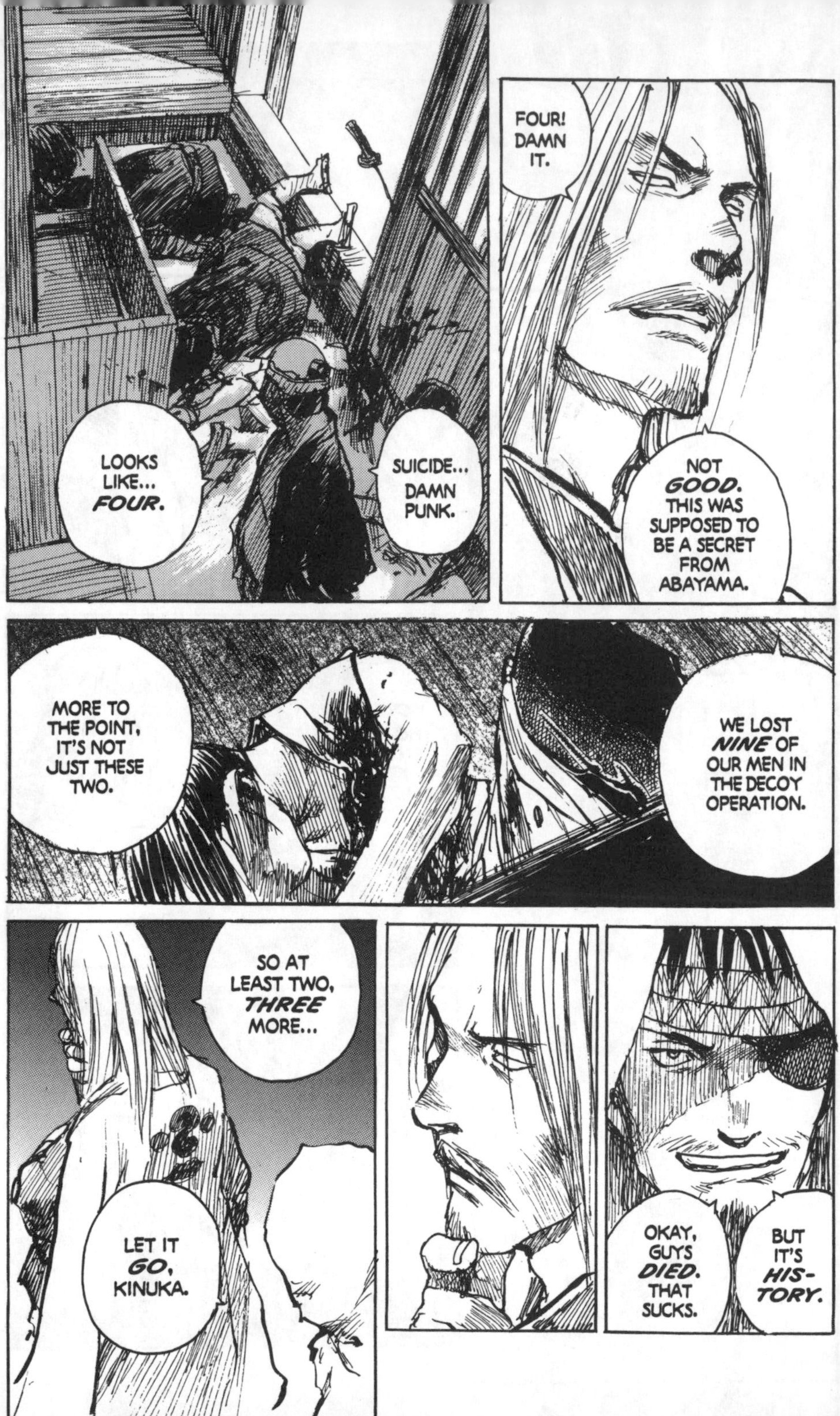
LOOKS LIKE... FOUR.
SUICIDE... DAMN PUNK.
FOUR! DAMN IT.
NOT GOOD. THIS WAS SUPPOSED TO BE A SECRET FROM ABAYAMA.
MORE TO THE POINT, IT'S NOT JUST THESE TWO.
WE LOST NINE OF OUR MEN IN THE DECOY OPERATION.
SO AT LEAST TWO, THREE MORE...
LET IT GO, KINUKA.
OKAY, GUYS DIED. THAT SUCKS.
BUT IT'S HIS-TORY.

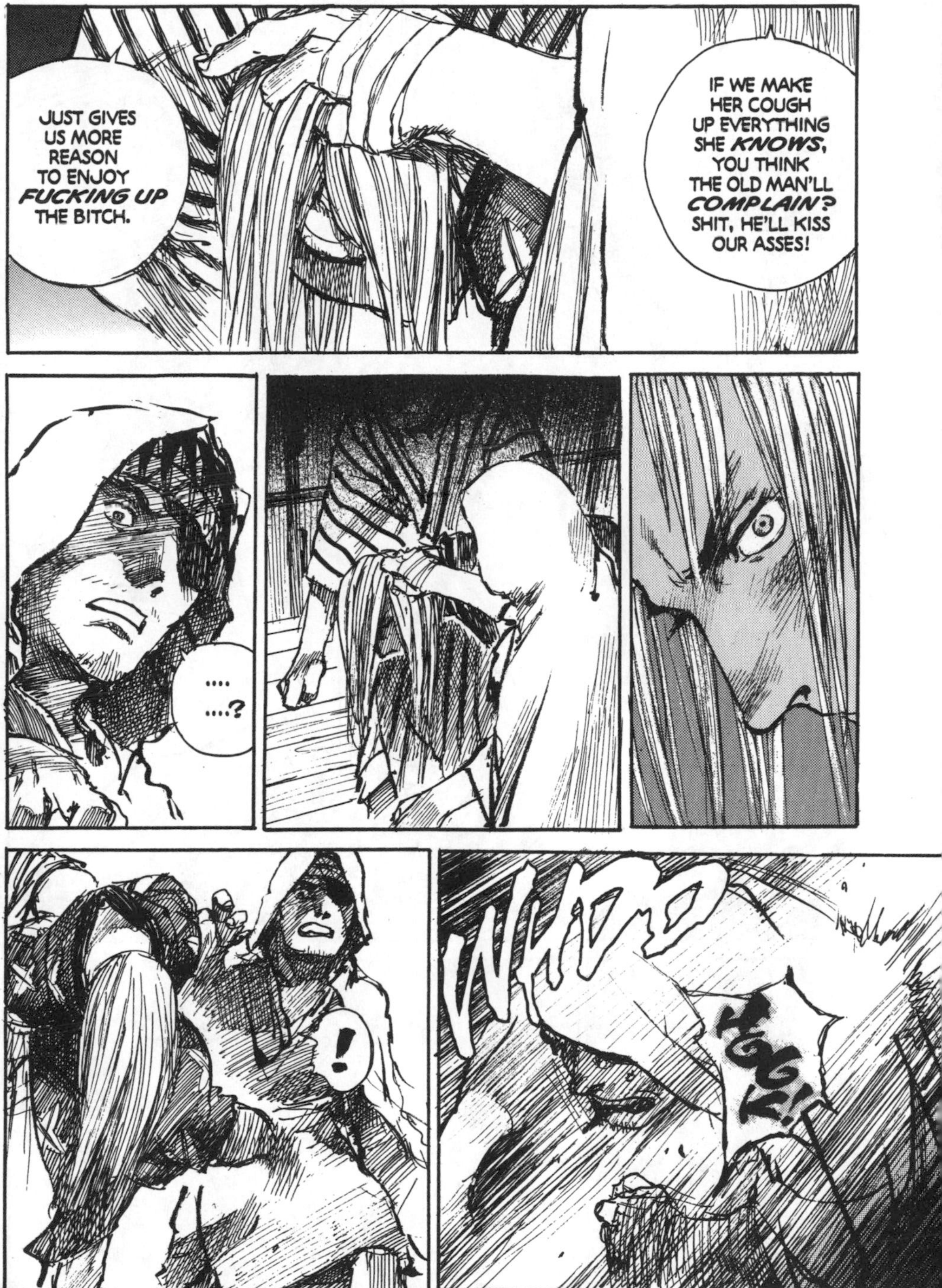
IF WE MAKE HER COUGH UP EVERYTHING SHE *KNOWS*, YOU THINK THE OLD MAN'LL *COMPLAIN?* SHIT, HE'LL KISS OUR ASSES!
JUST GIVES US MORE REASON TO ENJOY *FUCKING UP* THE BITCH.
....?
WHUD
HGGK!
!

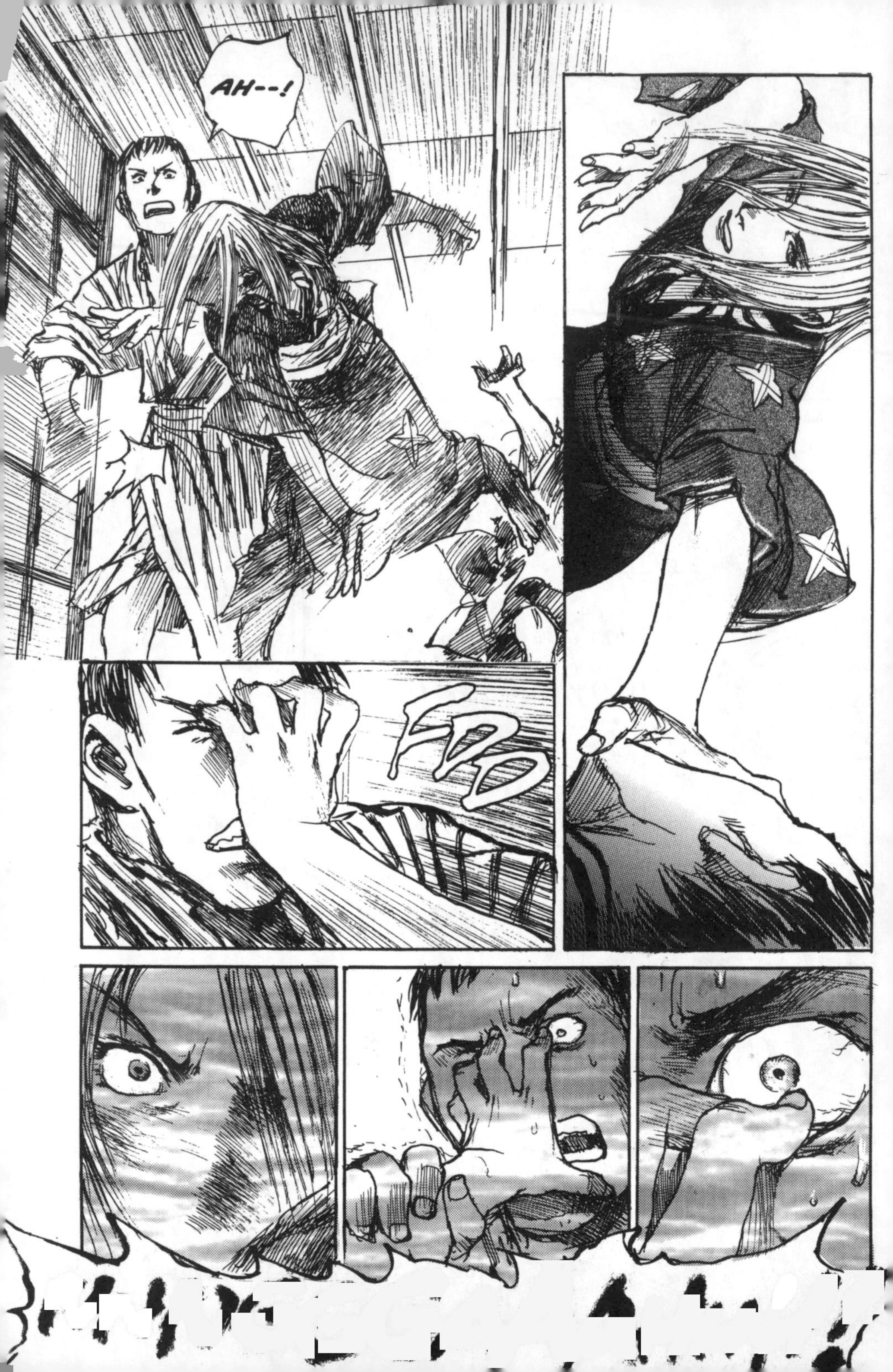
AH--!
FDD

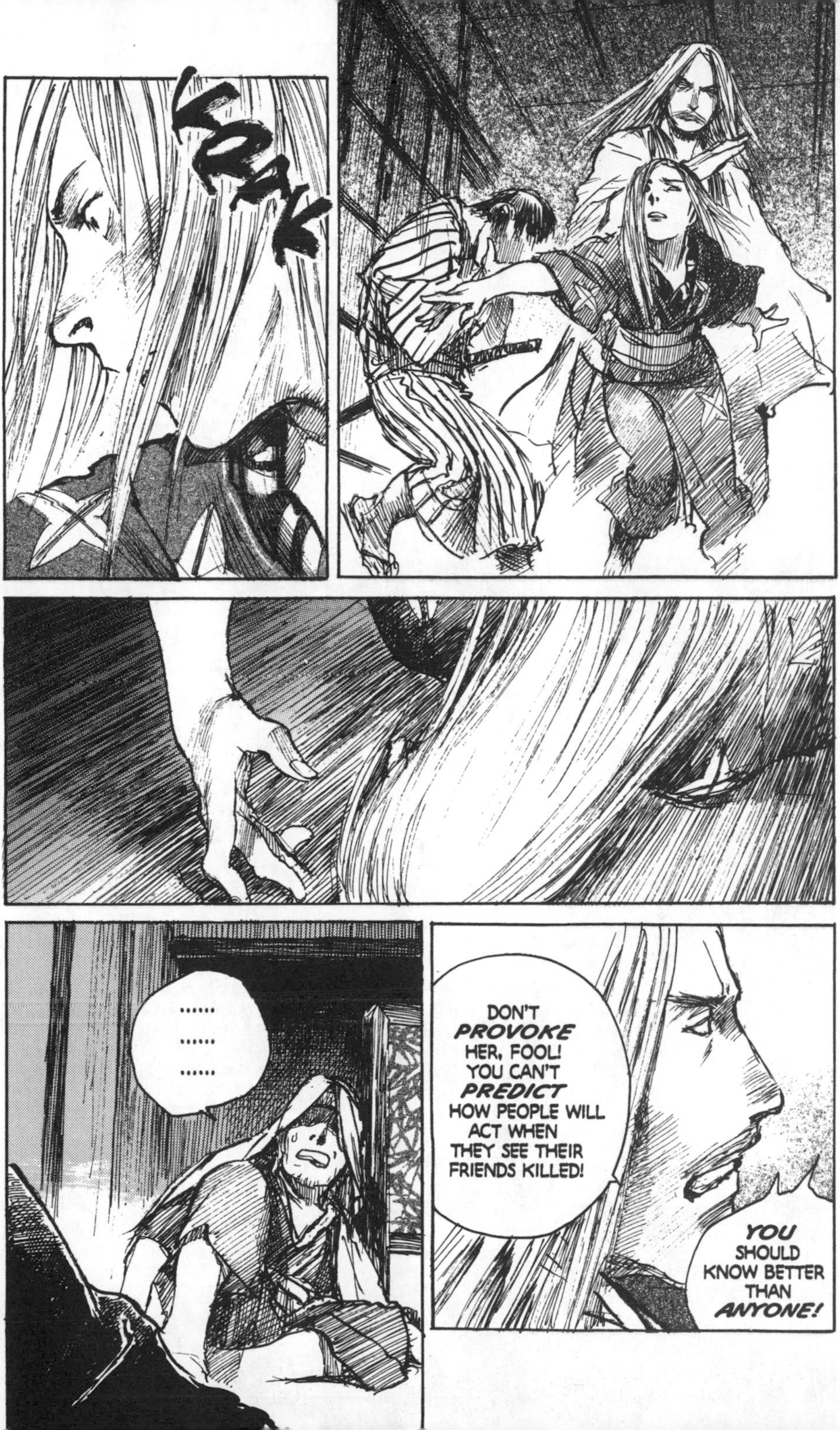
KRAK
DON'T *PROVOKE* HER, FOOL! YOU CAN'T *PREDICT* HOW PEOPLE WILL ACT WHEN THEY SEE THEIR FRIENDS KILLED!
YOU SHOULD KNOW BETTER THAN *ANYONE!*
....

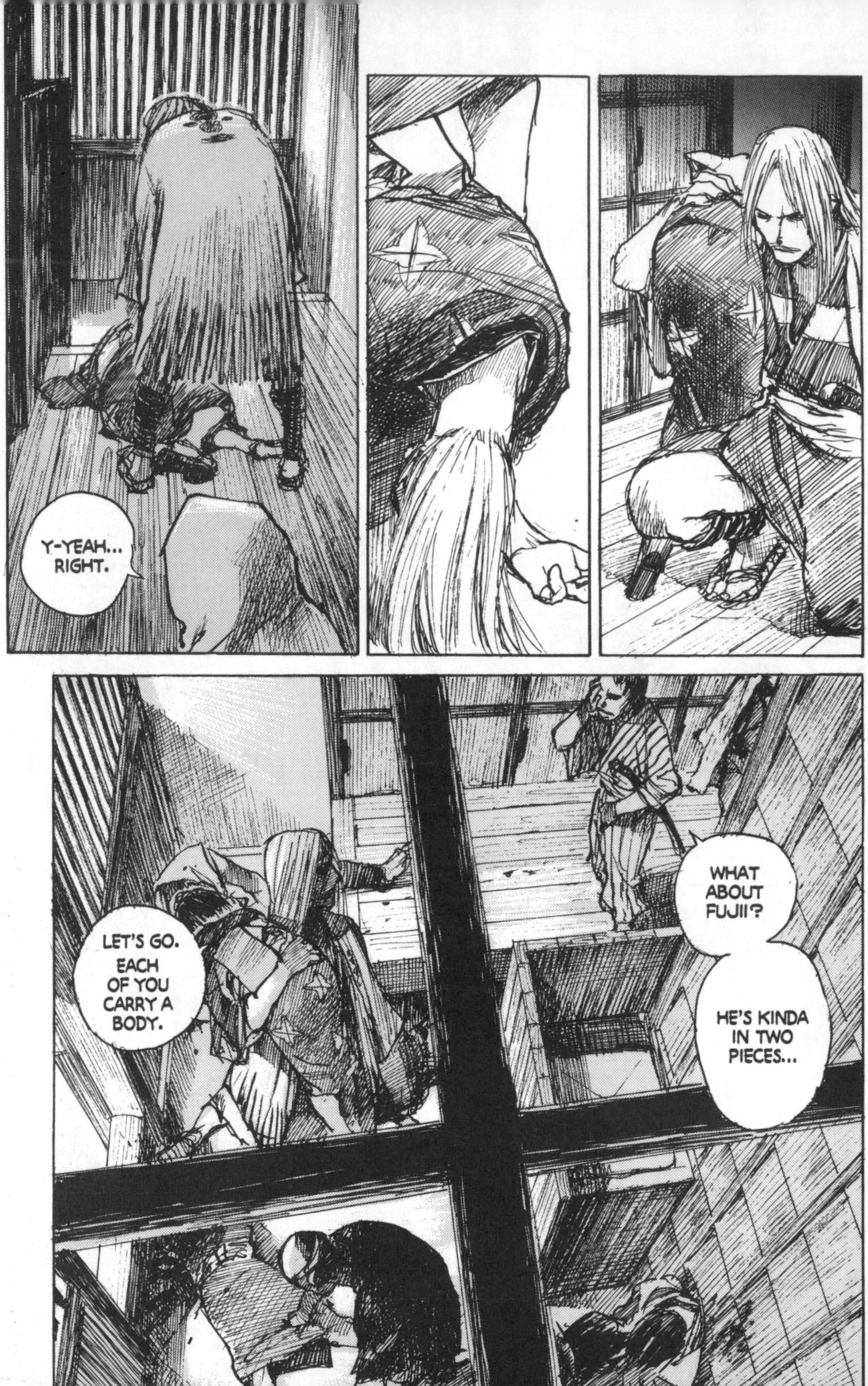
Y-YEAH... RIGHT.
LET'S GO. EACH OF YOU CARRY A BODY.
WHAT ABOUT FUJII?
HE'S KINDA IN TWO PIECES...

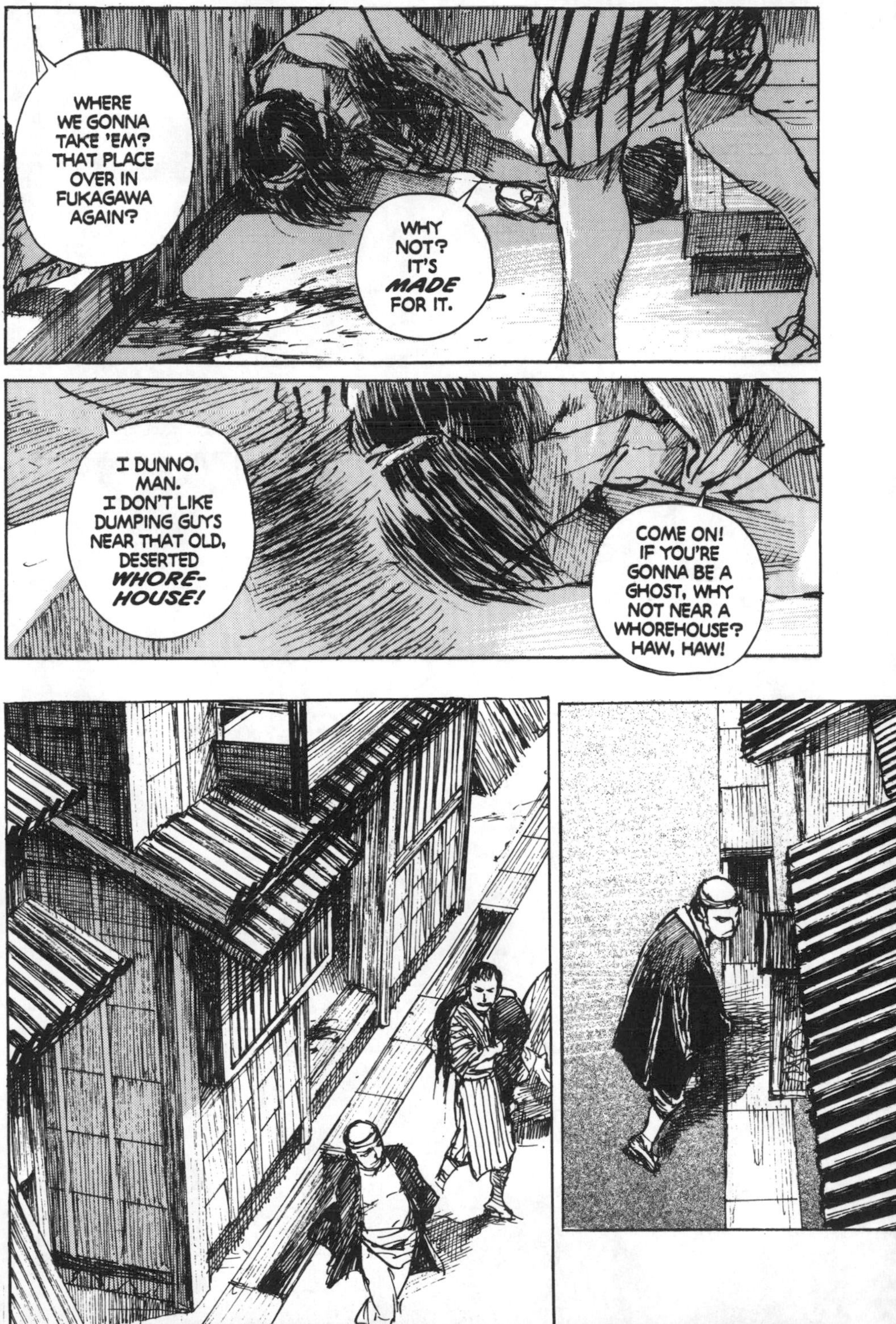
WHERE WE GONNA TAKE 'EM? THAT PLACE OVER IN FUKAGAWA AGAIN?
WHY NOT? IT'S MADE FOR IT.
I DUNNO, MAN. I DON'T LIKE DUMPING GUYS NEAR THAT OLD, DESERTED WHORE-HOUSE!
COME ON! IF YOU'RE GONNA BE A GHOST, WHY NOT NEAR A WHOREHOUSE? HAW, HAW!

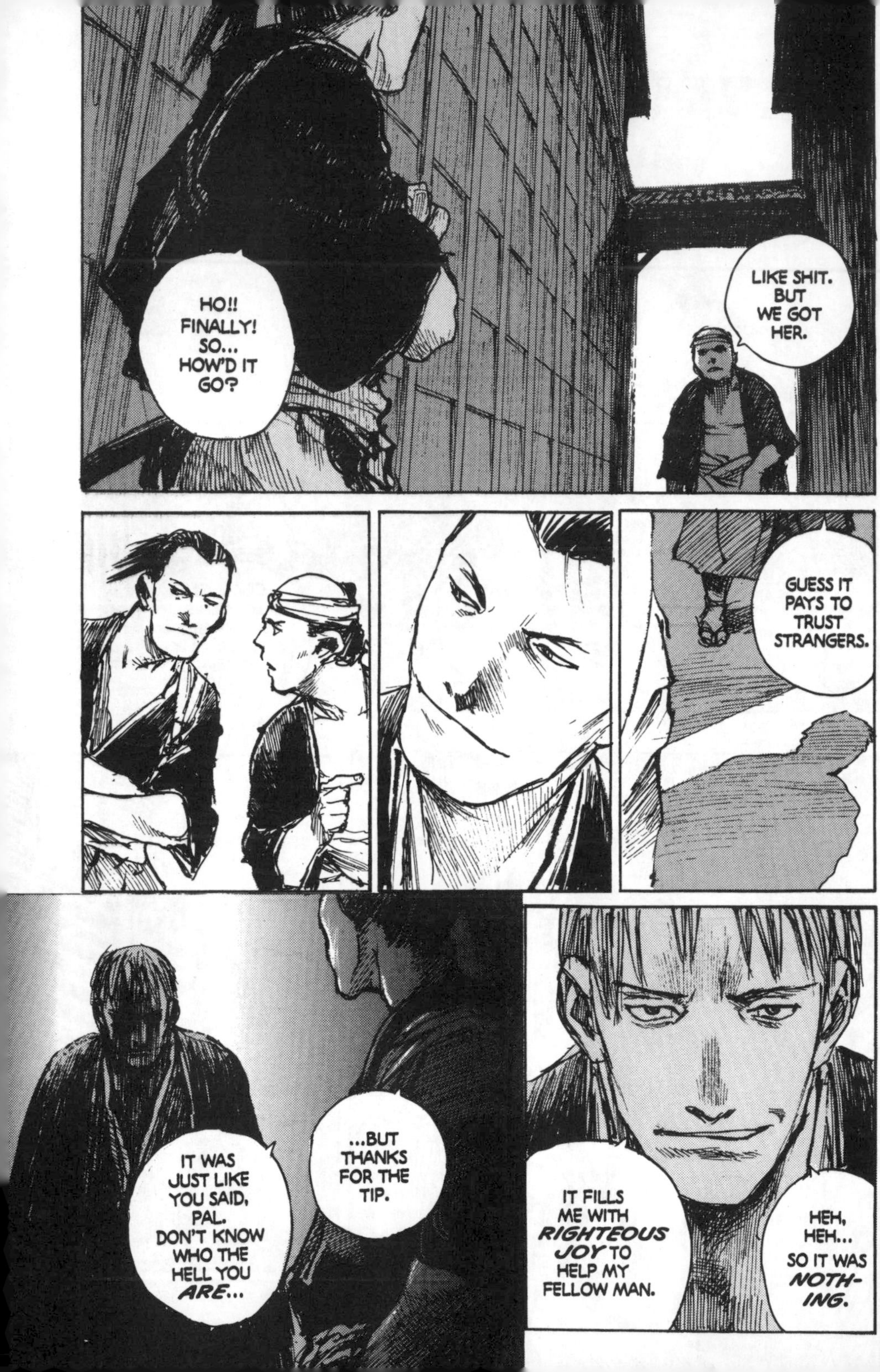
HO!! FINALLY! SO... HOW'D IT GO?
LIKE SHIT. BUT WE GOT HER.
GUESS IT PAYS TO TRUST STRANGERS.
IT WAS JUST LIKE YOU SAID, PAL. DON'T KNOW WHO THE HELL YOU ARE...
...BUT THANKS FOR THE TIP.
HEH, HEH... SO IT WAS NOTHING.
IT FILLS ME WITH RIGHTEOUS JOY TO HELP MY FELLOW MAN.

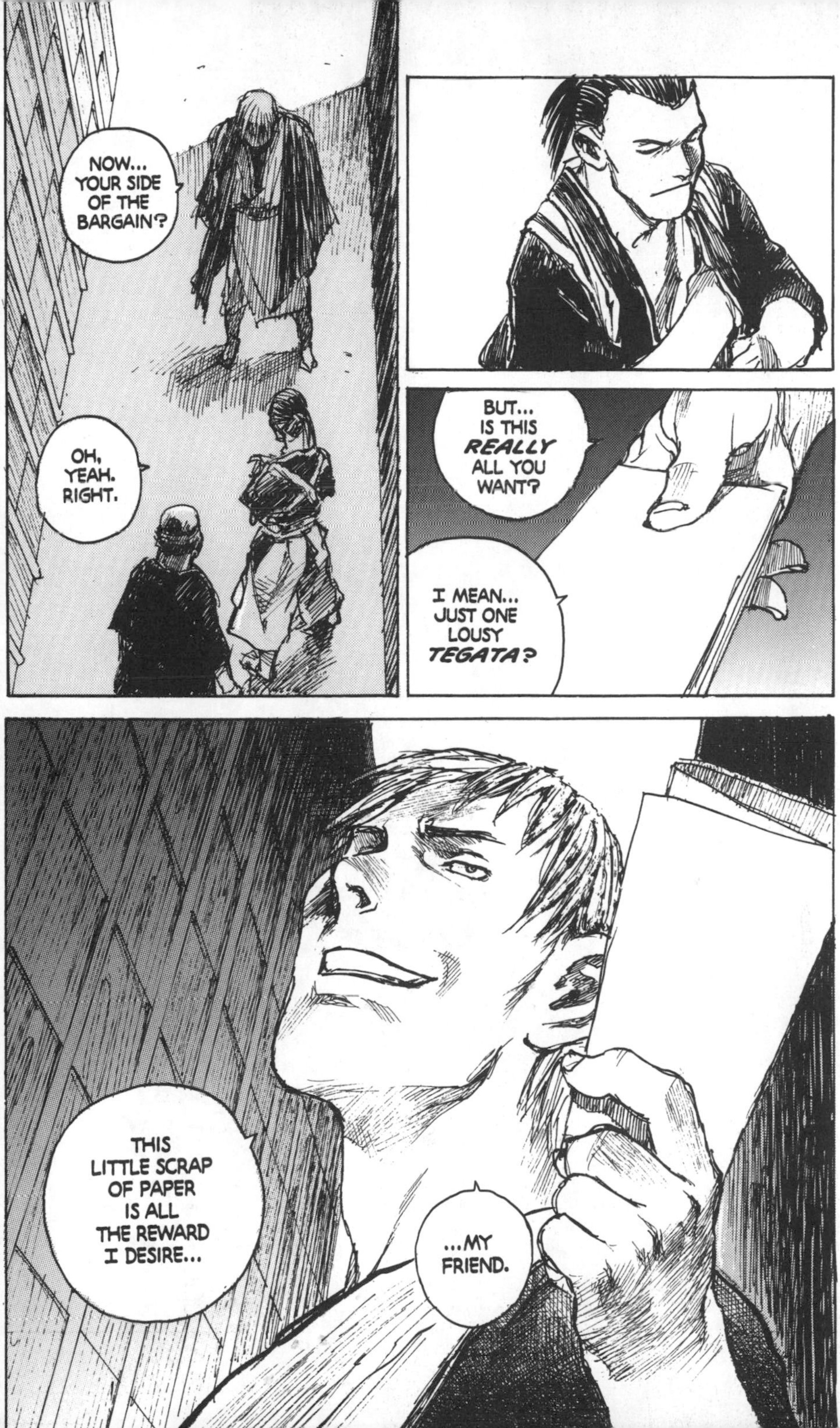
NOW... YOUR SIDE OF THE BARGAIN?
OH, YEAH. RIGHT.
BUT... IS THIS *REALLY* ALL YOU WANT?
I MEAN... JUST ONE LOUSY *TEGATA*?
THIS LITTLE SCRAP OF PAPER IS ALL THE REWARD I DESIRE...
...MY FRIEND.

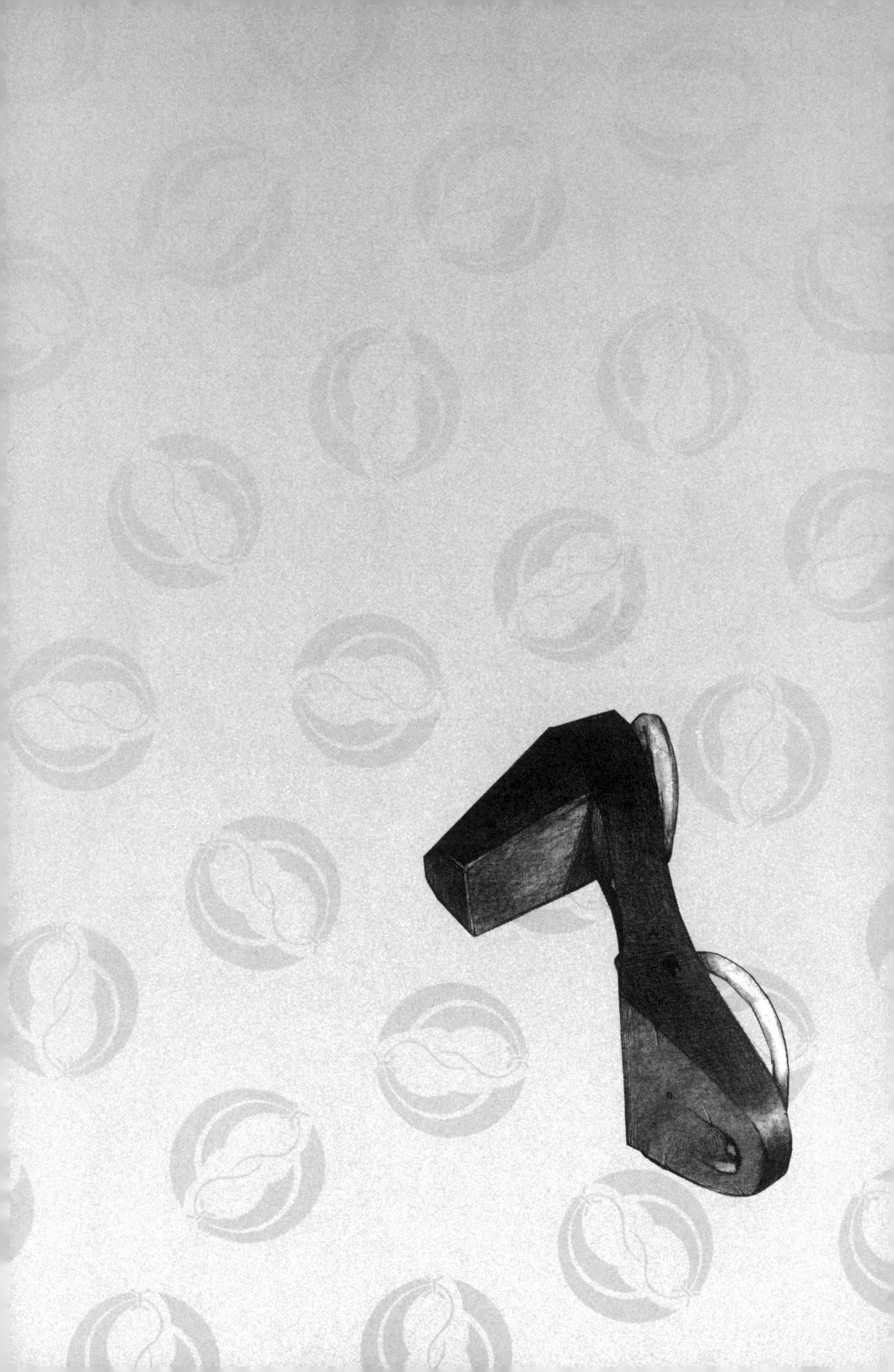

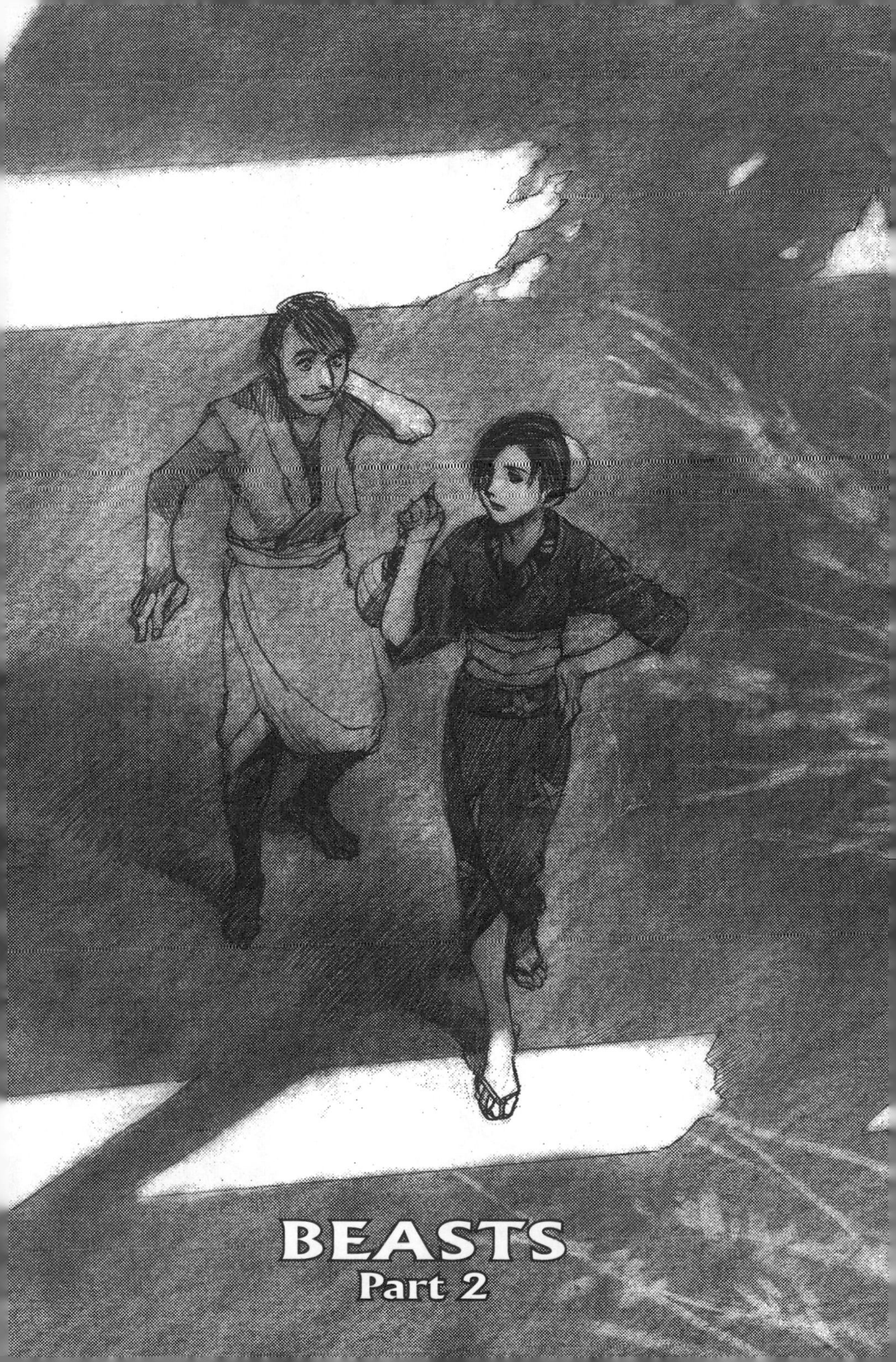
BEASTS
Part 2

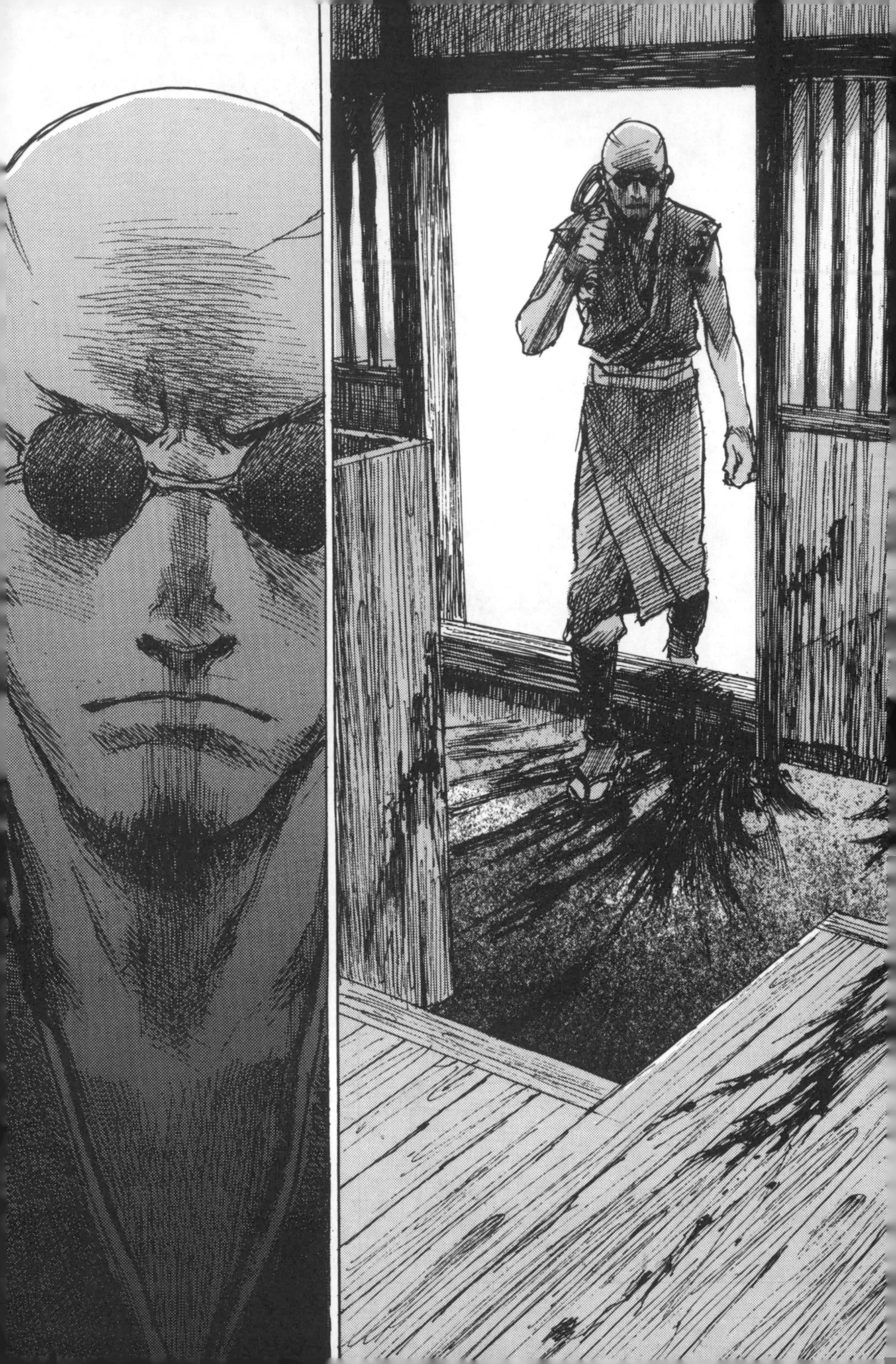

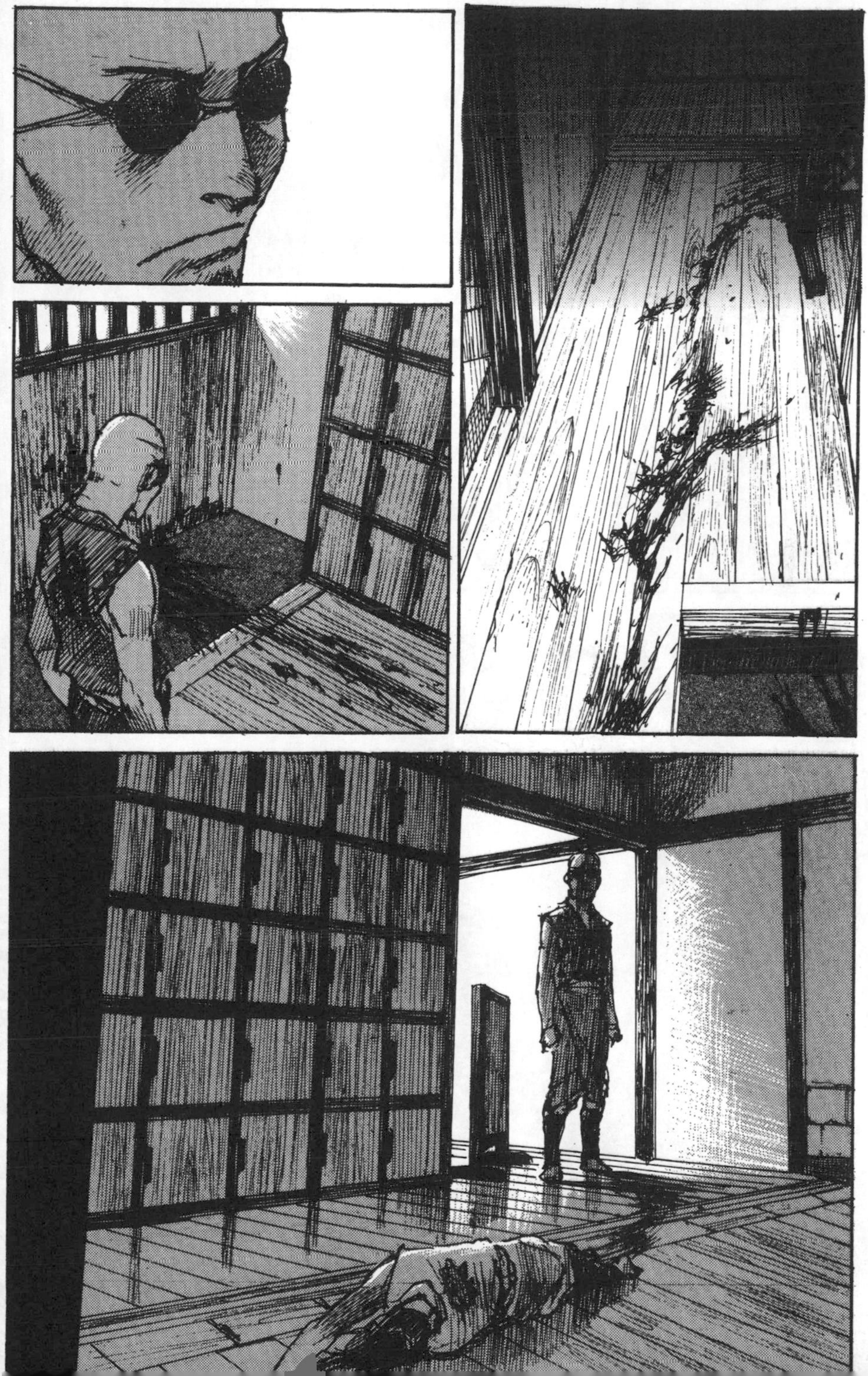

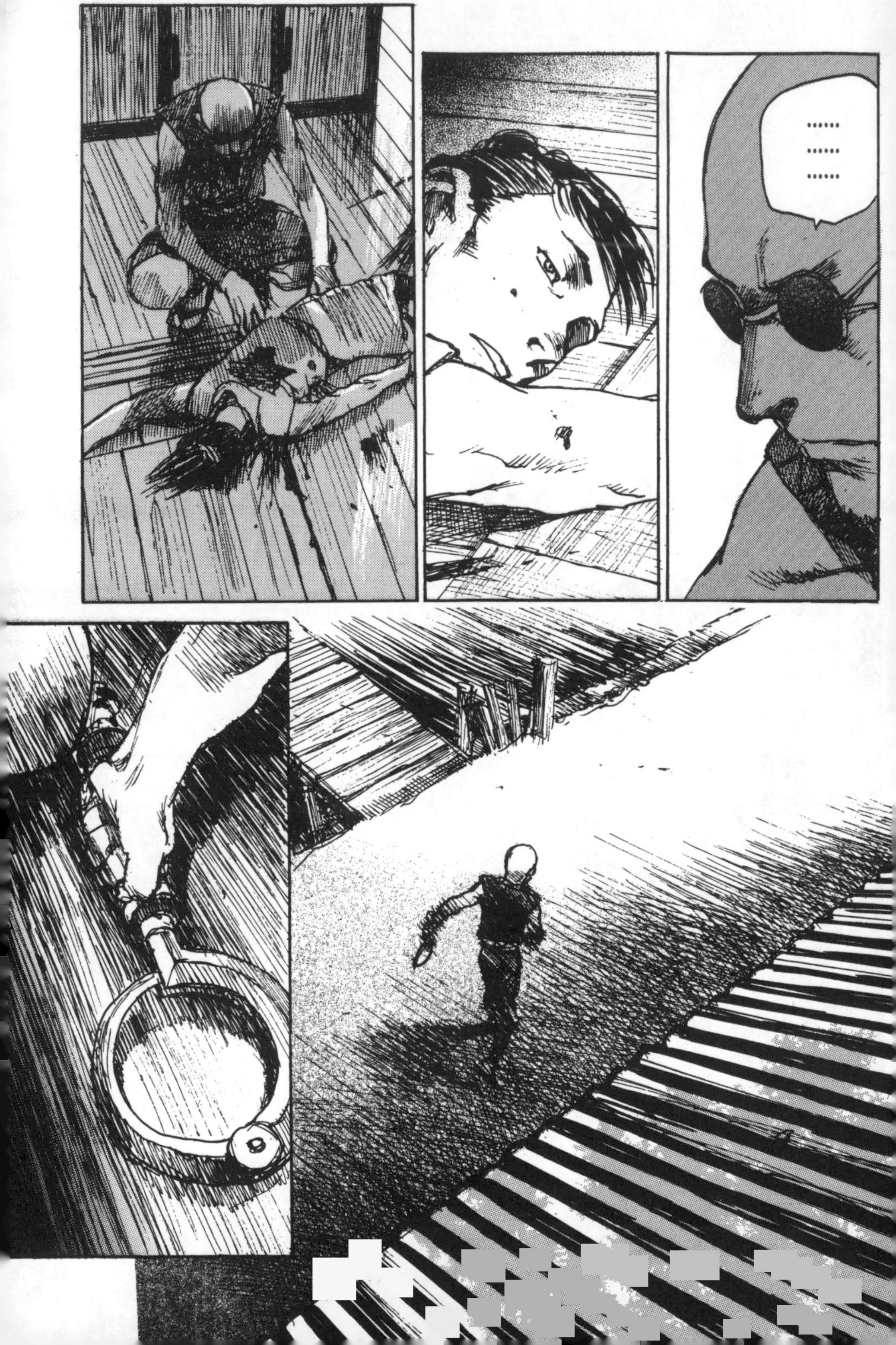
......

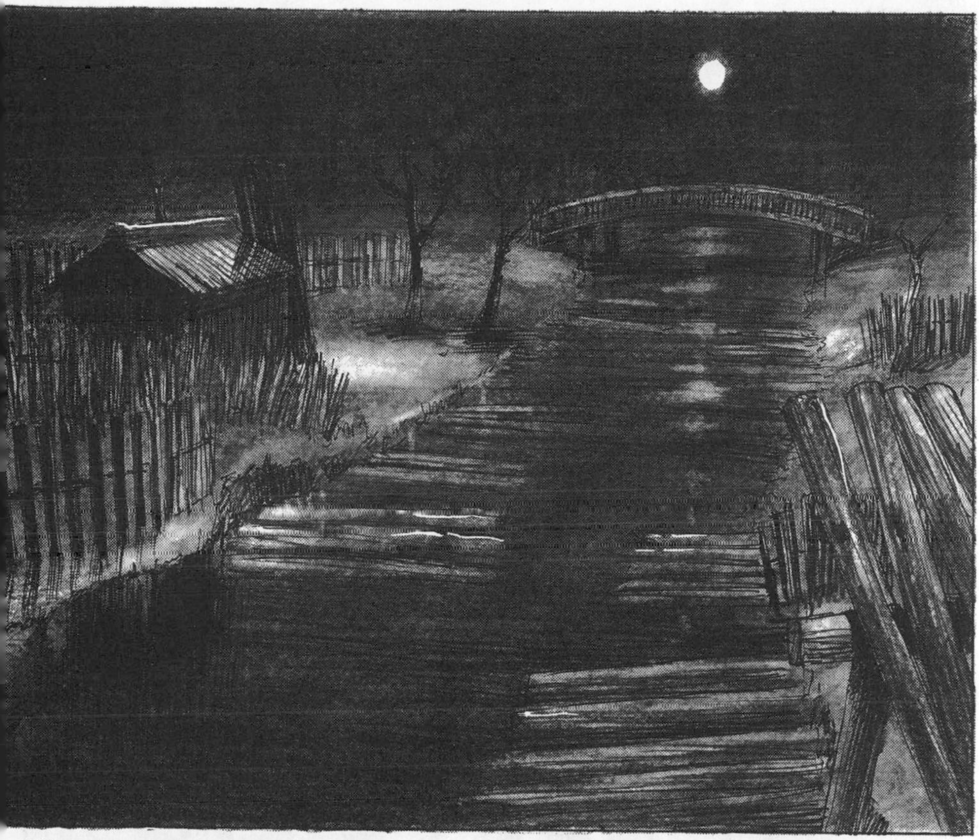

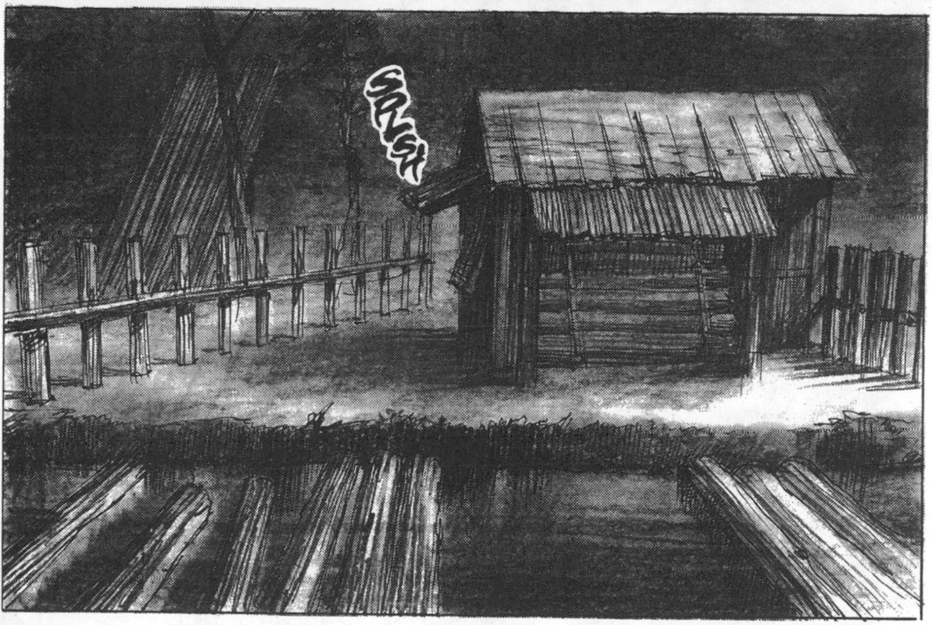
SPLISH

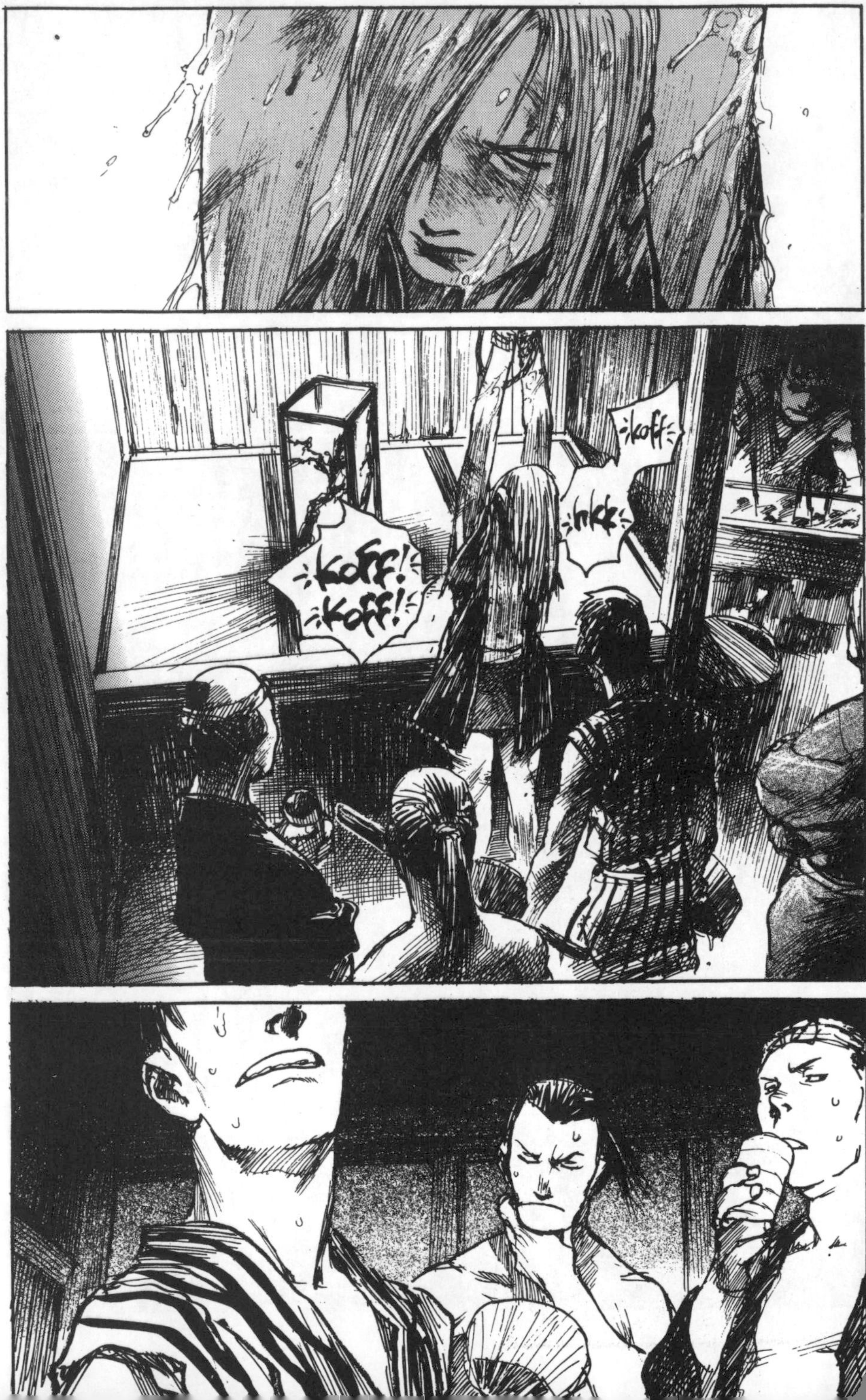
koff
hkk
KOFF! KOFF!

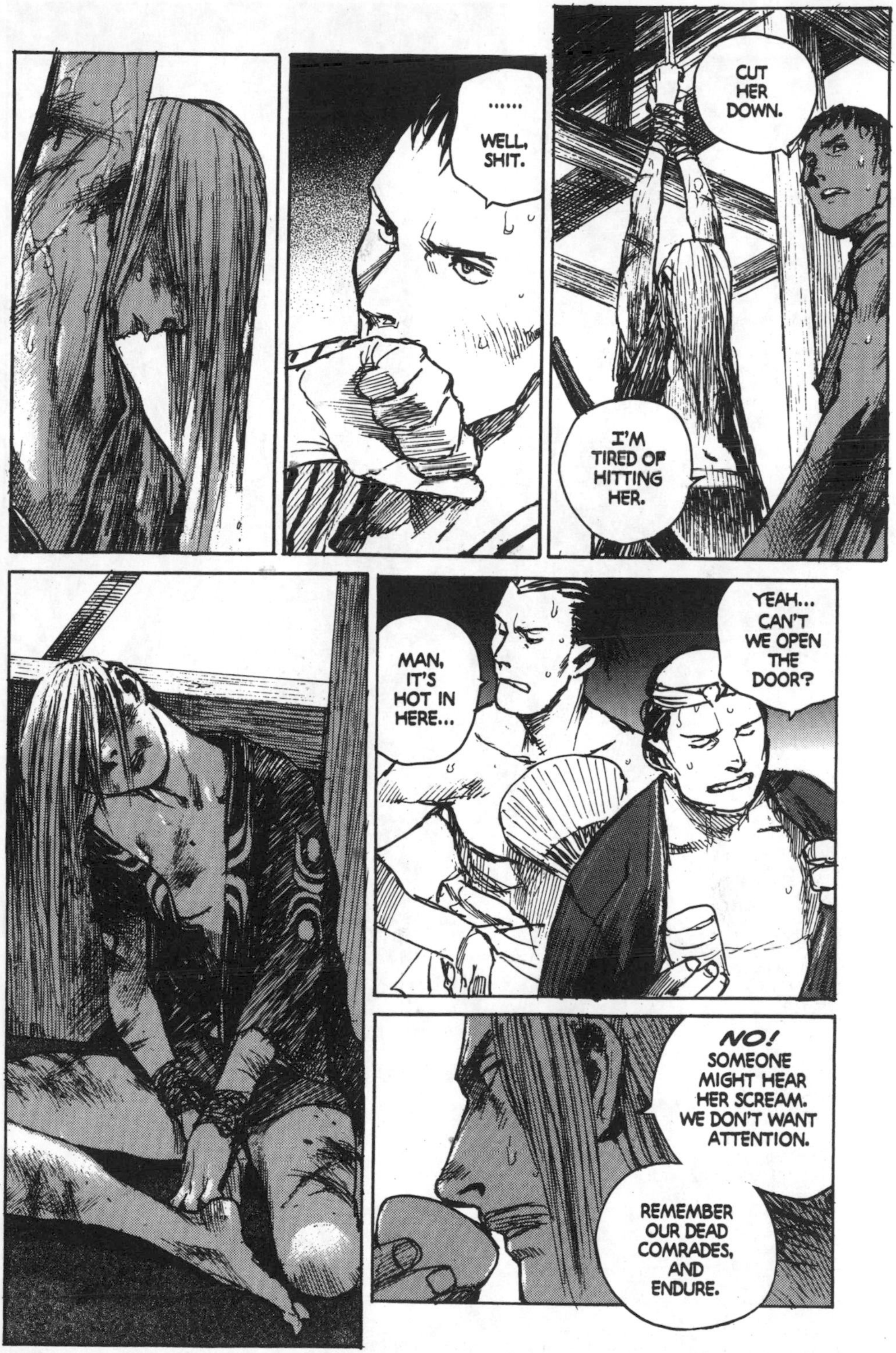
......
WELL, SHIT.
CUT HER DOWN.
I'M TIRED OF HITTING HER.
MAN, IT'S HOT IN HERE...
YEAH... CAN'T WE OPEN THE DOOR?
NO! SOMEONE MIGHT HEAR HER SCREAM. WE DON'T WANT ATTENTION.
REMEMBER OUR DEAD COMRADES, AND ENDURE.

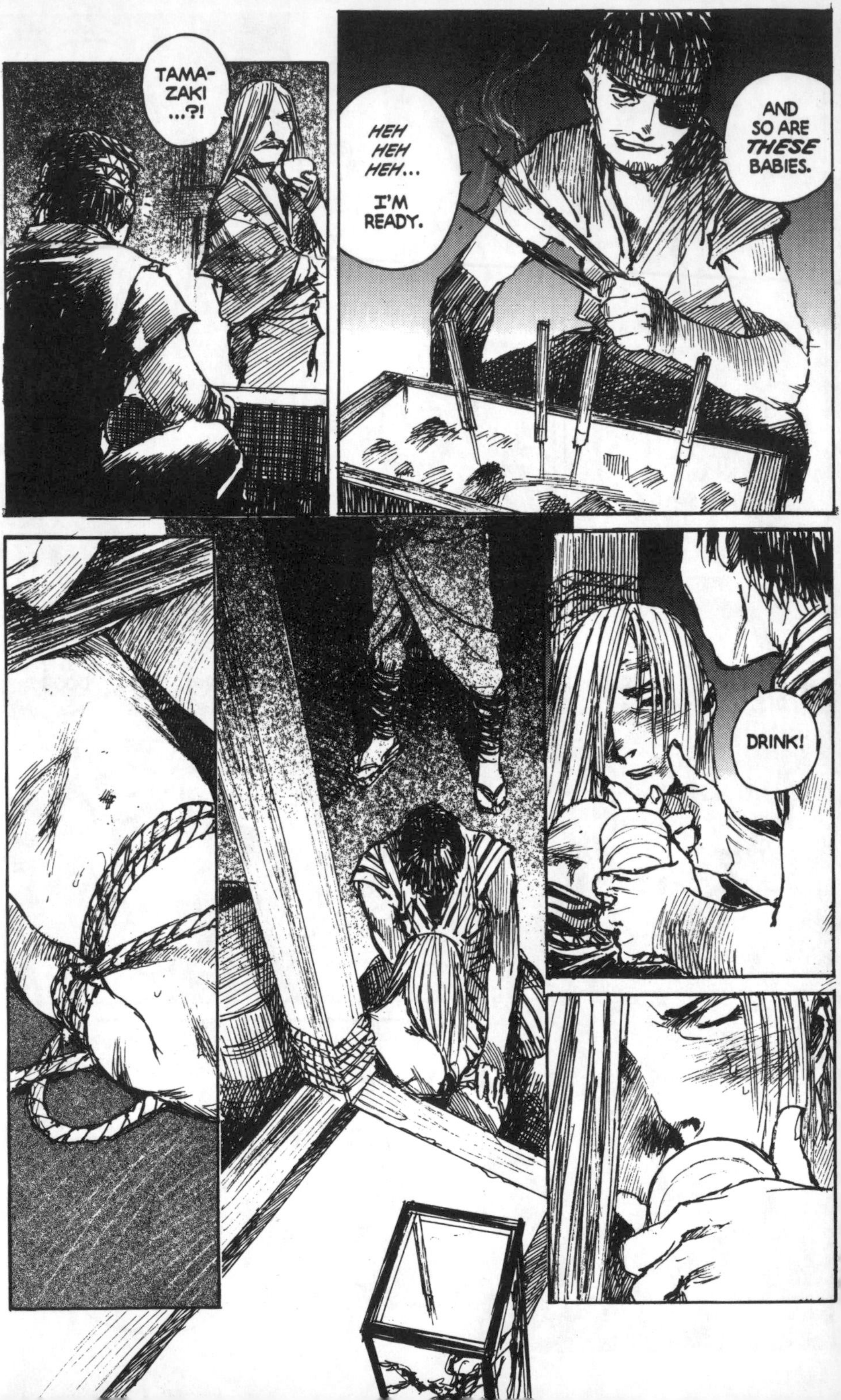
HEH HEH HEH... I'M READY.
AND SO ARE *THESE* BABIES.
TAMA-ZAKI ...?!
DRINK!

GOOD...
STILL
GOT SOME
LIFE
IN YOU.

EXCELLENT.
BE A
BITCH IF
YOU CROAKED
TOO
EASY.

Y'KNOW...BEFORE
I JOINED THE
ITTŌ-RYŪ, I GOT
TO HELP TORTURE
CHRISTIANS. NOW,
THAT WAS SOME
SERIOUS SHIT.
PEELING OFF
THEIR SKIN...

RAPING
AND SLICING
UP GIRLS, RIGHT
IN FRONT OF
THEIR PARENTS...
MOLTEN
SULFUR DOWN
THE THROAT...
YEAH.

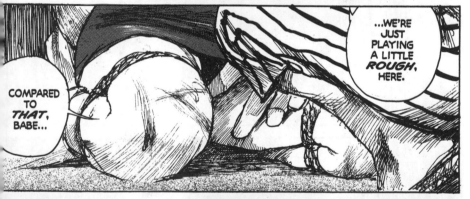

COMPARED
TO
THAT,
BABE...

...WE'RE
JUST
PLAYING
A LITTLE
ROUGH,
HERE.

......
......

SHIT...
I DON'T
GET IT.
YOU *OWE*
THESE GUYS
SO BAD...

...YOU'D
DIE
FOR
THEM?

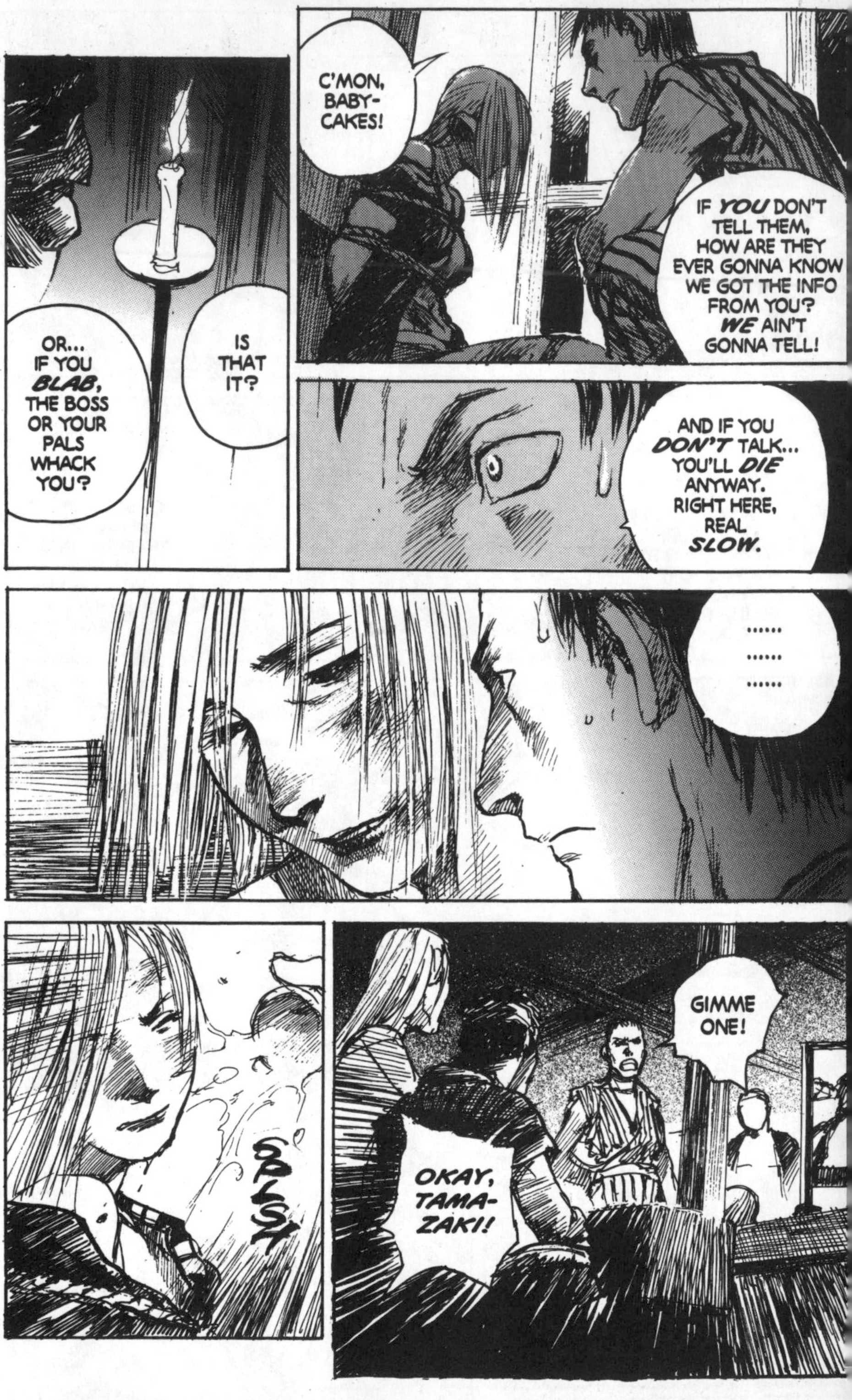
C'MON, BABY-CAKES!
IF YOU DON'T TELL THEM, HOW ARE THEY EVER GONNA KNOW WE GOT THE INFO FROM YOU? WE AIN'T GONNA TELL!
IS THAT IT?
OR... IF YOU BLAB, THE BOSS OR YOUR PALS WHACK YOU?
AND IF YOU DON'T TALK... YOU'LL DIE ANYWAY. RIGHT HERE, REAL SLOW.
......
......
......
GIMME ONE!
OKAY, TAMA-ZAKI!
SPLSH

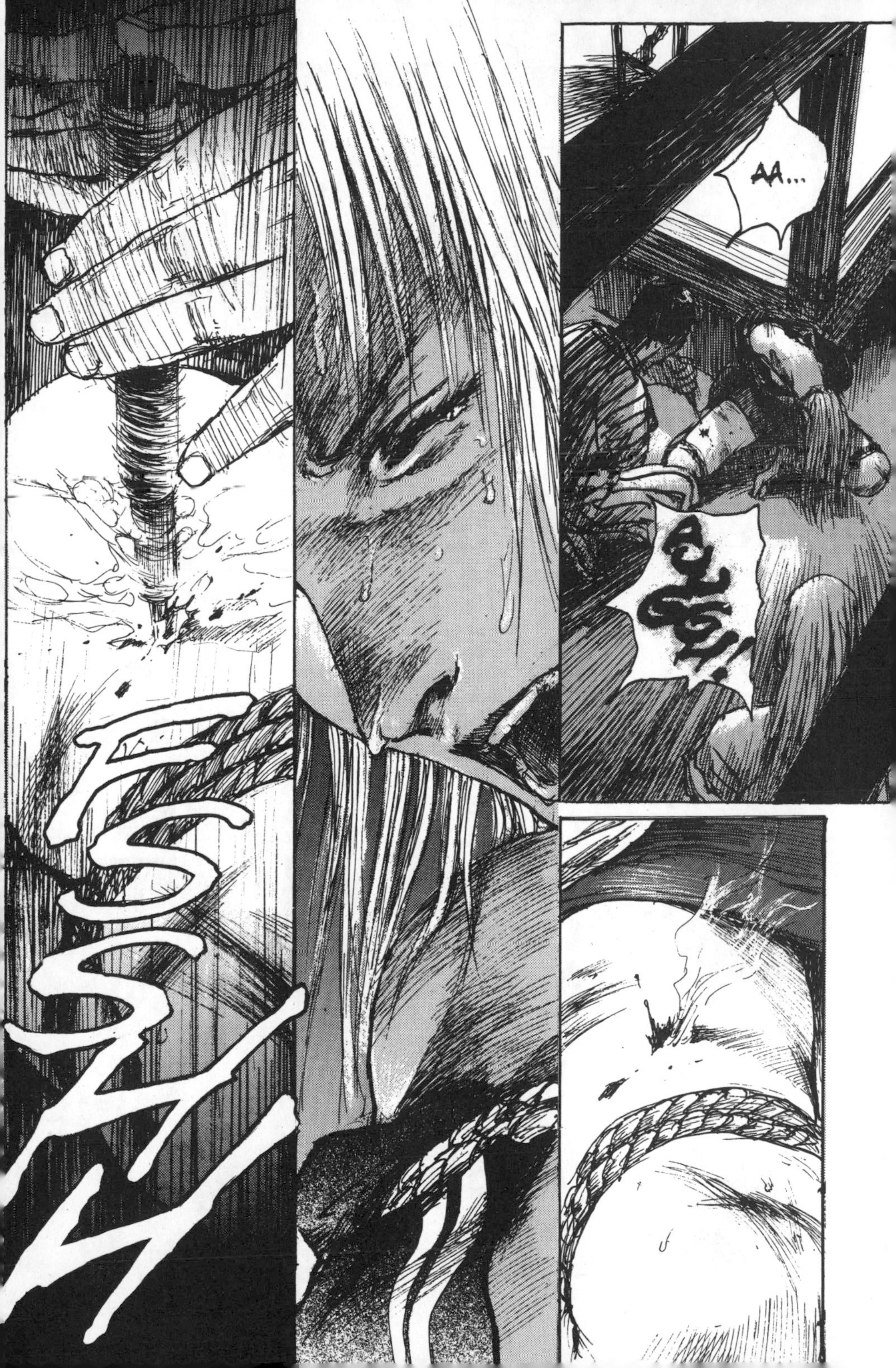
AA...

MMM, TASTY!

LOVE THE SMELL...

...OF BARBE-QUED MEAT.

BUT YOU GOTTA *SPICE* IT WHILE IT'S HOT, YEAH?

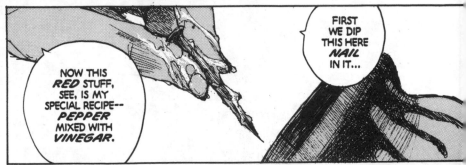

NOW THIS *RED* STUFF, SEE, IS MY SPECIAL RECIPE-- *PEPPER* MIXED WITH *VINEGAR*.

FIRST WE DIP THIS HERE *NAIL* IN IT...

NOW... LET'S PLUG THAT HOLE UP SO IT DON'T *BLEED*.

AH...!

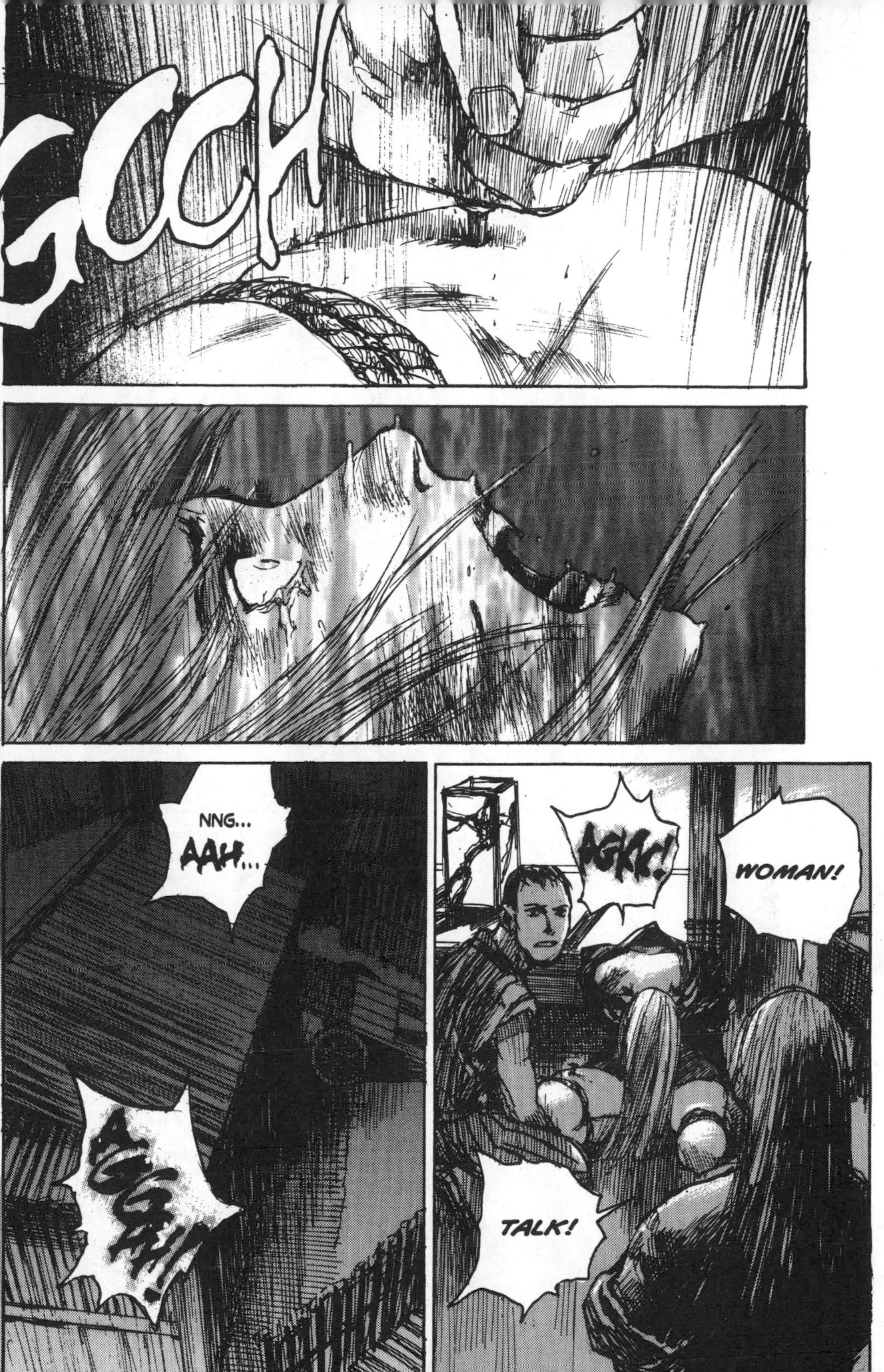
GCCH
WOMAN!
AGKK!
TALK!
NNG... AAH...
AGGH!

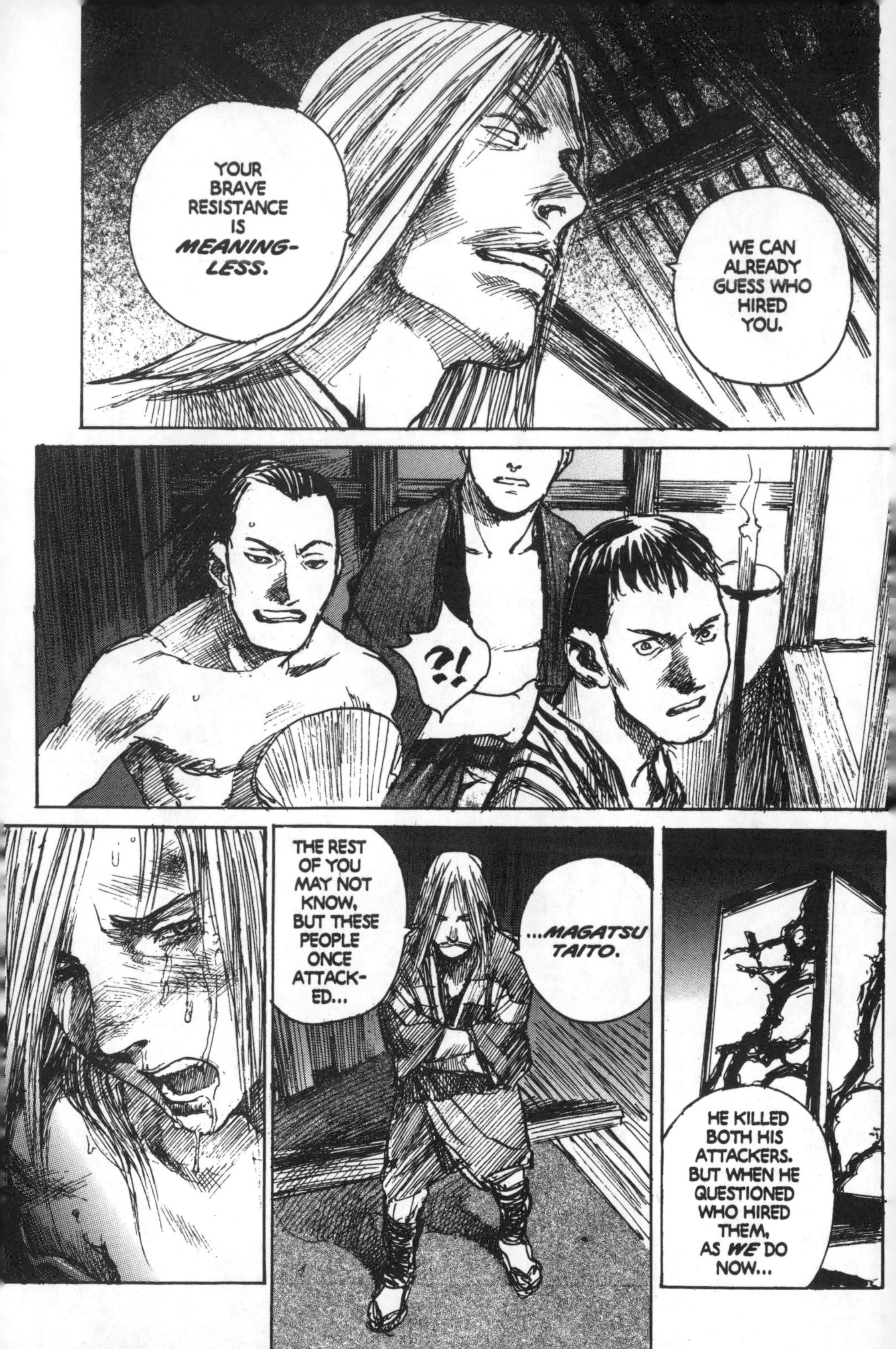
YOUR BRAVE RESISTANCE IS *MEANING-LESS.*
WE CAN ALREADY GUESS WHO HIRED YOU.
?!
THE REST OF YOU MAY NOT KNOW, BUT THESE PEOPLE ONCE ATTACK-ED...
...*MAGATSU TAITO.*
HE KILLED BOTH HIS ATTACKERS. BUT WHEN HE QUESTIONED WHO HIRED THEM, AS *WE* DO NOW...

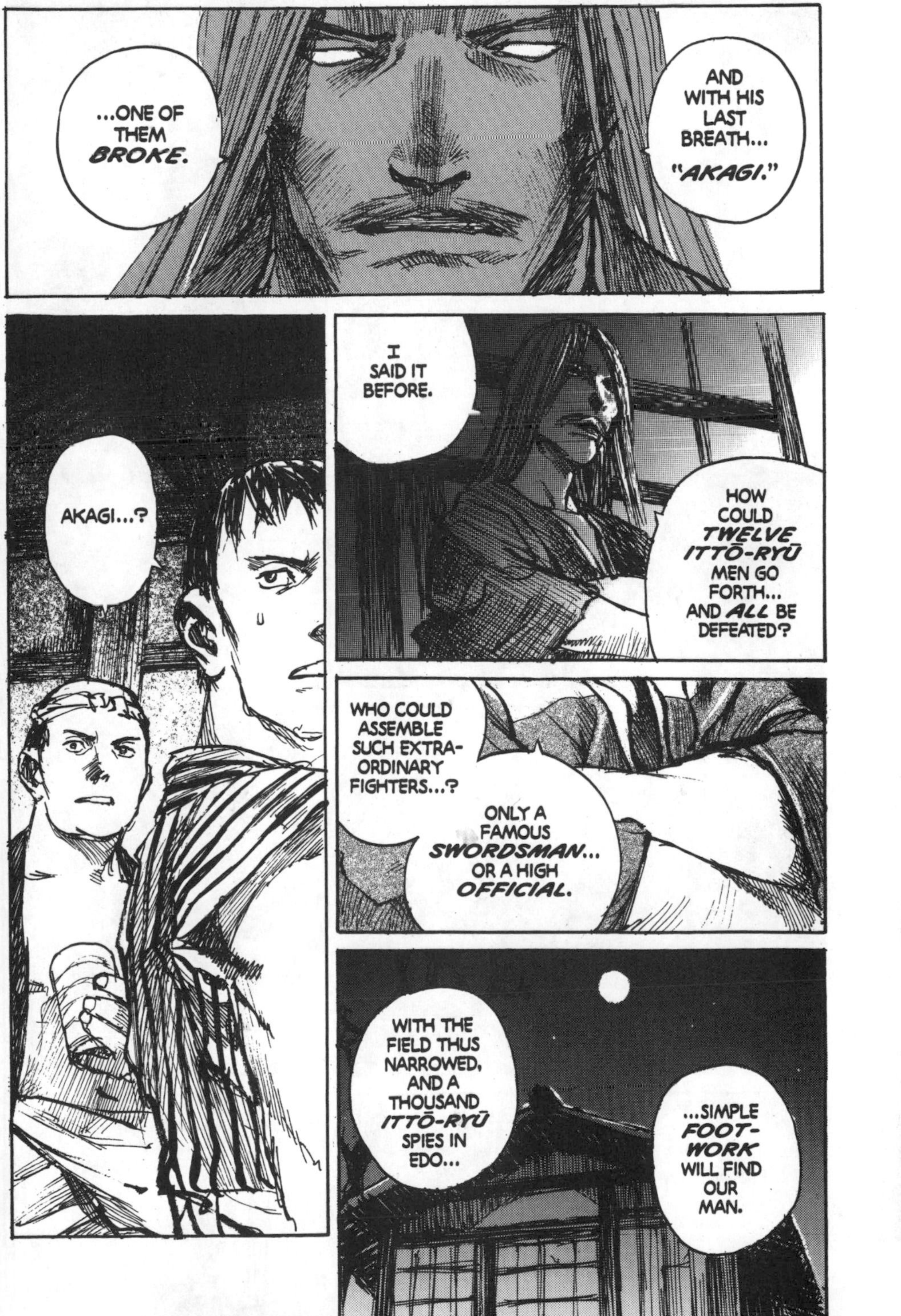
...ONE OF THEM BROKE.
AND WITH HIS LAST BREATH... "AKAGI."
AKAGI...?
I SAID IT BEFORE.
HOW COULD TWELVE ITTŌ-RYŪ MEN GO FORTH... AND ALL BE DEFEATED?
WHO COULD ASSEMBLE SUCH EXTRA-ORDINARY FIGHTERS...?
ONLY A FAMOUS SWORDSMAN... OR A HIGH OFFICIAL.
WITH THE FIELD THUS NARROWED, AND A THOUSAND ITTŌ-RYŪ SPIES IN EDO...
...SIMPLE FOOT-WORK WILL FIND OUR MAN.

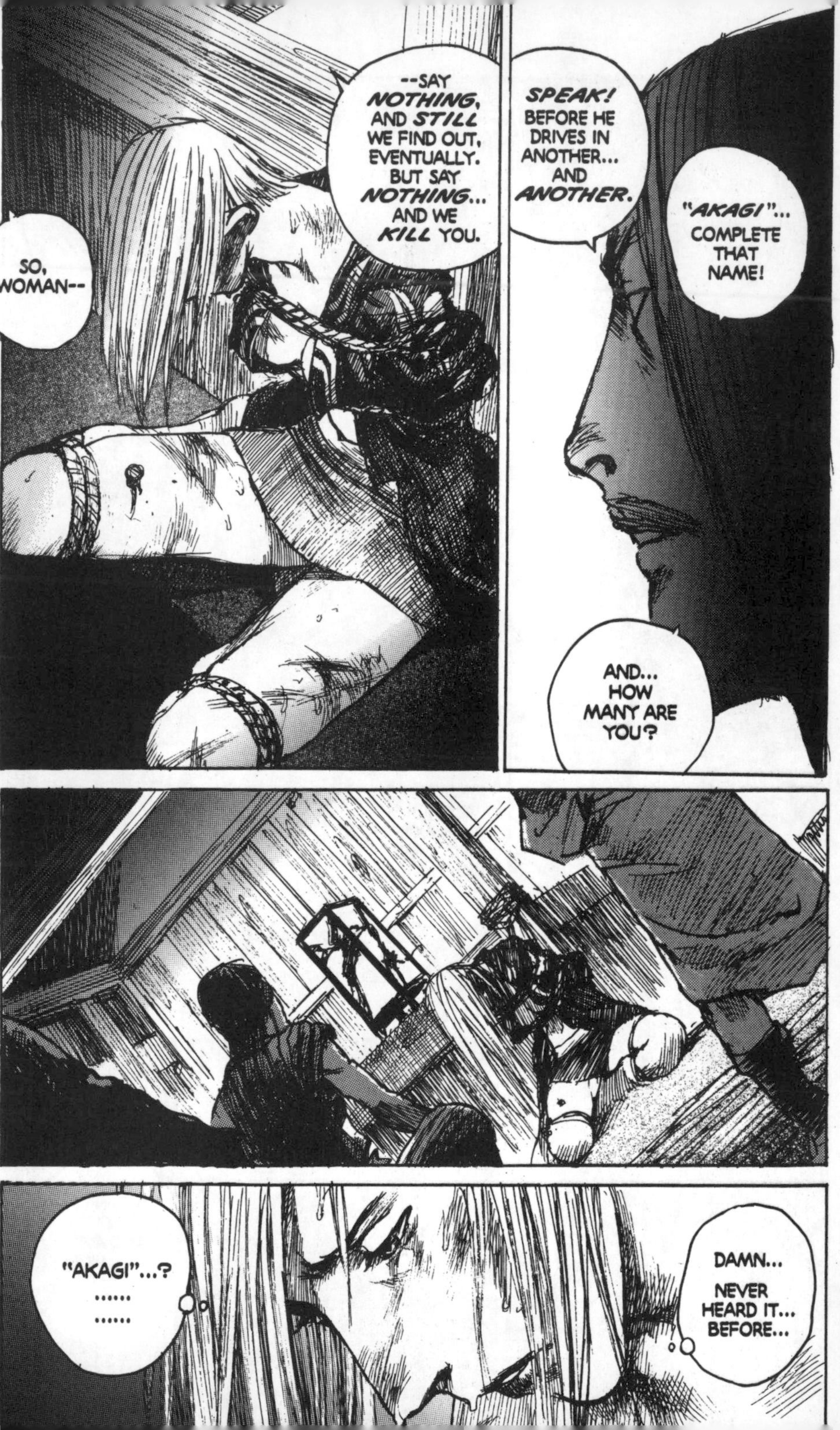
SO, WOMAN--
--SAY NOTHING, AND STILL WE FIND OUT, EVENTUALLY. BUT SAY NOTHING... AND WE KILL YOU.
SPEAK! BEFORE HE DRIVES IN ANOTHER... AND ANOTHER.
"AKAGI"... COMPLETE THAT NAME!
AND... HOW MANY ARE YOU?
"AKAGI"...? ....
DAMN... NEVER HEARD IT... BEFORE...

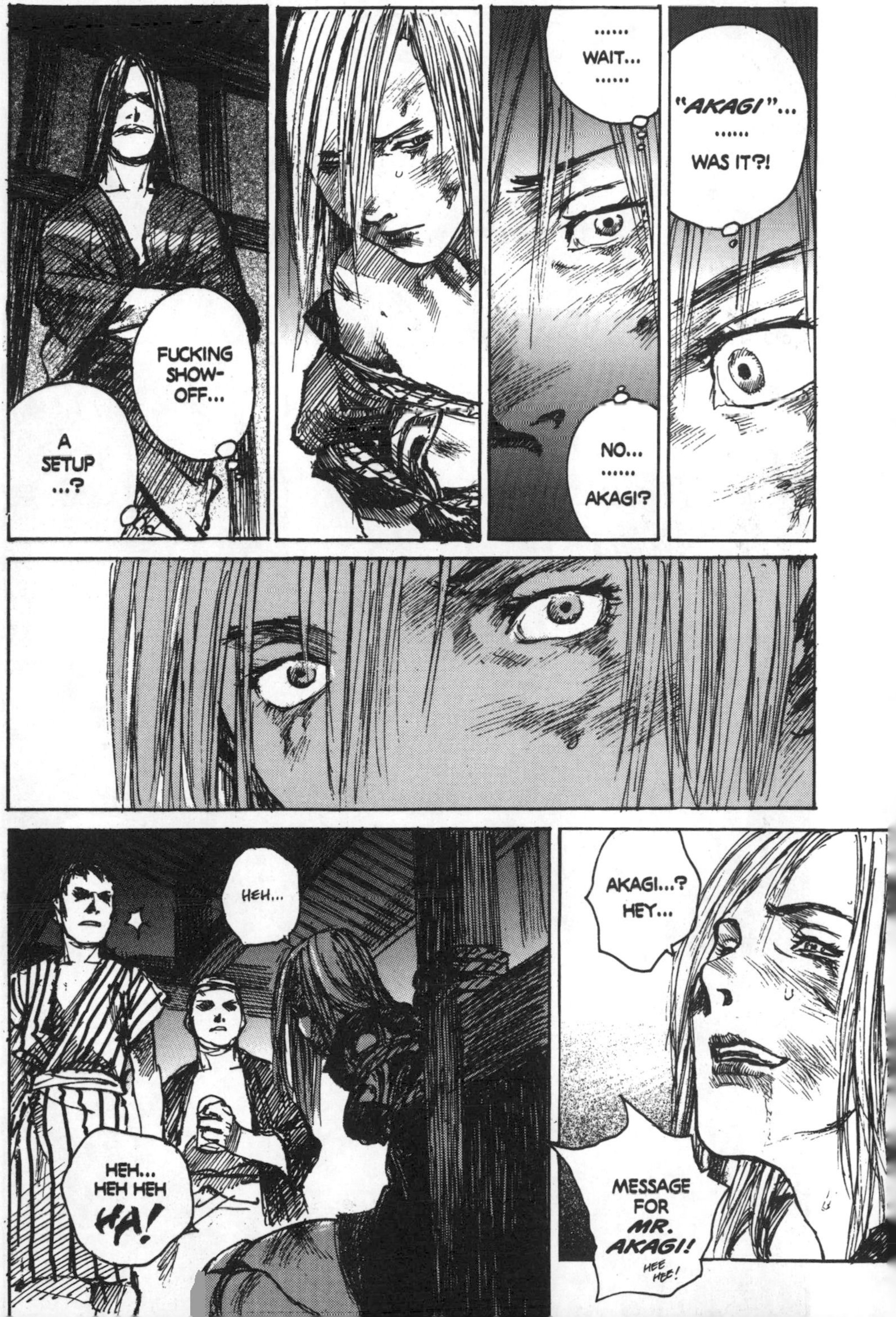
"AKAGI"... ...... WAS IT?!
...... WAIT... ......
NO... ...... AKAGI?
FUCKING SHOW-OFF...
A SETUP ...?
AKAGI...? HEY...
MESSAGE FOR MR. AKAGI!
HEE HEE!
HEH...
HEH... HEH HEH HA!

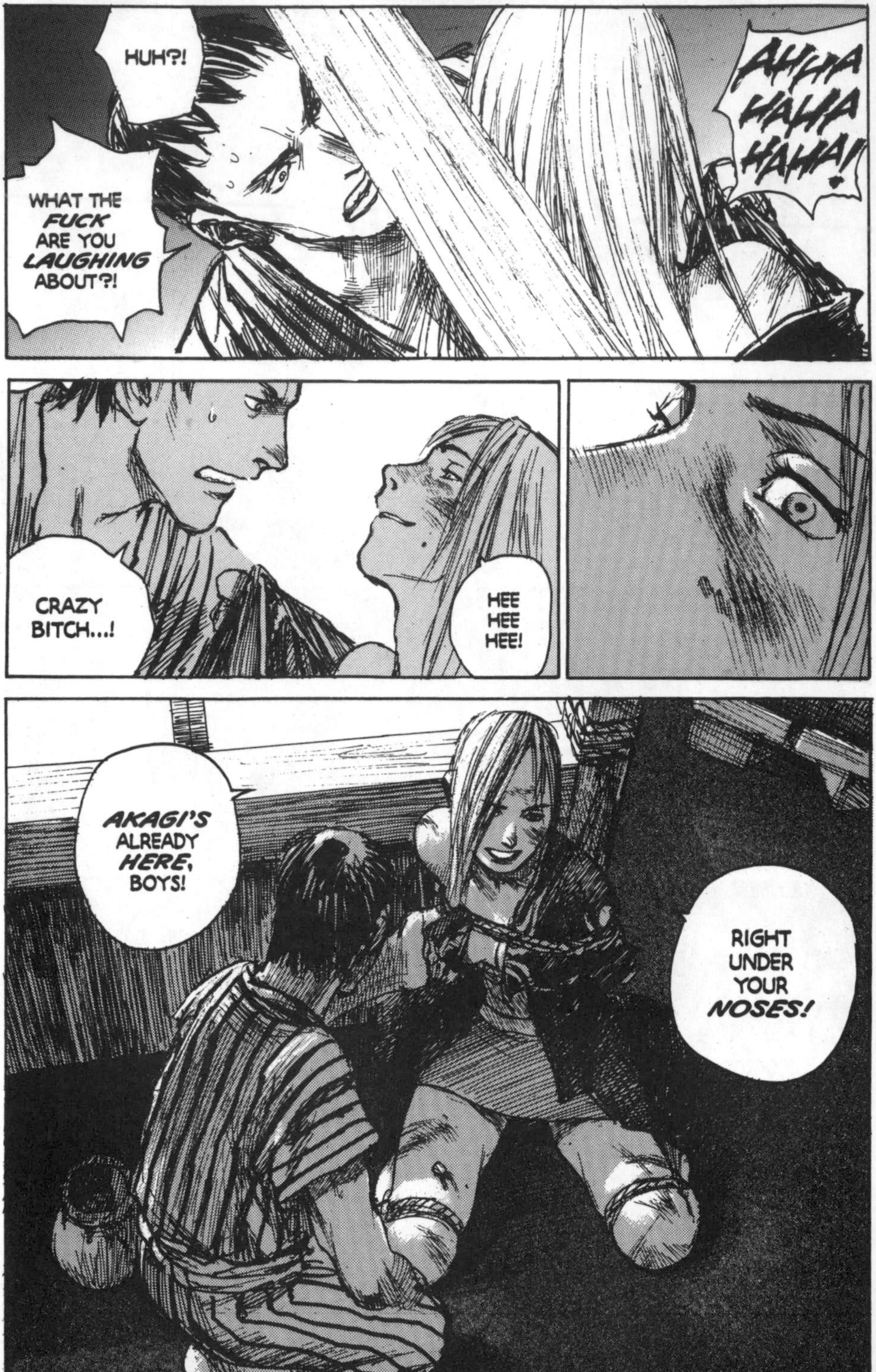
AHHA HAHA HAHA!
HUH?!
WHAT THE FUCK ARE YOU LAUGHING ABOUT?!
HEE HEE HEE!
CRAZY BITCH...!
AKAGI'S ALREADY HERE, BOYS!
RIGHT UNDER YOUR NOSES!

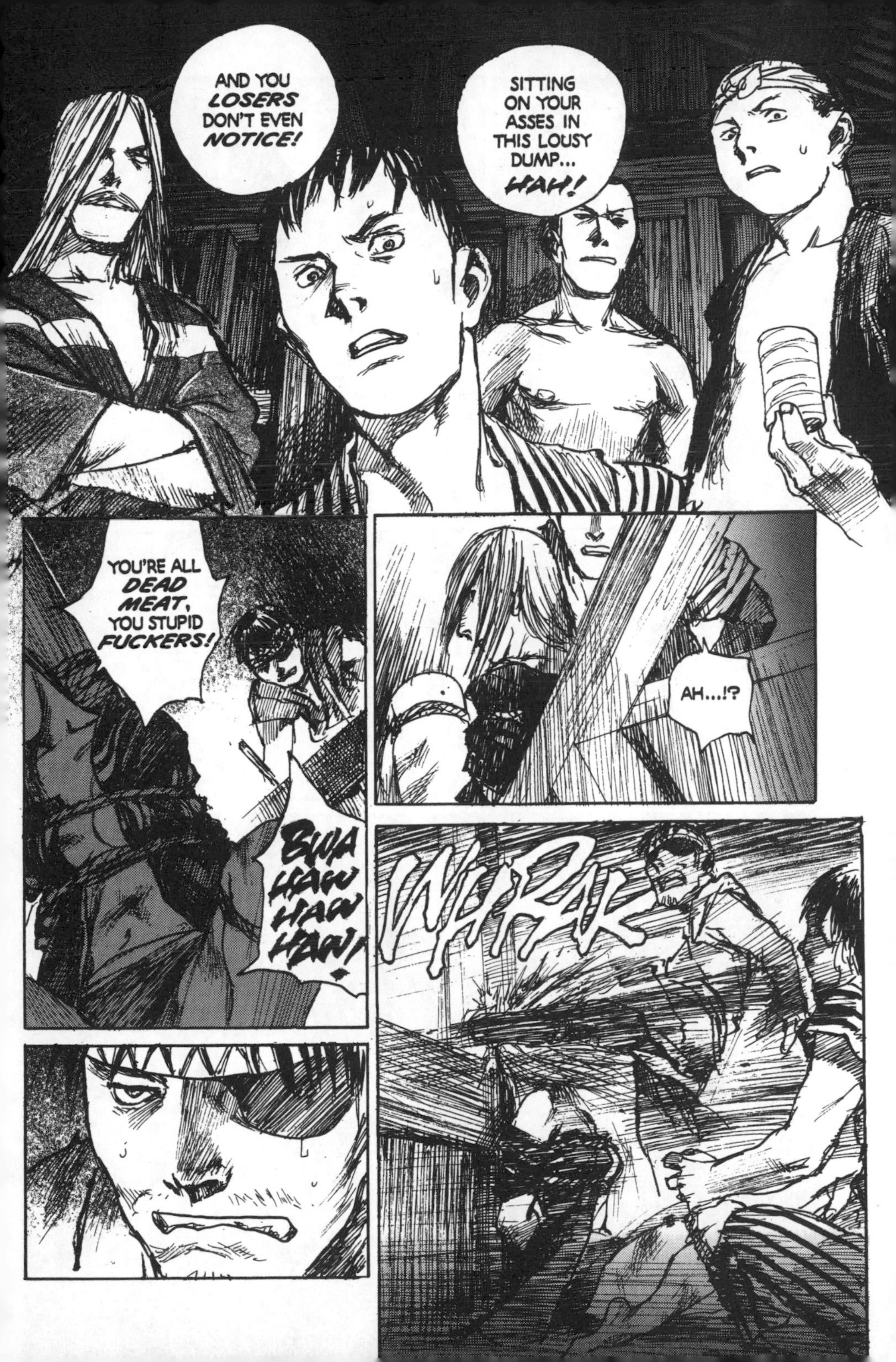
AND YOU LOSERS DON'T EVEN NOTICE!
SITTING ON YOUR ASSES IN THIS LOUSY DUMP... HAH!
YOU'RE ALL DEAD MEAT, YOU STUPID FUCKERS!
BWA HAW HAW HAW!
AH...!?

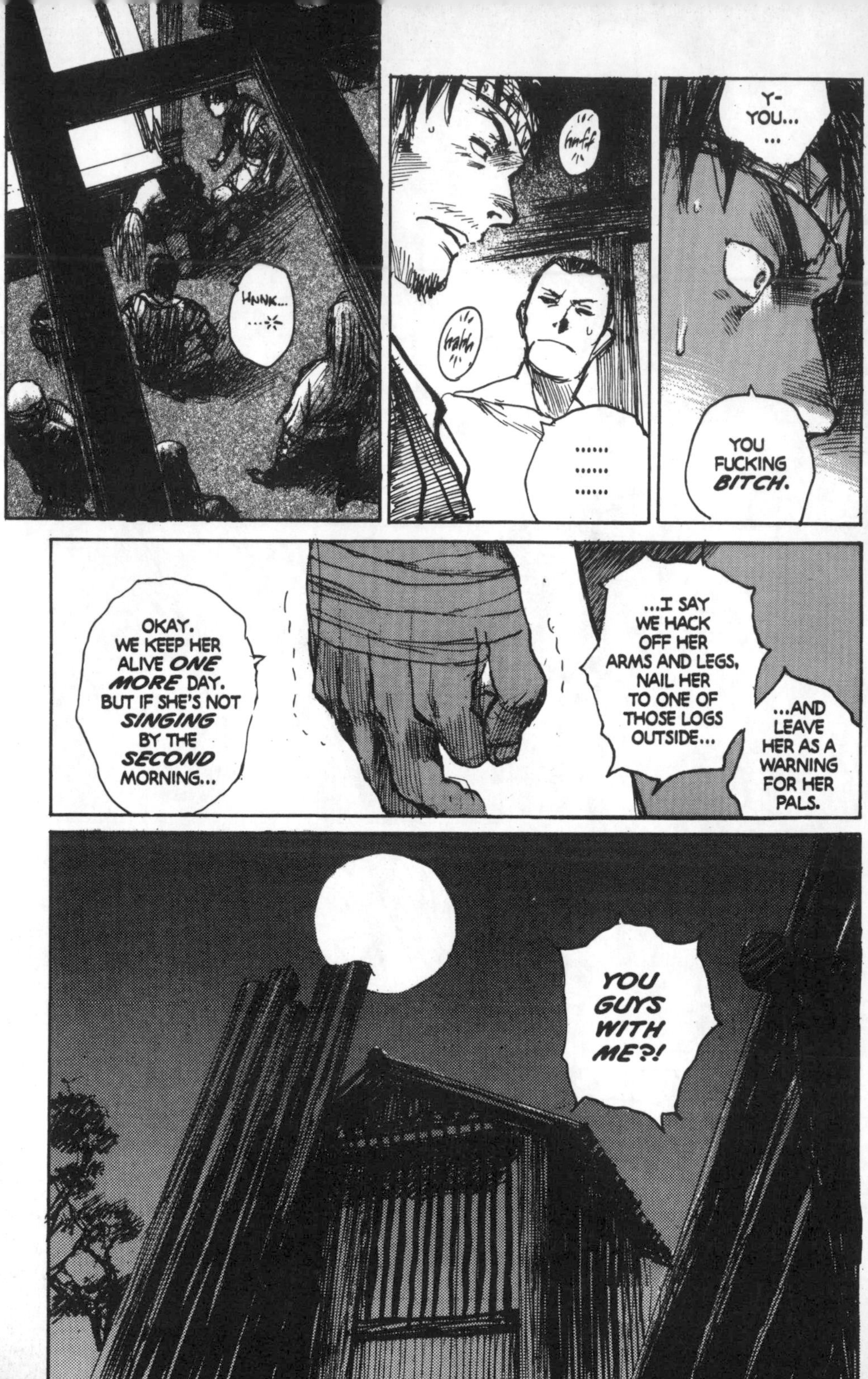
HNNK... ...
hmff
hahh
....
Y- YOU... ...
YOU FUCKING BITCH.
OKAY. WE KEEP HER ALIVE ONE MORE DAY. BUT IF SHE'S NOT SINGING BY THE SECOND MORNING...
...I SAY WE HACK OFF HER ARMS AND LEGS, NAIL HER TO ONE OF THOSE LOGS OUTSIDE...
...AND LEAVE HER AS A WARNING FOR HER PALS.
YOU GUYS WITH ME?!

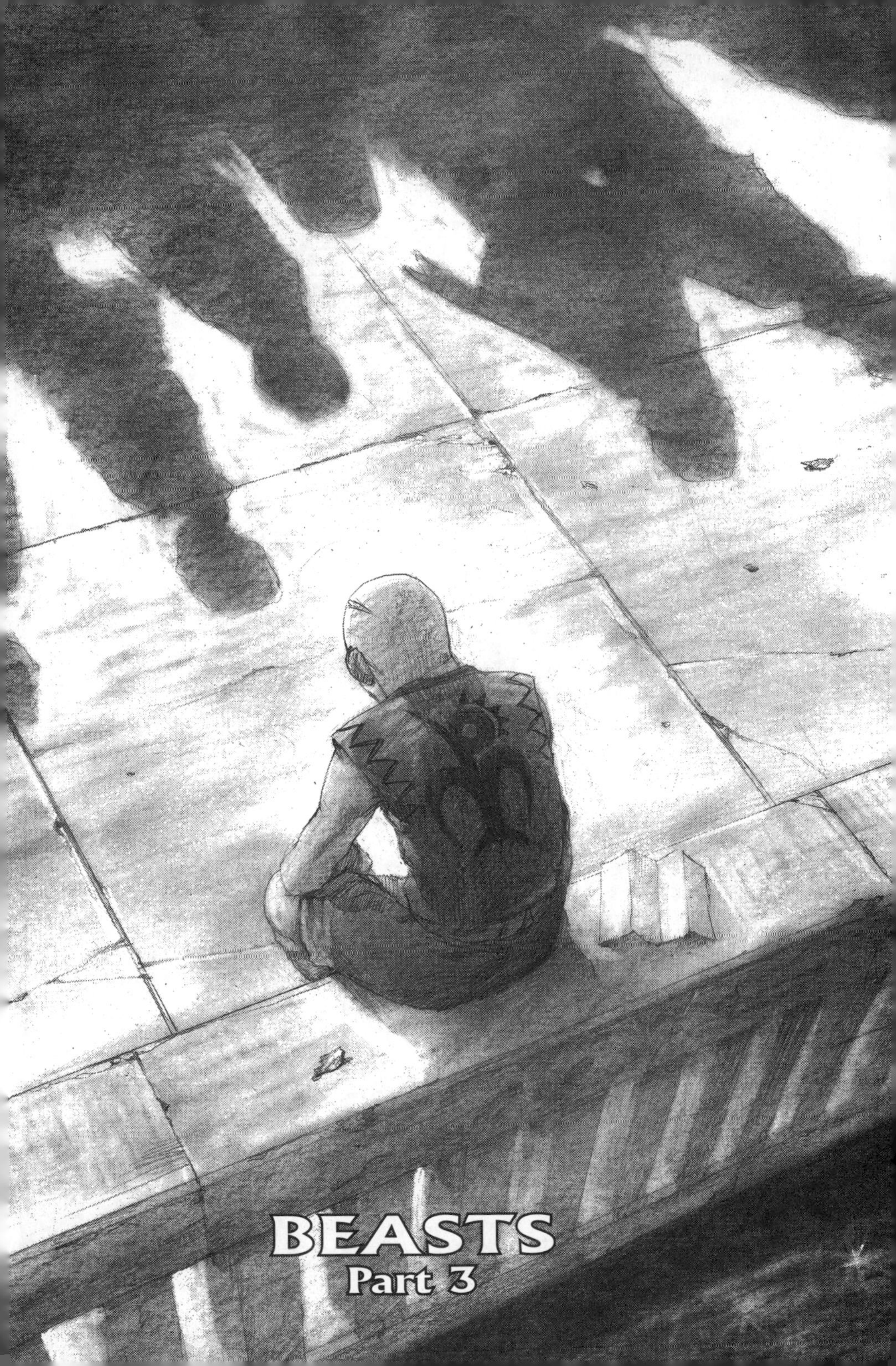
BEASTS
Part 3

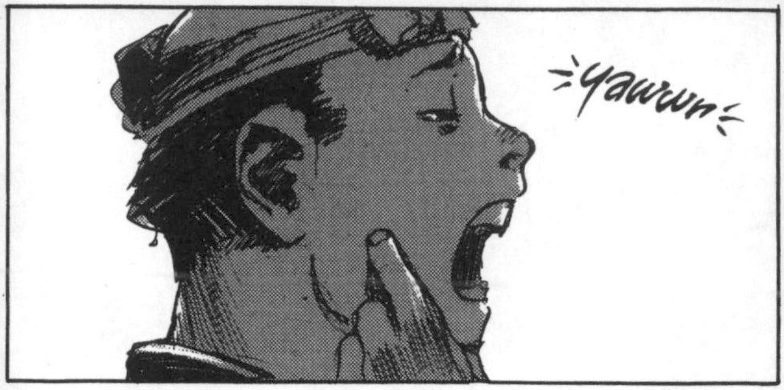
Yawwn
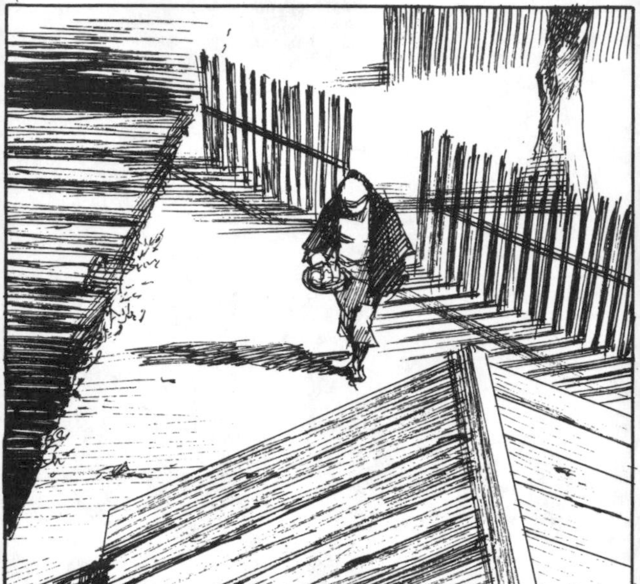
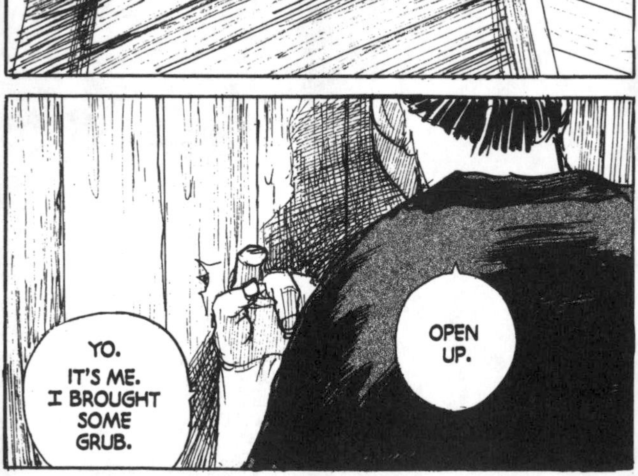
OPEN UP.
YO. IT'S ME. I BROUGHT SOME GRUB.
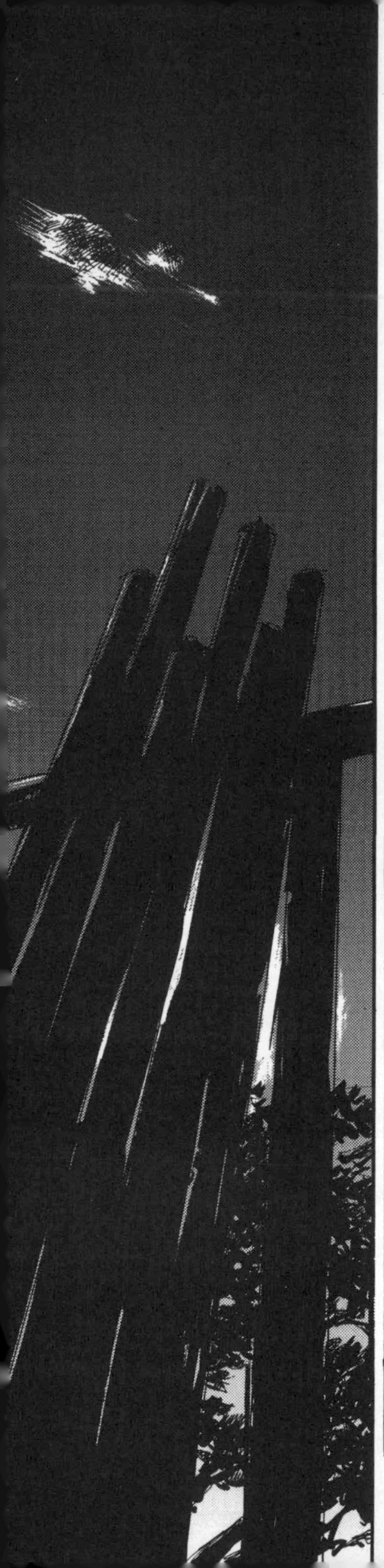

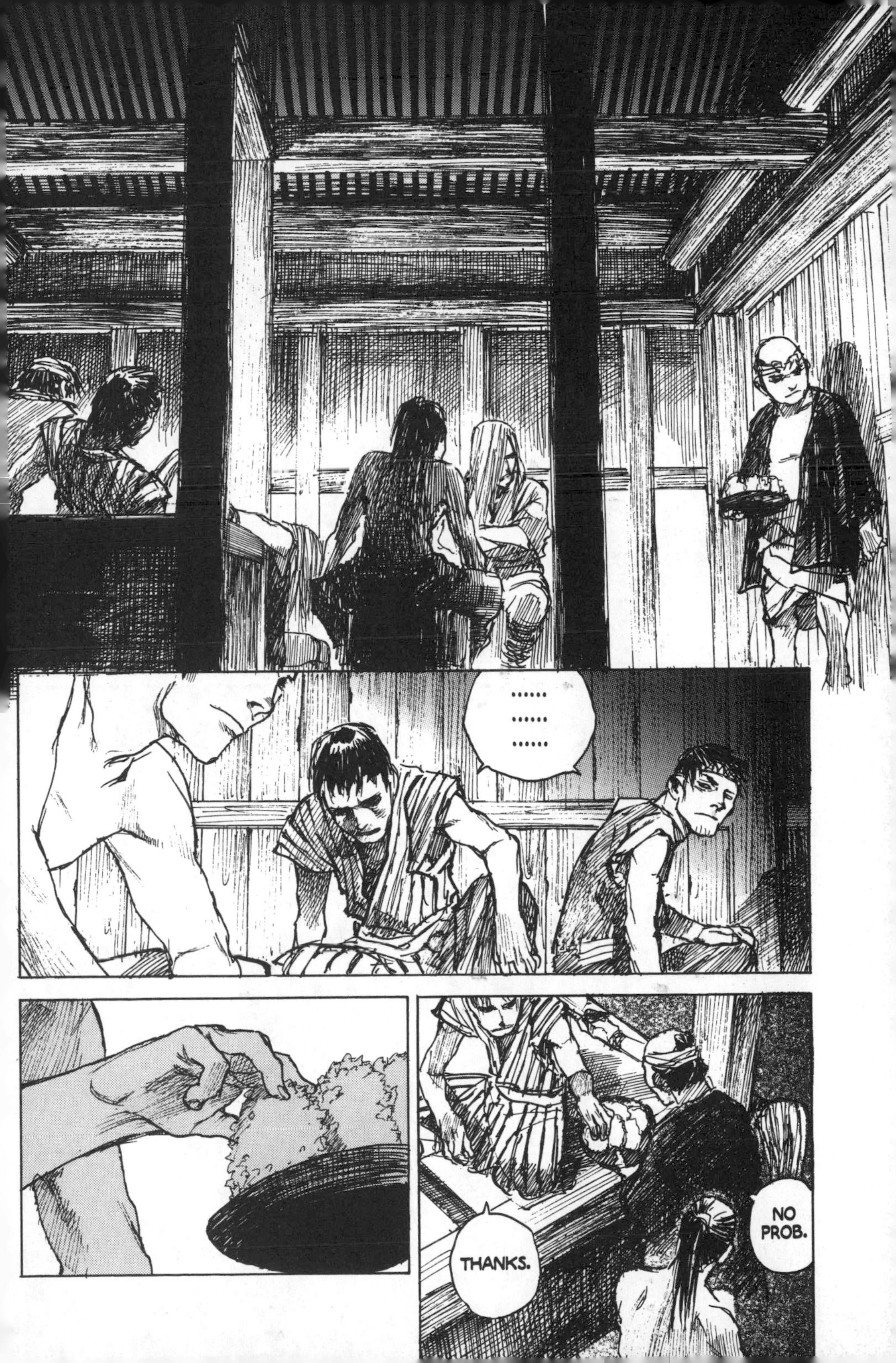

......
......
......
NO PROB.
THANKS.

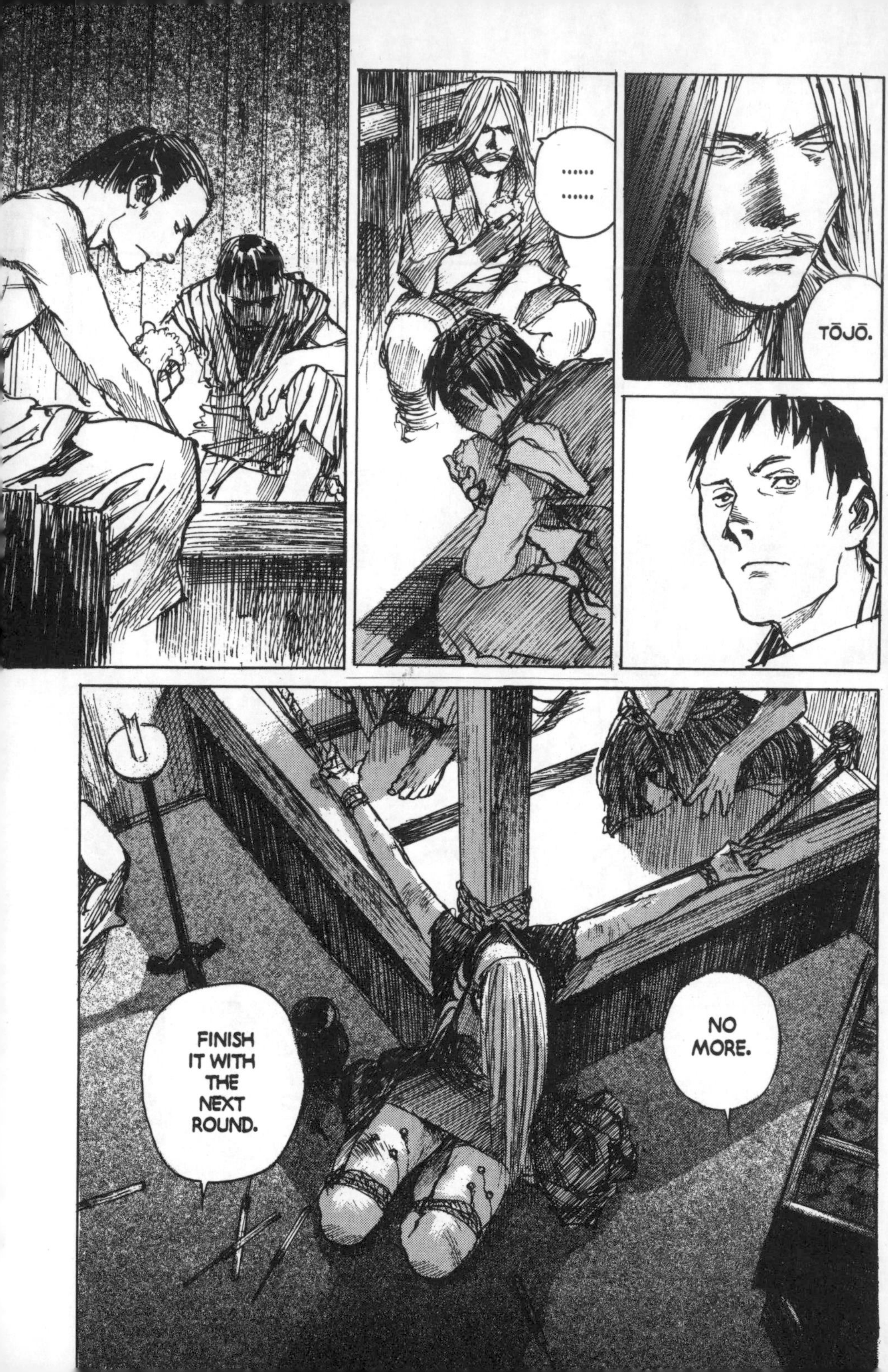
TŌJŌ.
......
......
NO MORE.
FINISH IT WITH THE NEXT ROUND.

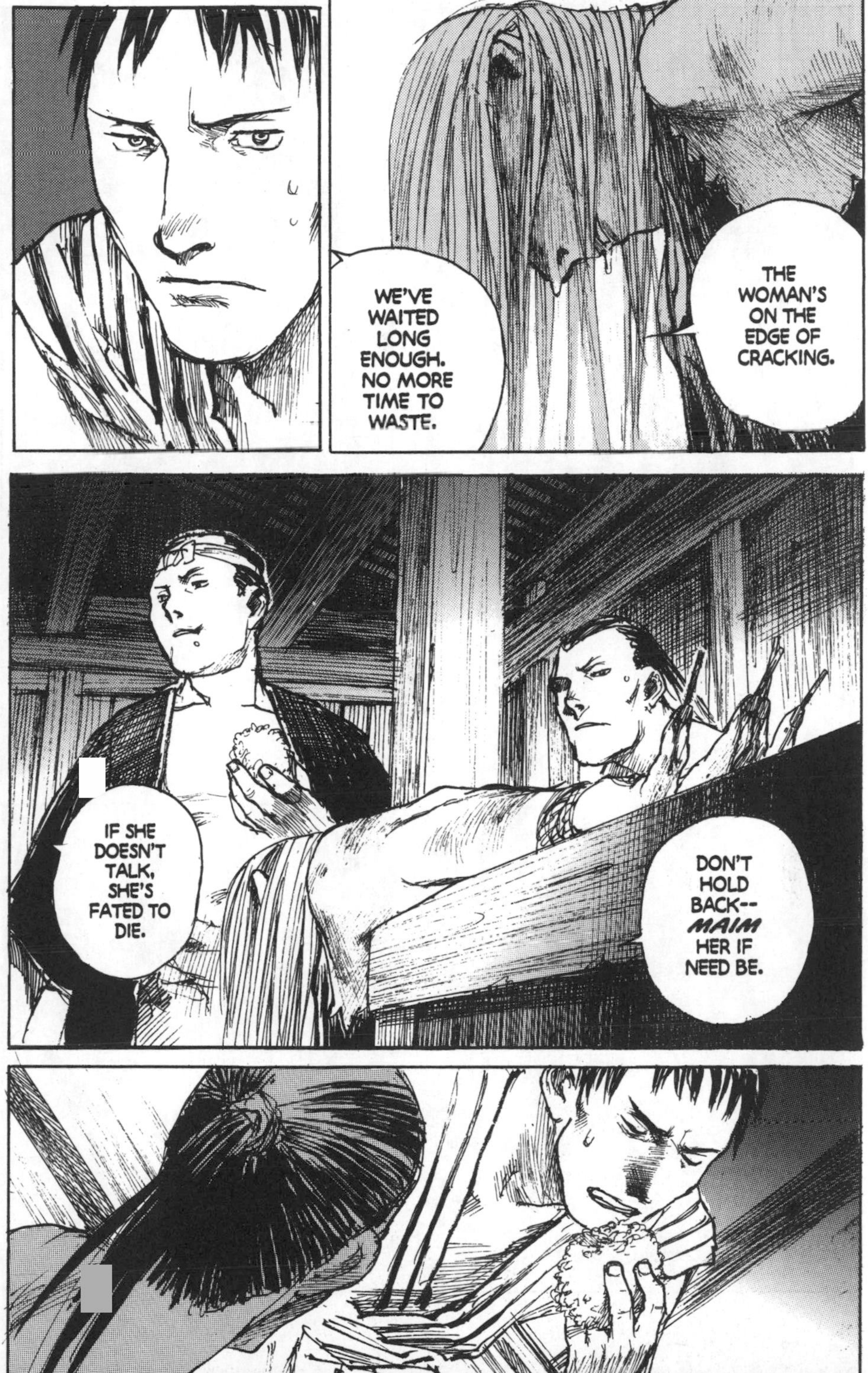
THE WOMAN'S ON THE EDGE OF CRACKING.
WE'VE WAITED LONG ENOUGH. NO MORE TIME TO WASTE.
DON'T HOLD BACK-- *MAIM* HER IF NEED BE.
IF SHE DOESN'T TALK, SHE'S FATED TO DIE.

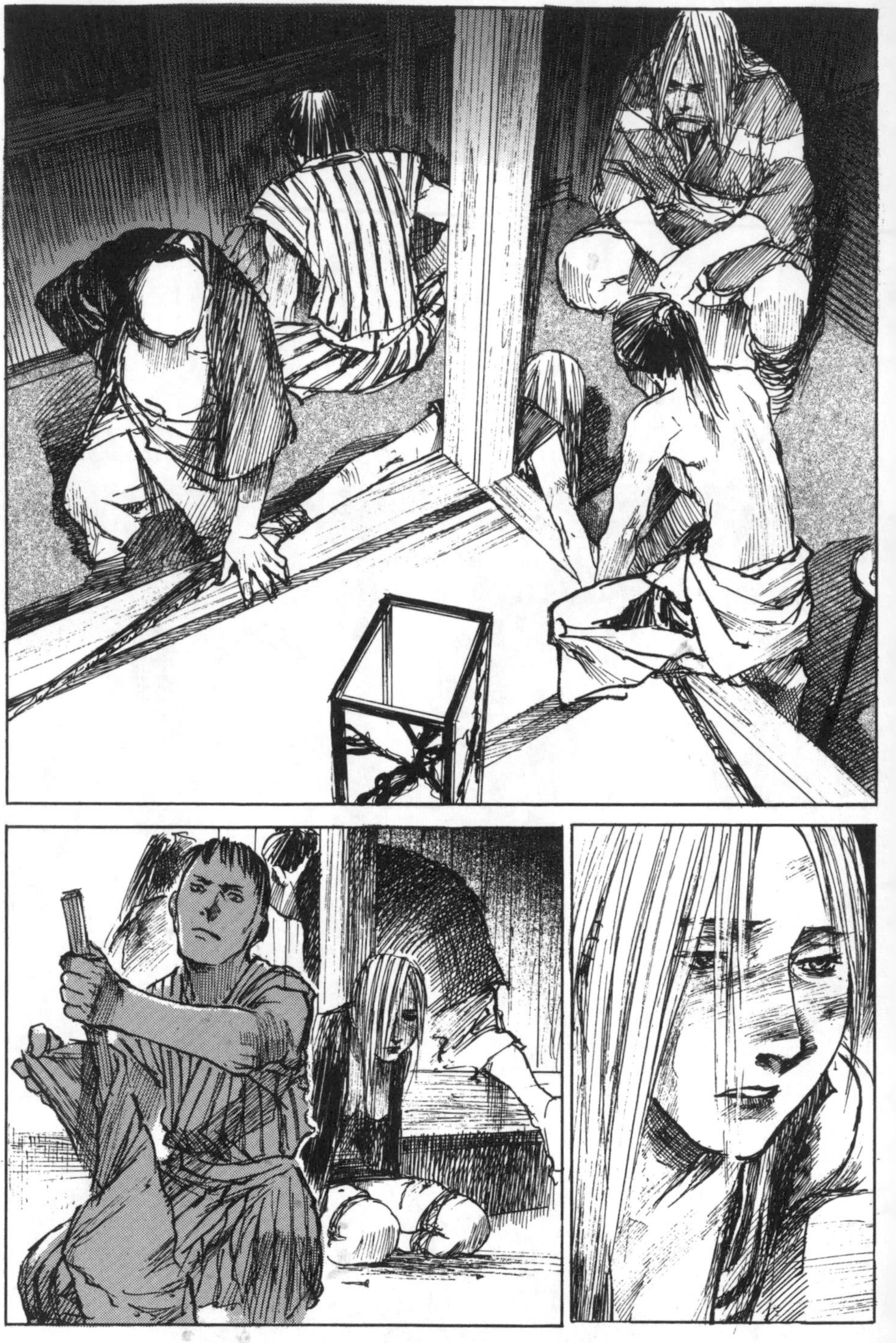

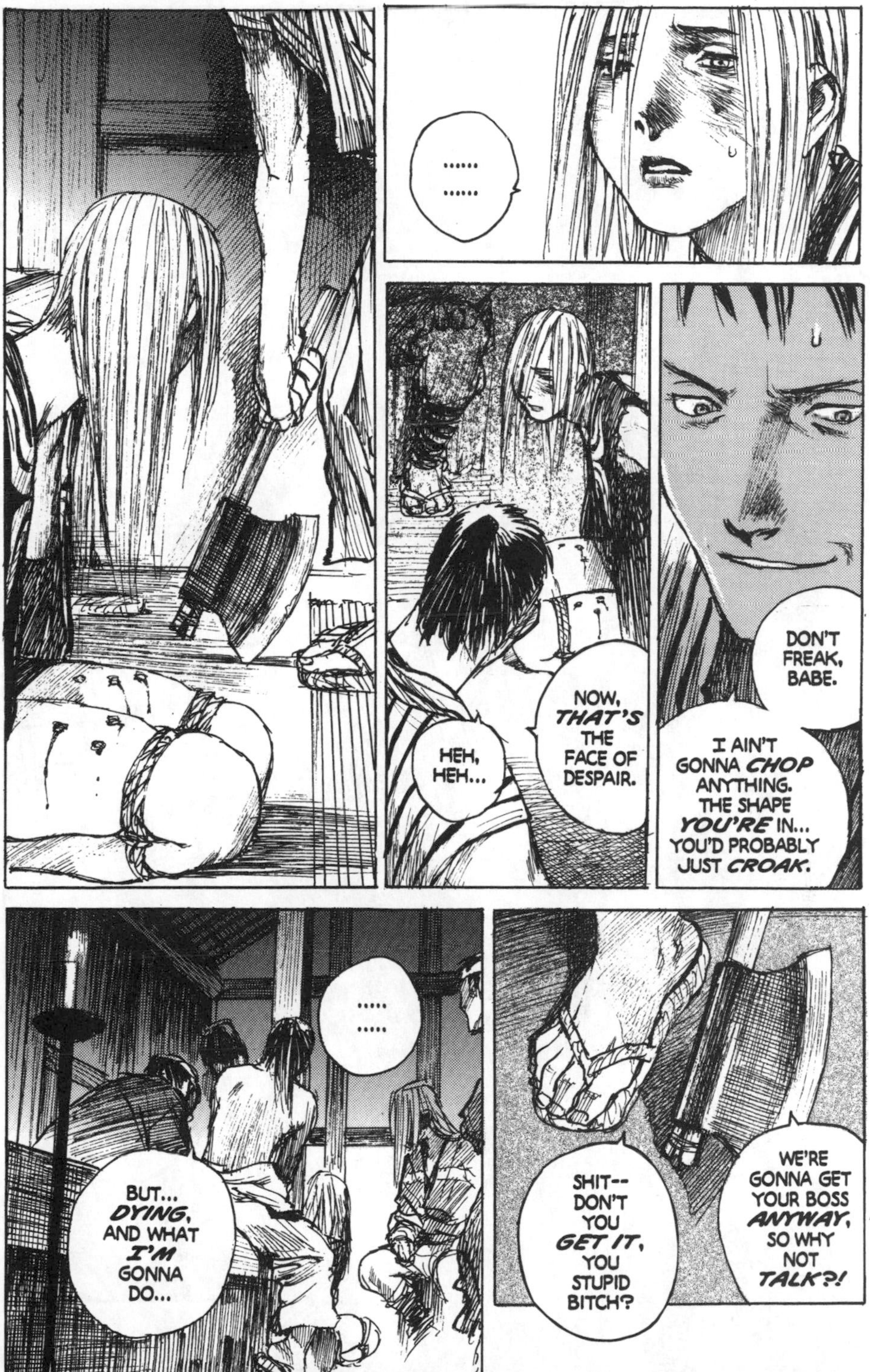

....
DON'T FREAK, BABE.
I AIN'T GONNA *CHOP* ANYTHING. THE SHAPE *YOU'RE* IN... YOU'D PROBABLY JUST *CROAK*.
NOW, *THAT'S* THE FACE OF DESPAIR.
HEH, HEH...
WE'RE GONNA GET YOUR BOSS *ANYWAY*, SO WHY NOT *TALK?!*
SHIT-- DON'T YOU *GET IT*, YOU STUPID BITCH?
....
BUT... *DYING*, AND WHAT *I'M* GONNA DO...

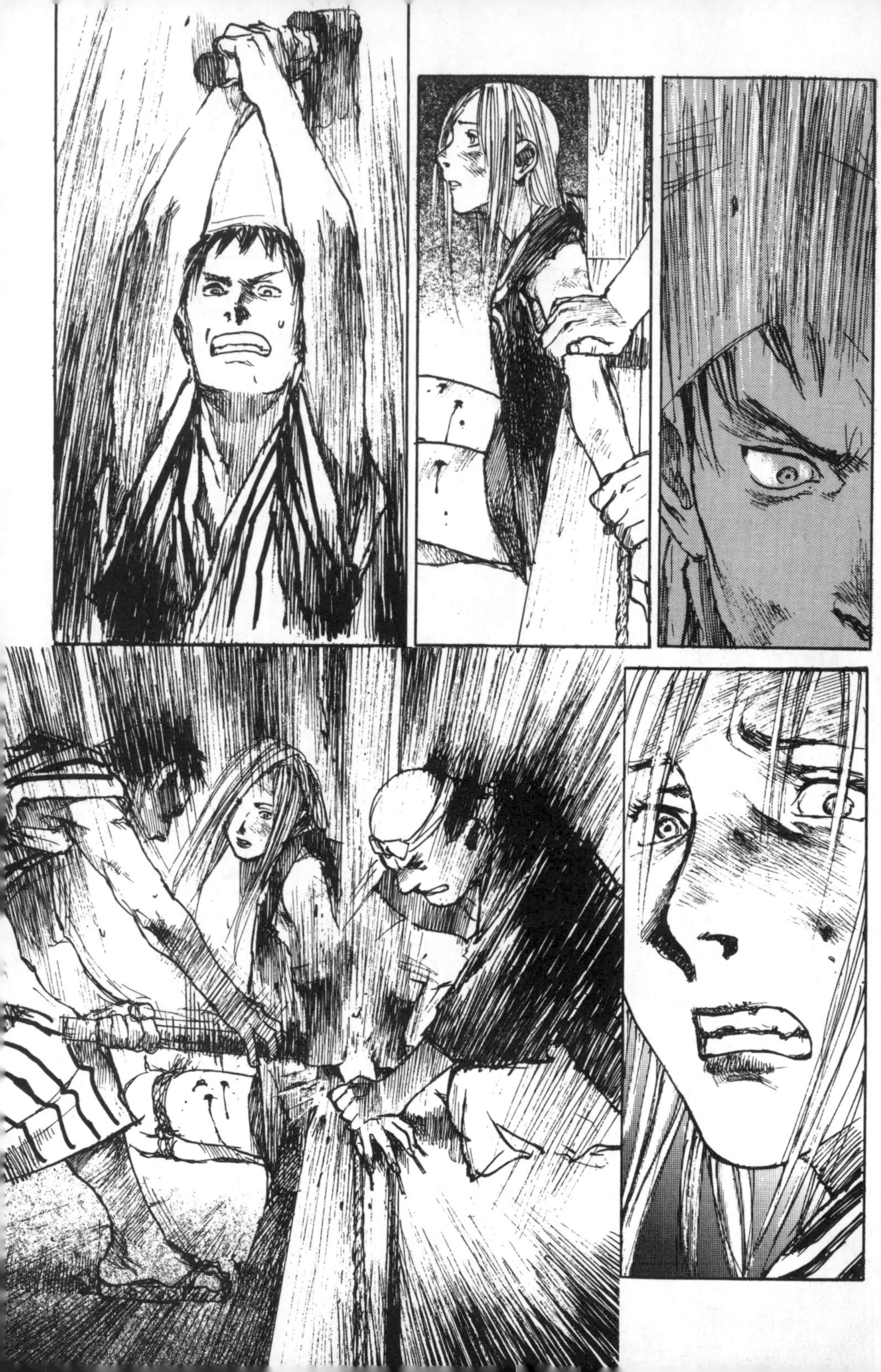

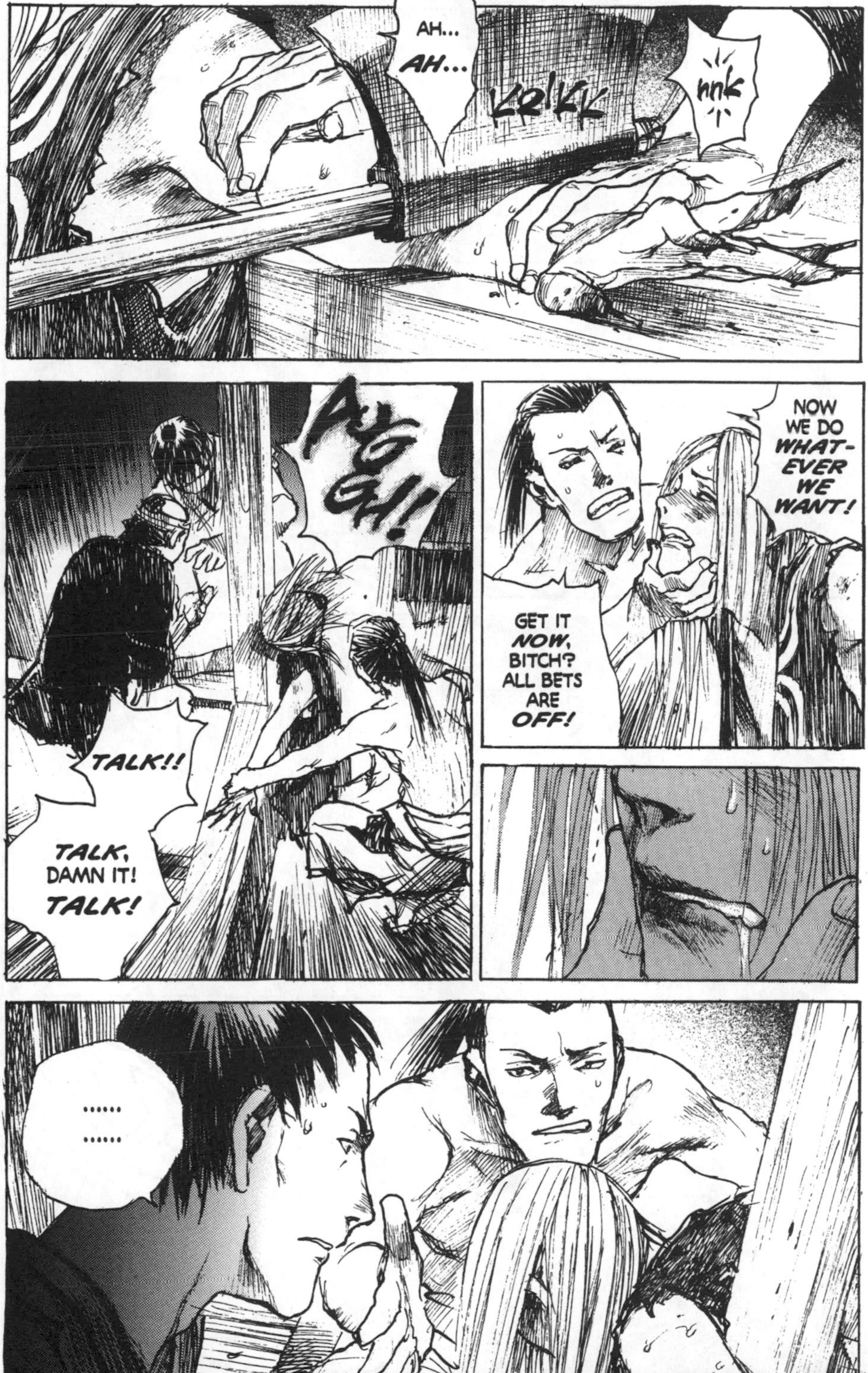
nnk
AH... AH...
KRIKK
NOW WE DO WHATEVER WE WANT!
GET IT NOW, BITCH? ALL BETS ARE OFF!
AUGGH!!
TALK!!
TALK, DAMN IT! TALK!
....

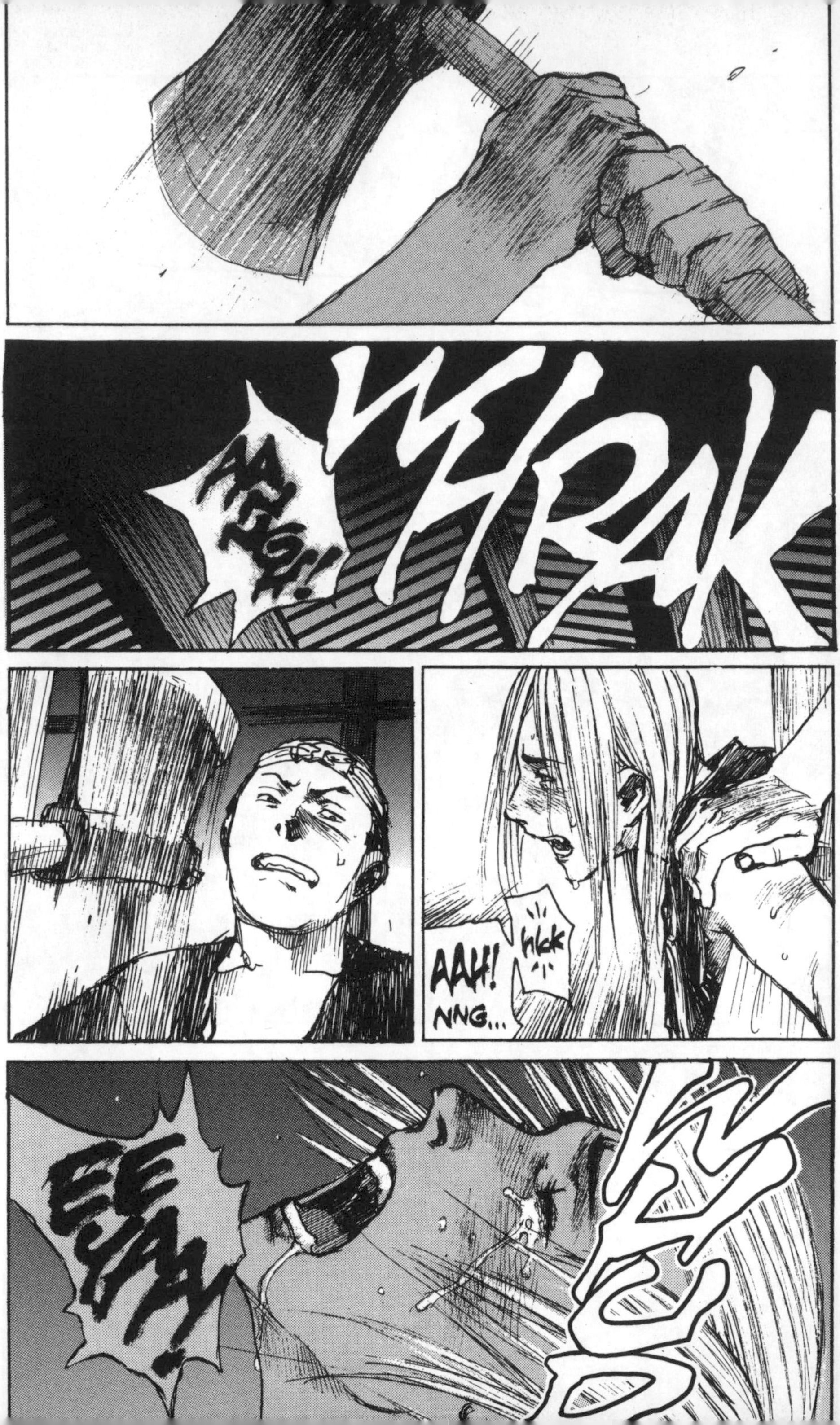
WHRAK
AARGH!!
hick
AAH!
NNG...
EEYA!

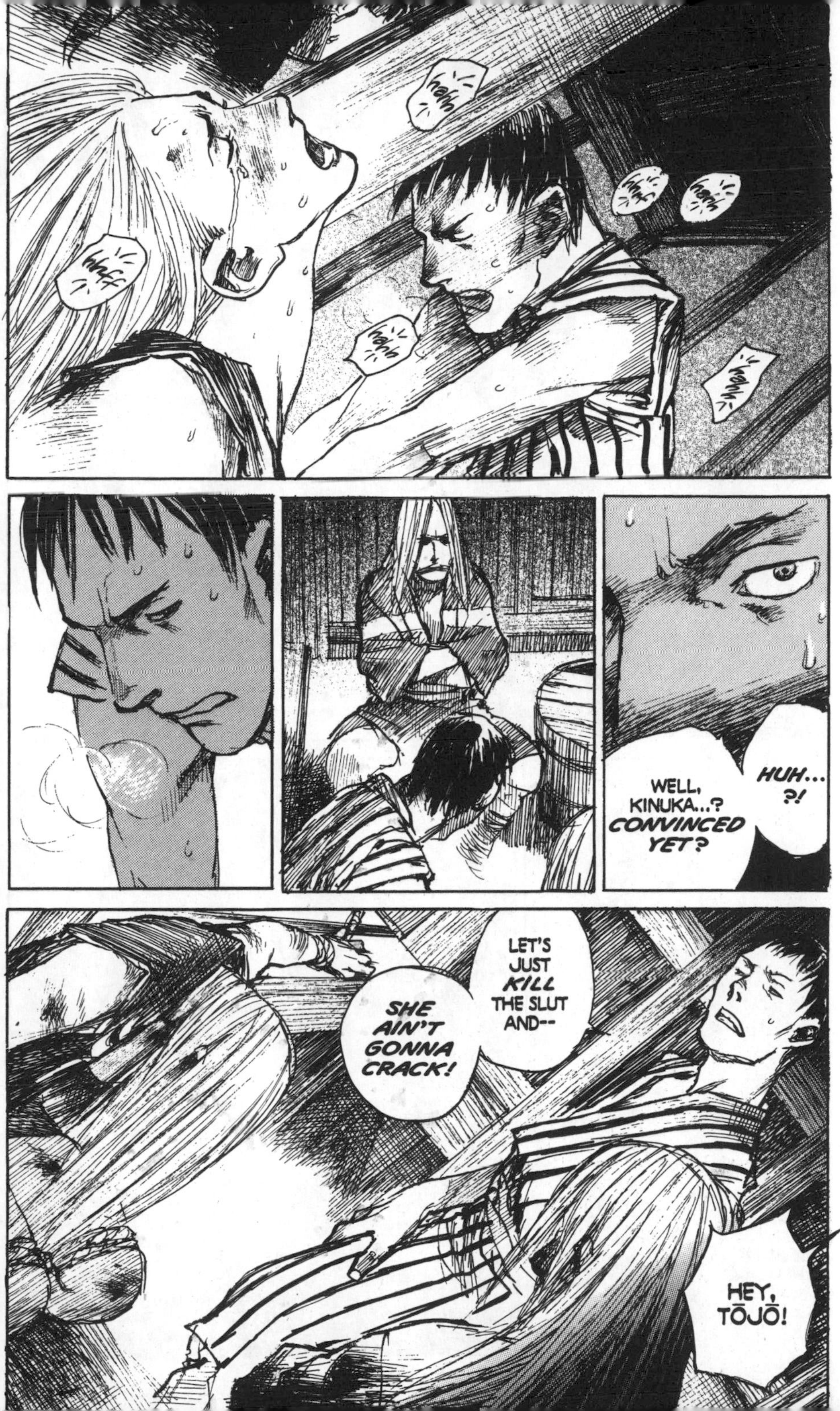
hehh
hehh
hehh
HUH...?!
WELL, KINUKA...? CONVINCED YET?
LET'S JUST KILL THE SLUT AND--
SHE AIN'T GONNA CRACK!
HEY, TŌJŌ!

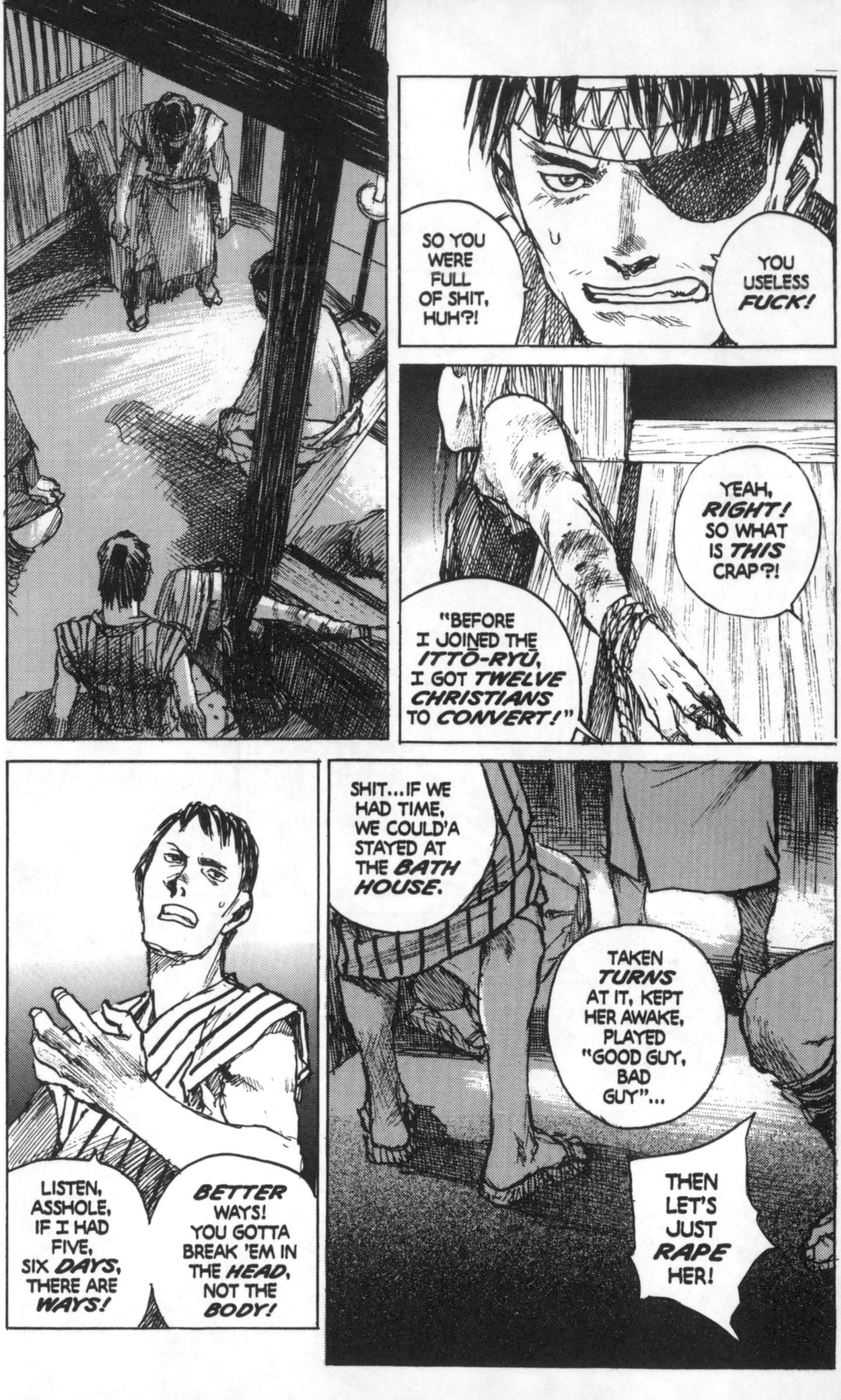
SO YOU WERE FULL OF SHIT, HUH?!
YOU USELESS FUCK!
YEAH, RIGHT! SO WHAT IS THIS CRAP?!
"BEFORE I JOINED THE ITTŌ-RYŪ, I GOT TWELVE CHRISTIANS TO CONVERT!"
LISTEN, ASSHOLE, IF I HAD FIVE, SIX DAYS, THERE ARE WAYS!
BETTER WAYS! YOU GOTTA BREAK 'EM IN THE HEAD, NOT THE BODY!
SHIT...IF WE HAD TIME, WE COULD'A STAYED AT THE BATH HOUSE.
TAKEN TURNS AT IT, KEPT HER AWAKE, PLAYED "GOOD GUY, BAD GUY"...
THEN LET'S JUST RAPE HER!

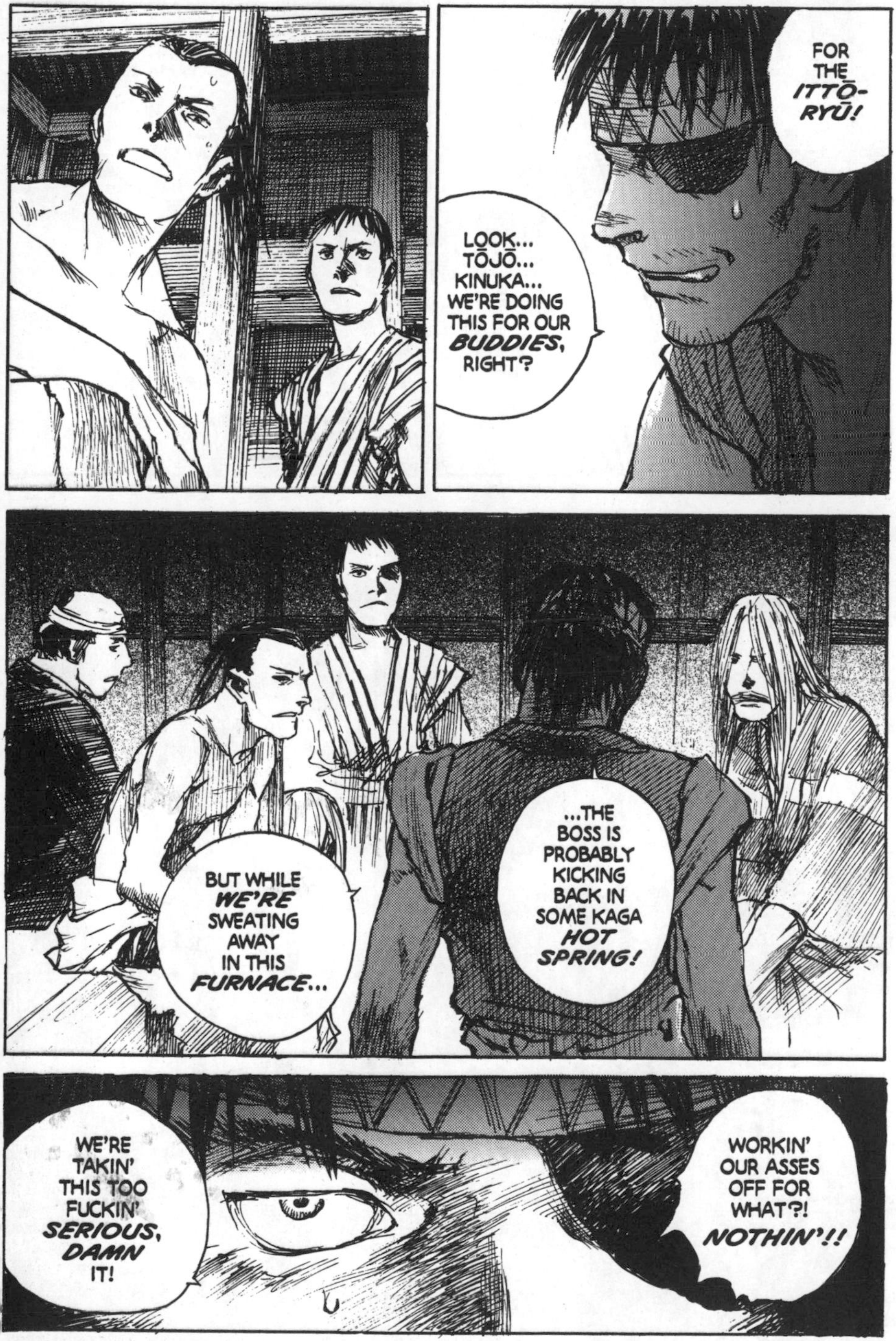
LOOK... TŌJŌ... KINUKA... WE'RE DOING THIS FOR OUR BUDDIES, RIGHT?
FOR THE ITTŌ-RYŪ!
BUT WHILE WE'RE SWEATING AWAY IN THIS FURNACE...
...THE BOSS IS PROBABLY KICKING BACK IN SOME KAGA HOT SPRING!
WE'RE TAKIN' THIS TOO FUCKIN' SERIOUS, DAMN IT!
WORKIN' OUR ASSES OFF FOR WHAT?! NOTHIN'!!

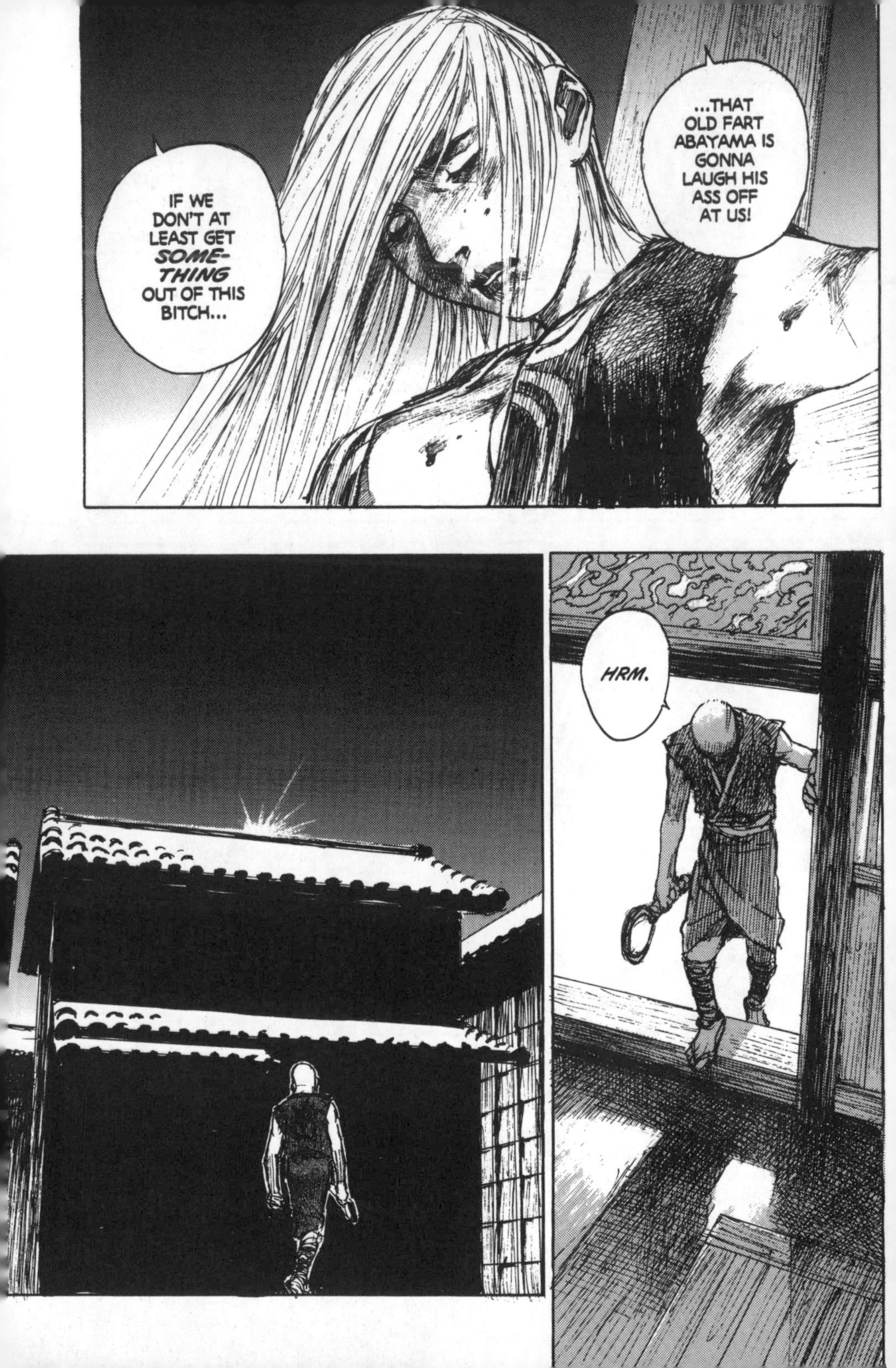
IF WE DON'T AT LEAST GET *SOME-THING* OUT OF THIS BITCH...
...THAT OLD FART ABAYAMA IS GONNA LAUGH HIS ASS OFF AT US!
HRM.

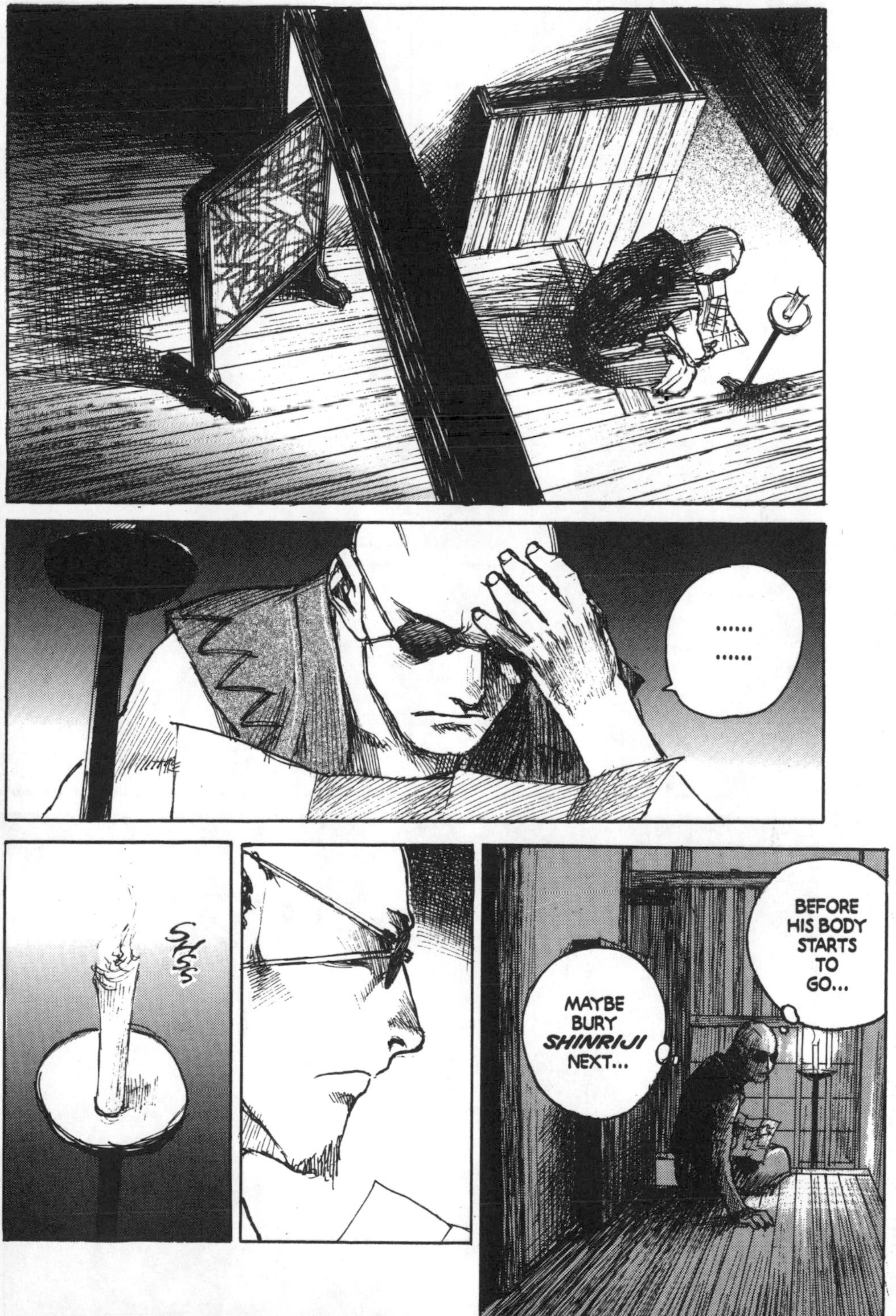
......
......
BEFORE HIS BODY STARTS TO GO...
MAYBE BURY SHINRIJI NEXT...
SHSSS

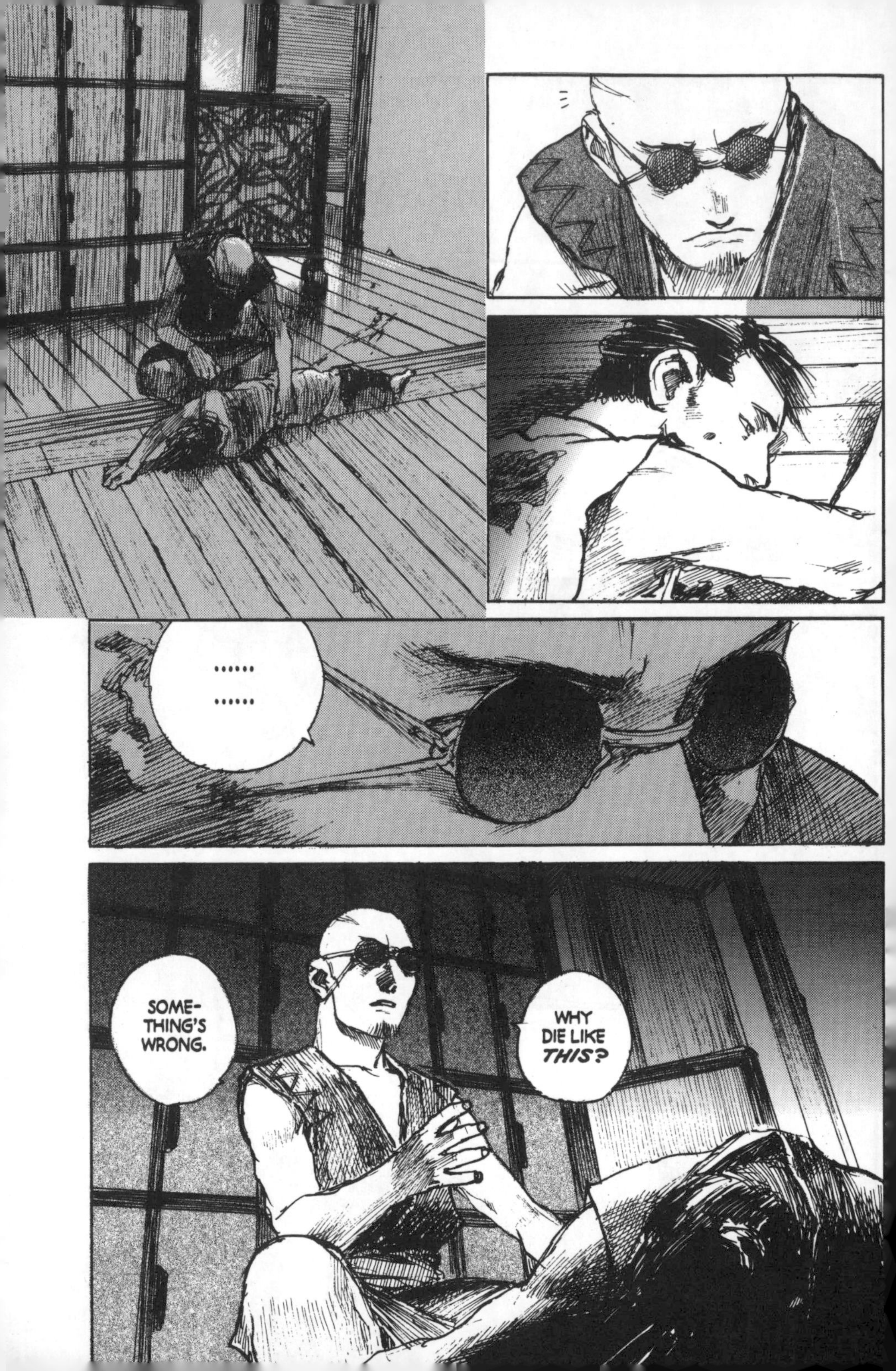
……
……
WHY DIE LIKE THIS?
SOME-THING'S WRONG.

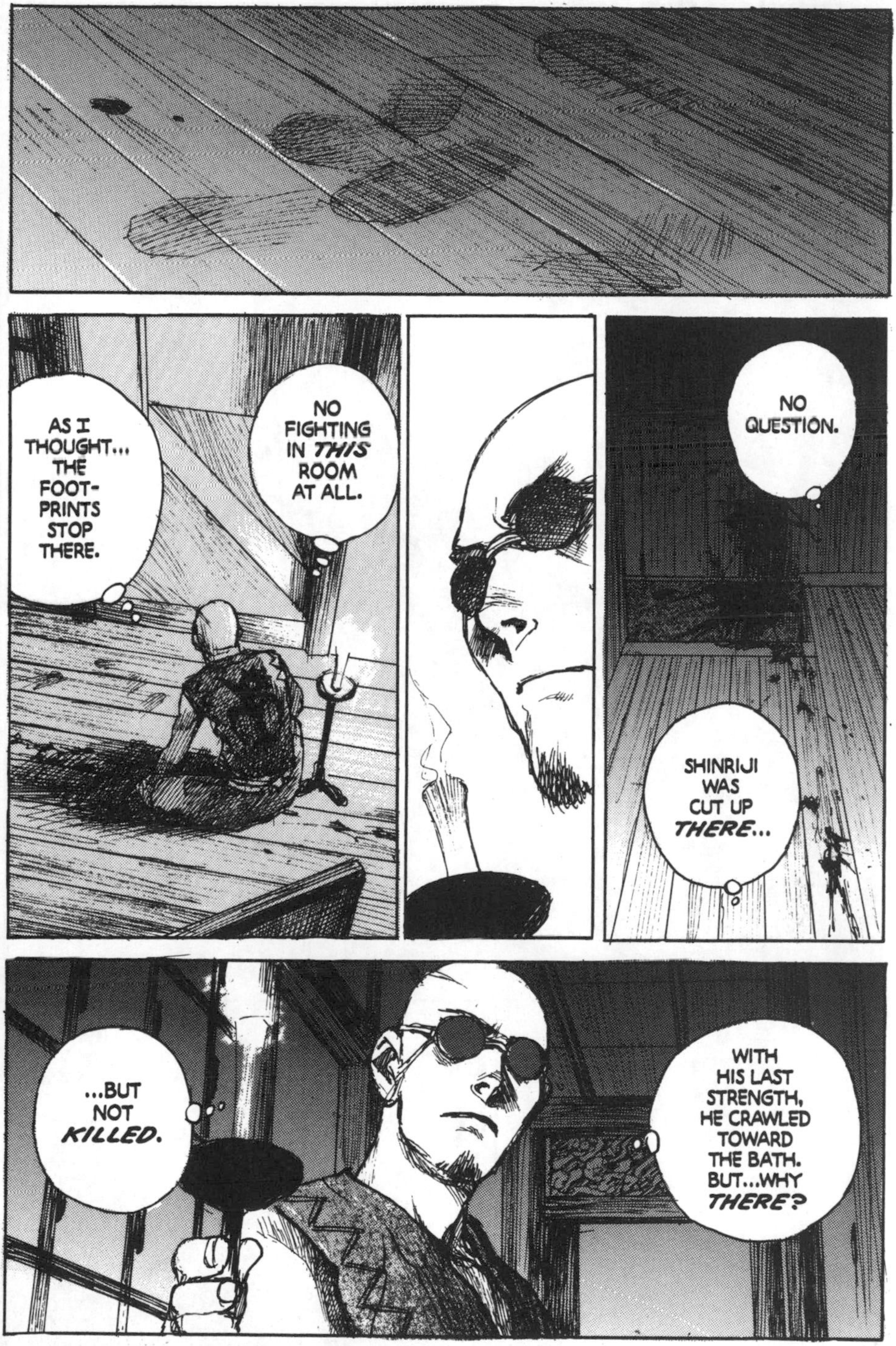
AS I THOUGHT... THE FOOT-PRINTS STOP THERE.
NO FIGHTING IN *THIS* ROOM AT ALL.
NO QUESTION.
SHINRIJI WAS CUT UP *THERE*...
...BUT NOT *KILLED*.
WITH HIS LAST STRENGTH, HE CRAWLED TOWARD THE BATH. BUT...WHY *THERE*?

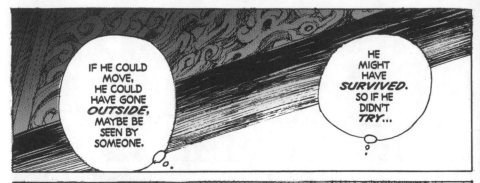

IF HE COULD MOVE, HE COULD HAVE GONE *OUTSIDE*, MAYBE BE SEEN BY SOMEONE.

HE MIGHT HAVE *SURVIVED*. SO IF HE DIDN'T *TRY*...

...HE WANTED *ME* TO SEE HIS CORPSE...?

SO I'D *LEARN* SOMETHING FROM HOW HE DIED...?

THEN... THIS *HAND*...

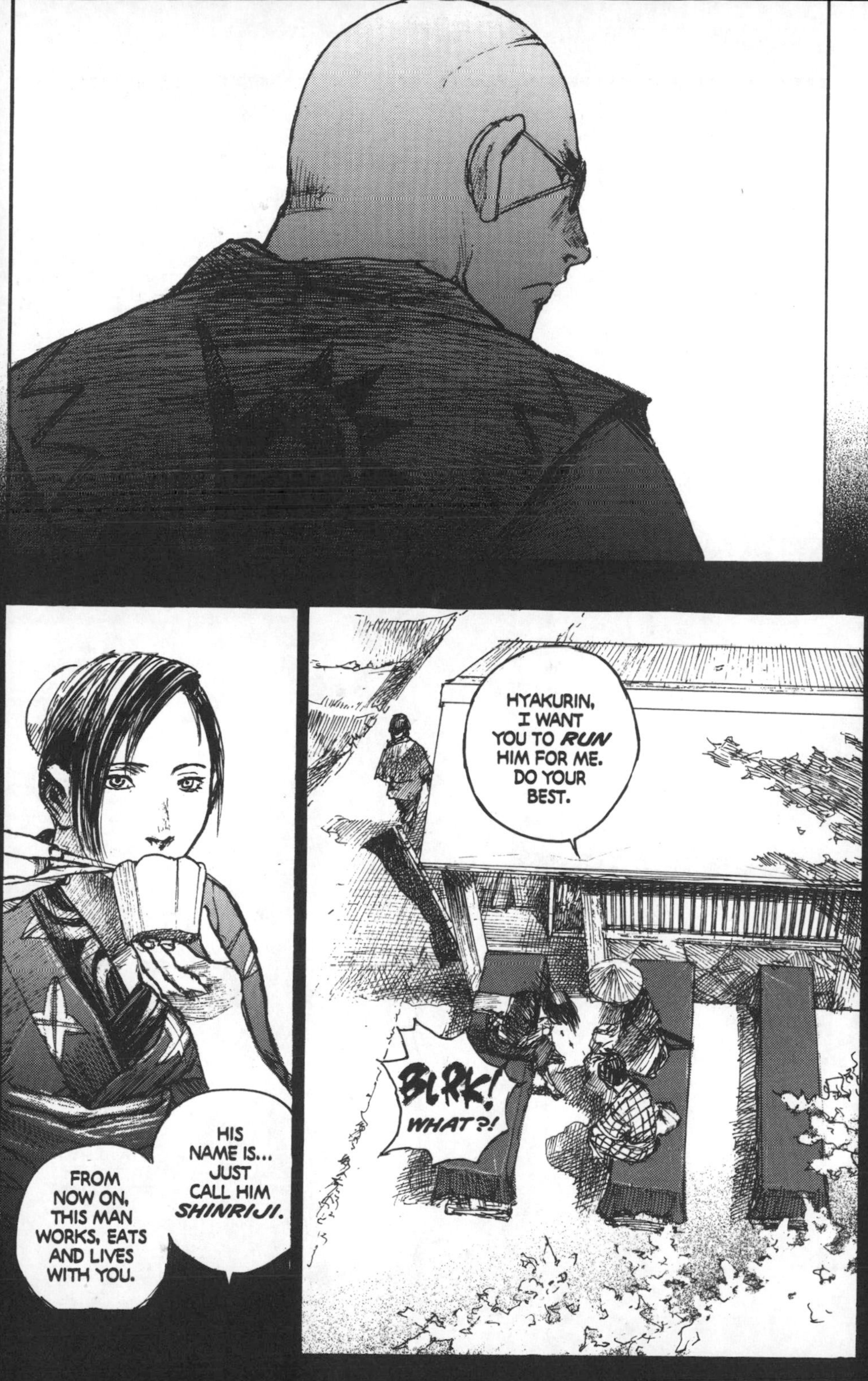
HYAKURIN, I WANT YOU TO *RUN* HIM FOR ME. DO YOUR BEST.
BLRK! *WHAT?!*
HIS NAME IS... JUST CALL HIM *SHINRIJI*.
FROM NOW ON, THIS MAN WORKS, EATS AND LIVES WITH YOU.

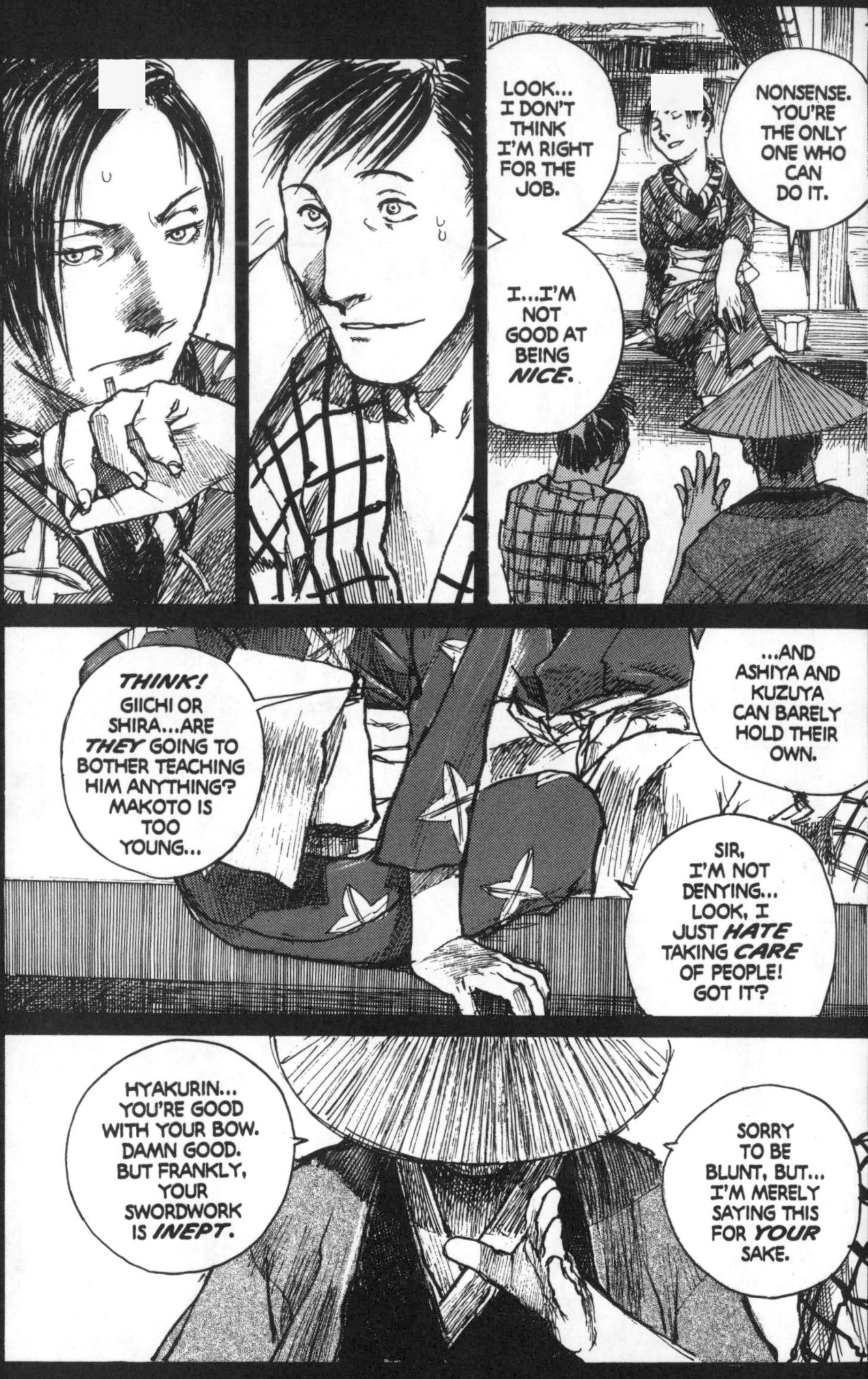
LOOK... I DON'T THINK I'M RIGHT FOR THE JOB.
NONSENSE. YOU'RE THE ONLY ONE WHO CAN DO IT.
I...I'M NOT GOOD AT BEING *NICE*.
THINK! GIICHI OR SHIRA...ARE *THEY* GOING TO BOTHER TEACHING HIM ANYTHING? MAKOTO IS TOO YOUNG...
...AND ASHIYA AND KUZUYA CAN BARELY HOLD THEIR OWN.
SIR, I'M NOT DENYING... LOOK, I JUST *HATE* TAKING *CARE* OF PEOPLE! GOT IT?
HYAKURIN... YOU'RE GOOD WITH YOUR BOW. DAMN GOOD. BUT FRANKLY, YOUR SWORDWORK IS *INEPT*.
SORRY TO BE BLUNT, BUT... I'M MERELY SAYING THIS FOR *YOUR* SAKE.

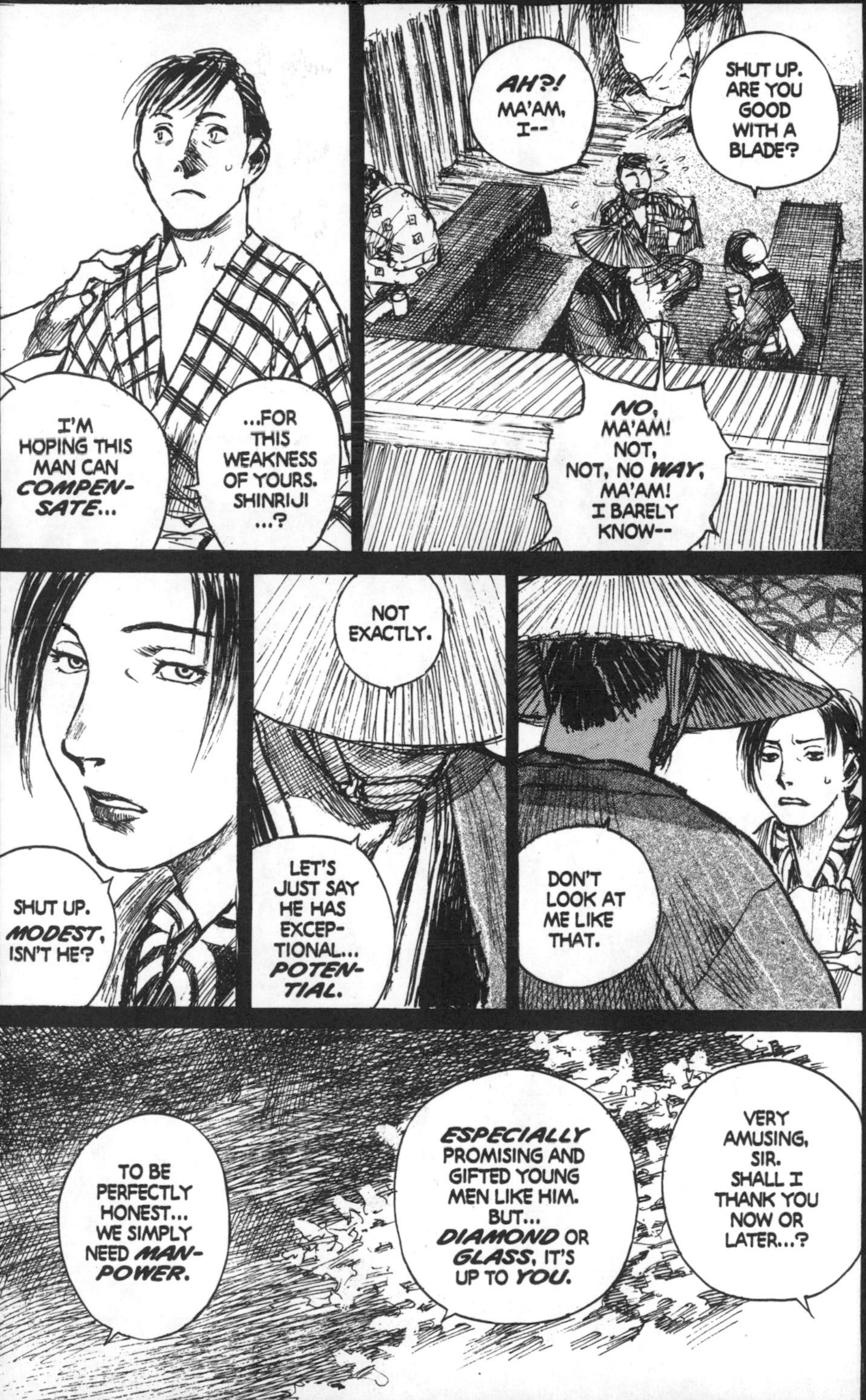
I'M HOPING THIS MAN CAN COMPENSATE...
...FOR THIS WEAKNESS OF YOURS. SHINRIJI ...?
AH?! MA'AM, I--
SHUT UP. ARE YOU GOOD WITH A BLADE?
NO, MA'AM! NOT, NOT, NO WAY, MA'AM! I BARELY KNOW--
SHUT UP. MODEST, ISN'T HE?
NOT EXACTLY.
LET'S JUST SAY HE HAS EXCEPTIONAL... POTENTIAL.
DON'T LOOK AT ME LIKE THAT.
TO BE PERFECTLY HONEST... WE SIMPLY NEED MANPOWER.
ESPECIALLY PROMISING AND GIFTED YOUNG MEN LIKE HIM. BUT... DIAMOND OR GLASS, IT'S UP TO YOU.
VERY AMUSING, SIR. SHALL I THANK YOU NOW OR LATER...?

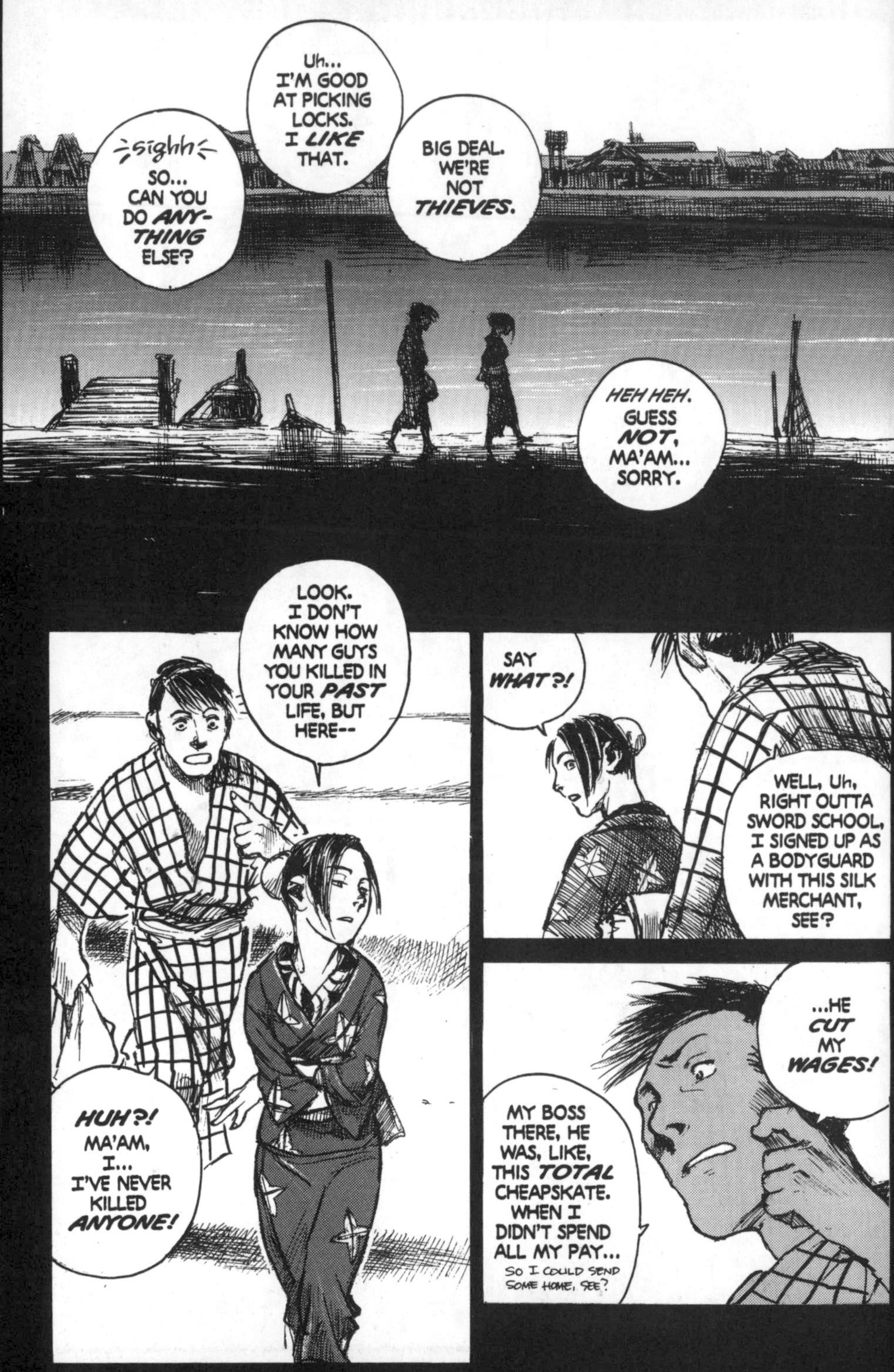
sighh
SO... CAN YOU DO ANYTHING ELSE?
Uh... I'M GOOD AT PICKING LOCKS. I LIKE THAT.
BIG DEAL. WE'RE NOT THIEVES.
HEH HEH. GUESS NOT, MA'AM... SORRY.
LOOK. I DON'T KNOW HOW MANY GUYS YOU KILLED IN YOUR PAST LIFE, BUT HERE--
HUH?! MA'AM, I... I'VE NEVER KILLED ANYONE!
SAY WHAT?!
WELL, Uh, RIGHT OUTTA SWORD SCHOOL, I SIGNED UP AS A BODYGUARD WITH THIS SILK MERCHANT, SEE?
MY BOSS THERE, HE WAS, LIKE, THIS TOTAL CHEAPSKATE. WHEN I DIDN'T SPEND ALL MY PAY...
SO I COULD SEND SOME HOME, SEE?
...HE CUT MY WAGES!

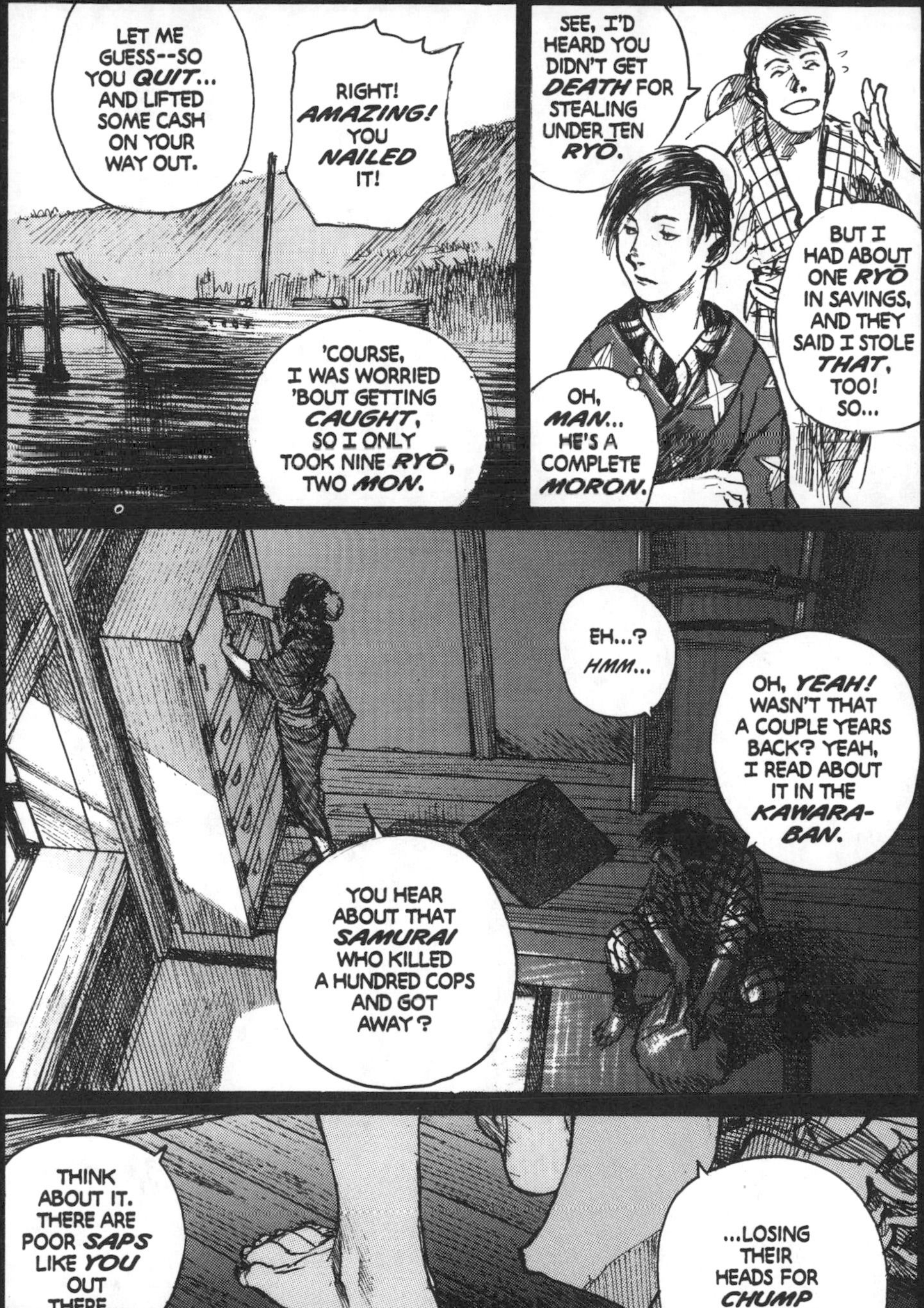
LET ME GUESS--SO YOU QUIT... AND LIFTED SOME CASH ON YOUR WAY OUT.
RIGHT! AMAZING! YOU NAILED IT!
'COURSE, I WAS WORRIED 'BOUT GETTING CAUGHT, SO I ONLY TOOK NINE RYŌ, TWO MON.
SEE, I'D HEARD YOU DIDN'T GET DEATH FOR STEALING UNDER TEN RYŌ.
BUT I HAD ABOUT ONE RYŌ IN SAVINGS, AND THEY SAID I STOLE THAT, TOO! SO...
OH, MAN... HE'S A COMPLETE MORON.
YOU HEAR ABOUT THAT SAMURAI WHO KILLED A HUNDRED COPS AND GOT AWAY?
EH...? HMM...
OH, YEAH! WASN'T THAT A COUPLE YEARS BACK? YEAH, I READ ABOUT IT IN THE KAWARA-BAN.
THINK ABOUT IT. THERE ARE POOR SAPS LIKE YOU OUT THERE...
...LOSING THEIR HEADS FOR CHUMP CHANGE.

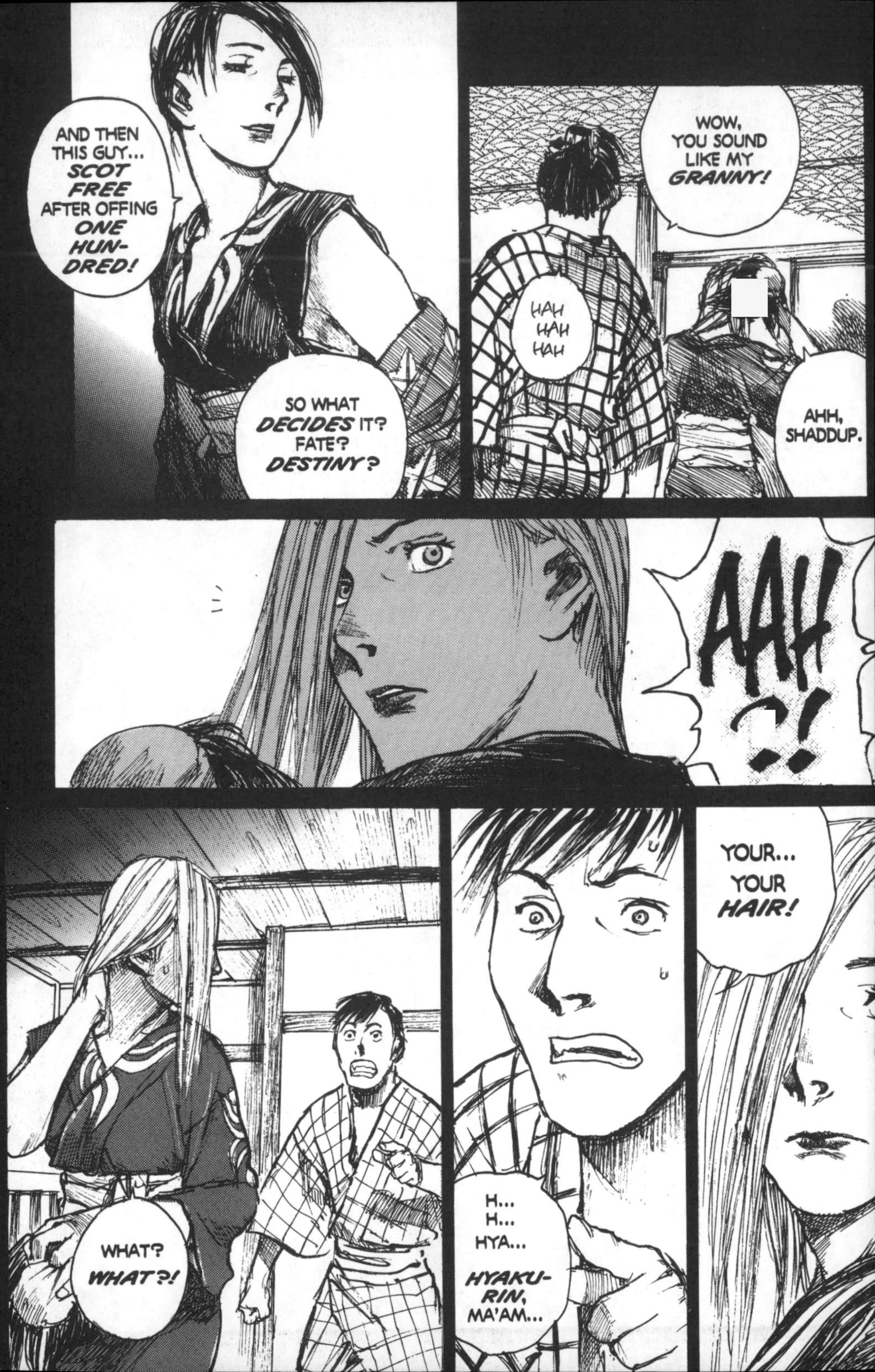
AND THEN THIS GUY... SCOT FREE AFTER OFFING ONE HUN-DRED!
SO WHAT DECIDES IT? FATE? DESTINY?
WOW, YOU SOUND LIKE MY GRANNY!
HAH HAH HAH
AHH, SHADDUP.
AAH ?!
WHAT? WHAT?!
H... H... HYA... HYAKU-RIN, MA'AM...
YOUR... YOUR HAIR!

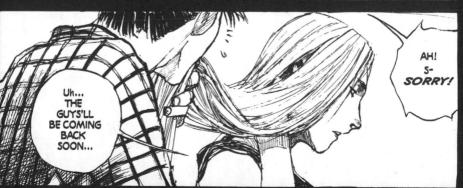

AH!
S-
SORRY!

Uh...
THE
GUYS'LL
BE COMING
BACK
SOON...

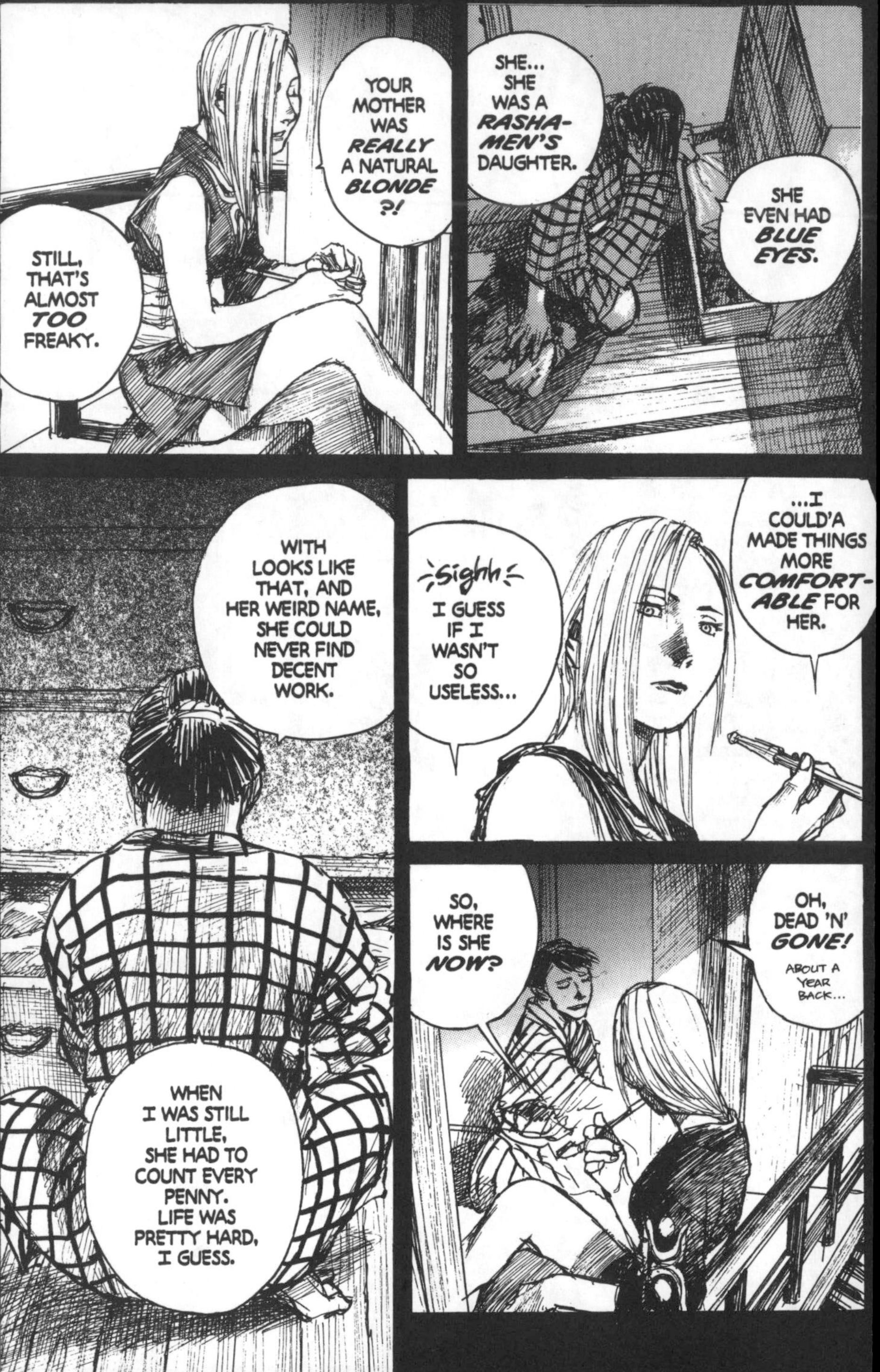
YOUR MOTHER WAS REALLY A NATURAL BLONDE ?!
STILL, THAT'S ALMOST TOO FREAKY.
SHE... SHE WAS A RASHAMEN'S DAUGHTER.
SHE EVEN HAD BLUE EYES.
WITH LOOKS LIKE THAT, AND HER WEIRD NAME, SHE COULD NEVER FIND DECENT WORK.
WHEN I WAS STILL LITTLE, SHE HAD TO COUNT EVERY PENNY. LIFE WAS PRETTY HARD, I GUESS.
Sighh
I GUESS IF I WASN'T SO USELESS...
...I COULD'A MADE THINGS MORE COMFORTABLE FOR HER.
SO, WHERE IS SHE NOW?
OH, DEAD 'N' GONE!
ABOUT A YEAR BACK...

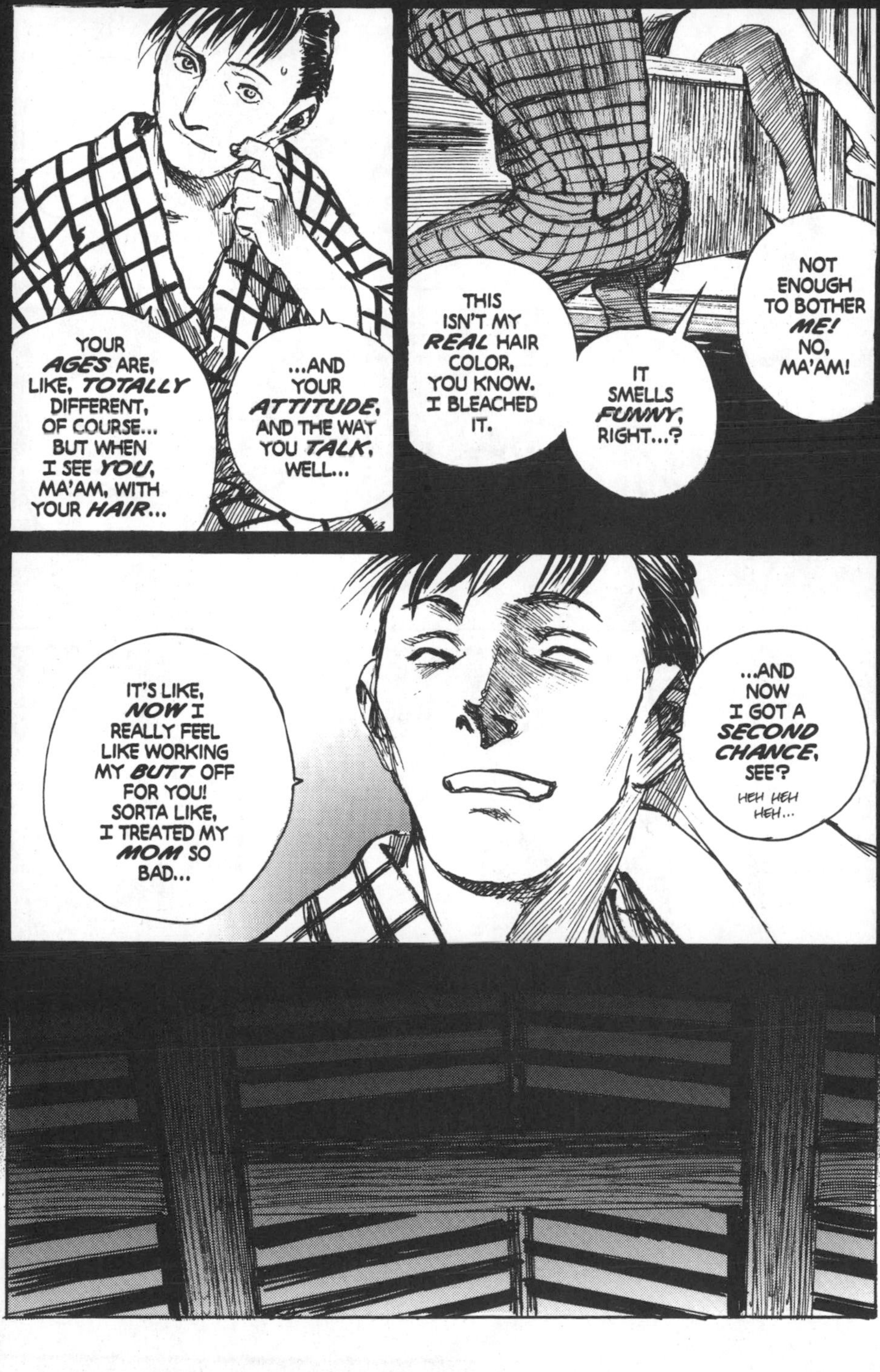
THIS ISN'T MY REAL HAIR COLOR, YOU KNOW. I BLEACHED IT.
IT SMELLS FUNNY, RIGHT...?
NOT ENOUGH TO BOTHER ME! NO, MA'AM!
YOUR AGES ARE, LIKE, TOTALLY DIFFERENT, OF COURSE... BUT WHEN I SEE YOU, MA'AM, WITH YOUR HAIR...
...AND YOUR ATTITUDE, AND THE WAY YOU TALK, WELL...
IT'S LIKE, NOW I REALLY FEEL LIKE WORKING MY BUTT OFF FOR YOU! SORTA LIKE, I TREATED MY MOM SO BAD...
...AND NOW I GOT A SECOND CHANCE, SEE?
HEH HEH HEH...

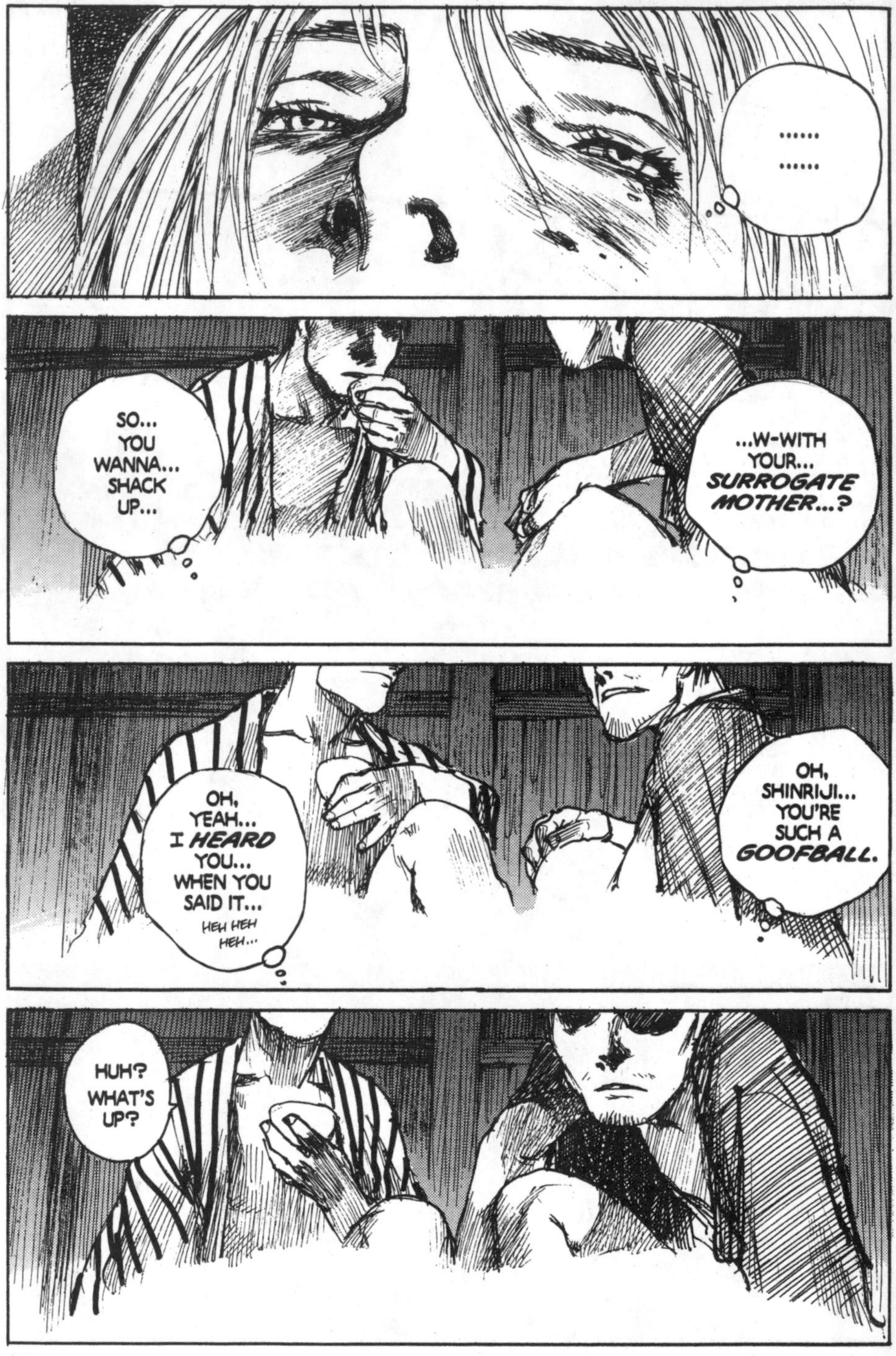
......
......
...W-WITH YOUR... SURROGATE MOTHER...?
SO... YOU WANNA... SHACK UP...
OH, SHINRIJI... YOU'RE SUCH A GOOFBALL.
OH, YEAH... I HEARD YOU... WHEN YOU SAID IT... HEH HEH HEH...
HUH? WHAT'S UP?

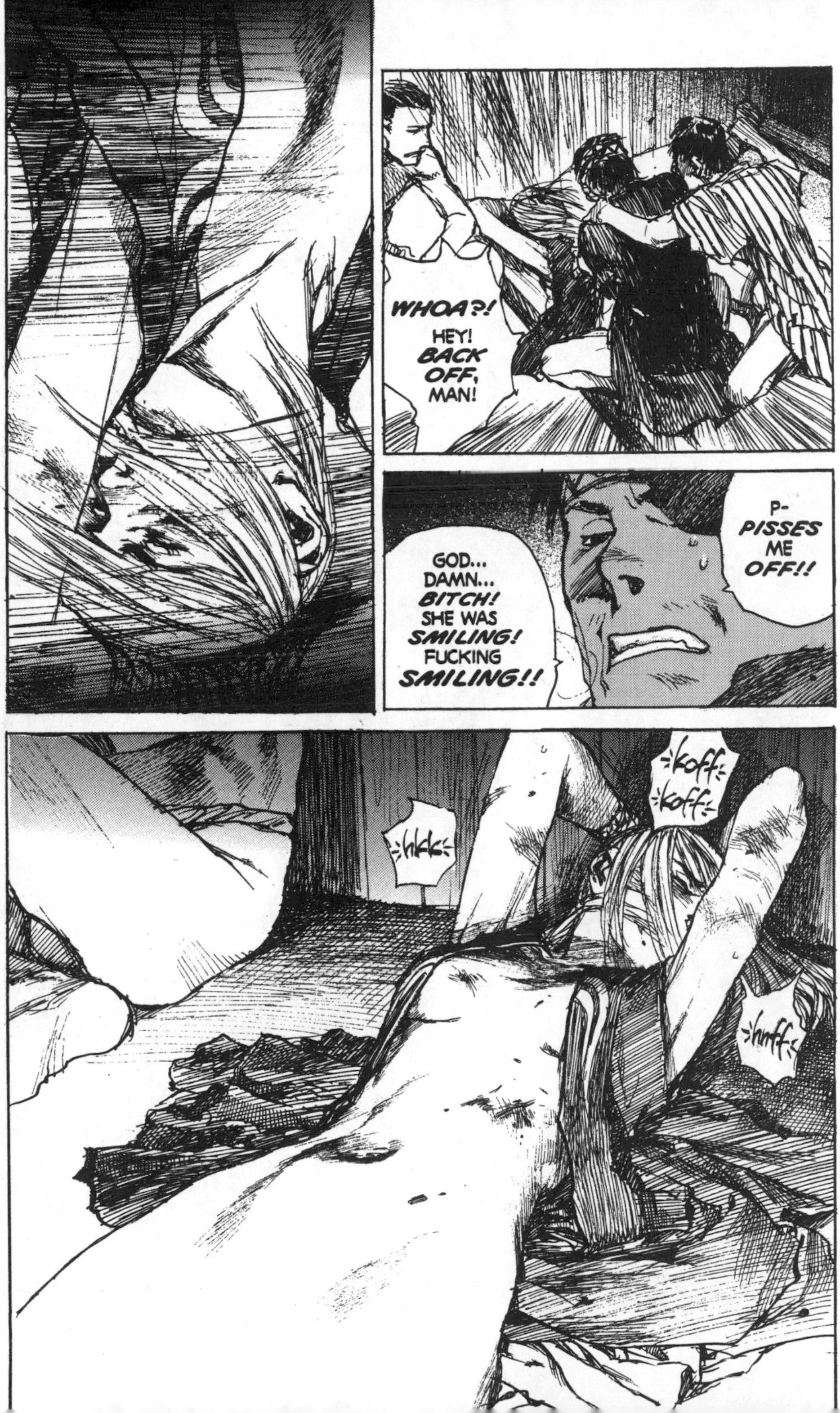
WHOA?!
HEY! BACK OFF, MAN!
P-PISSES ME OFF!!
GOD... DAMN... BITCH! SHE WAS SMILING! FUCKING SMILING!!
koff
koff
hkk
hnff

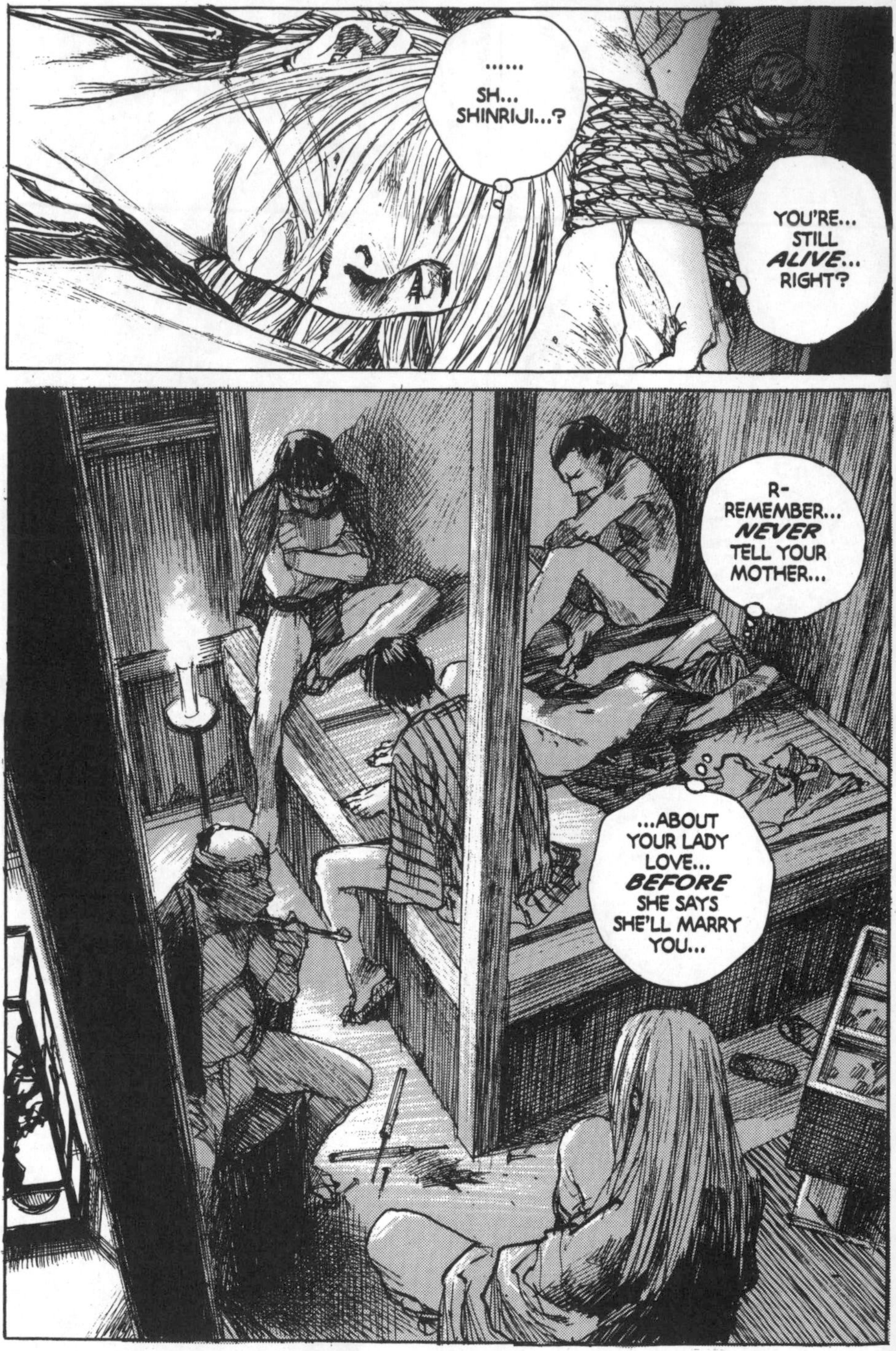
......
SH... SHINRIJI...?
YOU'RE... STILL ALIVE... RIGHT?
R- REMEMBER... NEVER TELL YOUR MOTHER...
...ABOUT YOUR LADY LOVE... BEFORE SHE SAYS SHE'LL MARRY YOU...

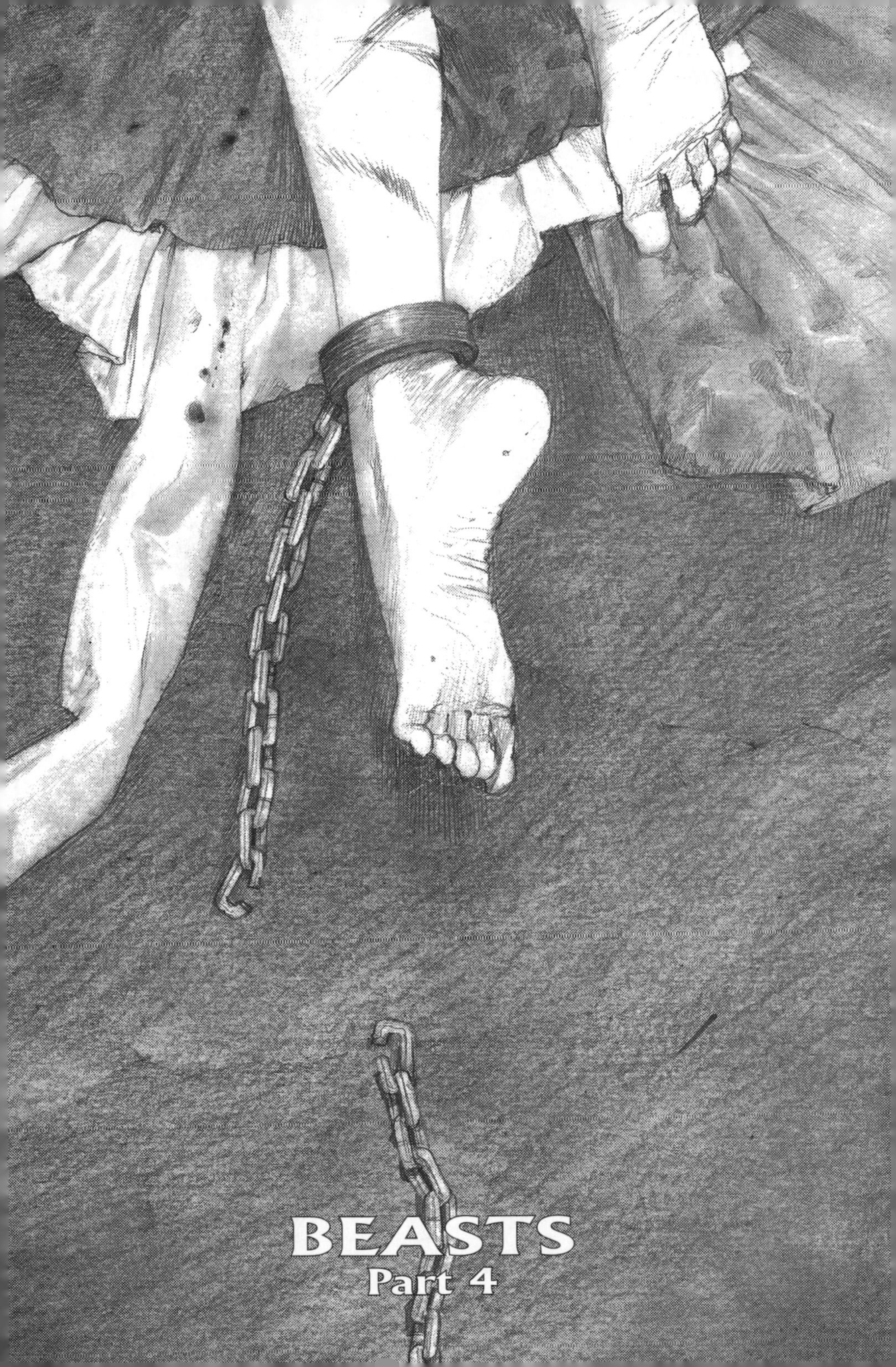
BEASTS
Part 4

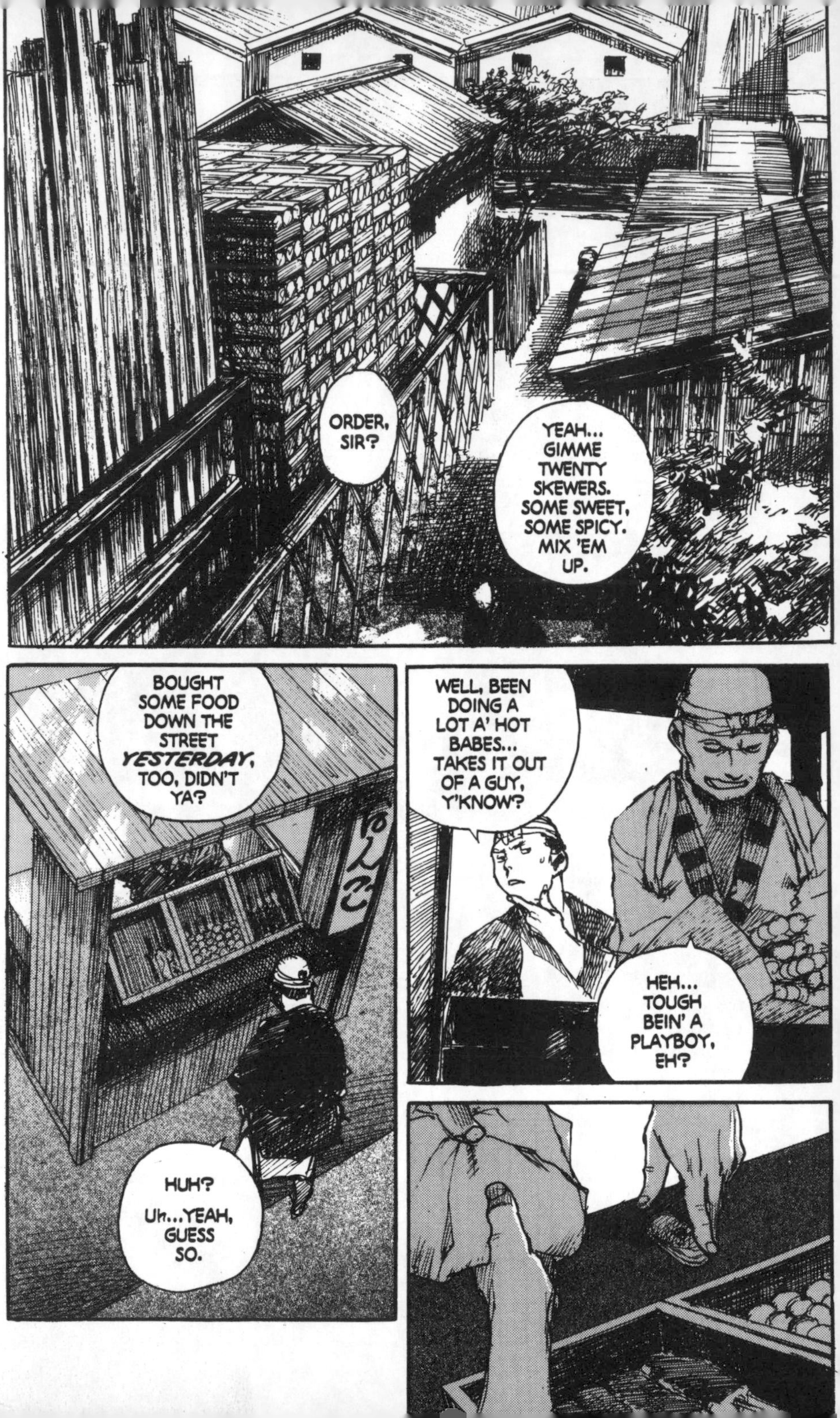
ORDER, SIR?
YEAH... GIMME TWENTY SKEWERS. SOME SWEET, SOME SPICY. MIX 'EM UP.
BOUGHT SOME FOOD DOWN THE STREET *YESTERDAY*, TOO, DIDN'T YA?
HUH? Uh...YEAH, GUESS SO.
WELL, BEEN DOING A LOT A' HOT BABES... TAKES IT OUT OF A GUY, Y'KNOW?
HEH... TOUGH BEIN' A PLAYBOY, EH?

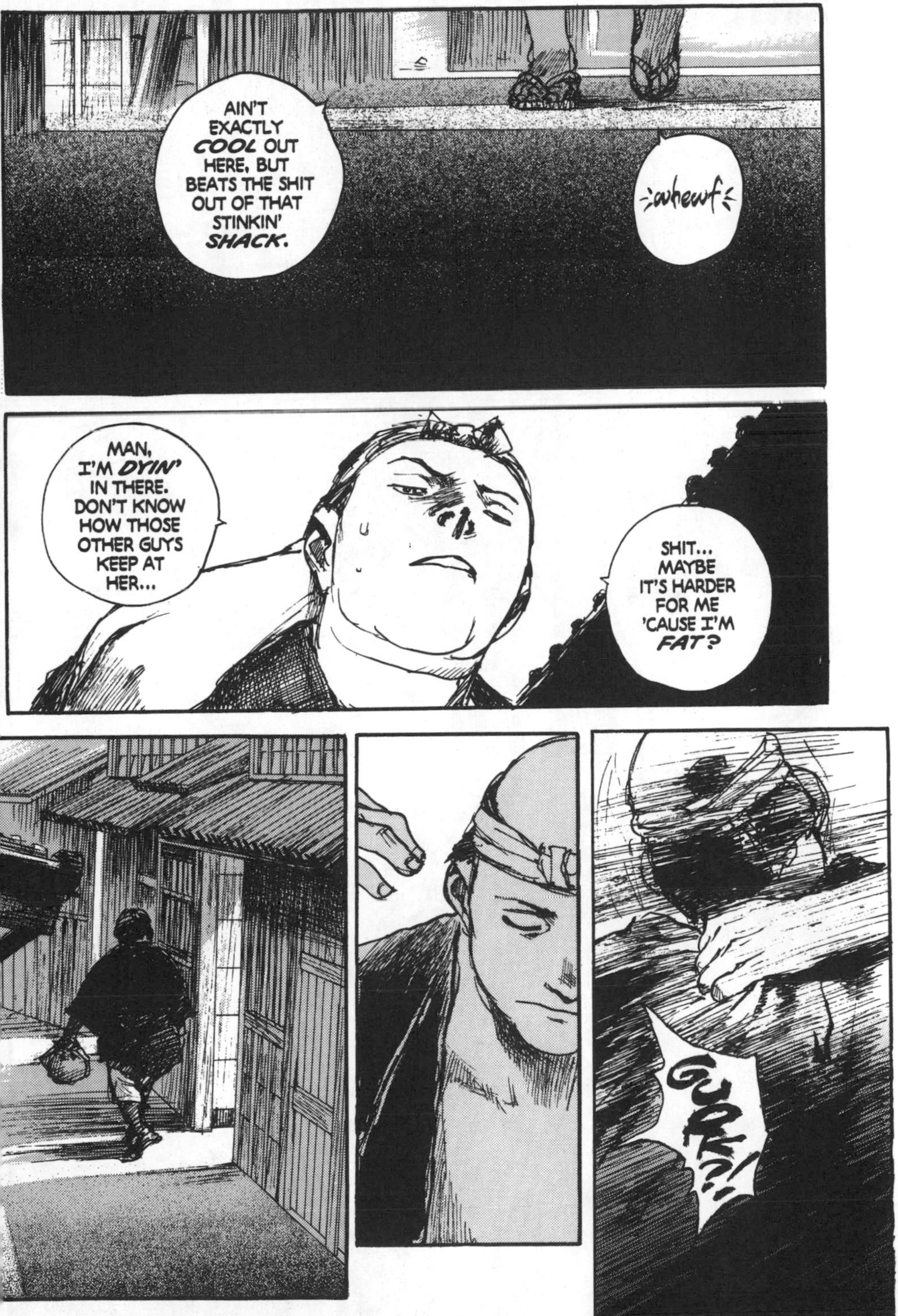
AIN'T EXACTLY COOL OUT HERE, BUT BEATS THE SHIT OUT OF THAT STINKIN' SHACK.
whewf
MAN, I'M DYIN' IN THERE. DON'T KNOW HOW THOSE OTHER GUYS KEEP AT HER...
SHIT... MAYBE IT'S HARDER FOR ME 'CAUSE I'M FAT?
GURK?!

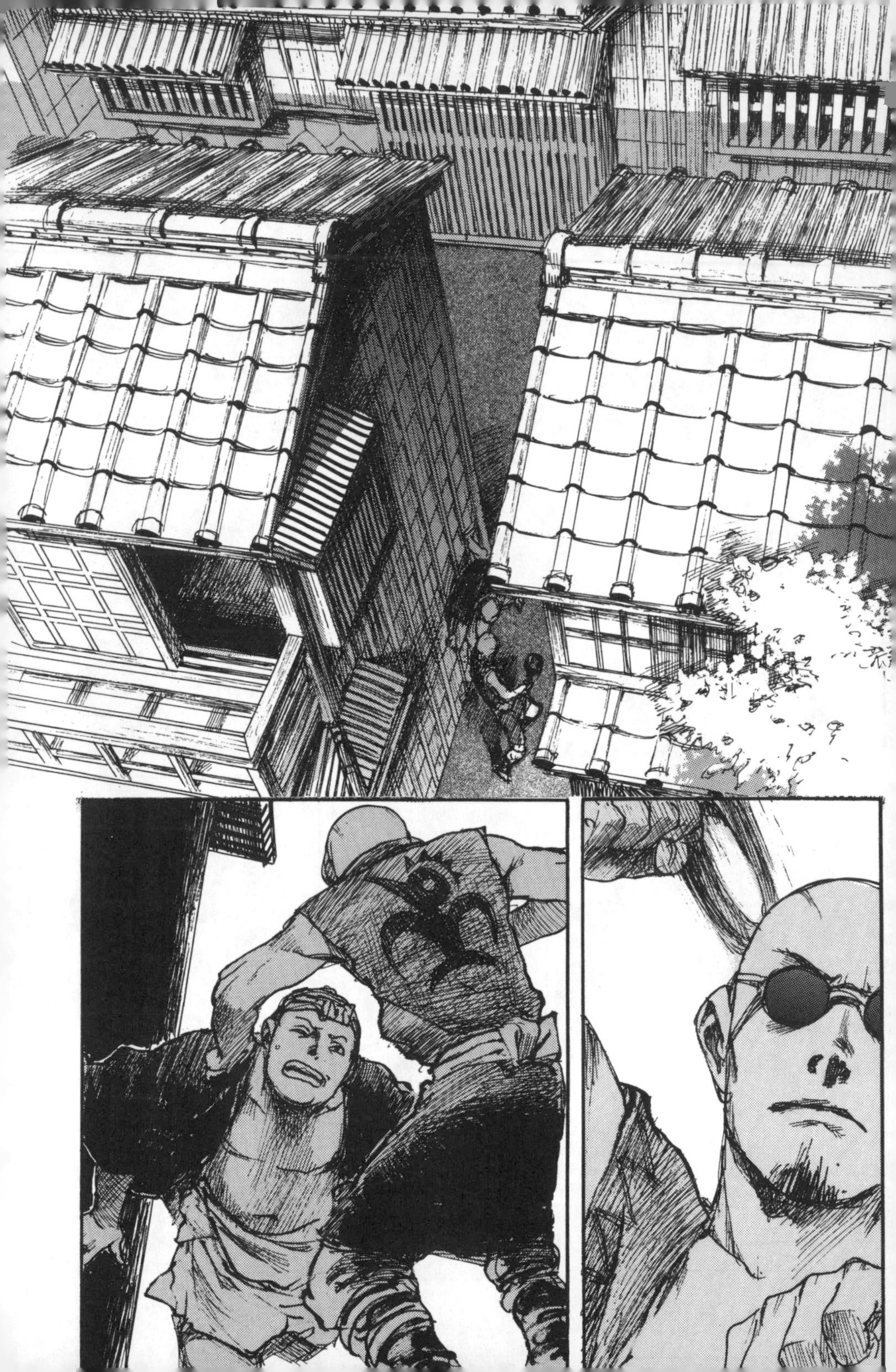

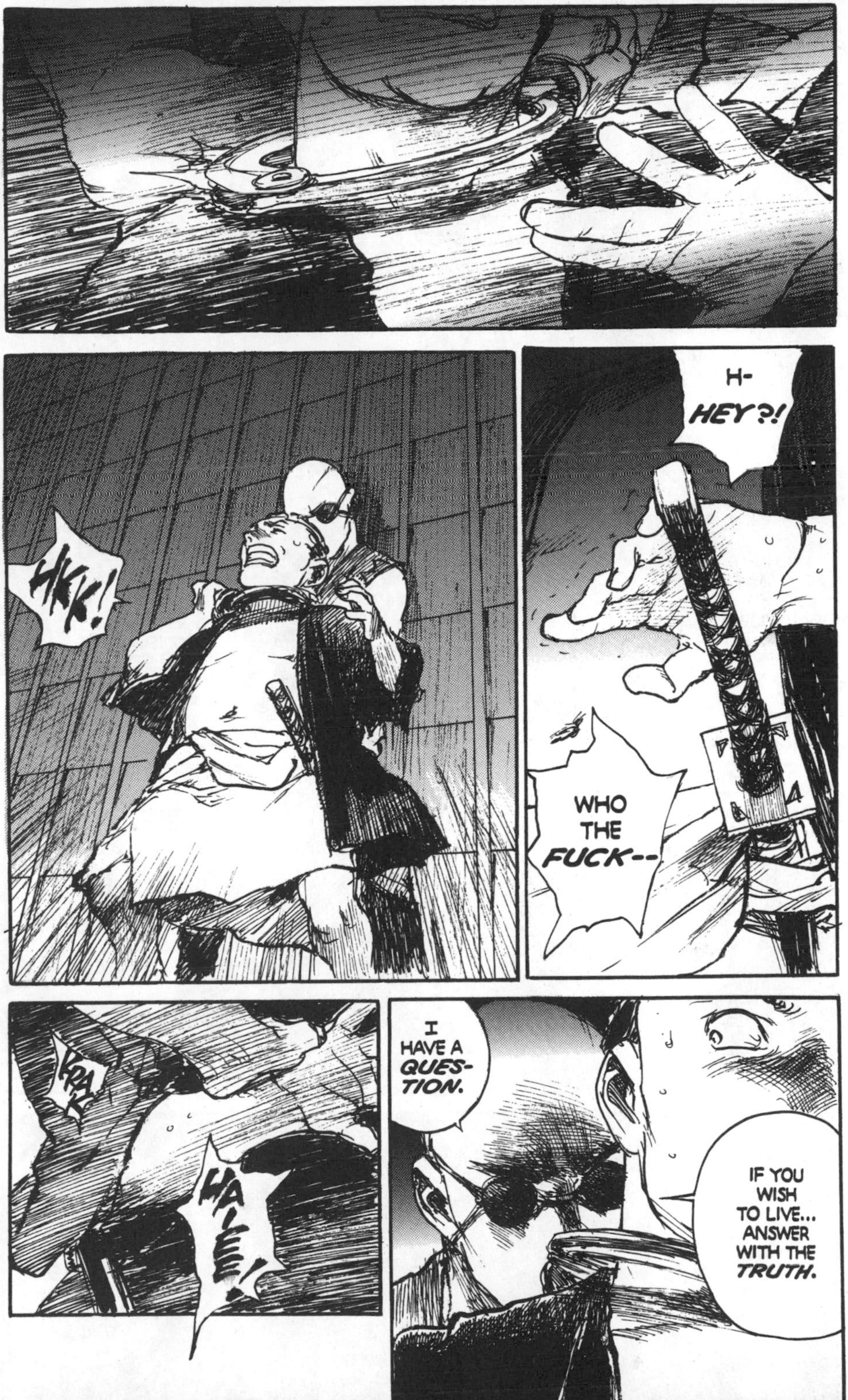
H- HEY?!
WHO THE FUCK--
HKK!
I HAVE A QUESTION.
IF YOU WISH TO LIVE... ANSWER WITH THE TRUTH.
KRAK

YOU ARE PART OF THE GANG THAT HIT A BATH HOUSE TWO NIGHTS AGO.

IT WAS IN *KODENMA-CHŌ.* THEY CUT DOWN ONE MAN, KIDNAPPED A WOMAN, AND VANISHED.

I DON'T KNOW *NOTHING!* I NEVER--

THAT IS NOT MY QUESTION.

I CONSIDER YOUR INVOLVE-MENT *FACT.*

NOW... THE FINGERS OF THE MAN YOU LEFT... POINTED A CERTAIN DIRECTION.

"*SOUTH-EAST,* TOWARDS *TATSUMI,* HERE IN FUKAGAWA.

"WOULD THEY CHOOSE THE RED LIGHT DISTRICT, OR THE LUMBER YARDS BEYOND...?"

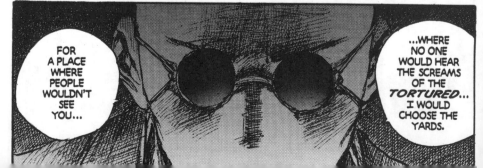

FOR A PLACE WHERE PEOPLE WOULDN'T SEE YOU...

...WHERE NO ONE WOULD HEAR THE SCREAMS OF THE *TORTURED...* I WOULD CHOOSE THE YARDS.

ON THIS BODY...

...*THREE SMELLS.*

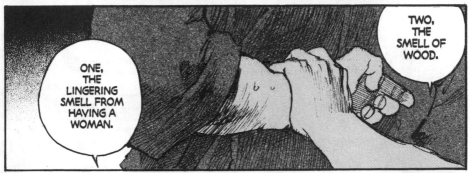

ONE, THE LINGERING SMELL FROM HAVING A WOMAN.

TWO, THE SMELL OF WOOD.

SO *WHAT?* I'VE LIVED HERE FOR *YEARS!*

WHAT THE HELL DO YOU *EXPECT?*

LUMBER YARDS OUT *BACK,* BROTHELS DOWN THE *STREET!*

WHAT'S SO STRANGE ABOUT--

YES. *PERSUA-SIVE.*

BUT THERE IS THE *THIRD* SMELL...

...OF WHICH I SPOKE. A UNIQUE ODOR.

THE WOMAN I SEEK USED A CERTAIN CHEMICAL TO BLEACH HER HAIR. IT IS A QUITE *UNMISTAKABLE* SMELL.

YOU HAVE BEEN... *CLOSE ENOUGH* TO THIS WOMAN TO HAVE ACQUIRED THE SCENT.

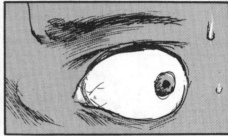

NOW TO THE QUESTION-- YOUR *FRIENDS* OR YOUR *LIFE*...

...WHICH DO YOU CHOOSE?

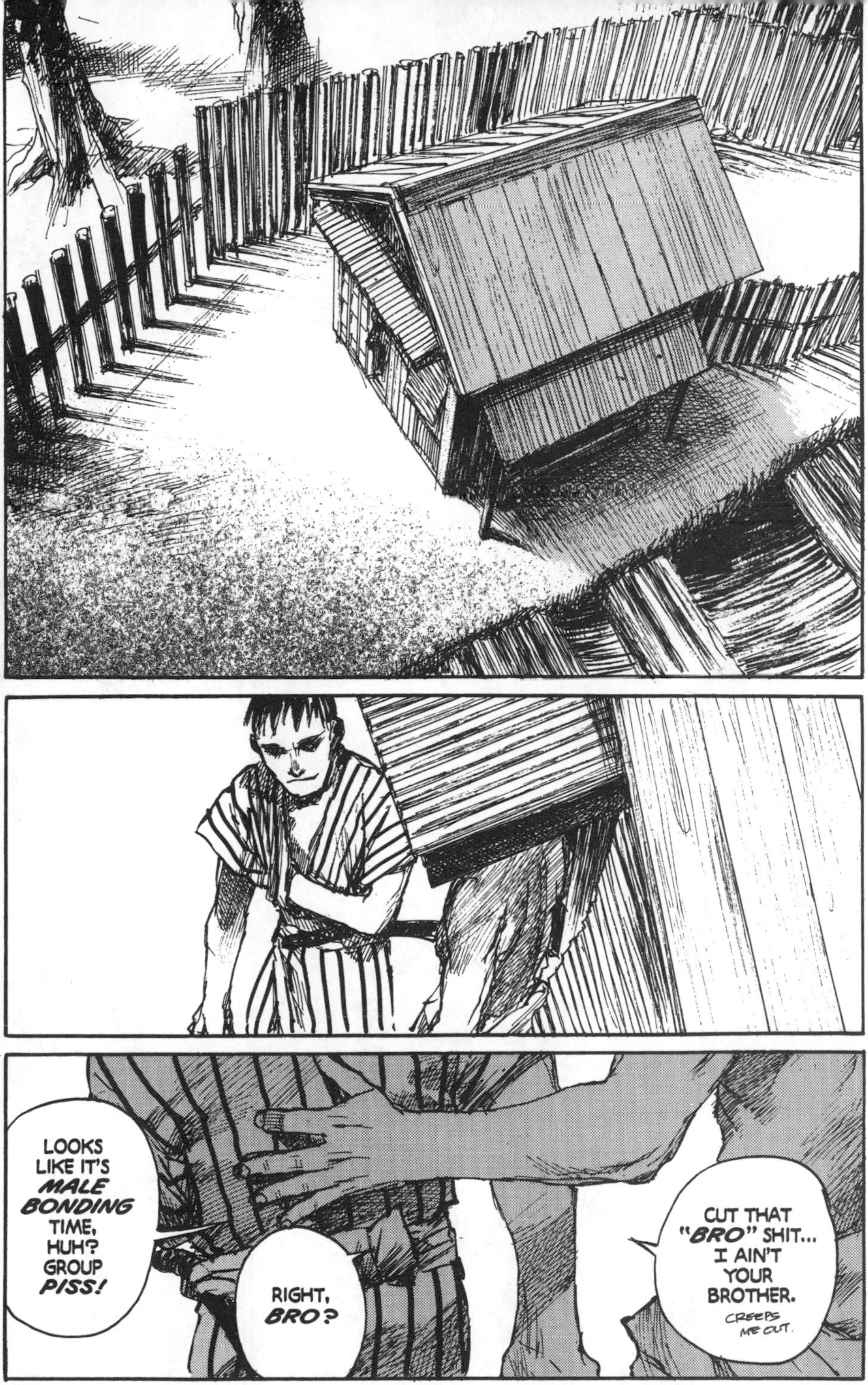
LOOKS LIKE IT'S MALE BONDING TIME, HUH? GROUP PISS!
RIGHT, BRO?
CUT THAT "BRO" SHIT... I AIN'T YOUR BROTHER.
CREEPS ME OUT.

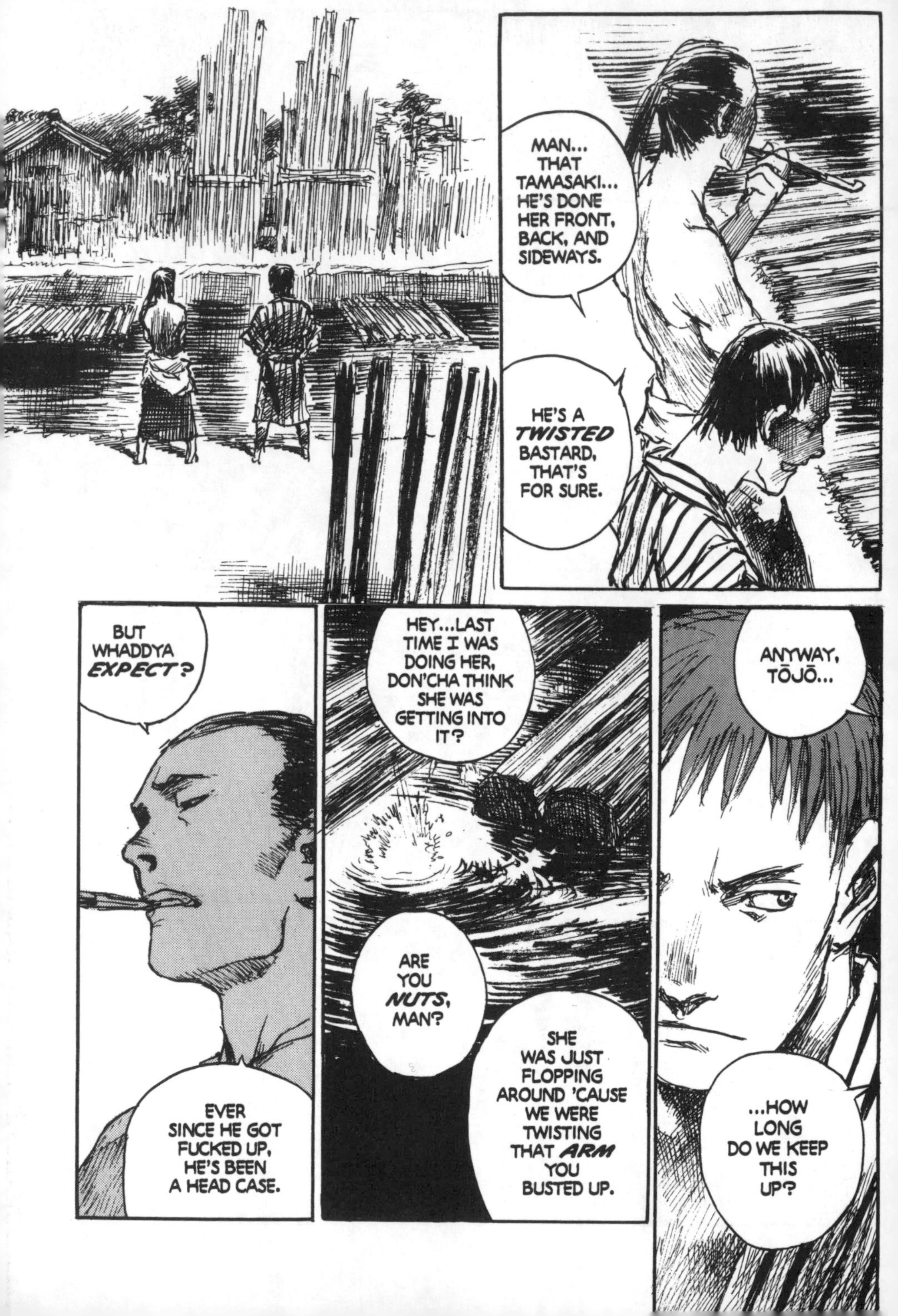
MAN... THAT TAMASAKI... HE'S DONE HER FRONT, BACK, AND SIDEWAYS.
HE'S A *TWISTED* BASTARD, THAT'S FOR SURE.
BUT WHADDYA *EXPECT*?
EVER SINCE HE GOT FUCKED UP, HE'S BEEN A HEAD CASE.
HEY...LAST TIME I WAS DOING HER, DON'CHA THINK SHE WAS GETTING INTO IT?
ARE YOU *NUTS*, MAN?
SHE WAS JUST FLOPPING AROUND 'CAUSE WE WERE TWISTING THAT *ARM* YOU BUSTED UP.
ANYWAY, TŌJŌ...
...HOW LONG DO WE KEEP THIS UP?

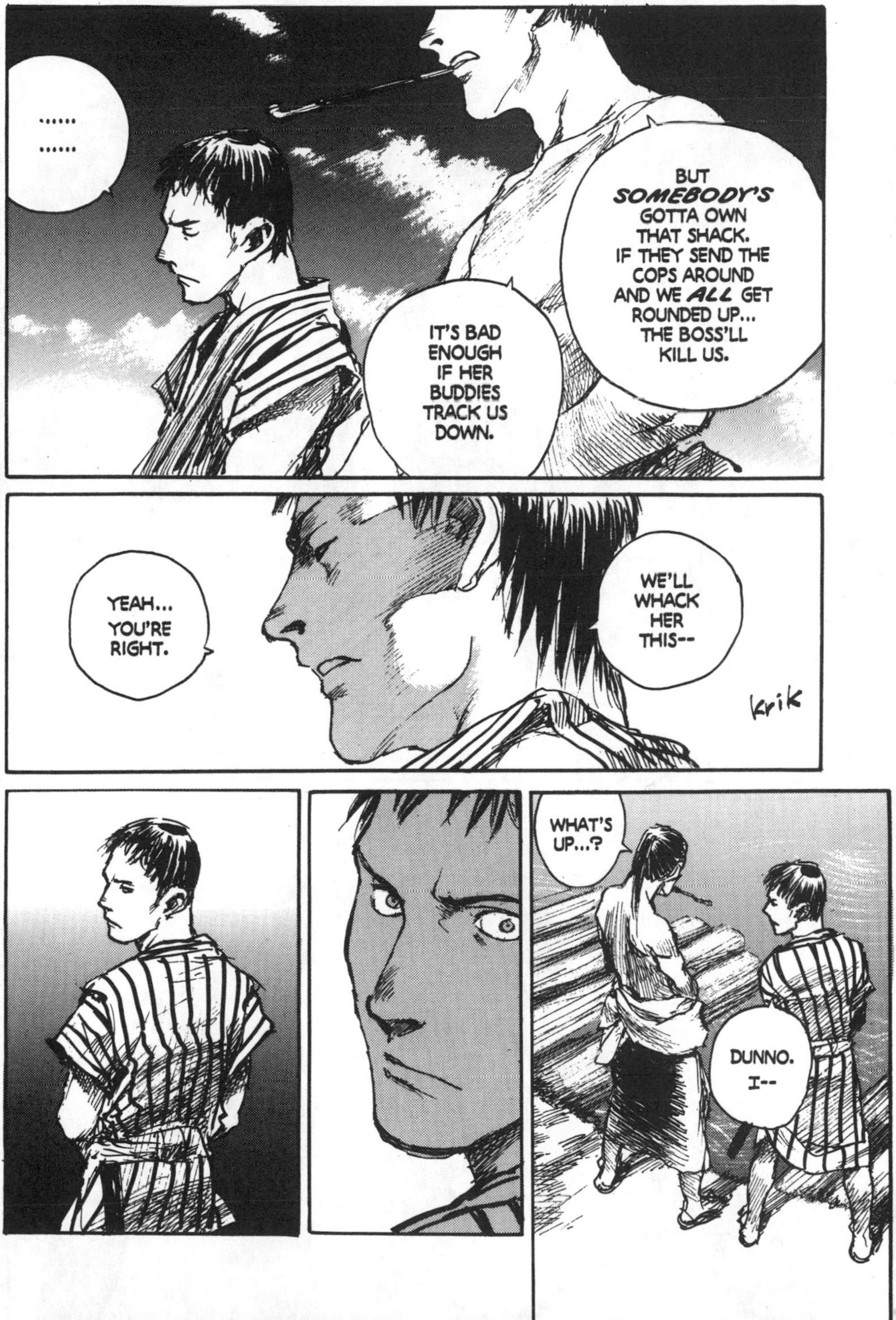
......
......
IT'S BAD ENOUGH IF HER BUDDIES TRACK US DOWN.
BUT *SOMEBODY'S* GOTTA OWN THAT SHACK. IF THEY SEND THE COPS AROUND AND WE *ALL* GET ROUNDED UP... THE BOSS'LL KILL US.
YEAH... YOU'RE RIGHT.
WE'LL WHACK HER THIS--
krik
WHAT'S UP...?
DUNNO. I--

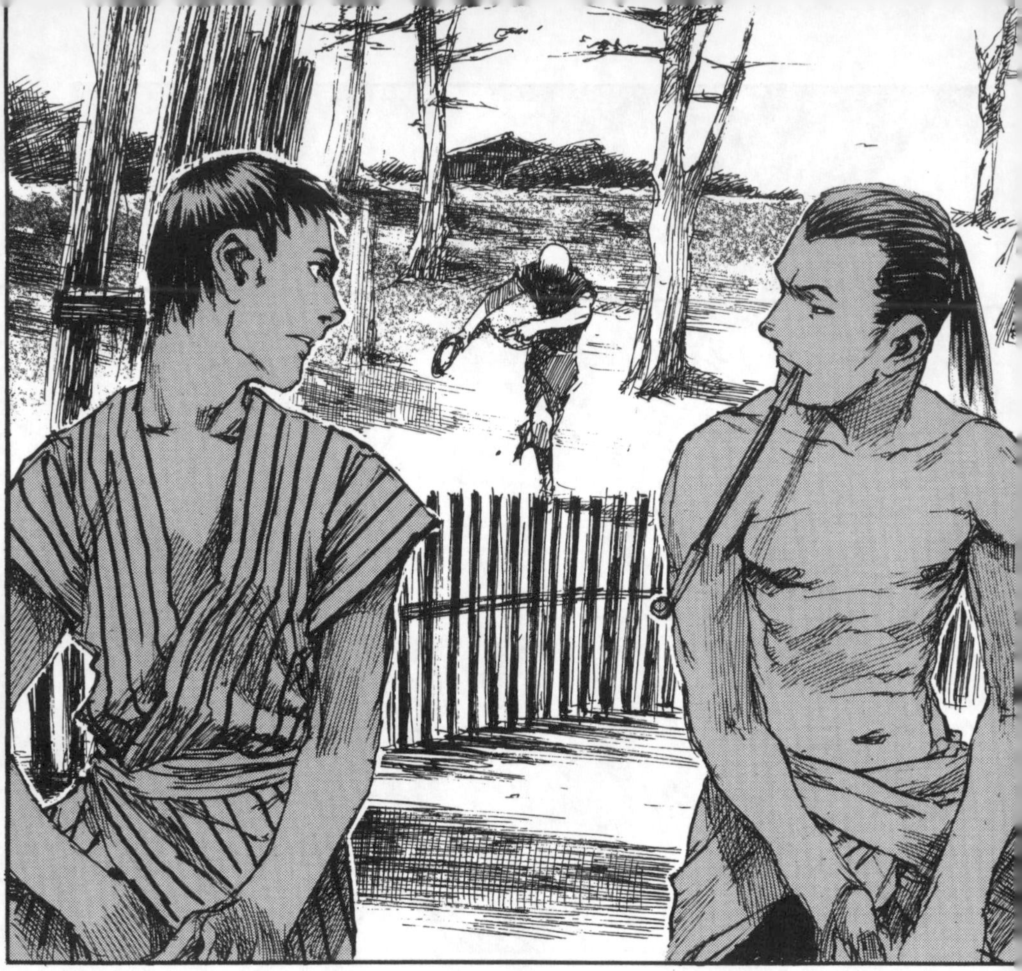
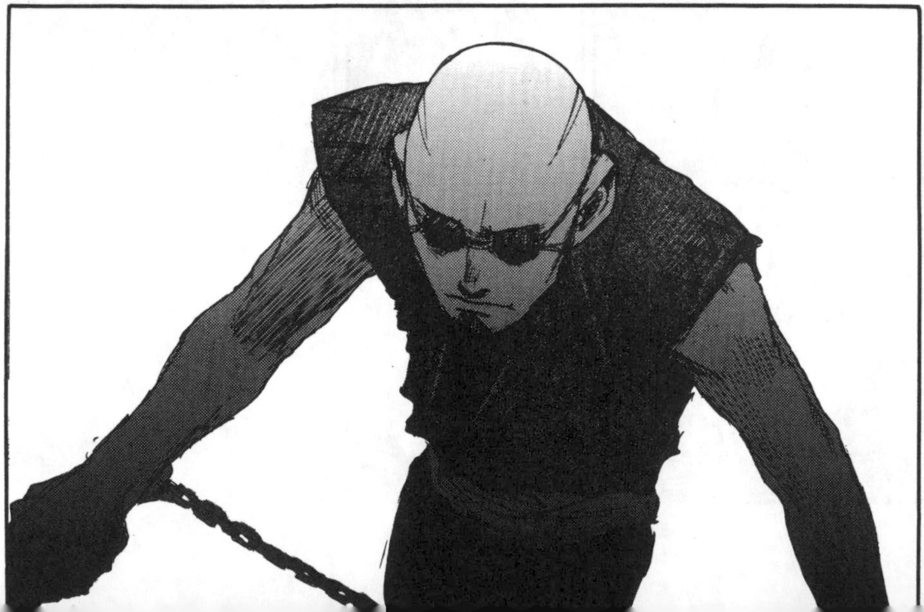

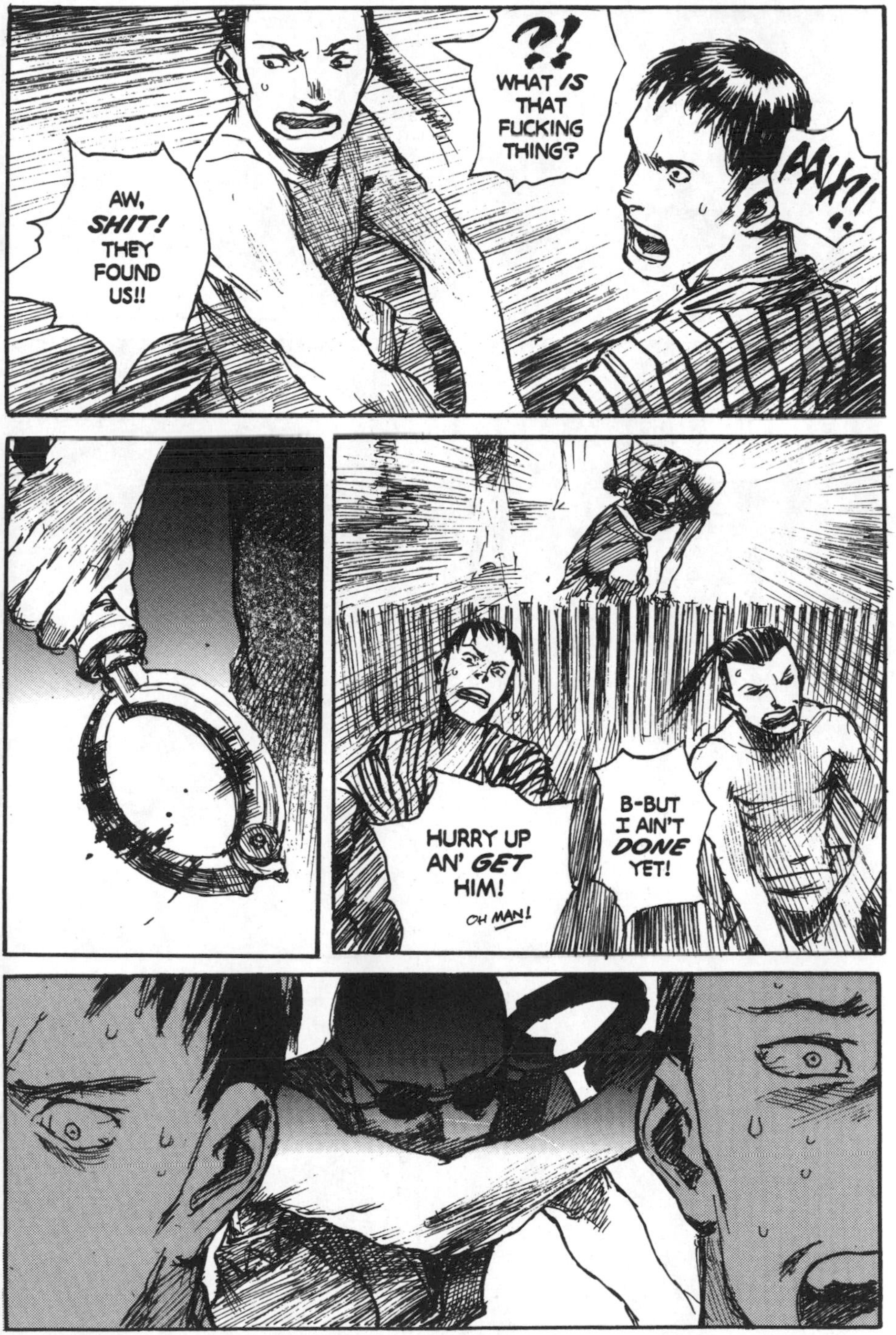
AAH?!
?!
WHAT *IS* THAT FUCKING THING?
AW, ***SHIT!*** THEY FOUND US!!
B-BUT I AIN'T ***DONE*** YET!
HURRY UP AN' ***GET*** HIM!
OH MAN!

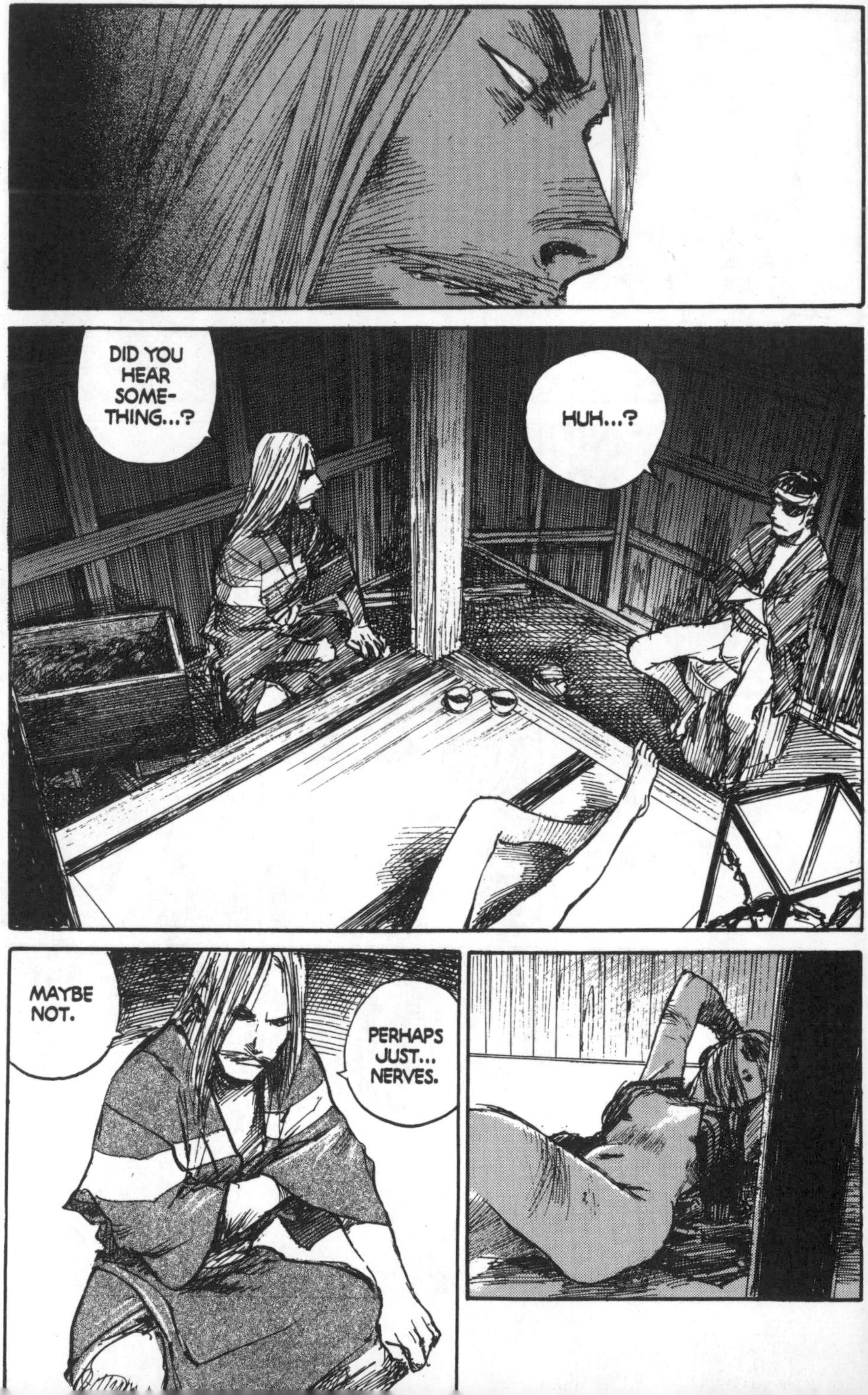
DID YOU HEAR SOME-THING...?
HUH...?
MAYBE NOT.
PERHAPS JUST... NERVES.

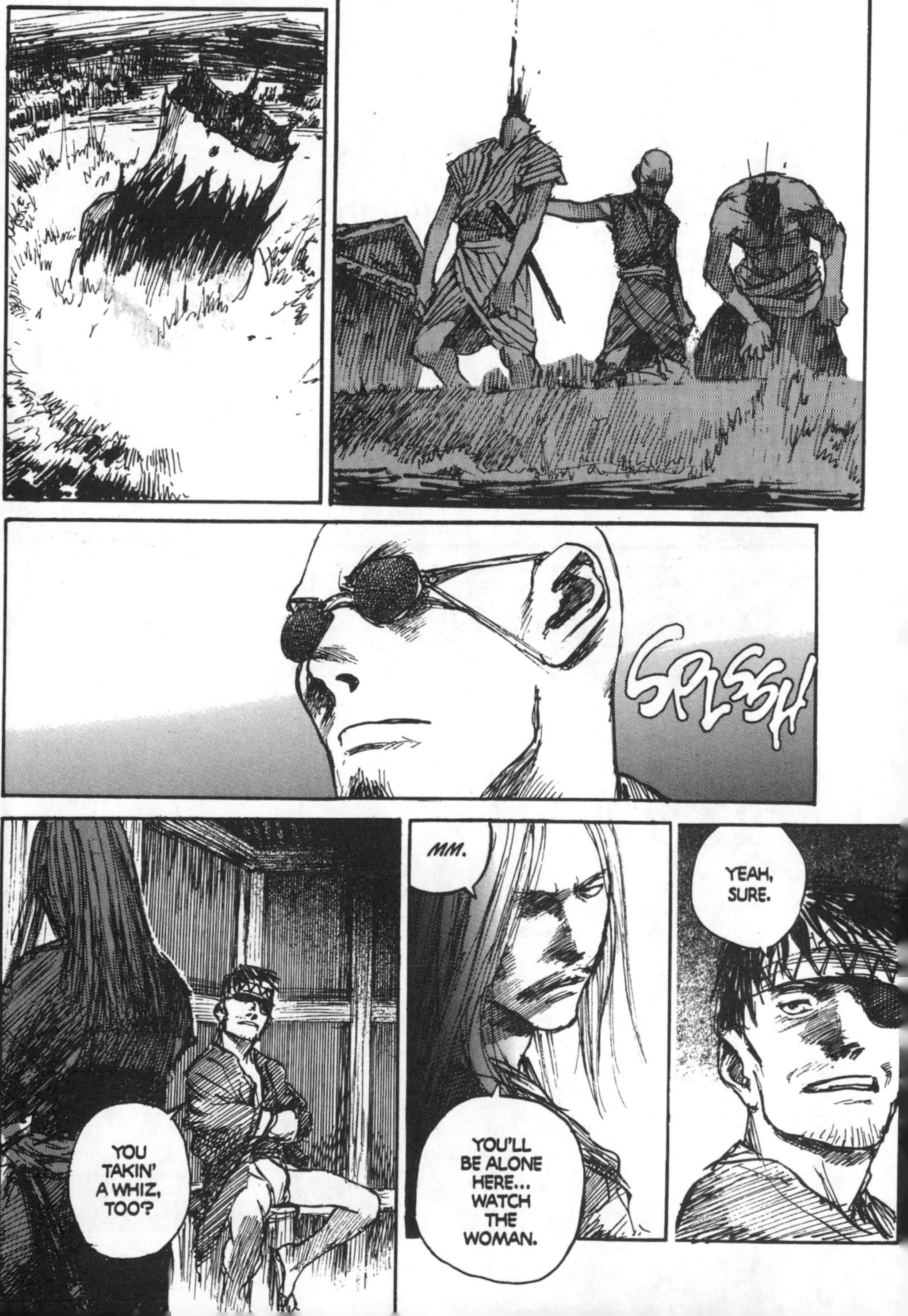
SPLSSH
YOU TAKIN' A WHIZ, TOO?
MM.
YOU'LL BE ALONE HERE... WATCH THE WOMAN.
YEAH, SURE.

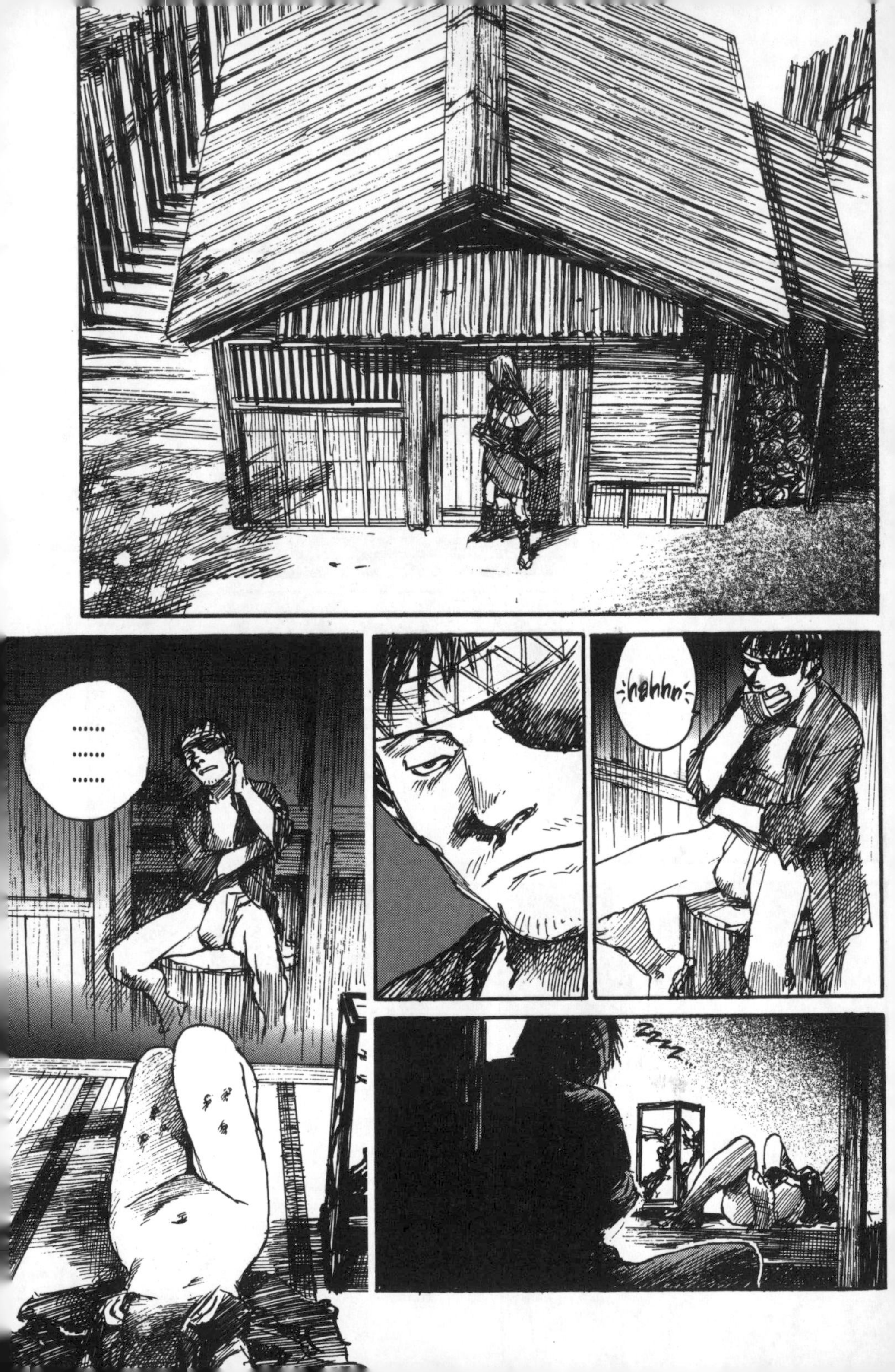
hahhn
……
……
……
zzzz…

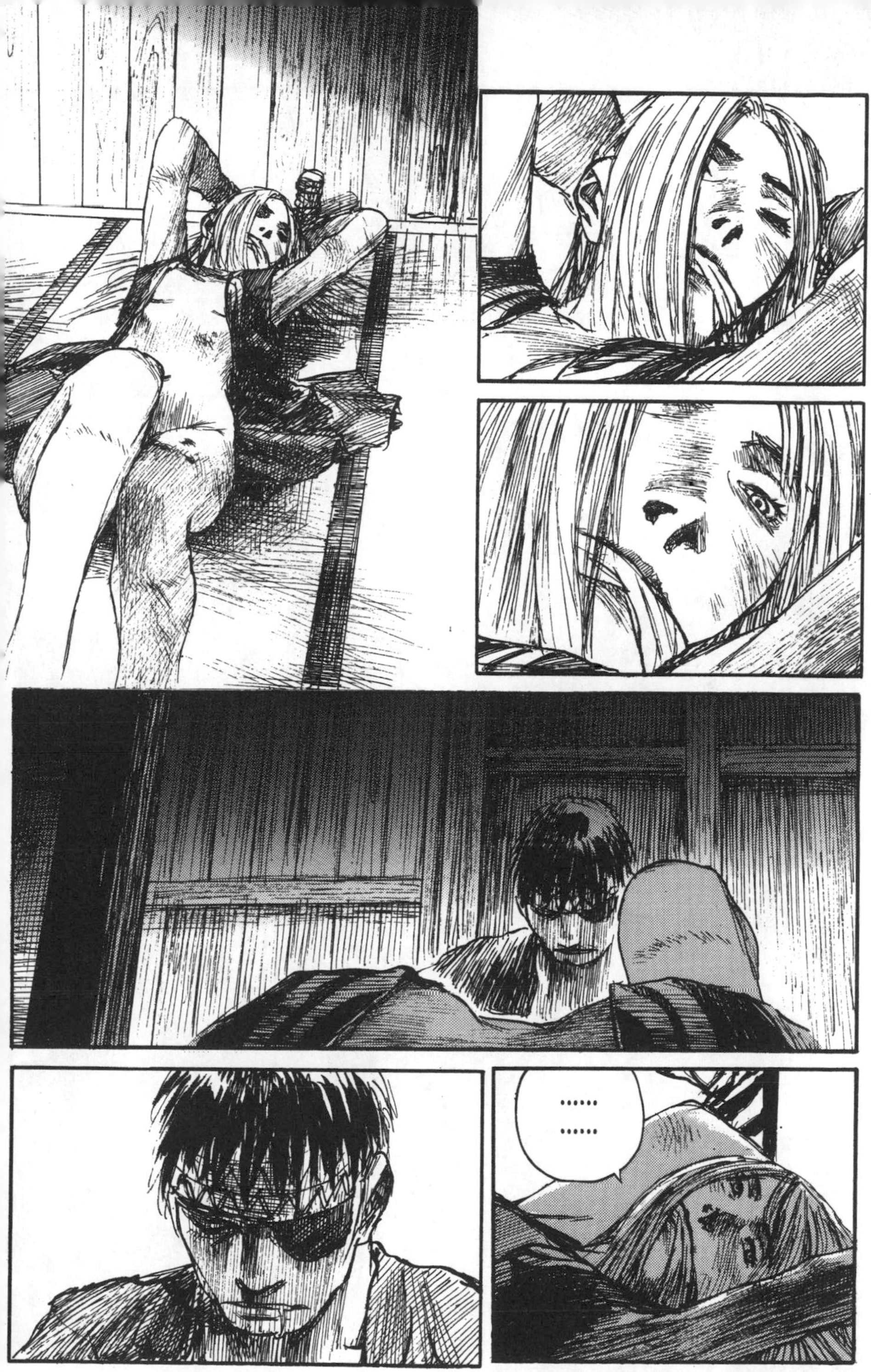
......
......

NNG...

......

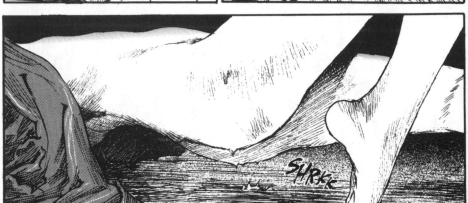

SHRKK

HKK...!

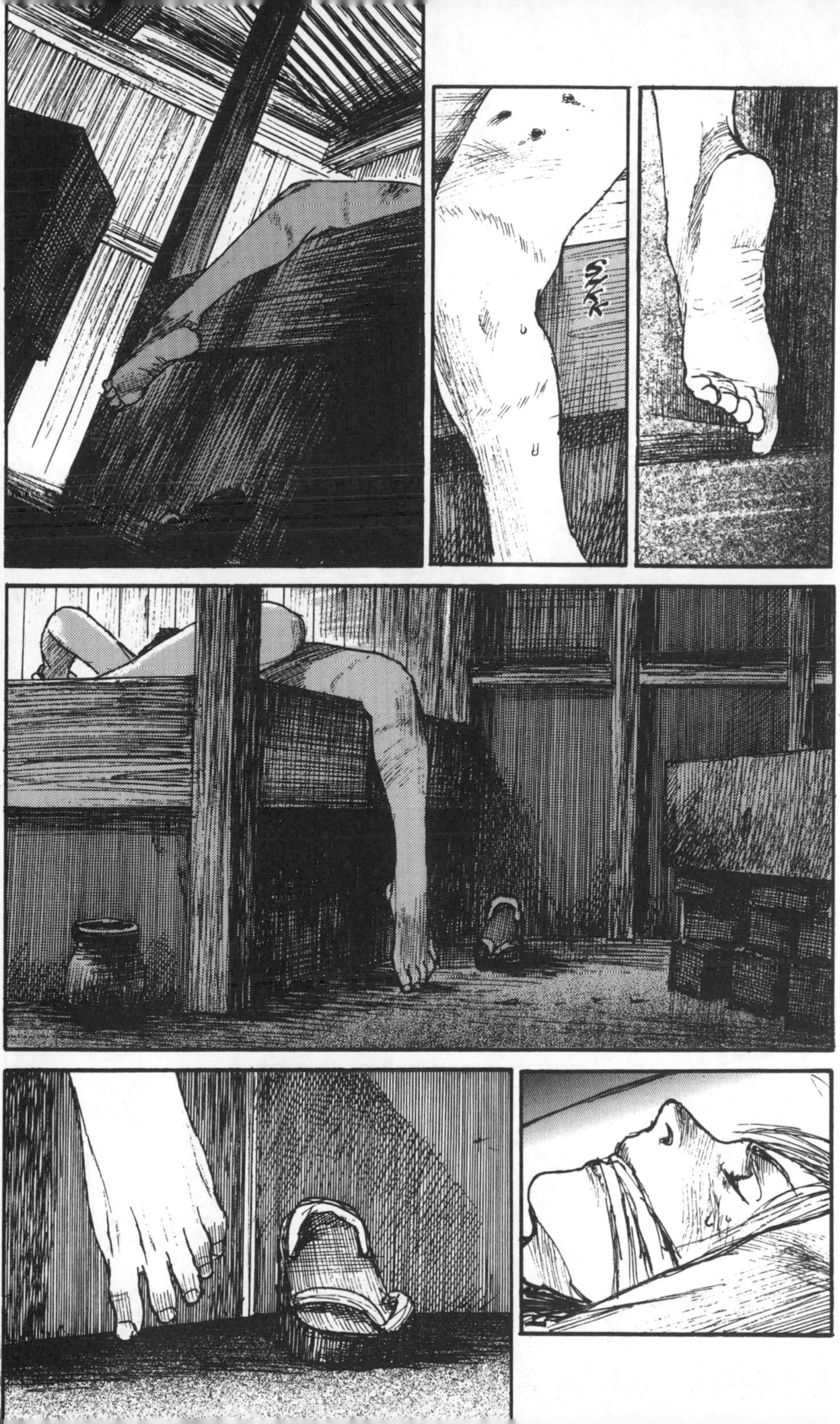
SZZK

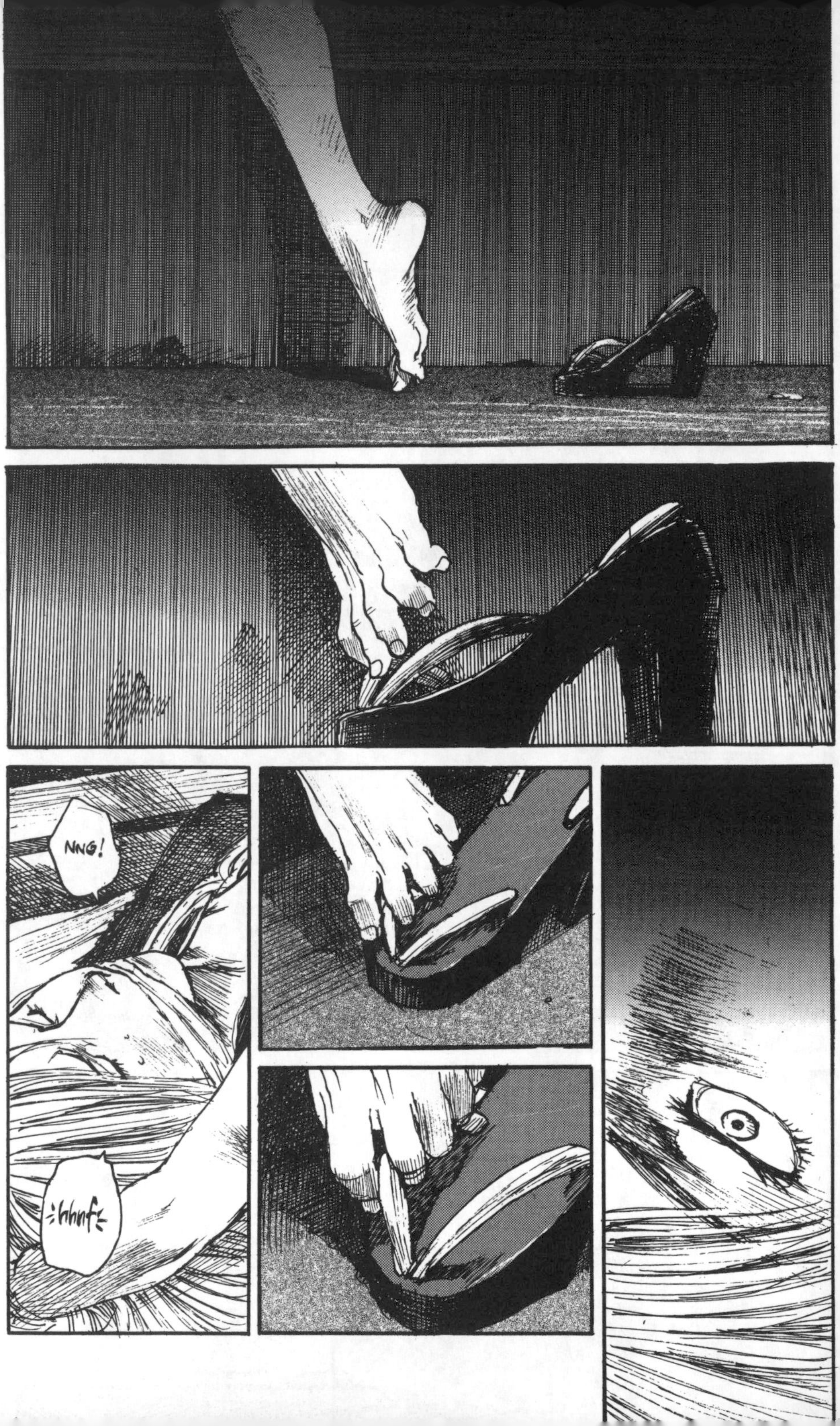
NNG!
hhnf

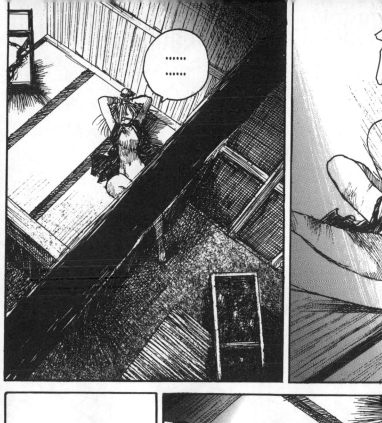

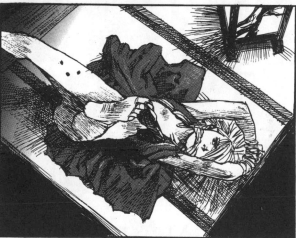

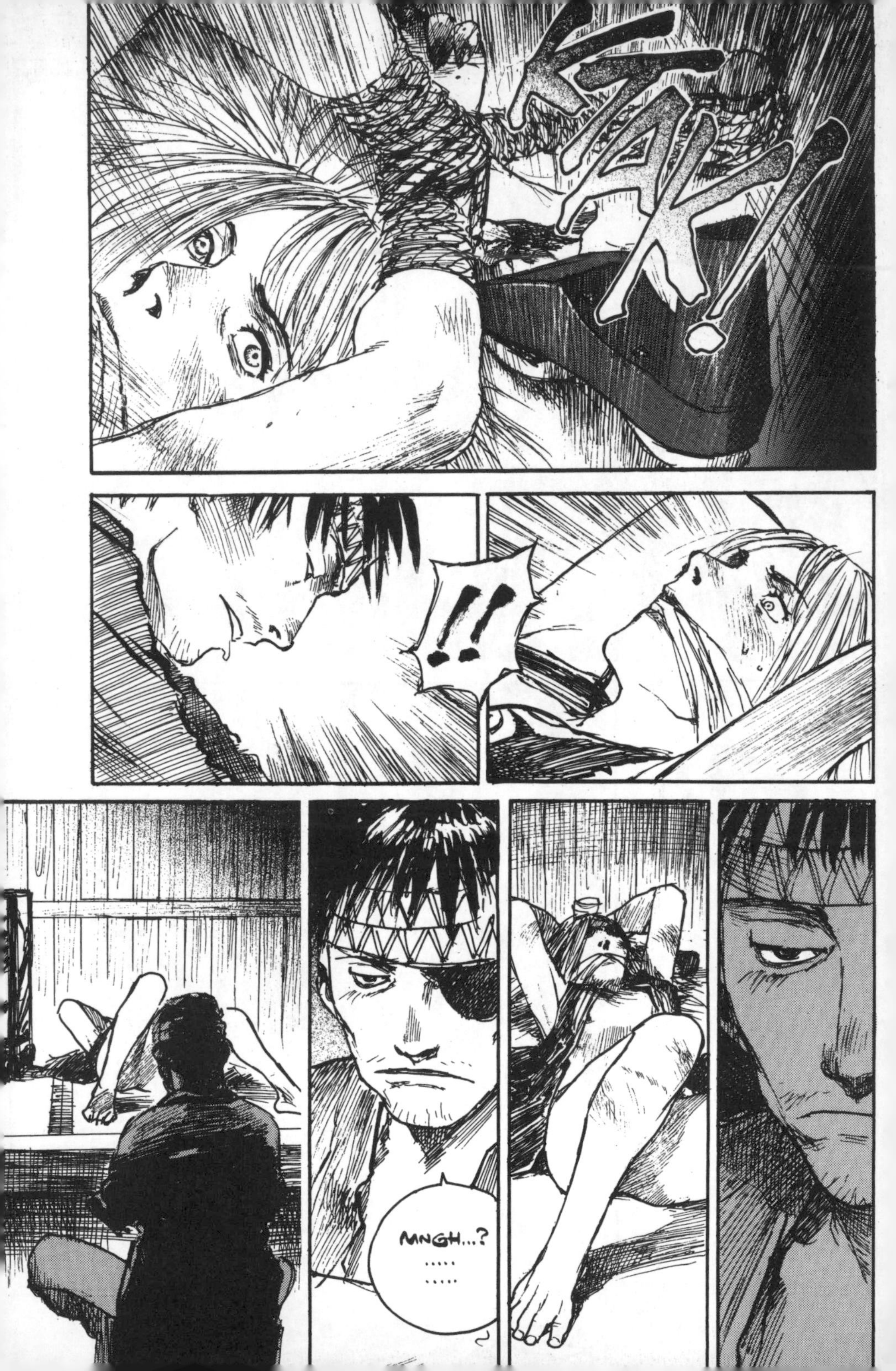
FWAP!
!!
MNGH...?
.....
.....

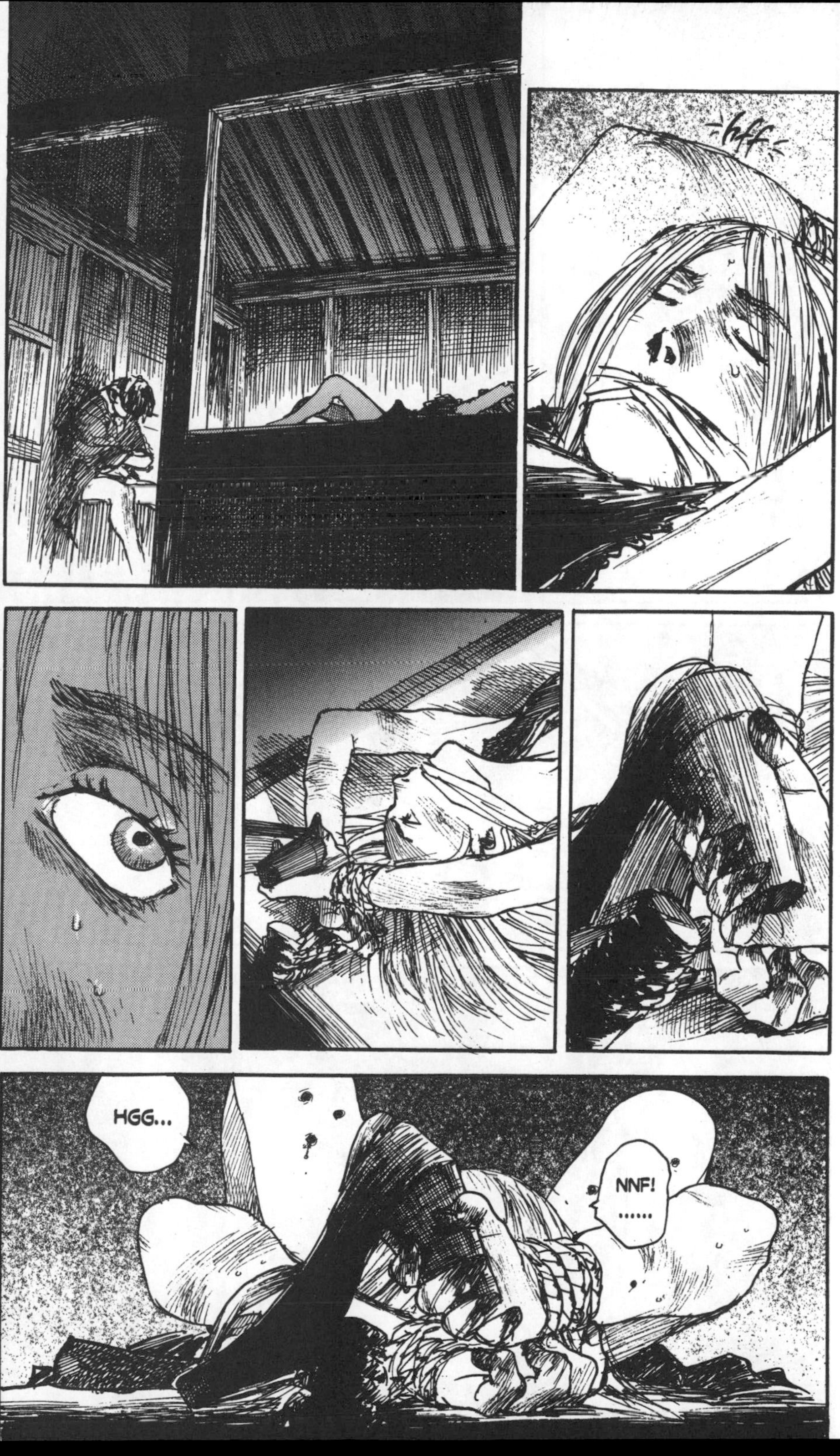
hff
HGG...
NNF!
......

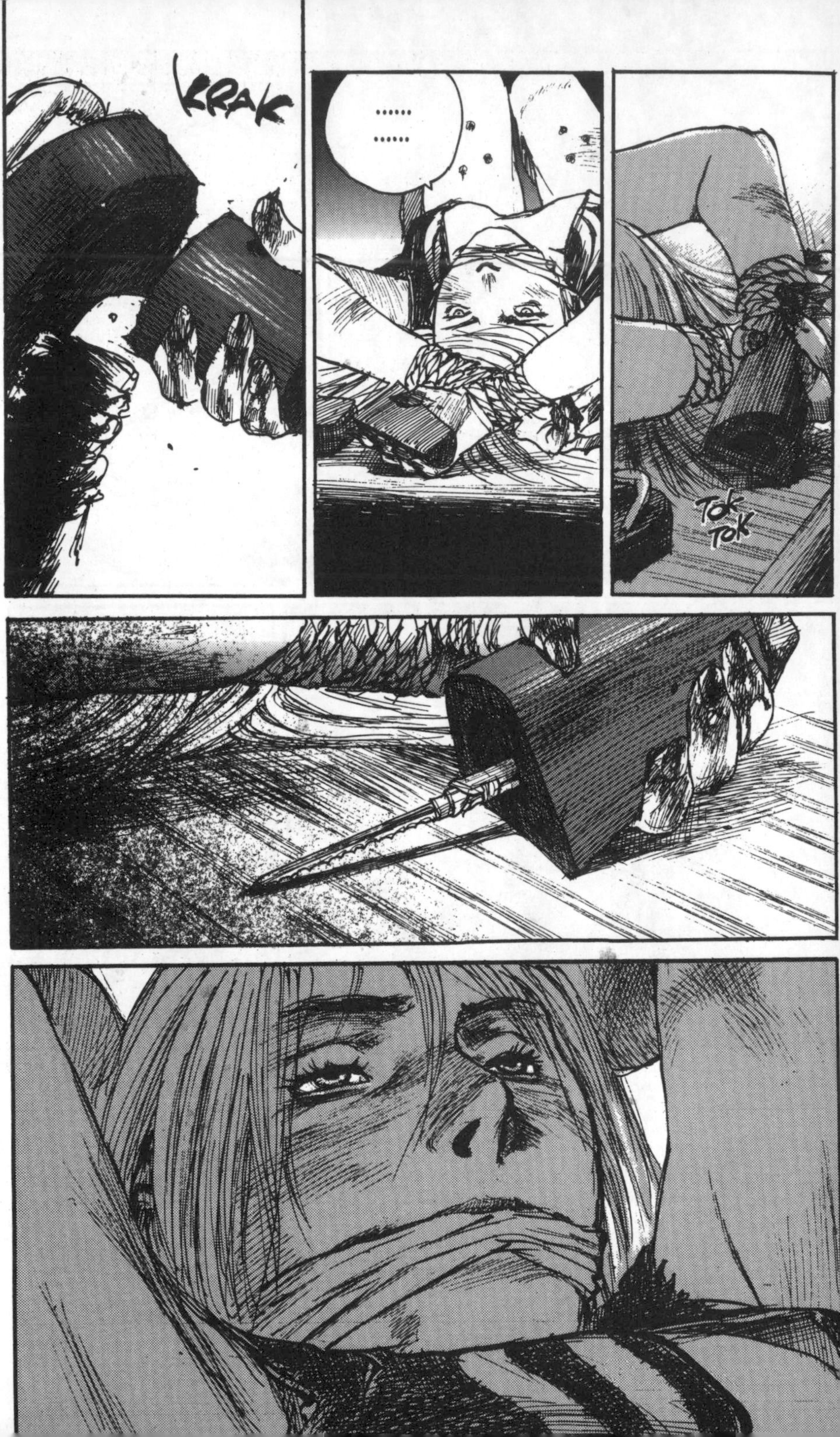
KRAK
......
......
TOK
TOK

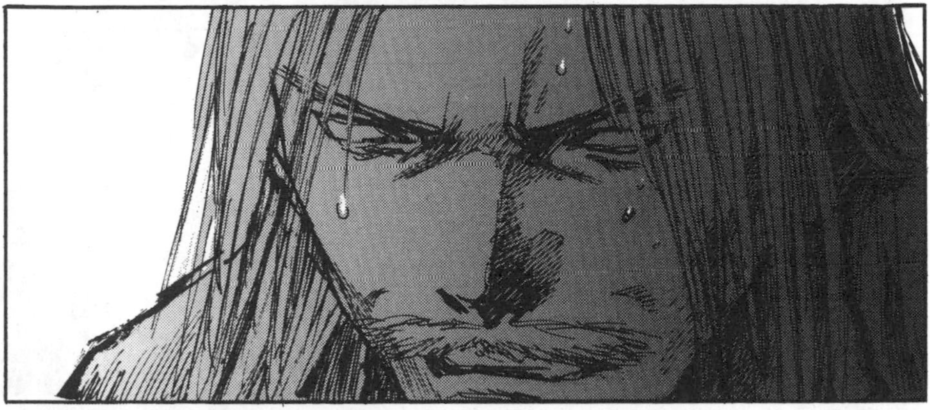
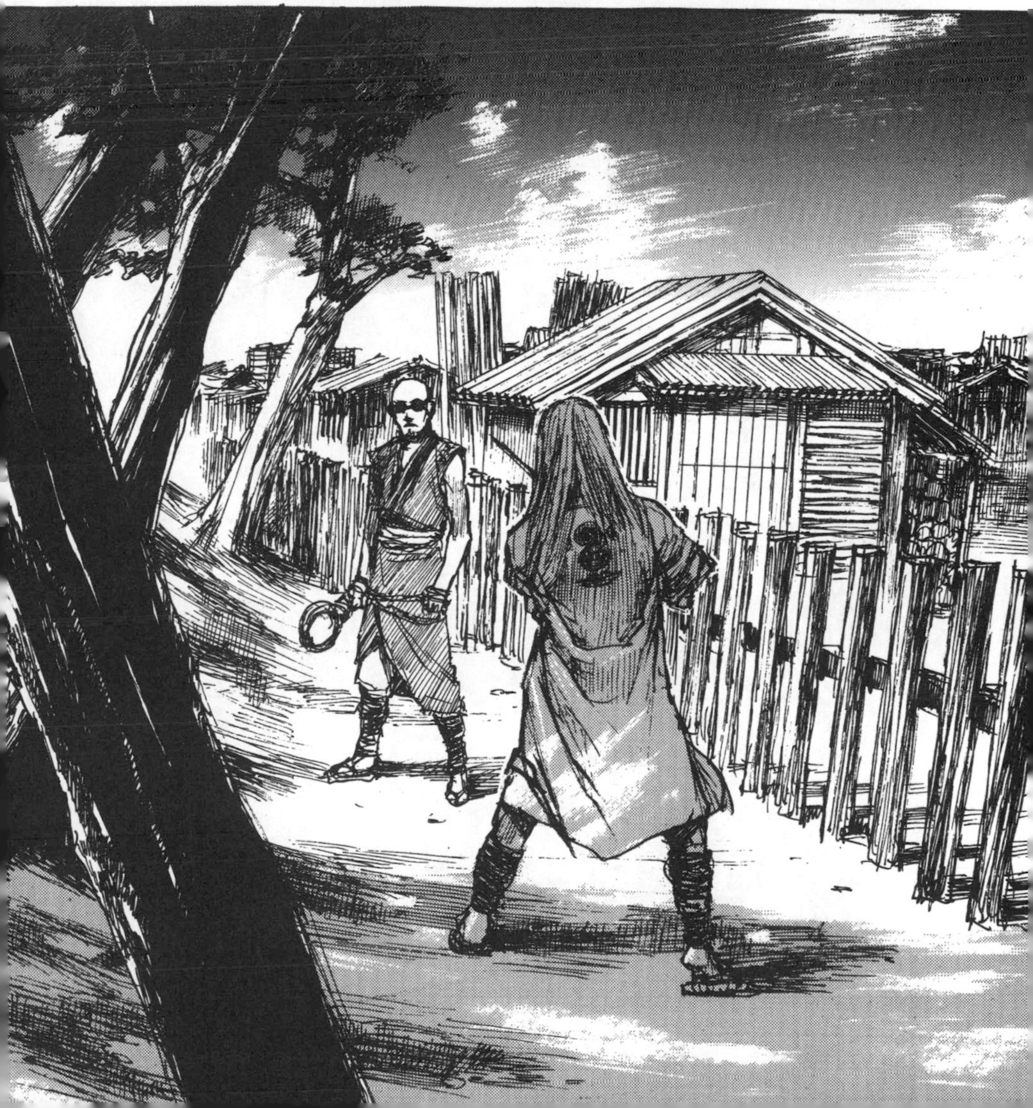

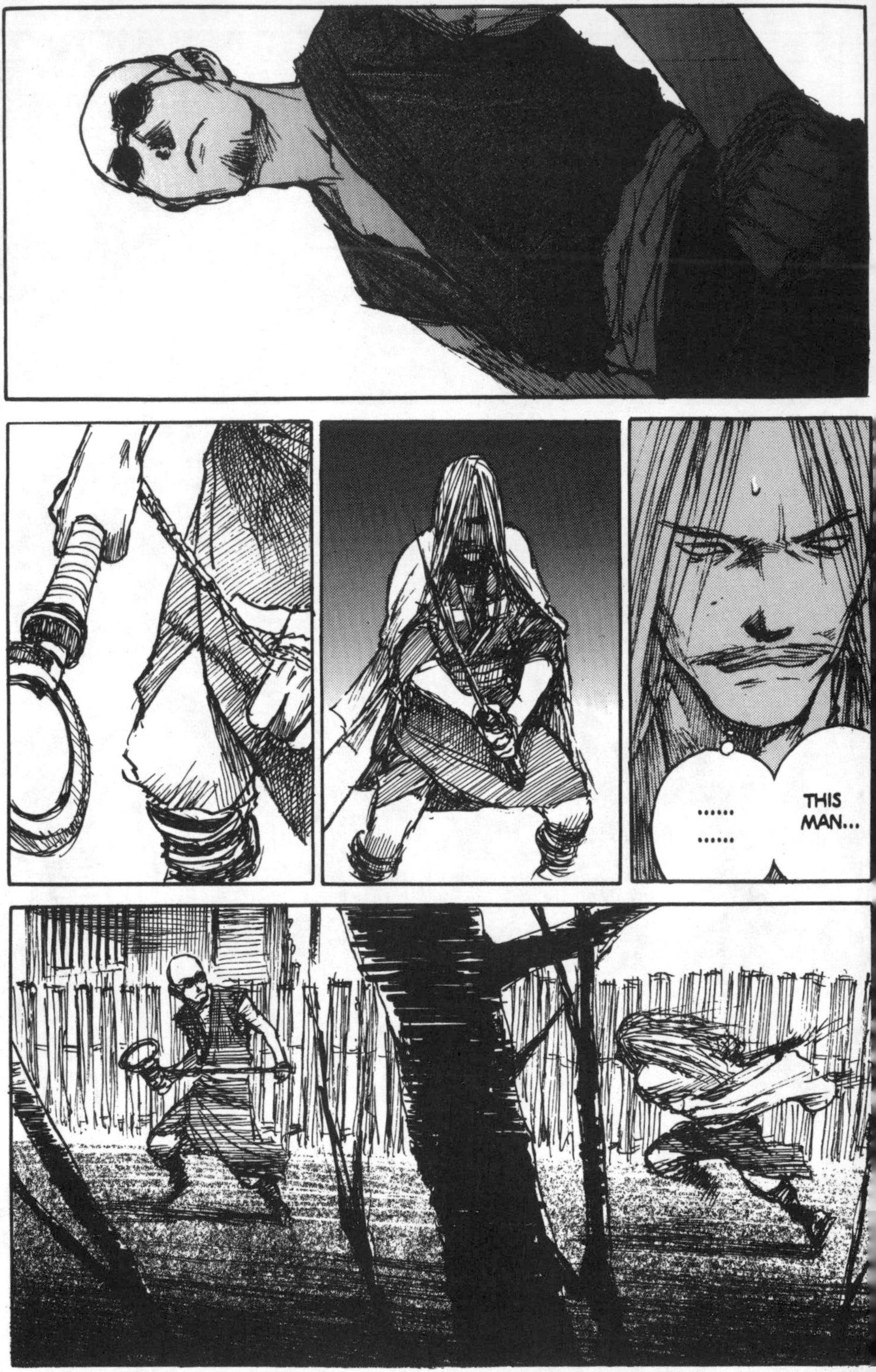
THIS MAN...
......
......

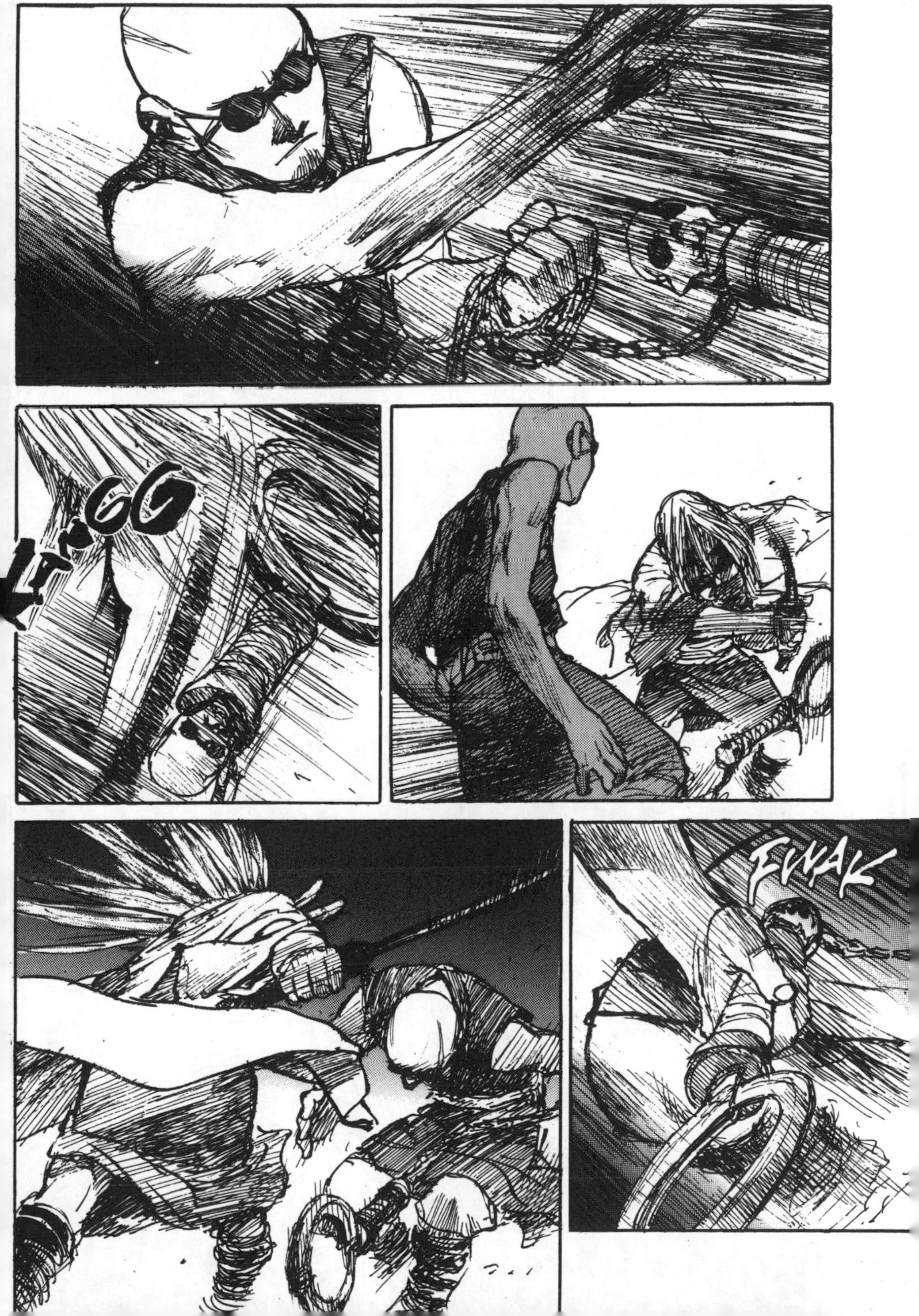
FWAK

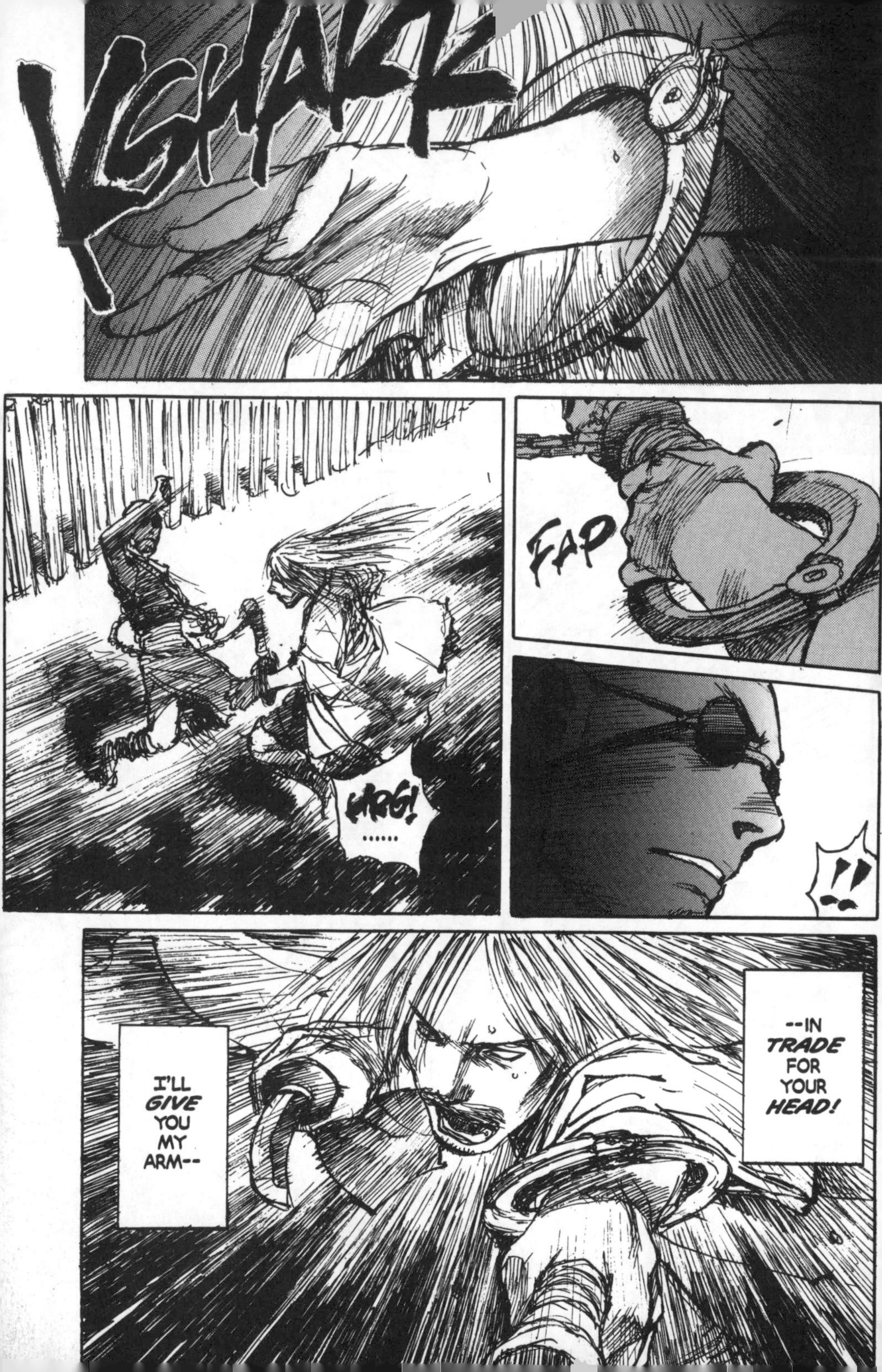
VSHAKK
FAP
!!
URG!
......
--IN *TRADE* FOR YOUR *HEAD!*
I'LL *GIVE* YOU MY ARM--

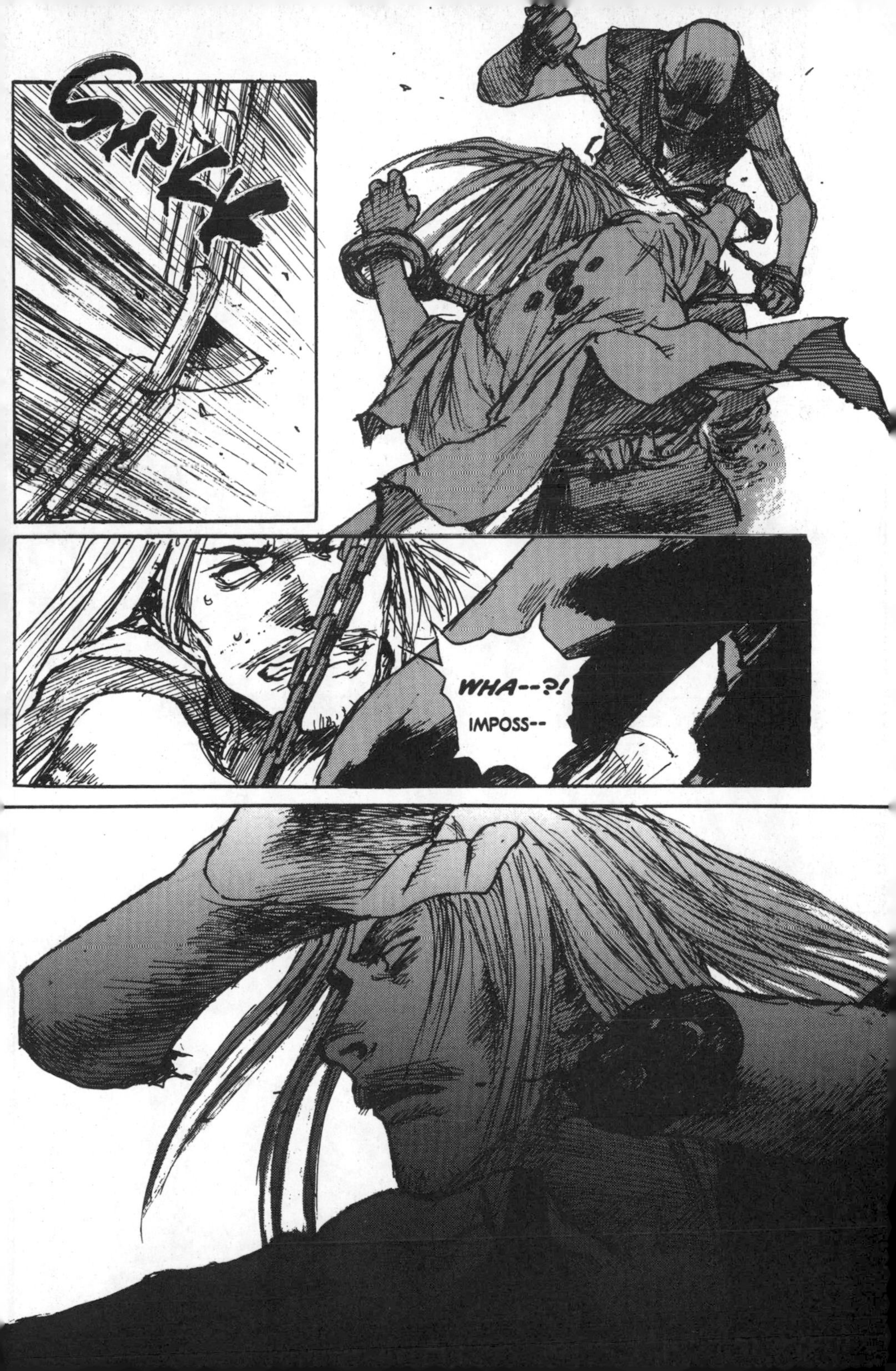
SHNKK
WHA--?!
IMPOSS--

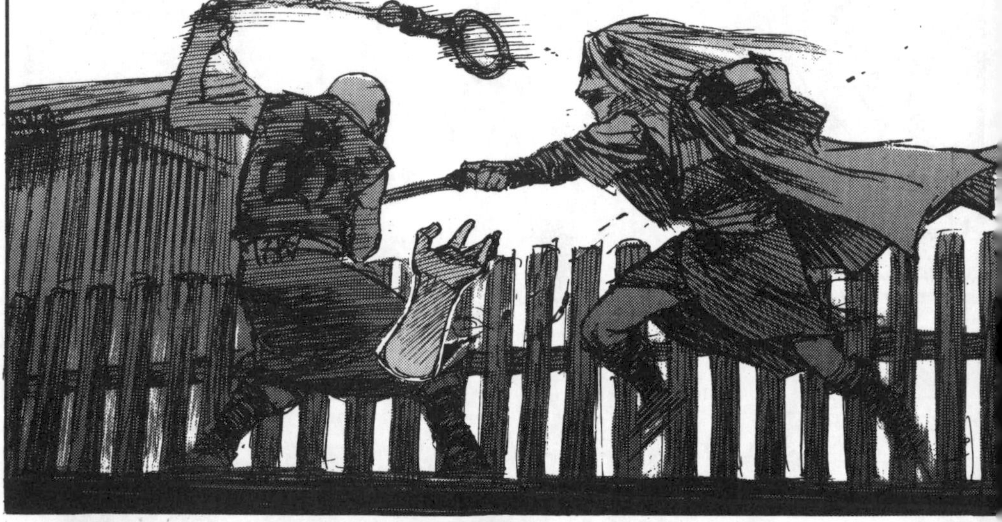
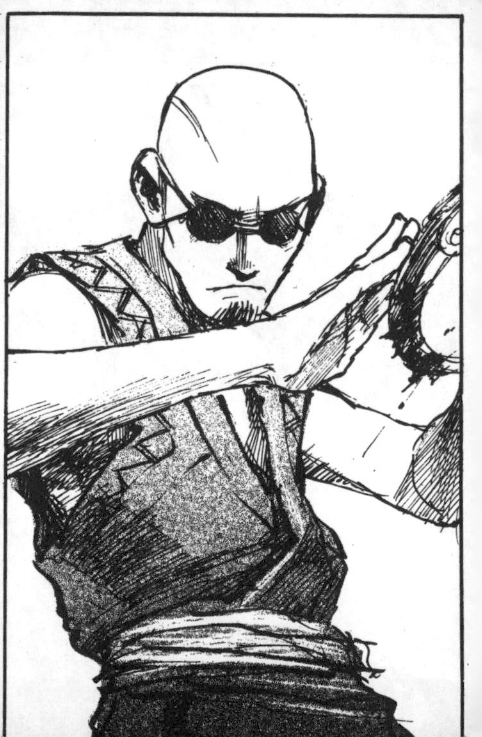
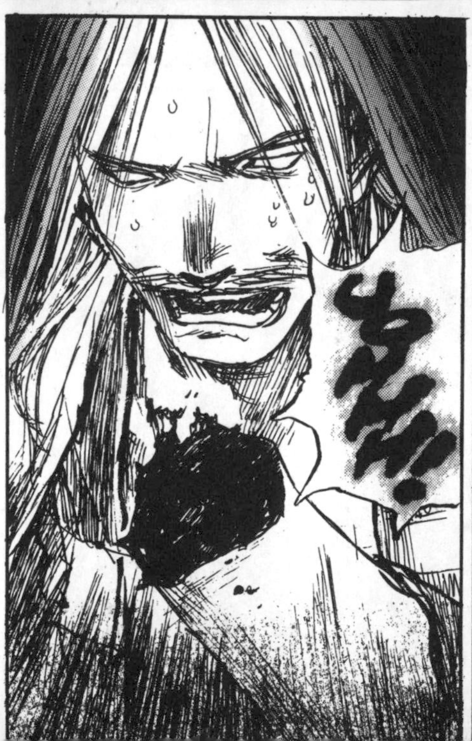

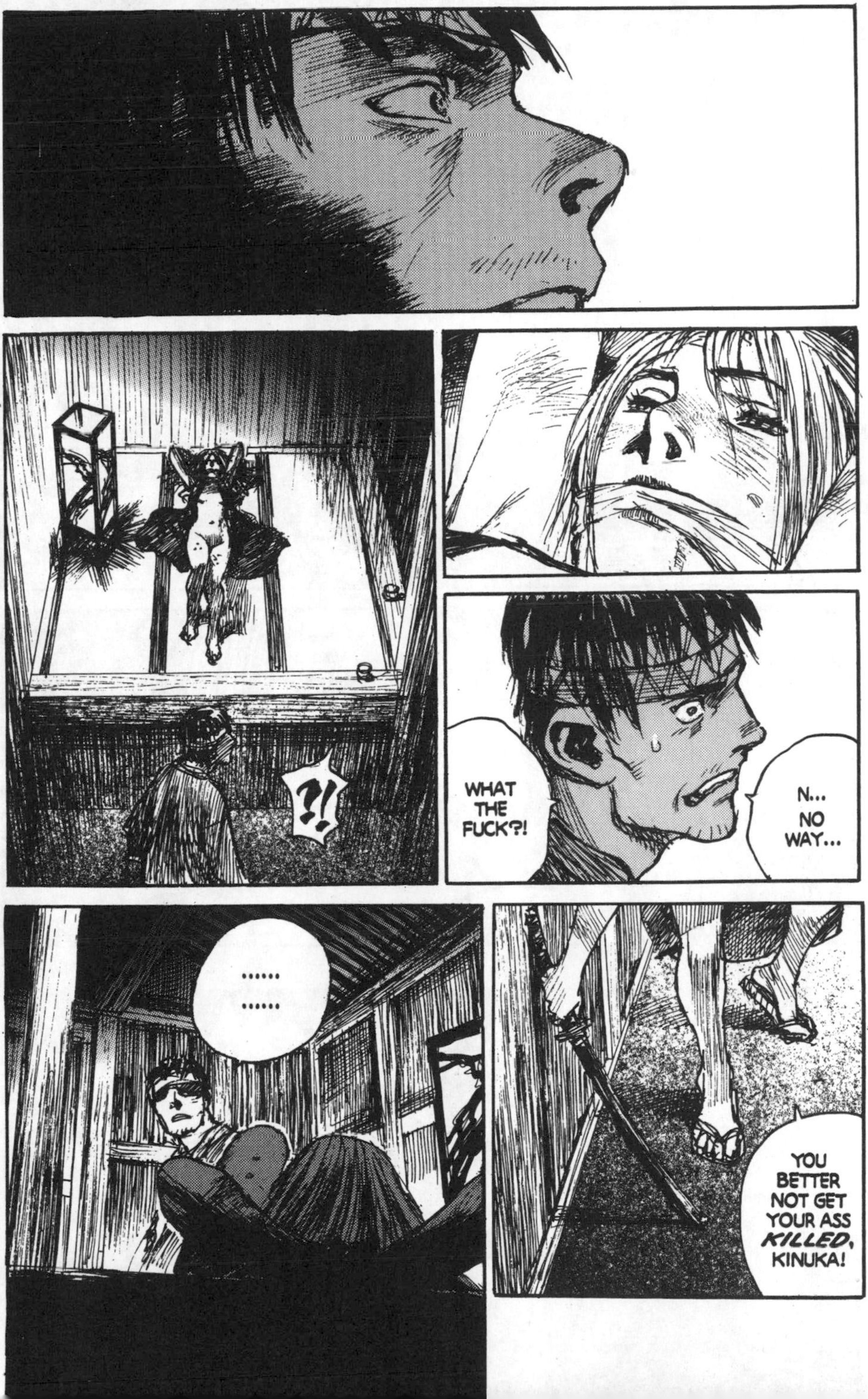
N... NO WAY...
WHAT THE FUCK?!
?!
YOU BETTER NOT GET YOUR ASS *KILLED*, KINUKA!
....

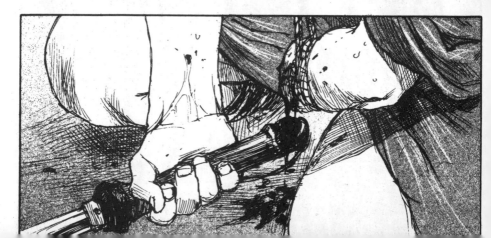

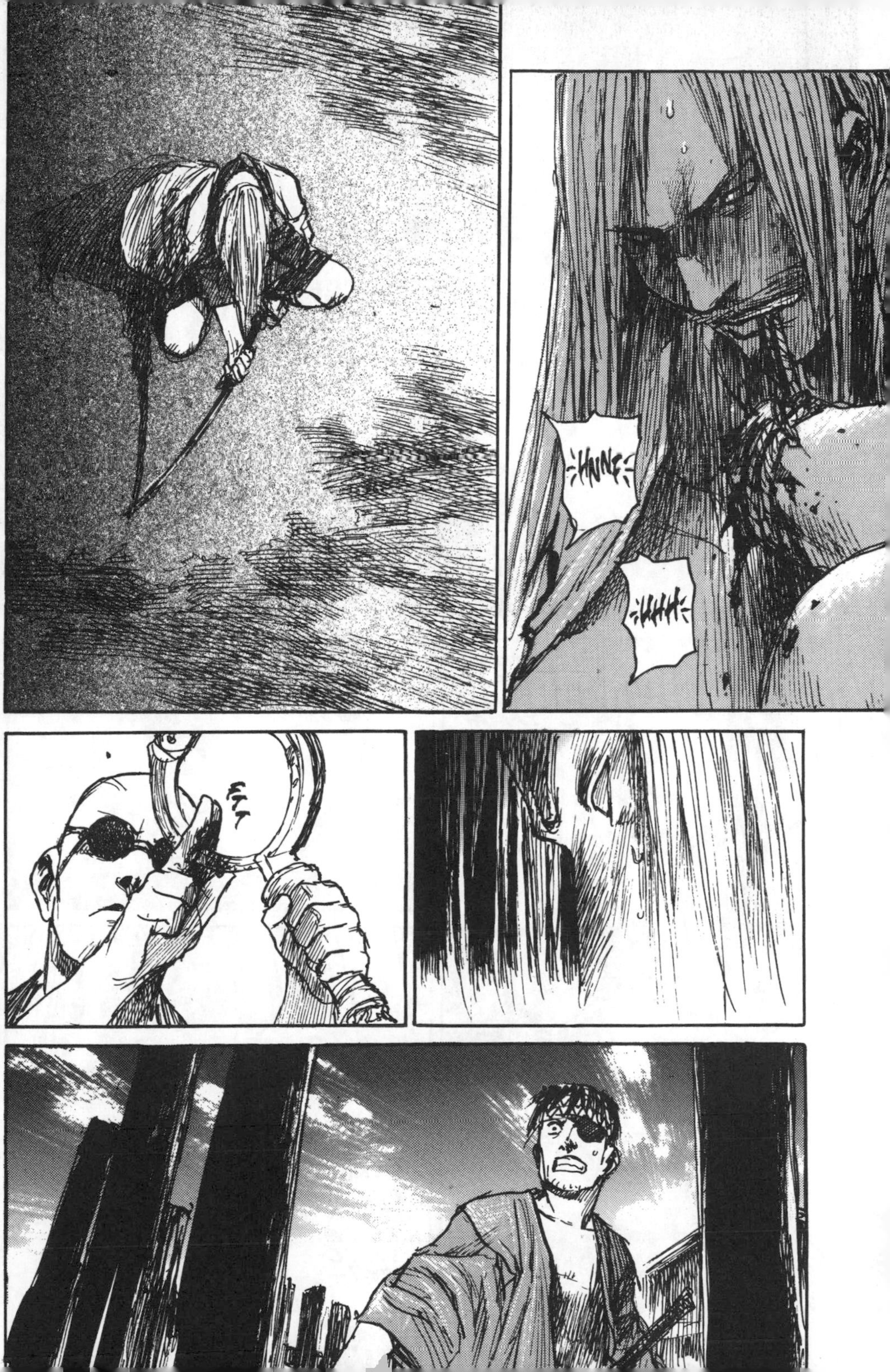
HNNG
UHH

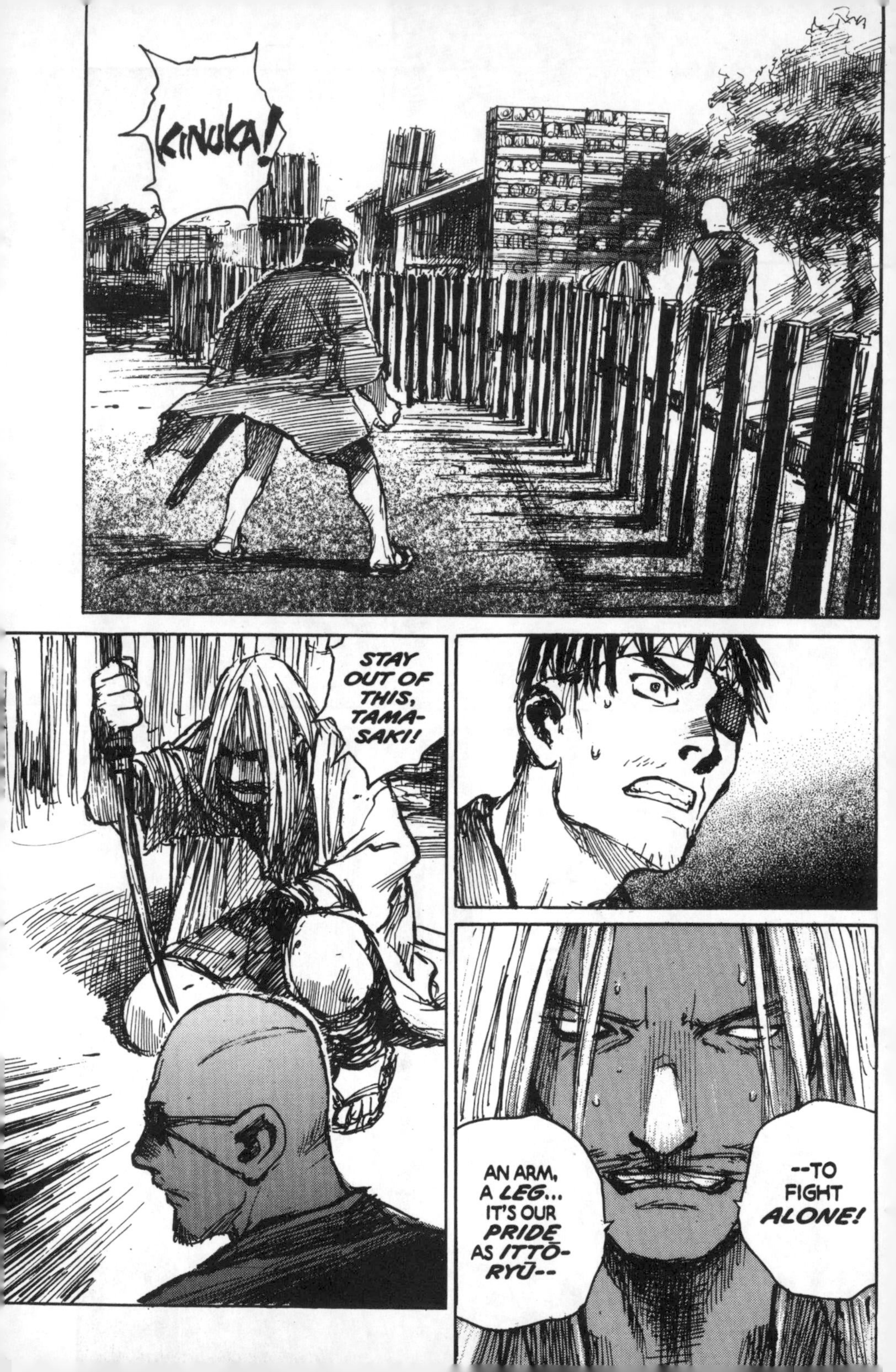
KINUKA!
STAY OUT OF THIS, TAMA-SAKI!
AN ARM, A LEG... IT'S OUR PRIDE AS ITTŌ-RYŪ--
--TO FIGHT ALONE!

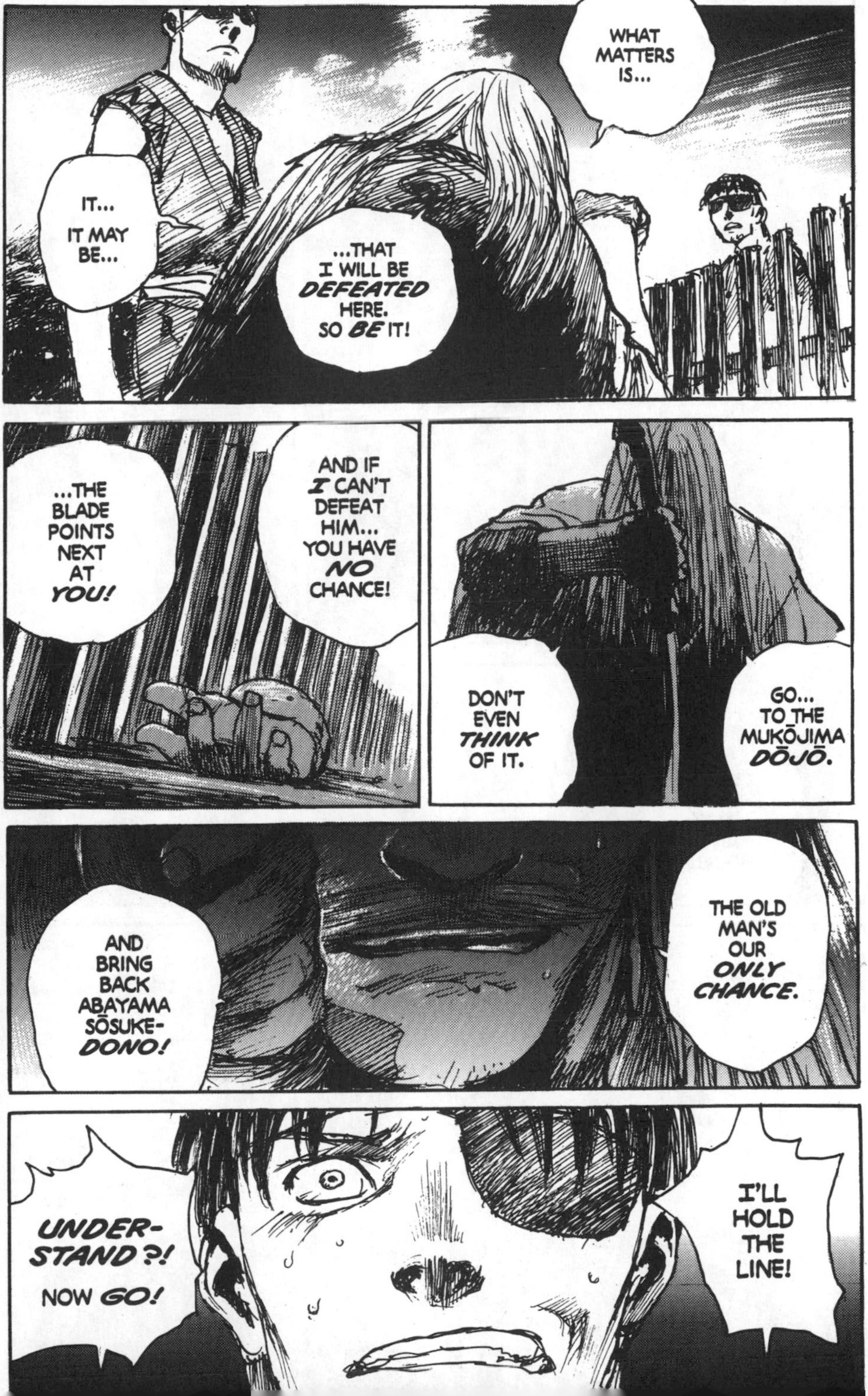

IT... IT MAY BE...
...THAT I WILL BE *DEFEATED* HERE. SO *BE* IT!
WHAT MATTERS IS...
...THE BLADE POINTS NEXT AT *YOU!*
AND IF *I* CAN'T DEFEAT HIM... YOU HAVE *NO* CHANCE!
DON'T EVEN *THINK* OF IT.
GO... TO THE MUKŌJIMA *DŌJŌ*.
AND BRING BACK ABAYAMA SŌSUKE-*DONO!*
THE OLD MAN'S OUR *ONLY CHANCE*.
UNDER-STAND?! NOW *GO!*
I'LL HOLD THE LINE!

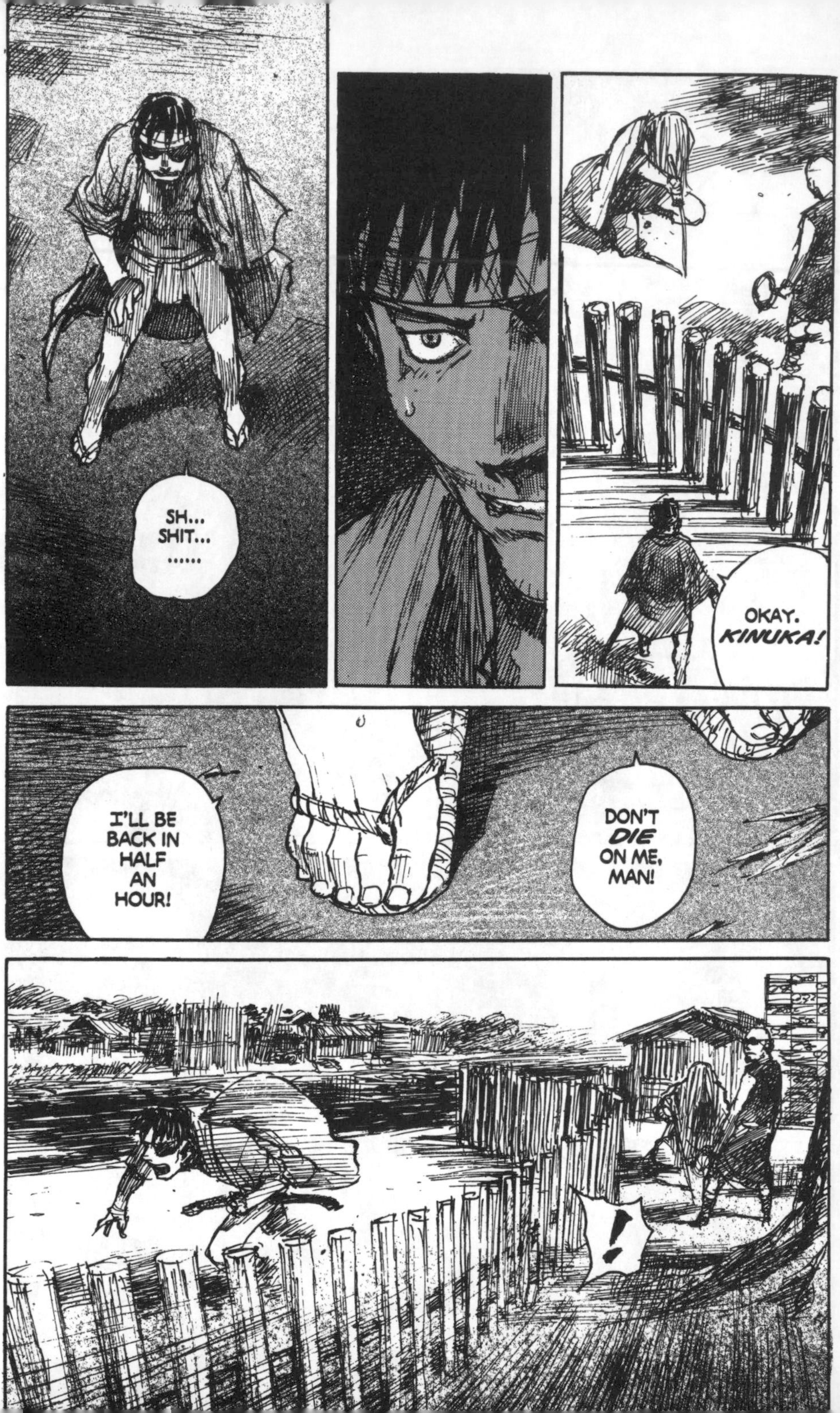

OKAY. *KINUKA!*
SH... SHIT... ......
DON'T *DIE* ON ME, MAN!
I'LL BE BACK IN HALF AN HOUR!
!

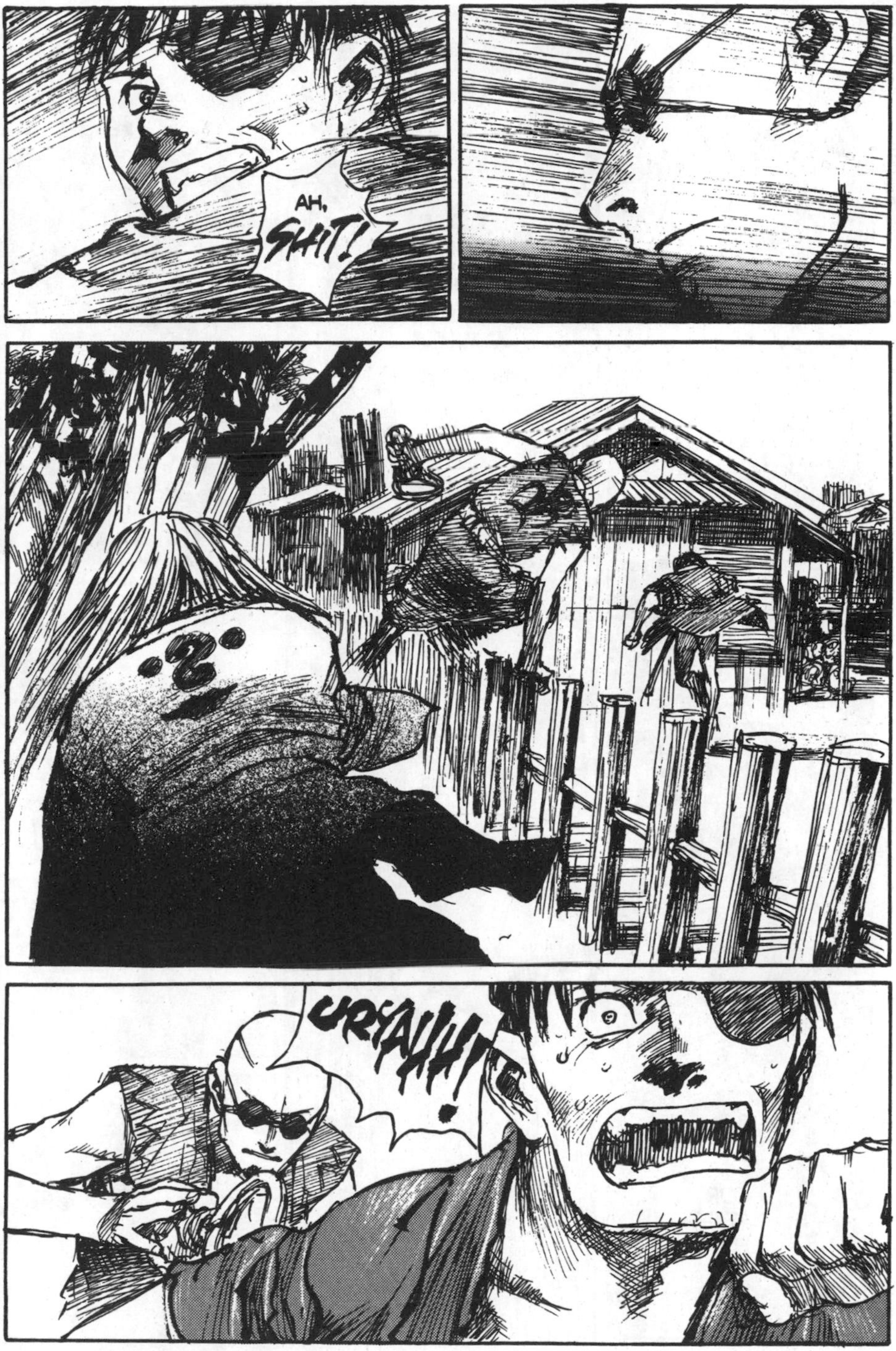
AH, SHIT!
URGAHHH!

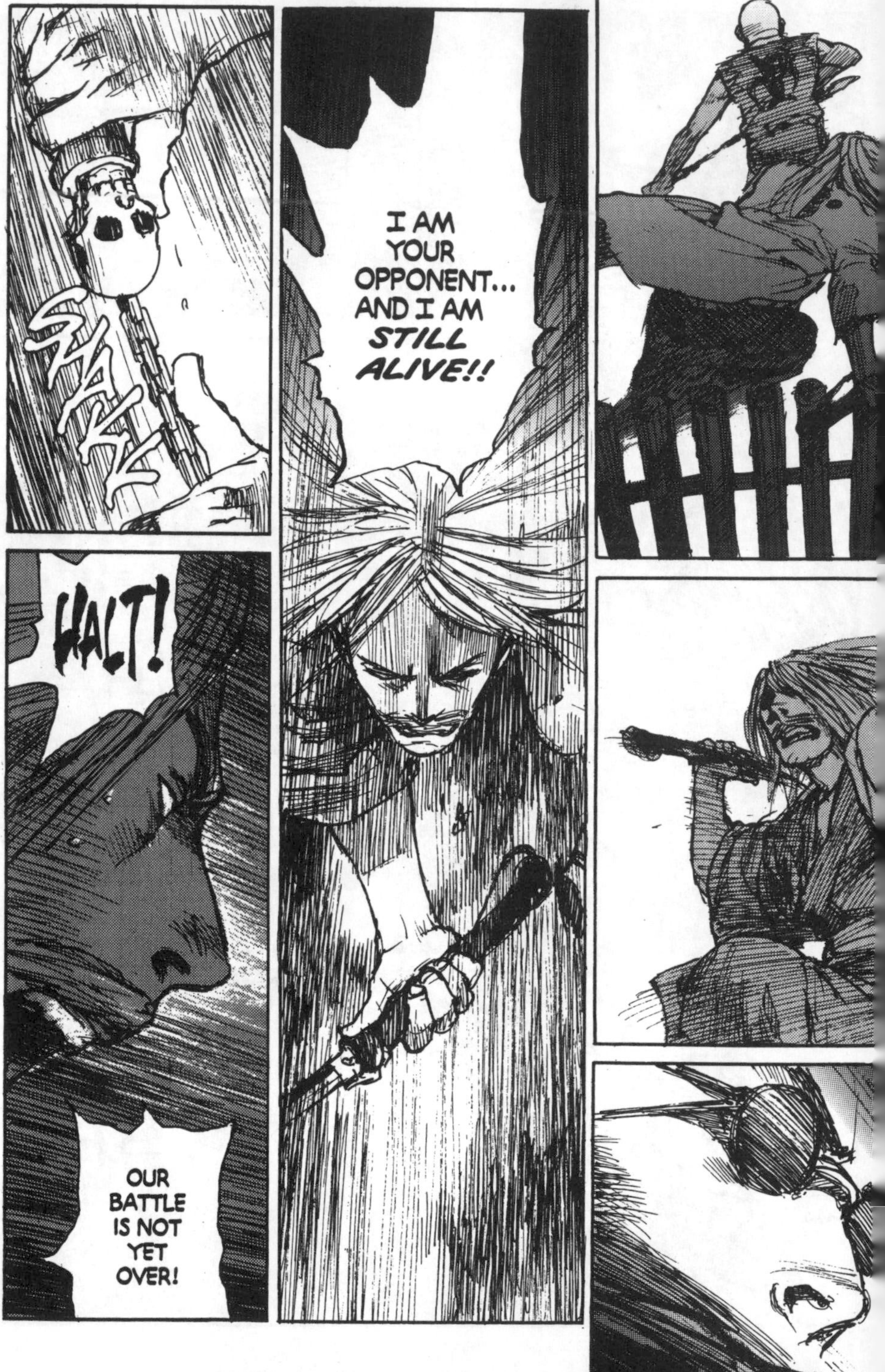
I AM YOUR OPPONENT... AND I AM *STILL ALIVE!!*
SHAKK
HALT!
OUR BATTLE IS NOT YET OVER!

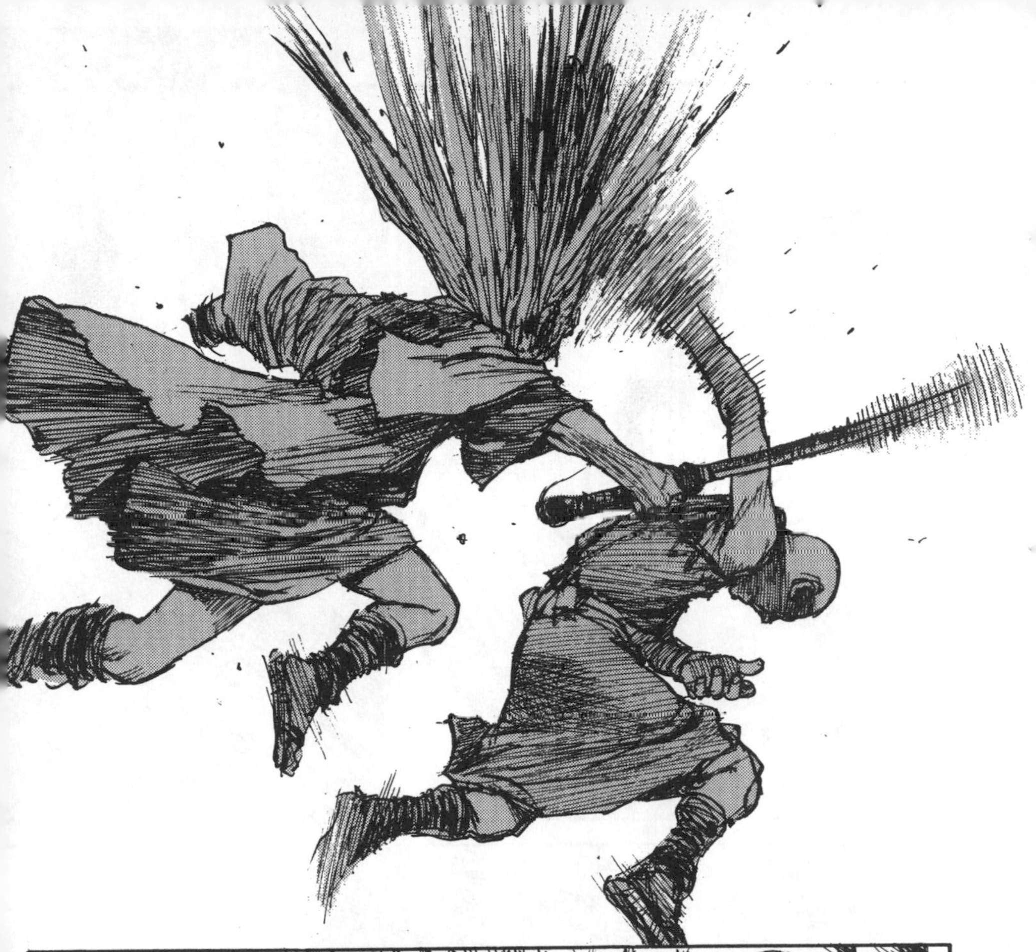
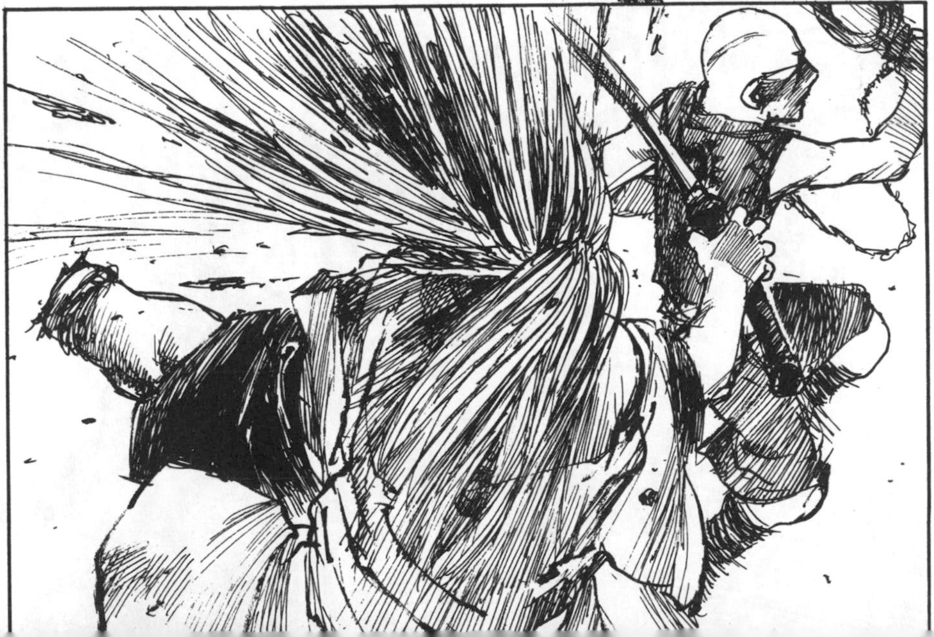

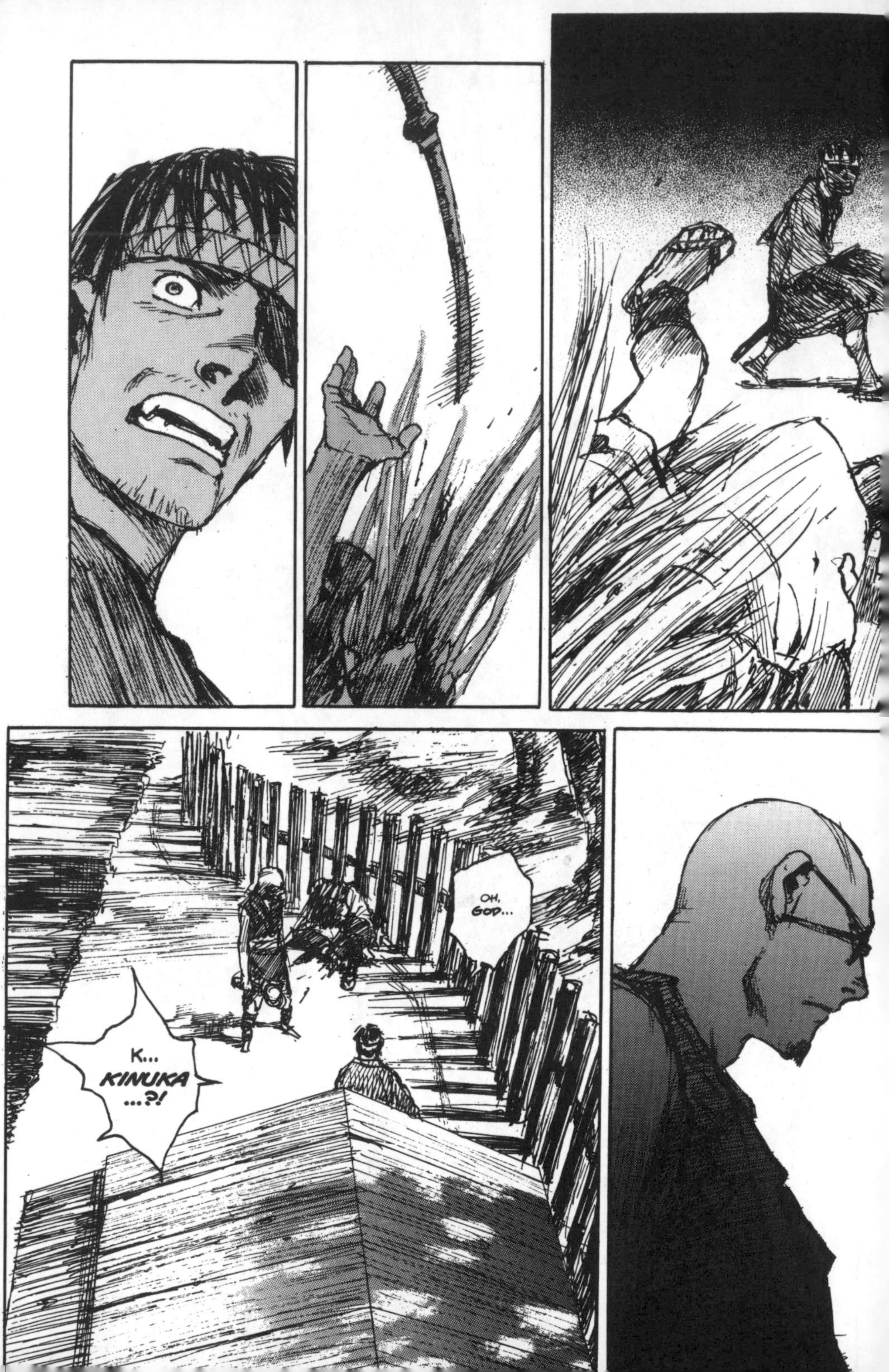
OH, GOD...
K... KINUKA ...?!

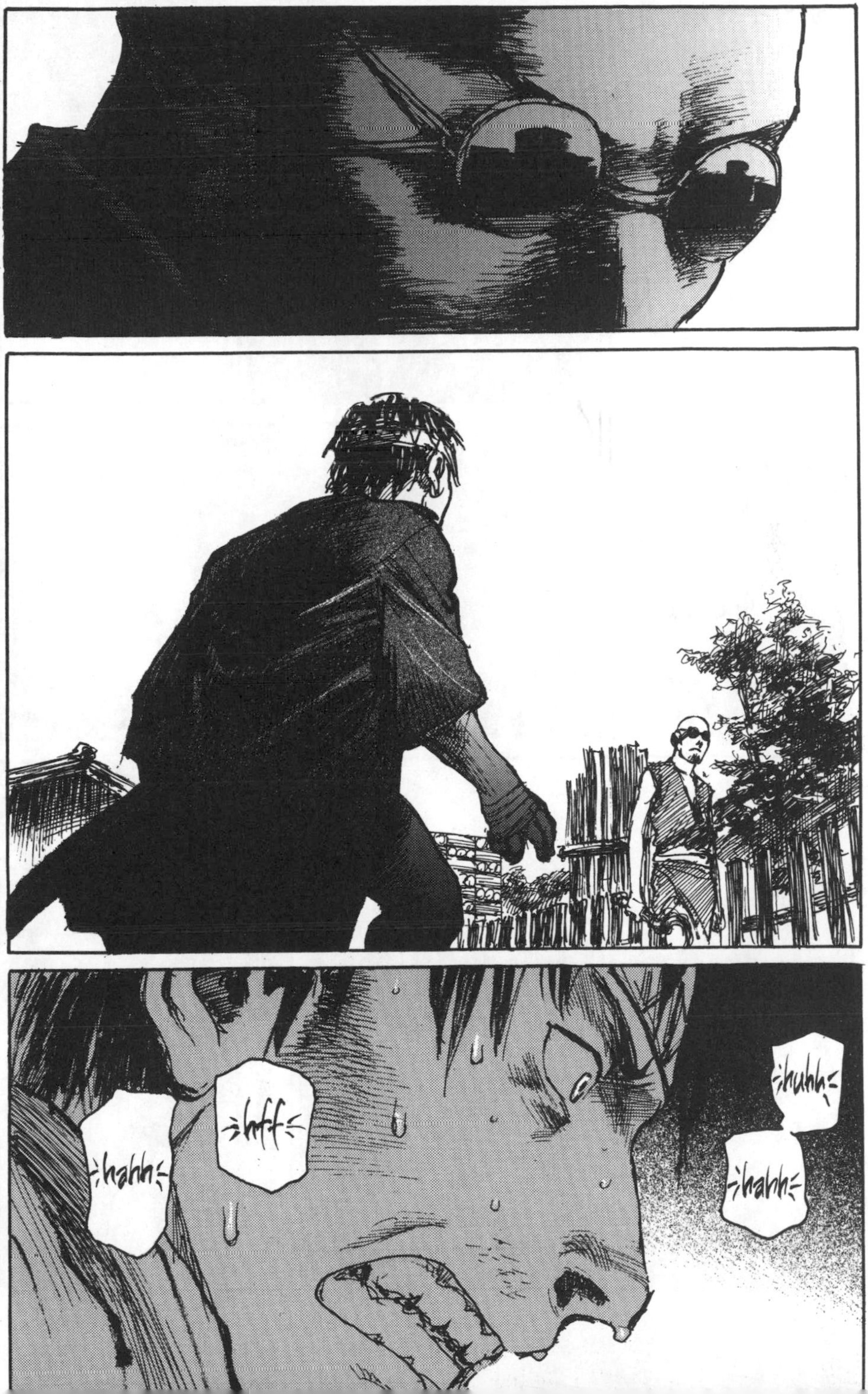
huhh
hahh
hff
hahh

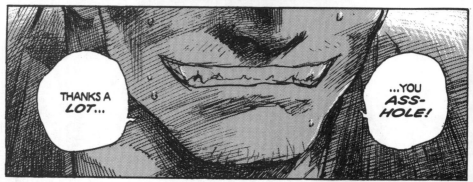

THANKS A *LOT*...

...YOU *ASS-HOLE!*

HEH, HEH... JUST *TWO* DAYS...

EIGHT OF US IN *TWO DAYS!*

NO WAY...

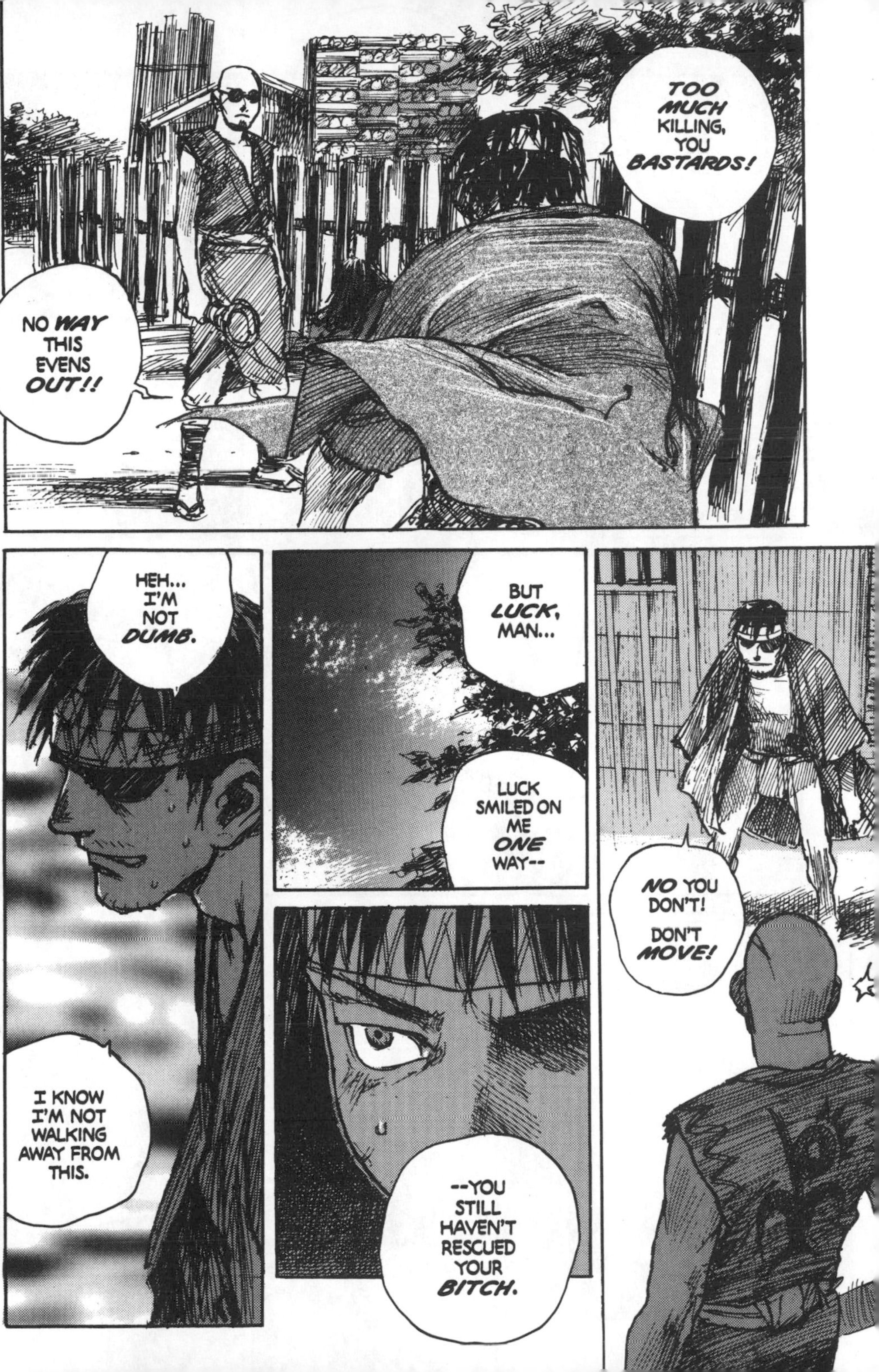
NO WAY THIS EVENS OUT!!
TOO MUCH KILLING, YOU BASTARDS!
HEH... I'M NOT DUMB.
I KNOW I'M NOT WALKING AWAY FROM THIS.
BUT LUCK, MAN...
LUCK SMILED ON ME ONE WAY--
--YOU STILL HAVEN'T RESCUED YOUR BITCH.
NO YOU DON'T! DON'T MOVE!

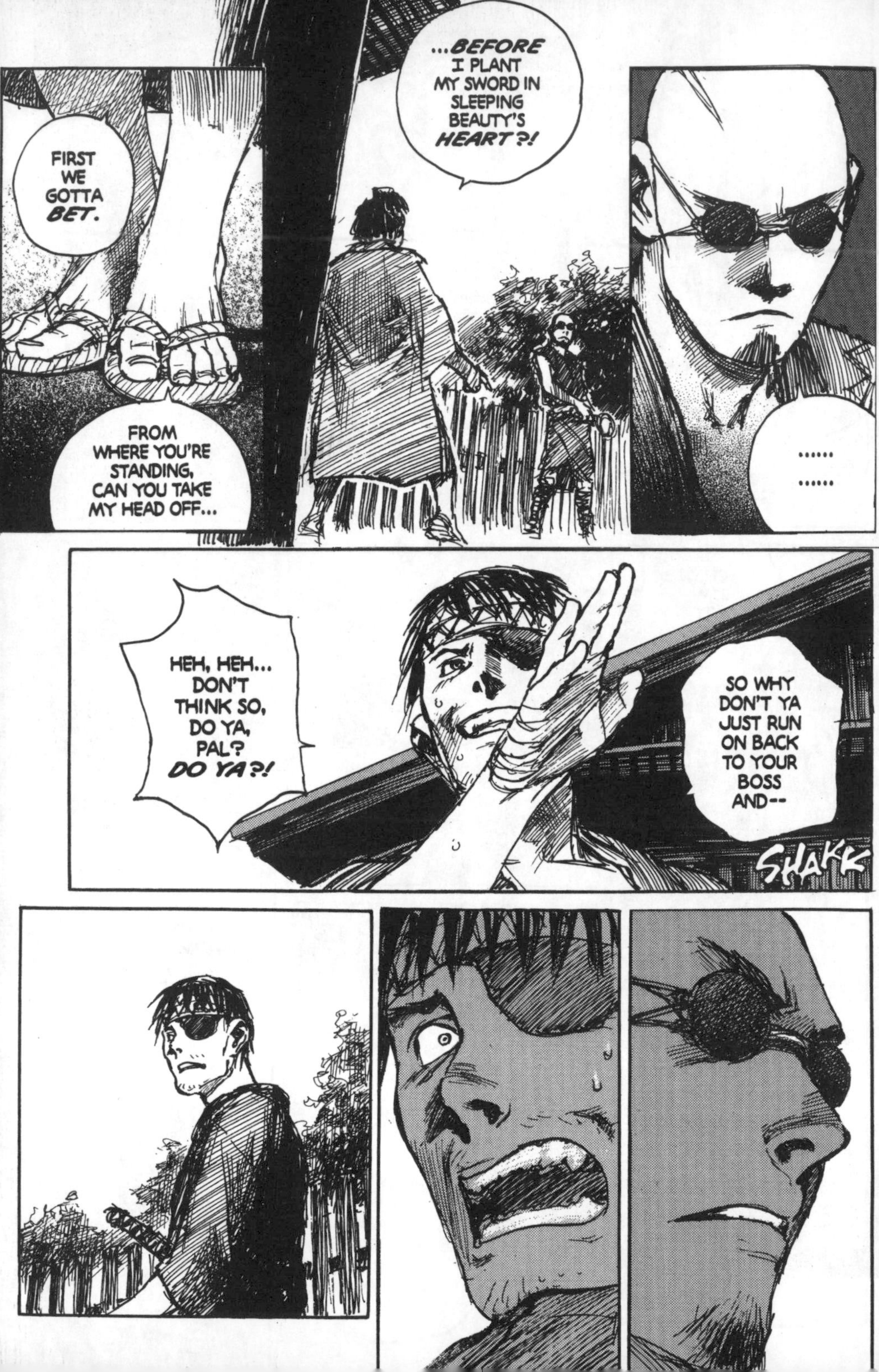
FIRST WE GOTTA BET.
FROM WHERE YOU'RE STANDING, CAN YOU TAKE MY HEAD OFF...
...BEFORE I PLANT MY SWORD IN SLEEPING BEAUTY'S HEART?!
......
......
HEH, HEH... DON'T THINK SO, DO YA, PAL? DO YA?!
SO WHY DON'T YA JUST RUN ON BACK TO YOUR BOSS AND--
SHAKK

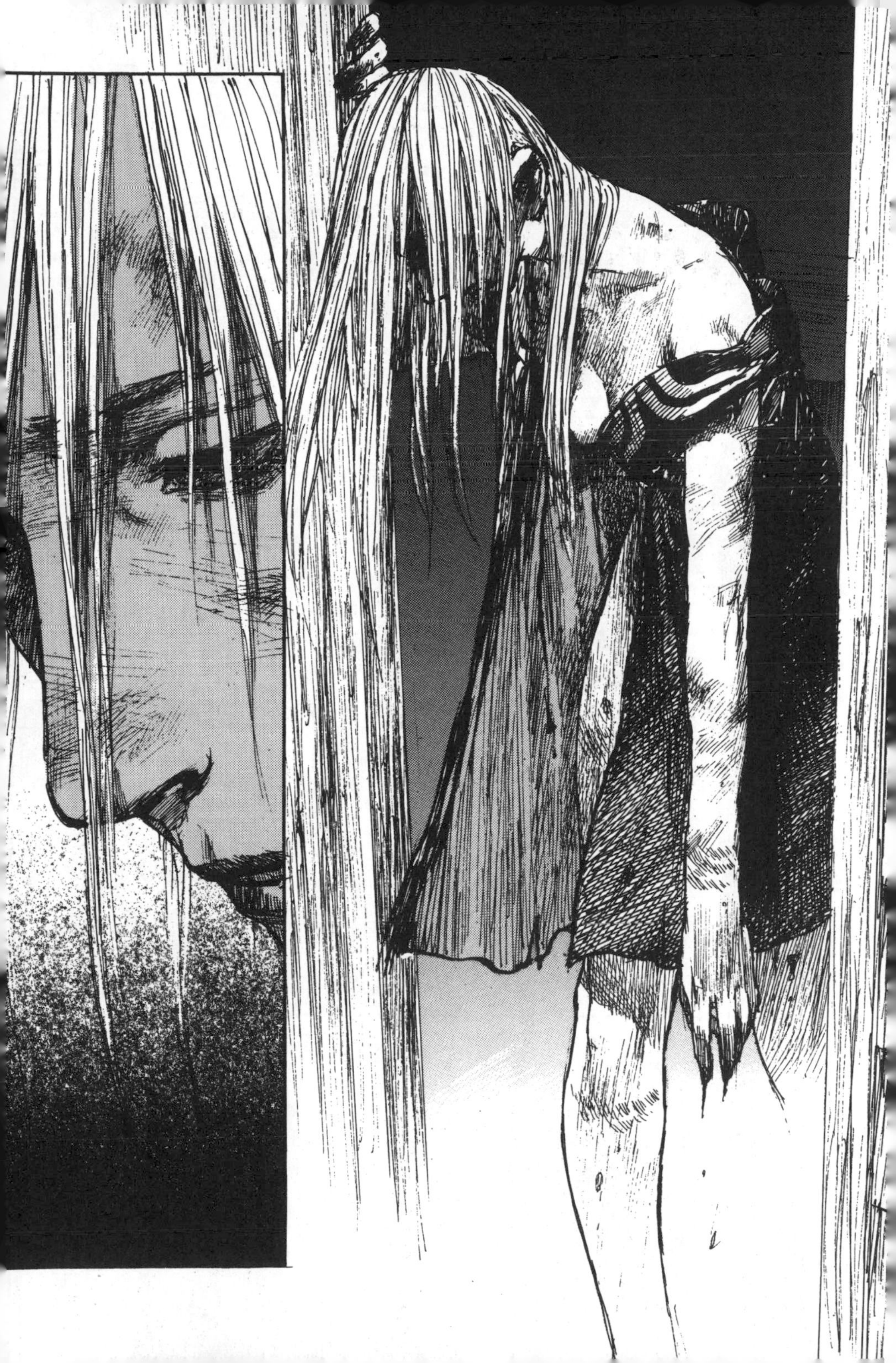

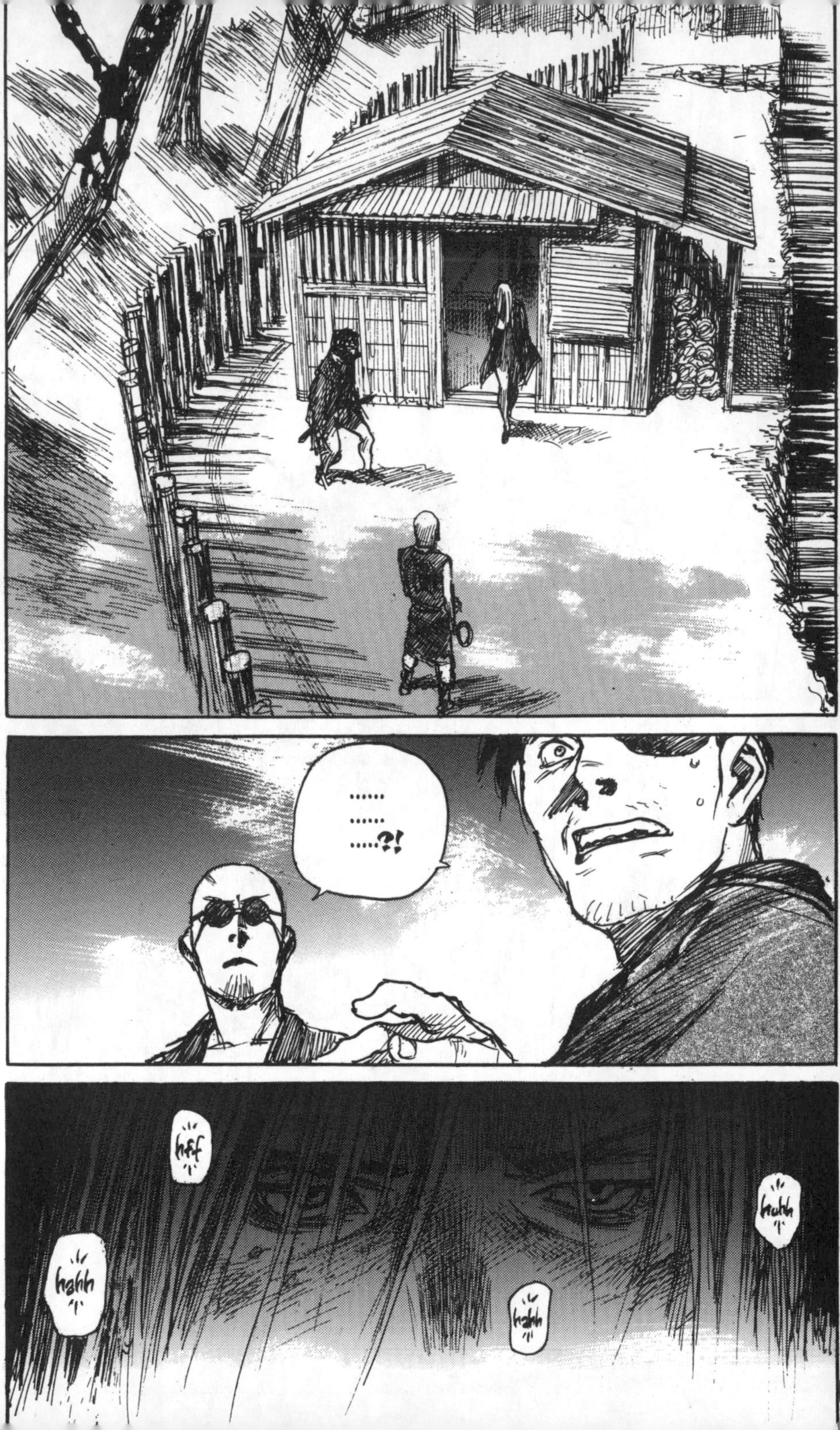
……
……
……?!
hff
hahh
hahh
hahh

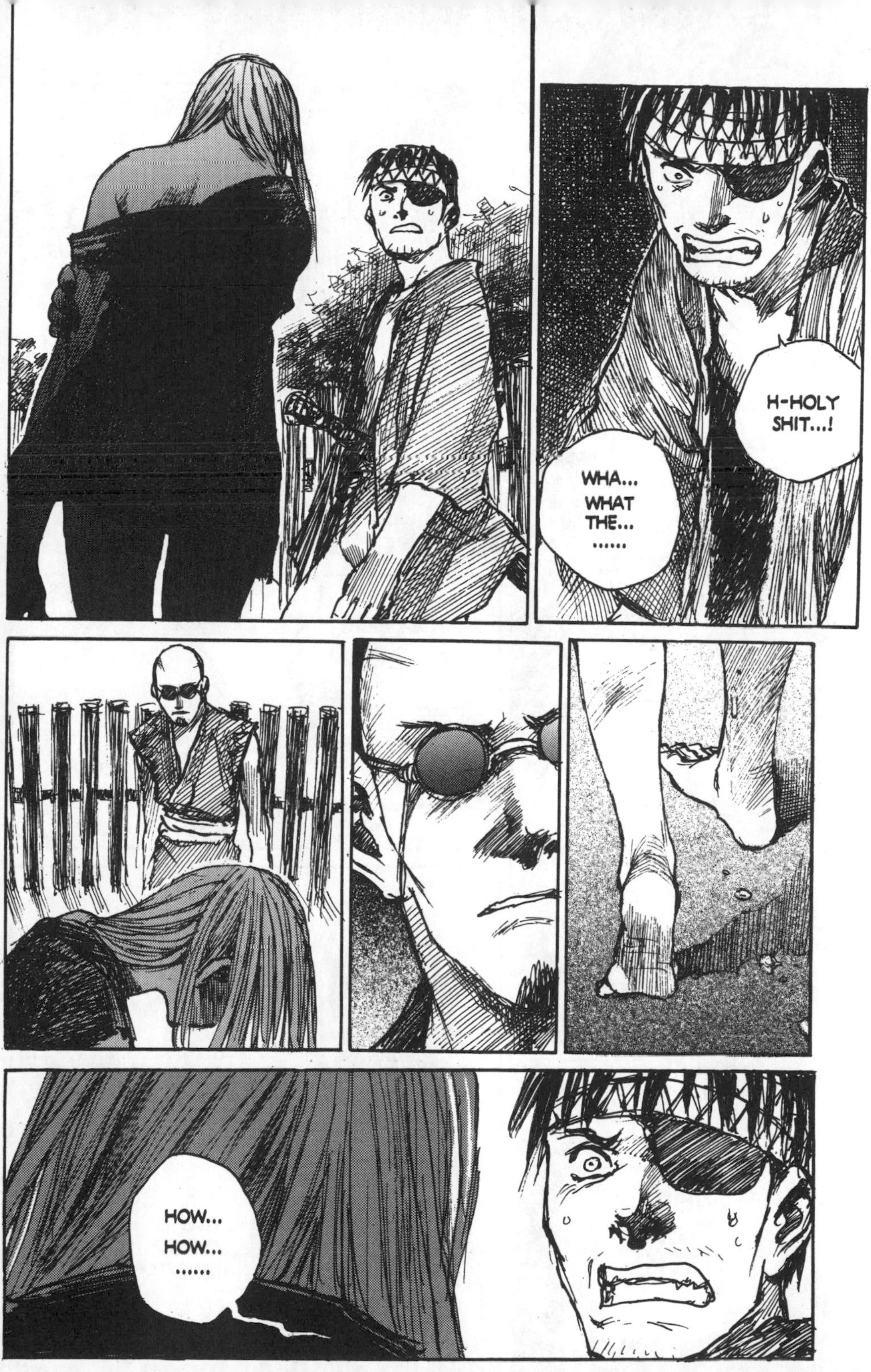
H-HOLY SHIT...!
WHA... WHAT THE... ......
HOW... HOW... ......

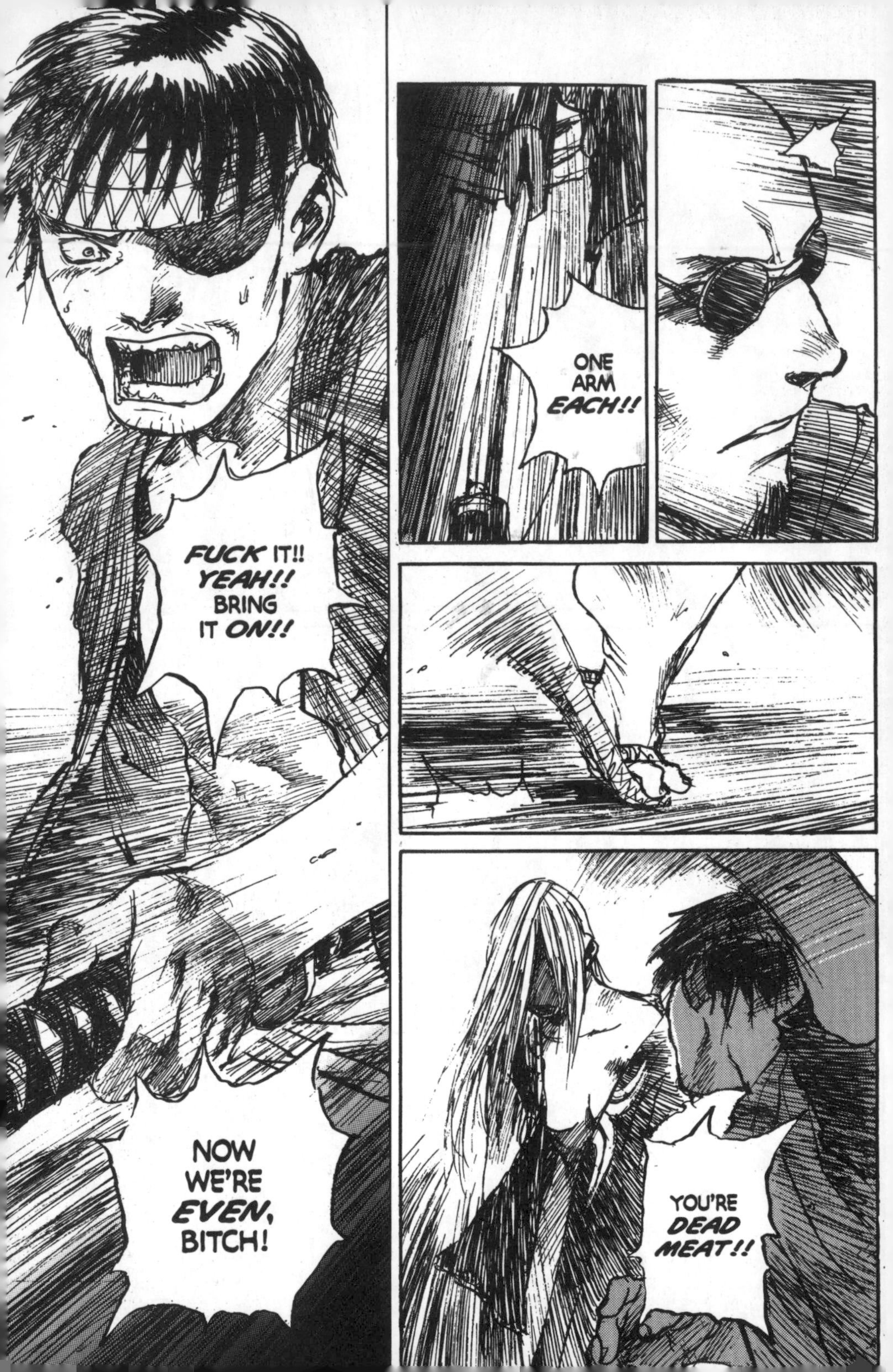
ONE ARM EACH!!
YOU'RE DEAD MEAT!!
FUCK IT!! YEAH!! BRING IT ON!!
NOW WE'RE EVEN, BITCH!

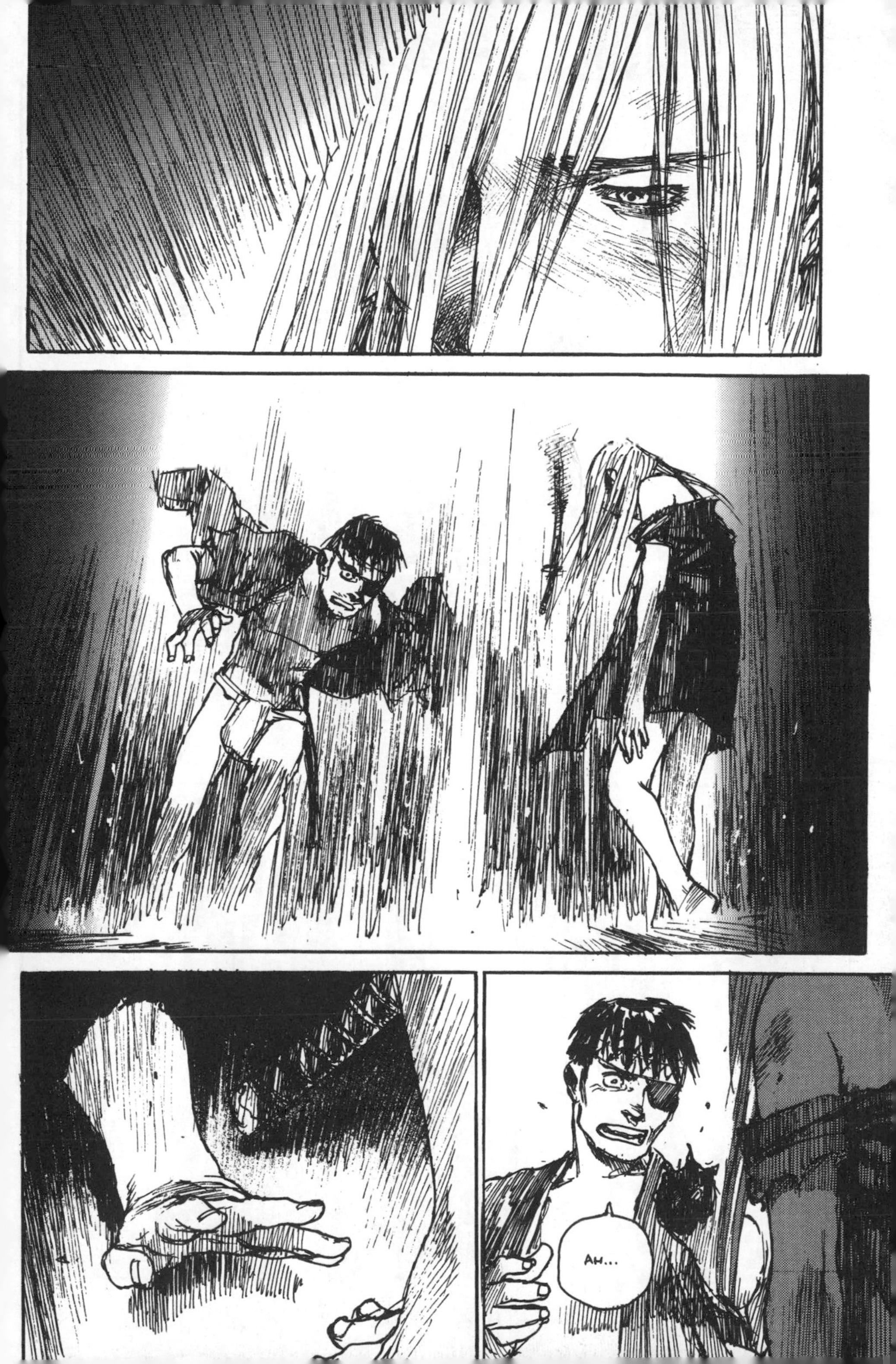
AH...

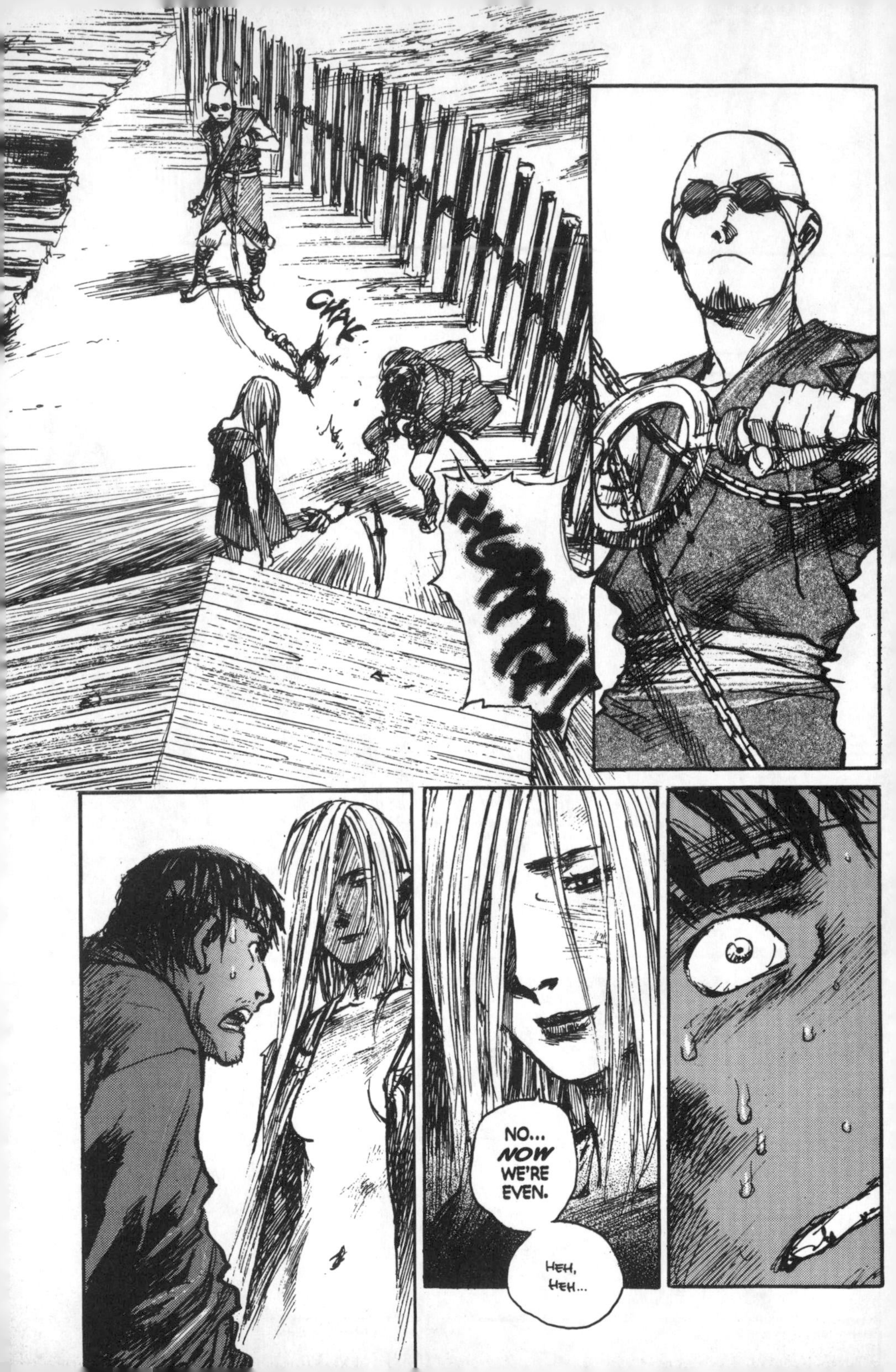
CHAK
NO... ***NOW*** WE'RE EVEN.
HEH, HEH...

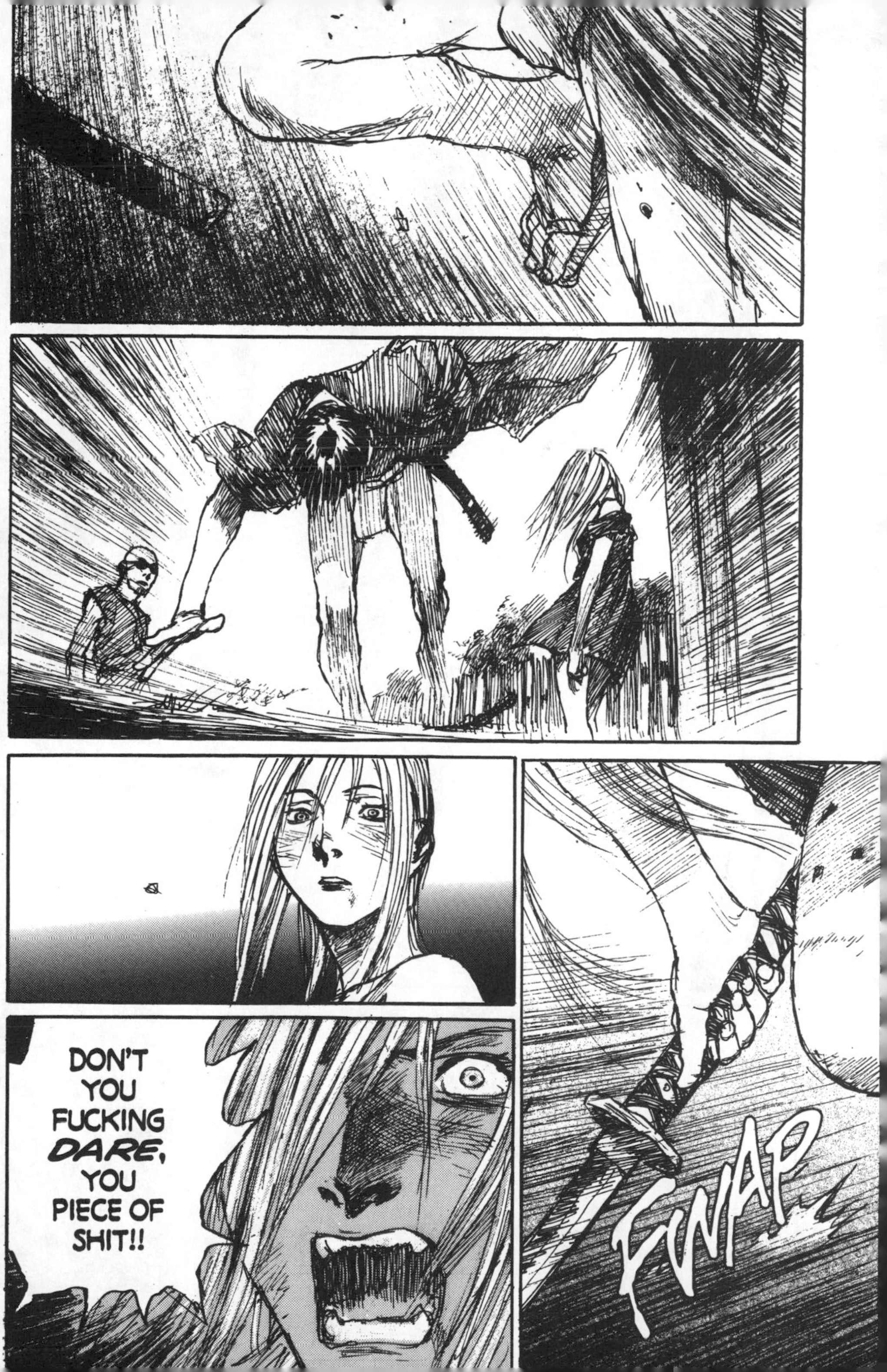
DON'T YOU FUCKING DARE, YOU PIECE OF SHIT!!
FWAP

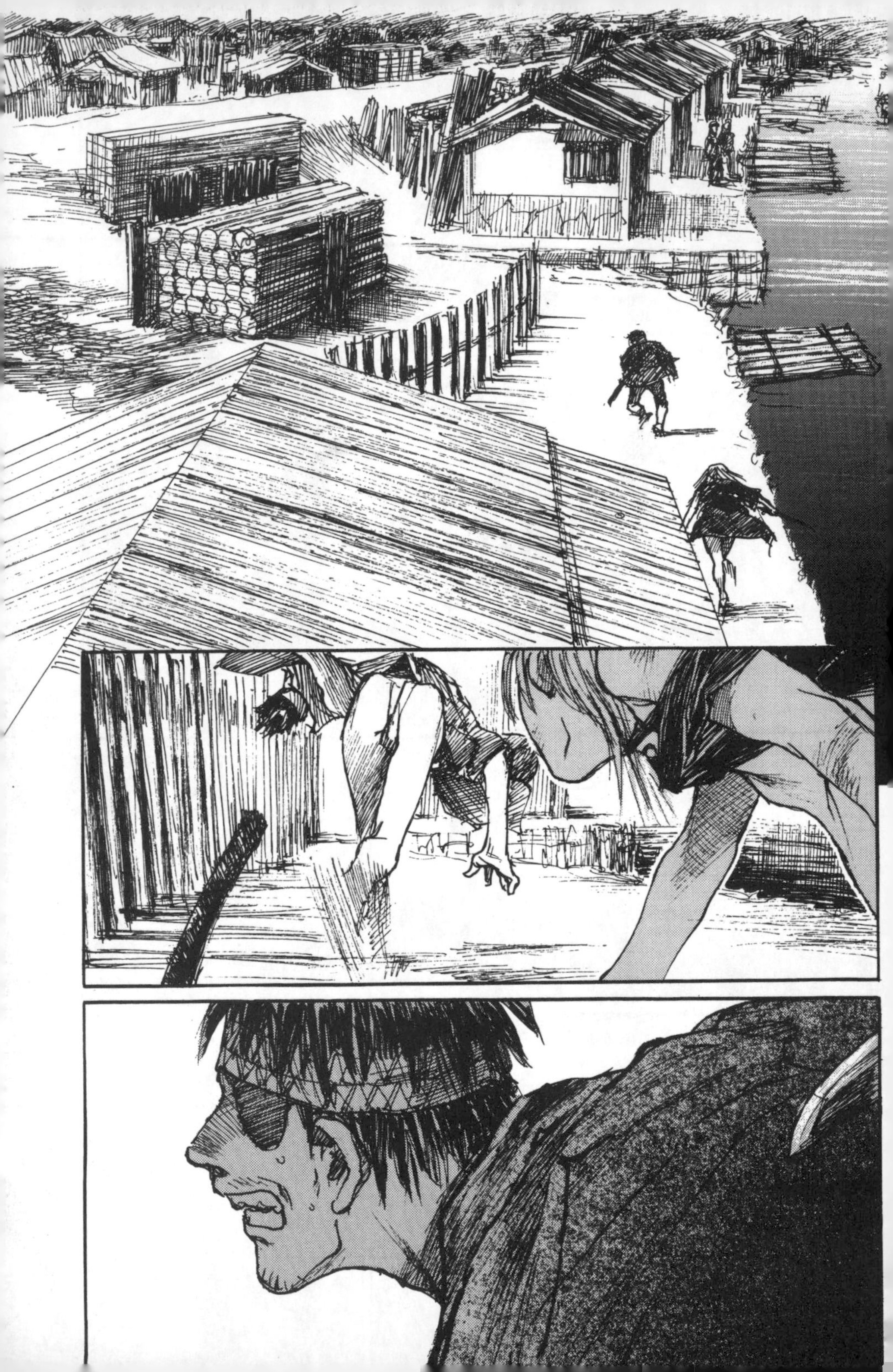

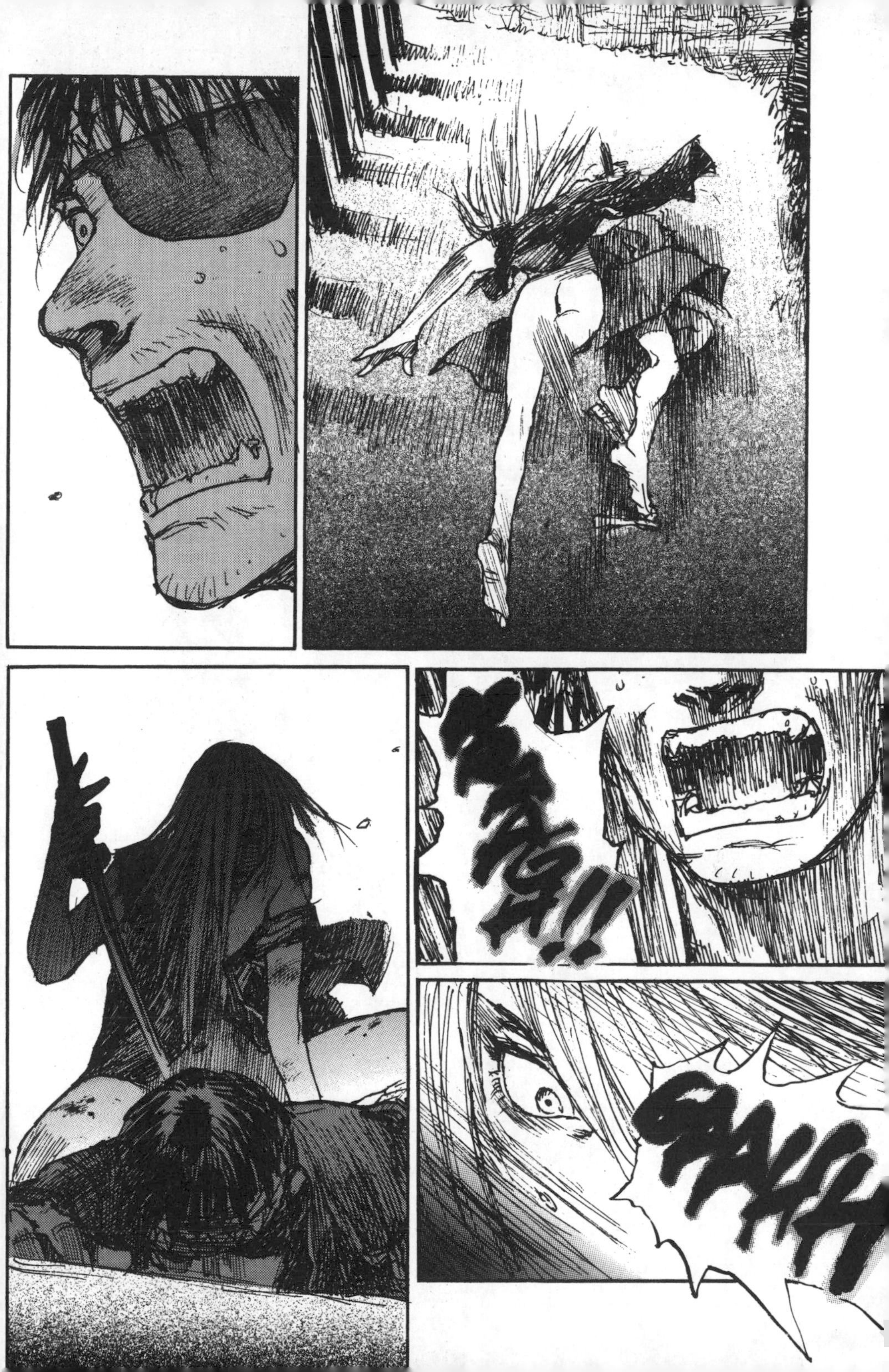

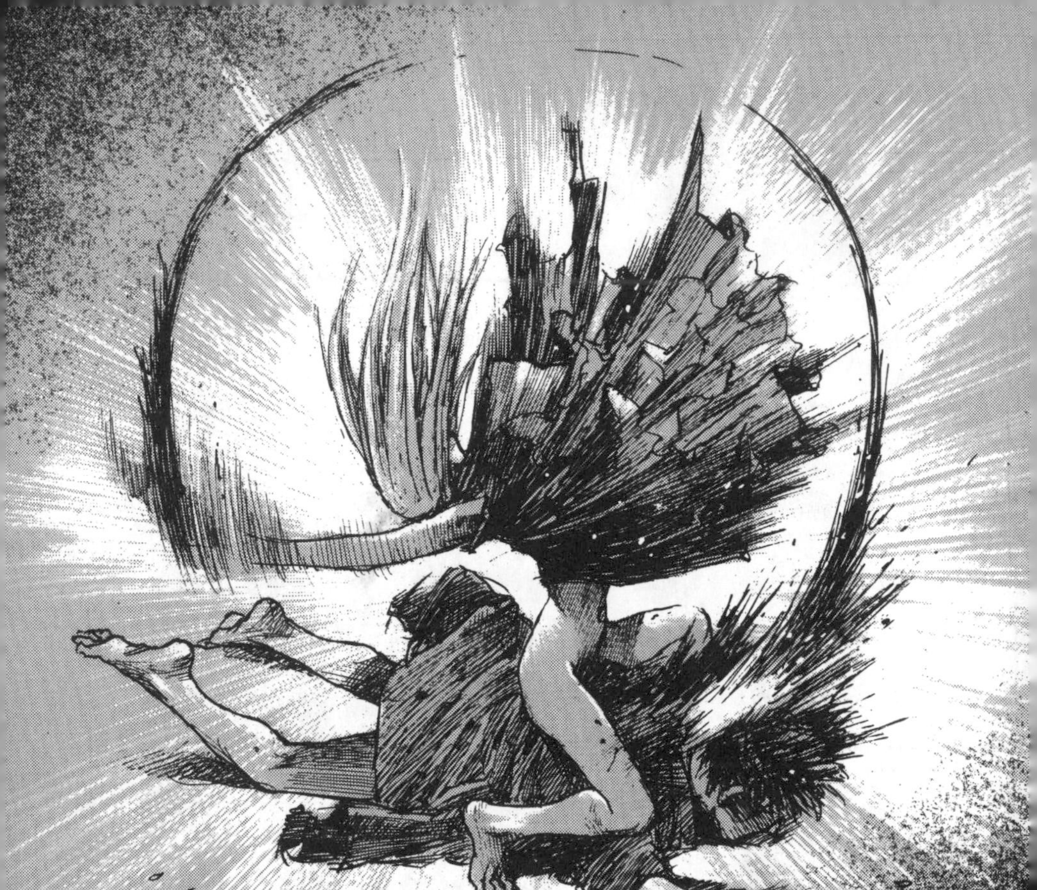
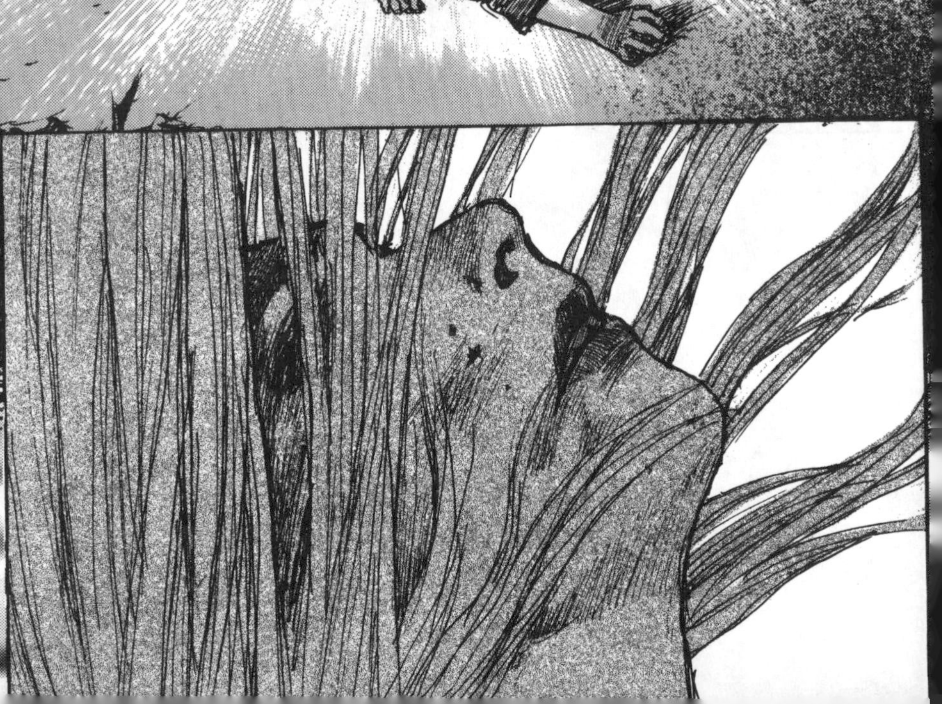

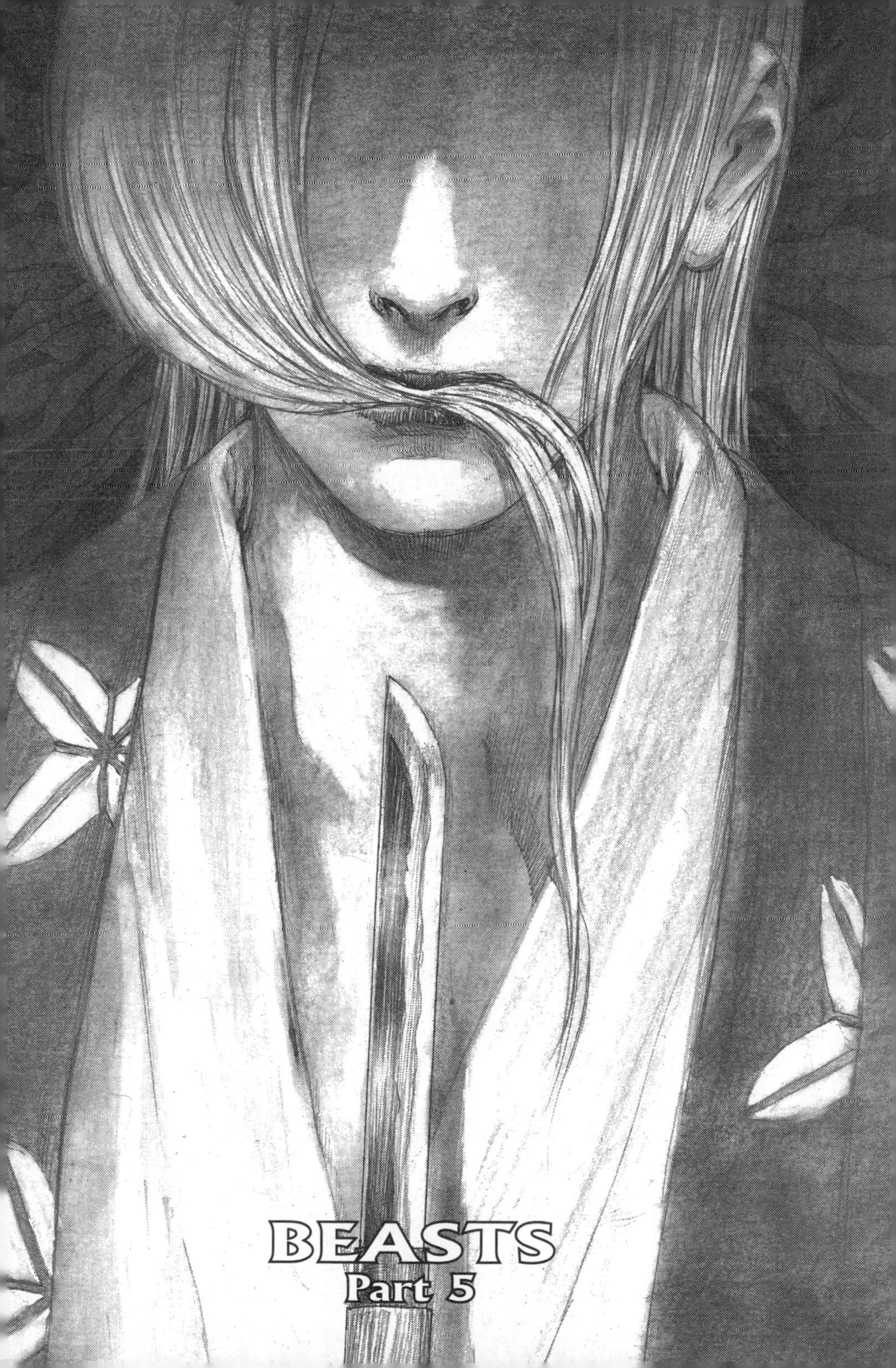
BEASTS
Part 5

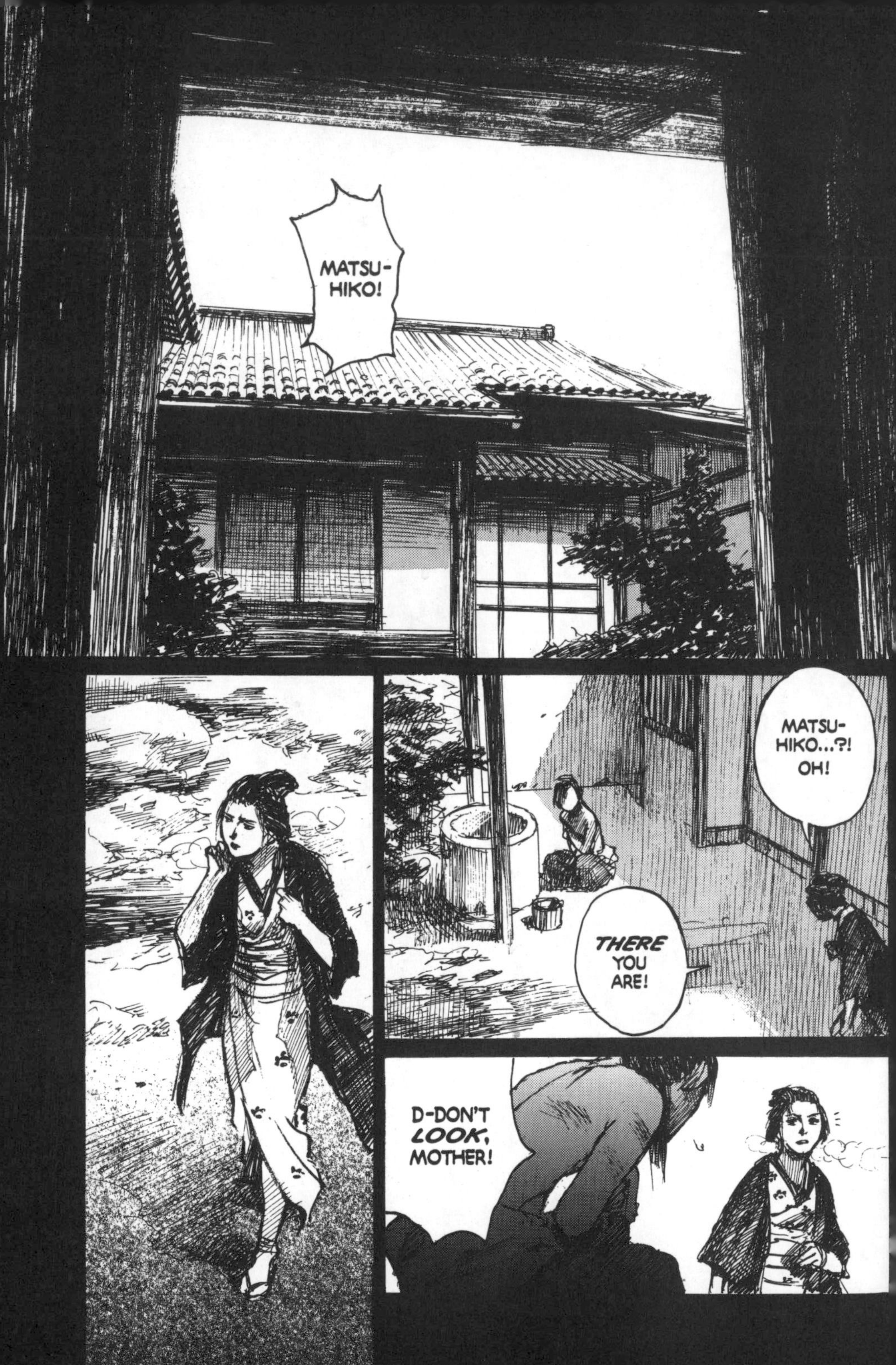
MATSU-HIKO!
MATSU-HIKO...?! OH!
THERE YOU ARE!
D-DON'T LOOK, MOTHER!

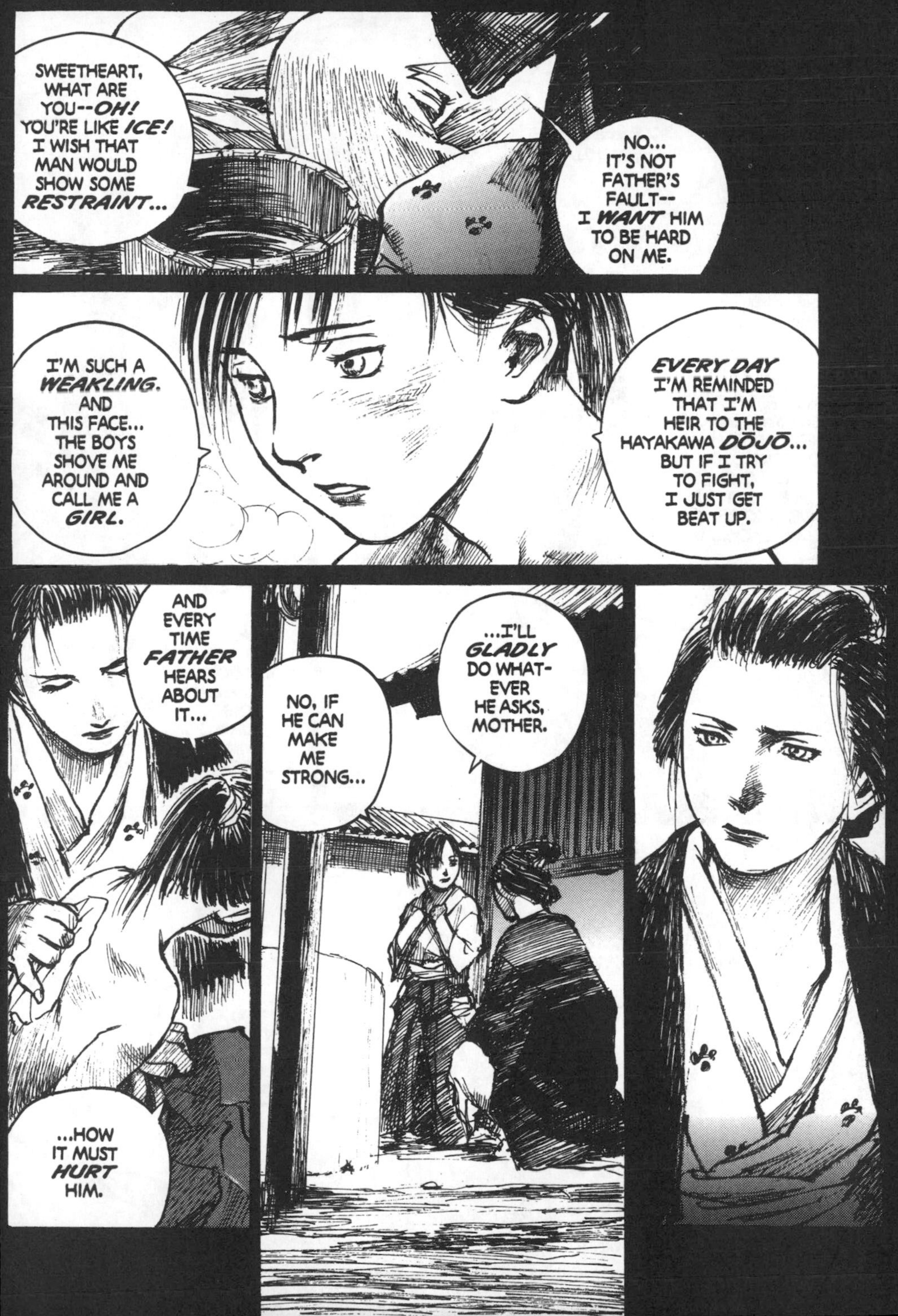
SWEETHEART, WHAT ARE YOU--OH! YOU'RE LIKE ICE! I WISH THAT MAN WOULD SHOW SOME RESTRAINT...
NO... IT'S NOT FATHER'S FAULT-- I WANT HIM TO BE HARD ON ME.
I'M SUCH A WEAKLING. AND THIS FACE... THE BOYS SHOVE ME AROUND AND CALL ME A GIRL.
EVERY DAY I'M REMINDED THAT I'M HEIR TO THE HAYAKAWA DŌJŌ... BUT IF I TRY TO FIGHT, I JUST GET BEAT UP.
AND EVERY TIME FATHER HEARS ABOUT IT...
...HOW IT MUST HURT HIM.
NO, IF HE CAN MAKE ME STRONG...
...I'LL GLADLY DO WHATEVER HE ASKS, MOTHER.

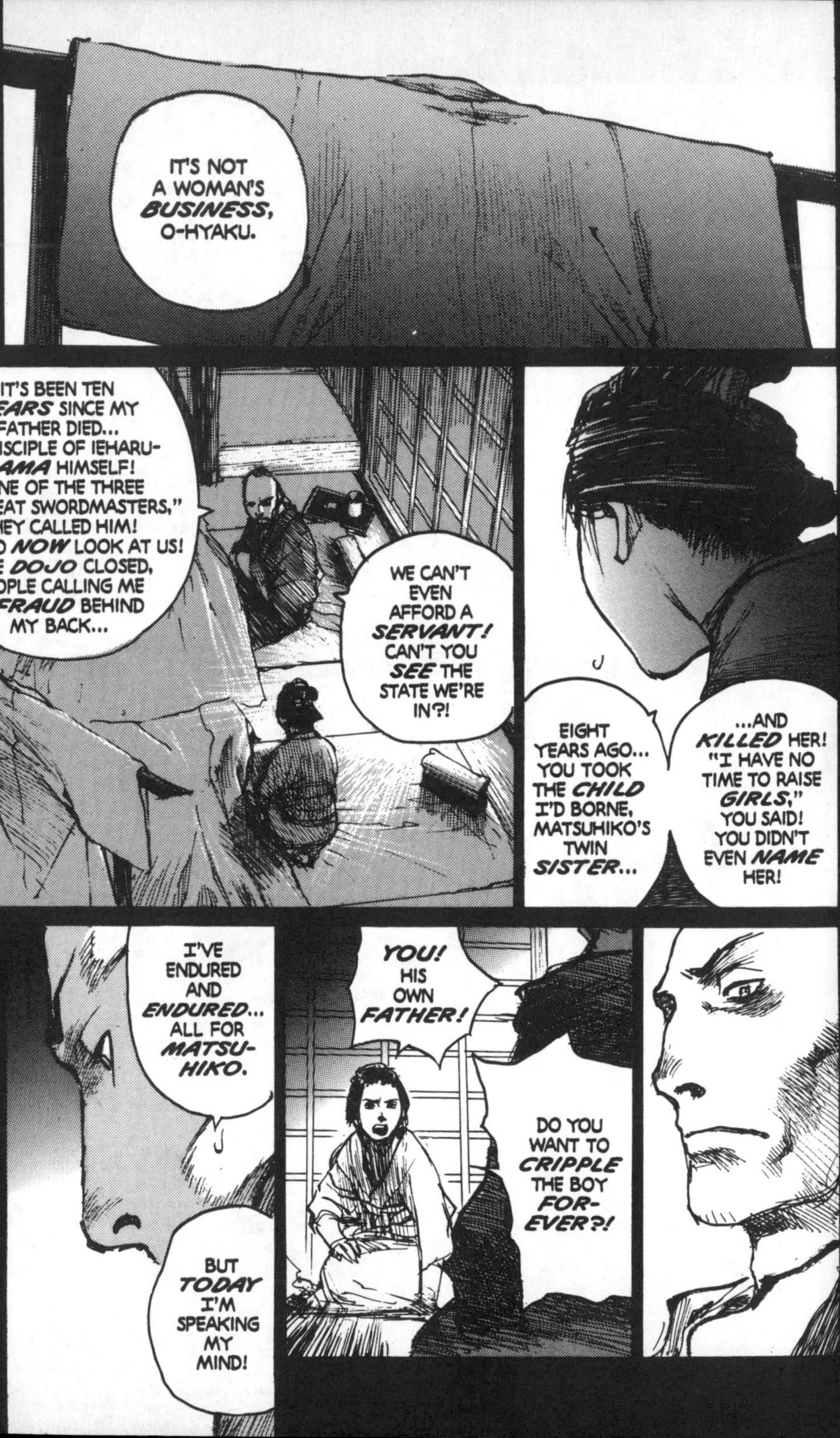
IT'S NOT A WOMAN'S BUSINESS, O-HYAKU.
IT'S BEEN TEN YEARS SINCE MY FATHER DIED... A DISCIPLE OF IEHARU-SAMA HIMSELF! "ONE OF THE THREE GREAT SWORDMASTERS," THEY CALLED HIM! AND NOW LOOK AT US! THE DOJO CLOSED, PEOPLE CALLING ME A FRAUD BEHIND MY BACK...
WE CAN'T EVEN AFFORD A SERVANT! CAN'T YOU SEE THE STATE WE'RE IN?!
EIGHT YEARS AGO... YOU TOOK THE CHILD I'D BORNE, MATSUHIKO'S TWIN SISTER...
...AND KILLED HER! "I HAVE NO TIME TO RAISE GIRLS," YOU SAID! YOU DIDN'T EVEN NAME HER!
I'VE ENDURED AND ENDURED... ALL FOR MATSU-HIKO.
BUT TODAY I'M SPEAKING MY MIND!
YOU! HIS OWN FATHER!
DO YOU WANT TO CRIPPLE THE BOY FOR-EVER?!

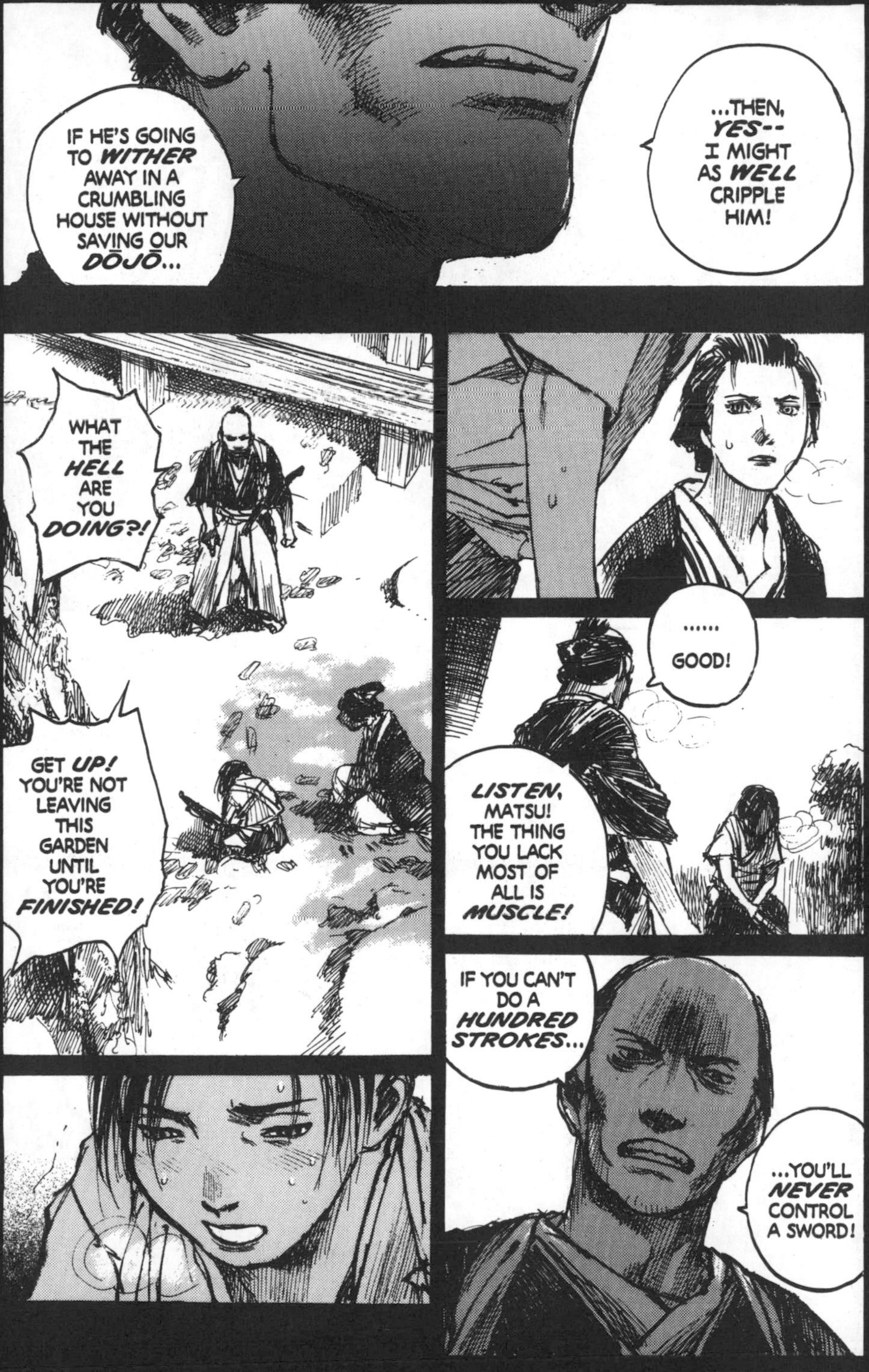
IF HE'S GOING TO WITHER AWAY IN A CRUMBLING HOUSE WITHOUT SAVING OUR DŌJŌ...
...THEN, YES-- I MIGHT AS WELL CRIPPLE HIM!
WHAT THE HELL ARE YOU DOING?!
GET UP! YOU'RE NOT LEAVING THIS GARDEN UNTIL YOU'RE FINISHED!
......
GOOD!
LISTEN, MATSU! THE THING YOU LACK MOST OF ALL IS MUSCLE!
IF YOU CAN'T DO A HUNDRED STROKES...
...YOU'LL NEVER CONTROL A SWORD!

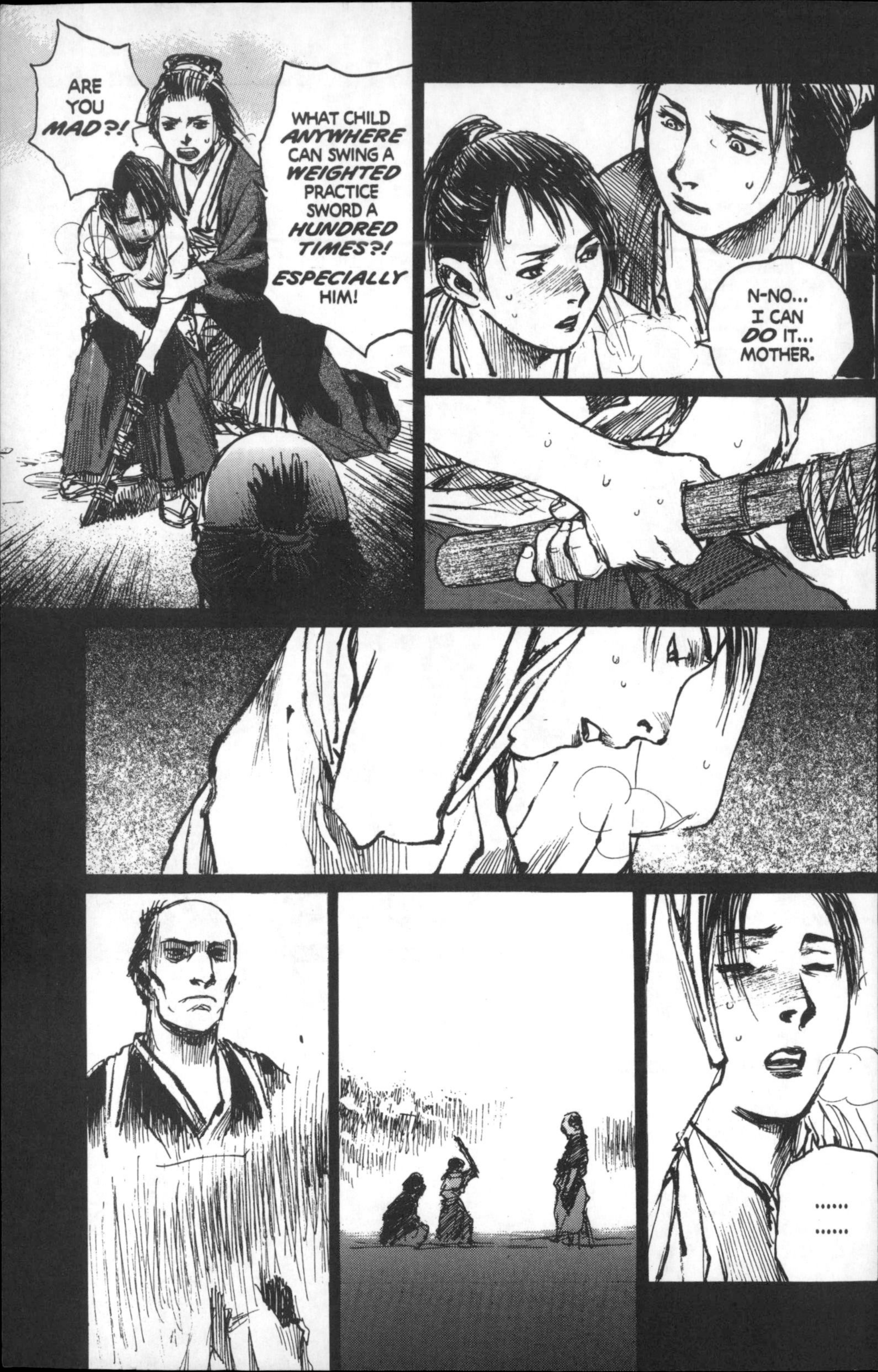
ARE YOU MAD?!
WHAT CHILD ANYWHERE CAN SWING A WEIGHTED PRACTICE SWORD A HUNDRED TIMES?!
ESPECIALLY HIM!
N-NO... I CAN DO IT... MOTHER.
......
......

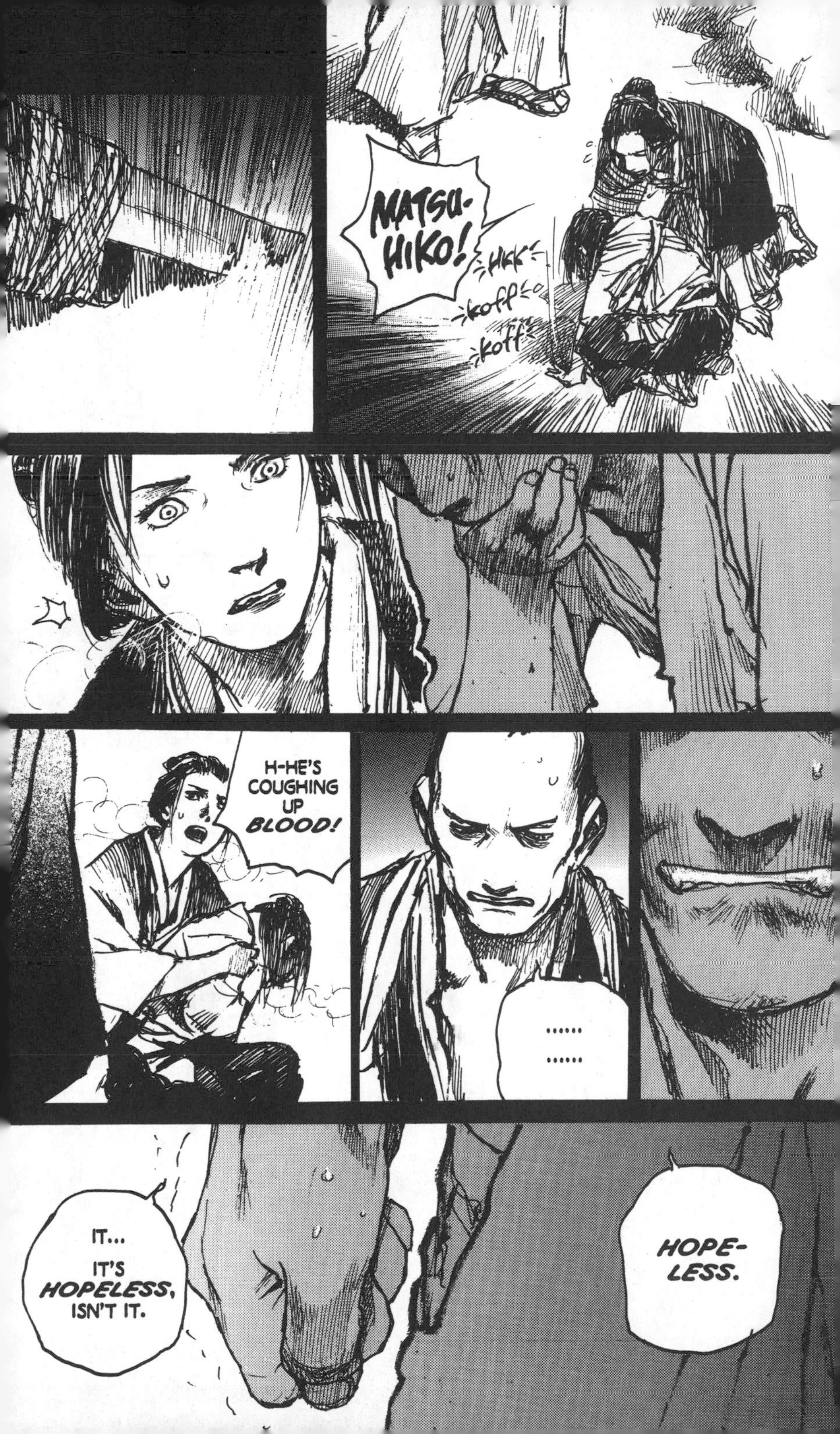
MATSU-HIKO!
HKK
koff
koff
H-HE'S COUGHING UP BLOOD!
......
......
HOPE-LESS.
IT...
IT'S HOPELESS, ISN'T IT.

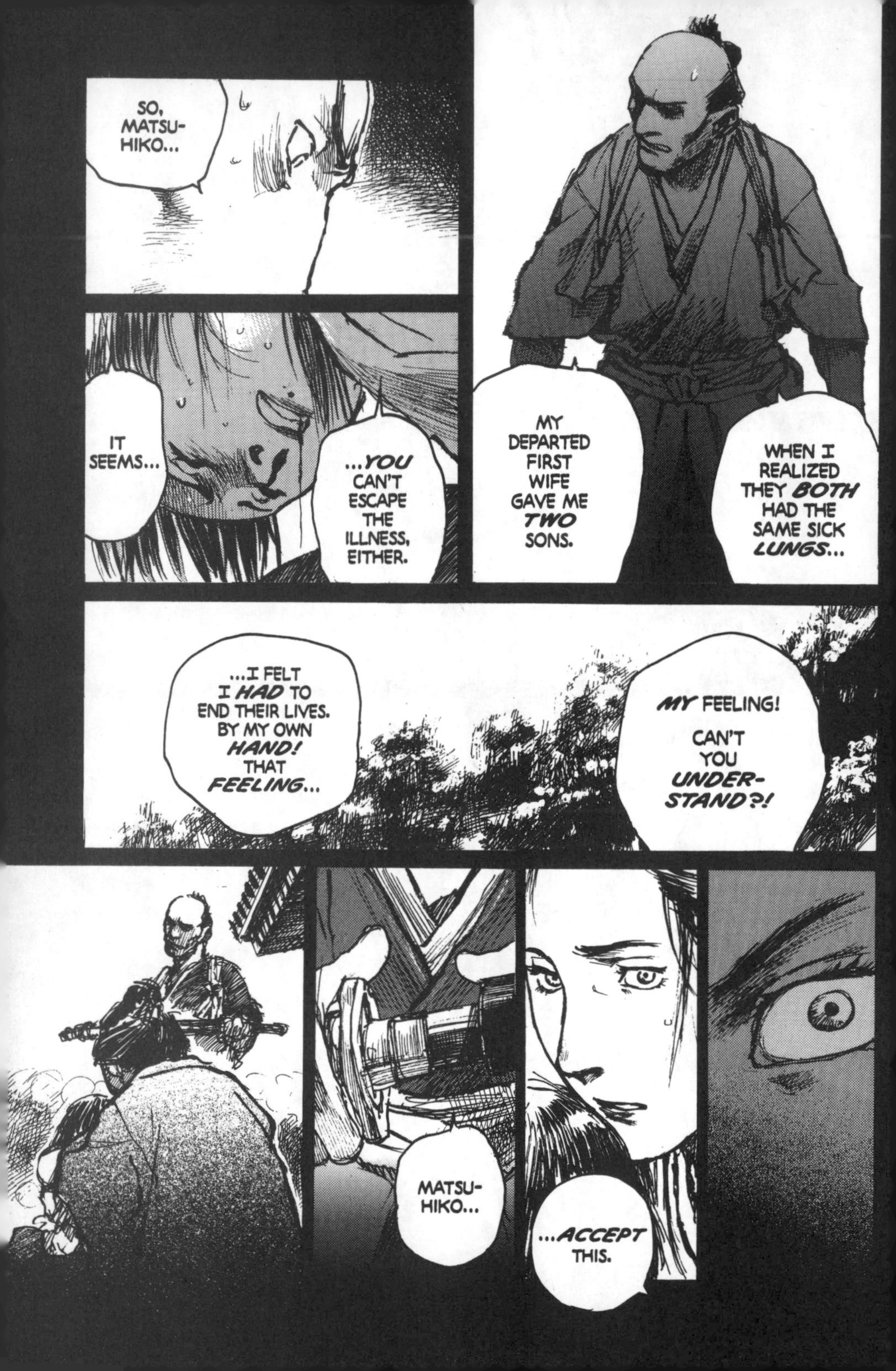
SO, MATSU-HIKO...
IT SEEMS...
...YOU CAN'T ESCAPE THE ILLNESS, EITHER.
MY DEPARTED FIRST WIFE GAVE ME TWO SONS.
WHEN I REALIZED THEY BOTH HAD THE SAME SICK LUNGS...
...I FELT I HAD TO END THEIR LIVES. BY MY OWN HAND! THAT FEELING...
MY FEELING! CAN'T YOU UNDER-STAND?!
MATSU-HIKO...
...ACCEPT THIS.

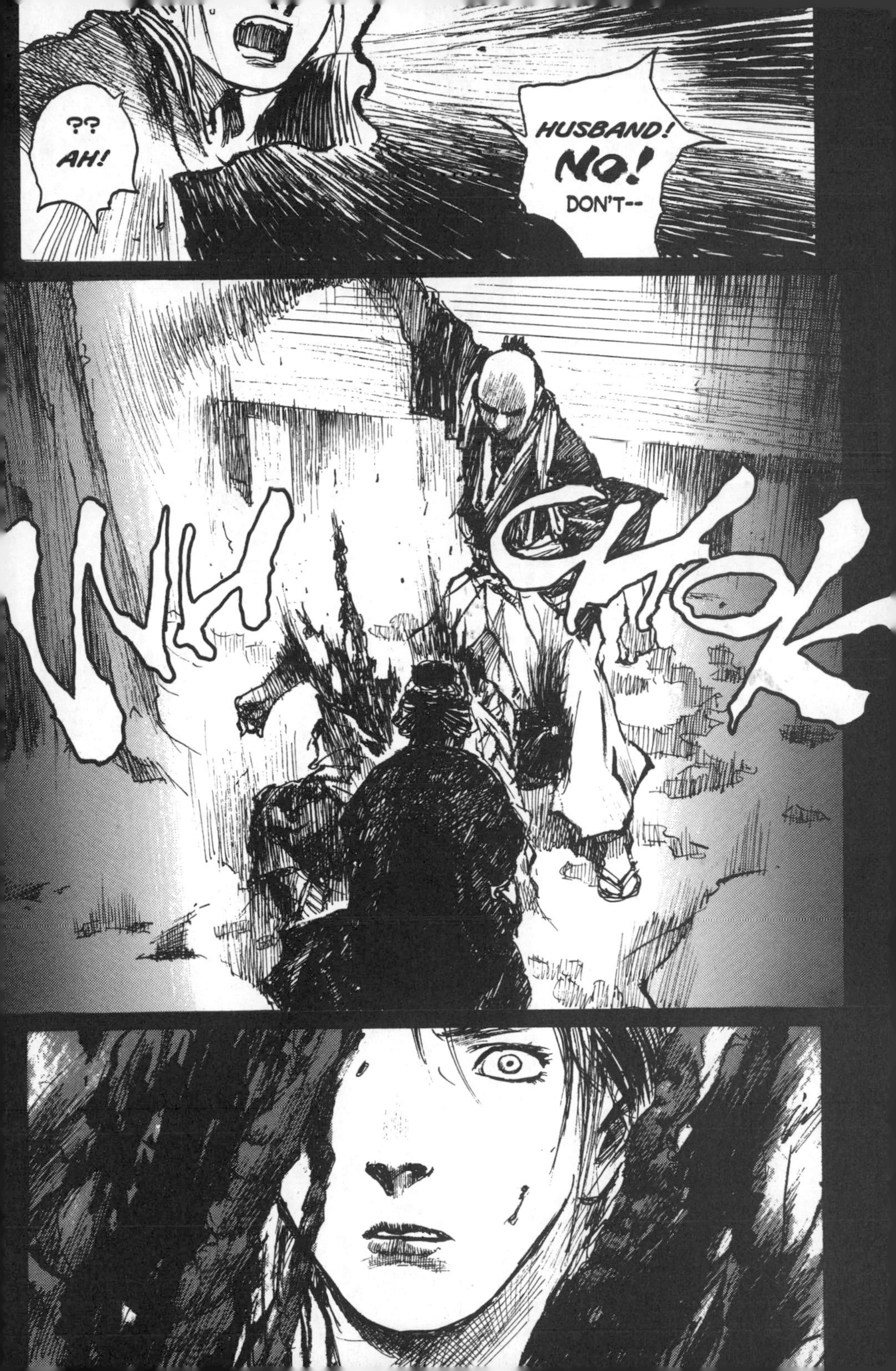
HUSBAND! NO! DON'T--
?? AH!
WHCHK

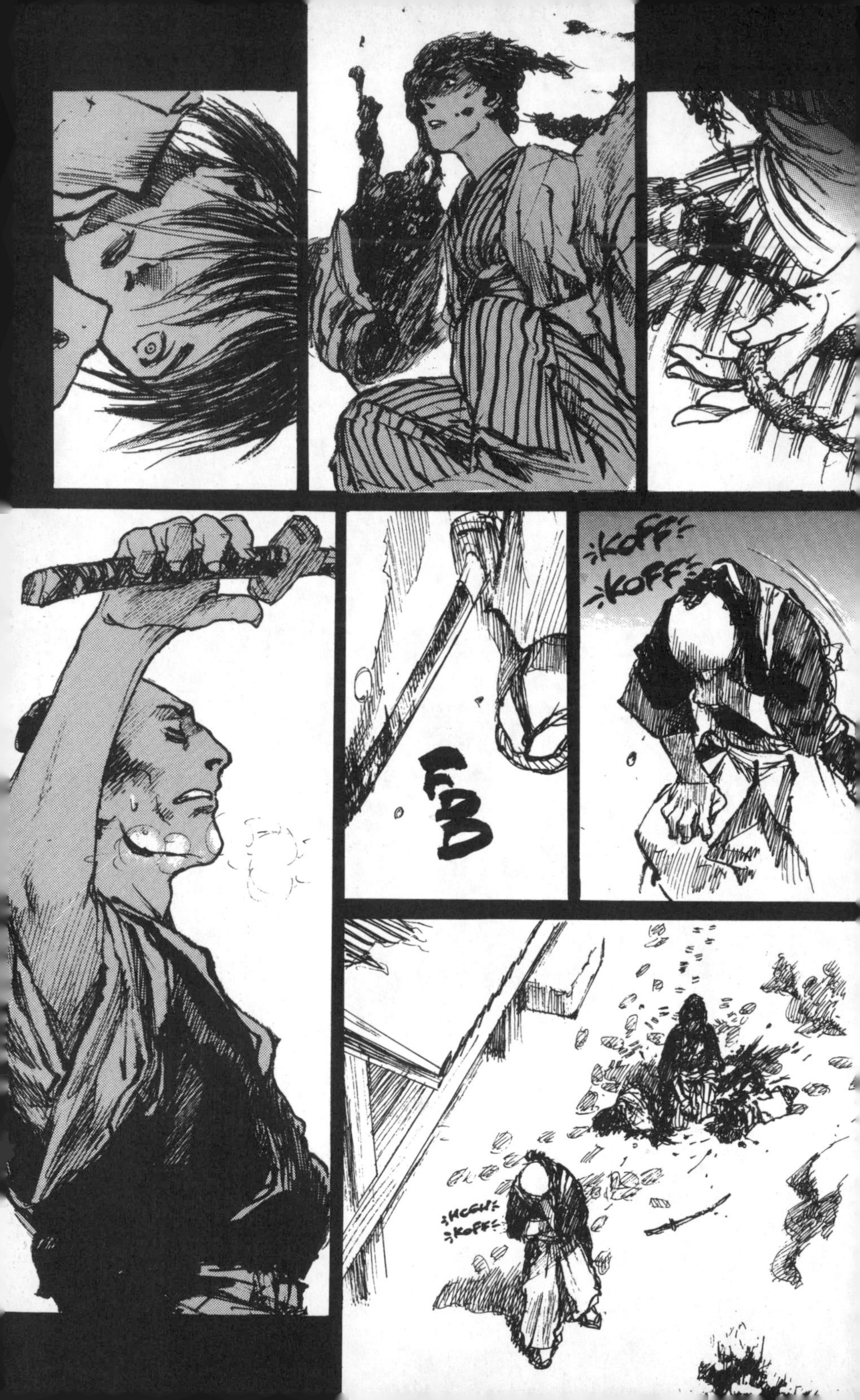
KOFF
KOFF
FBD
HGGH!
KOFF

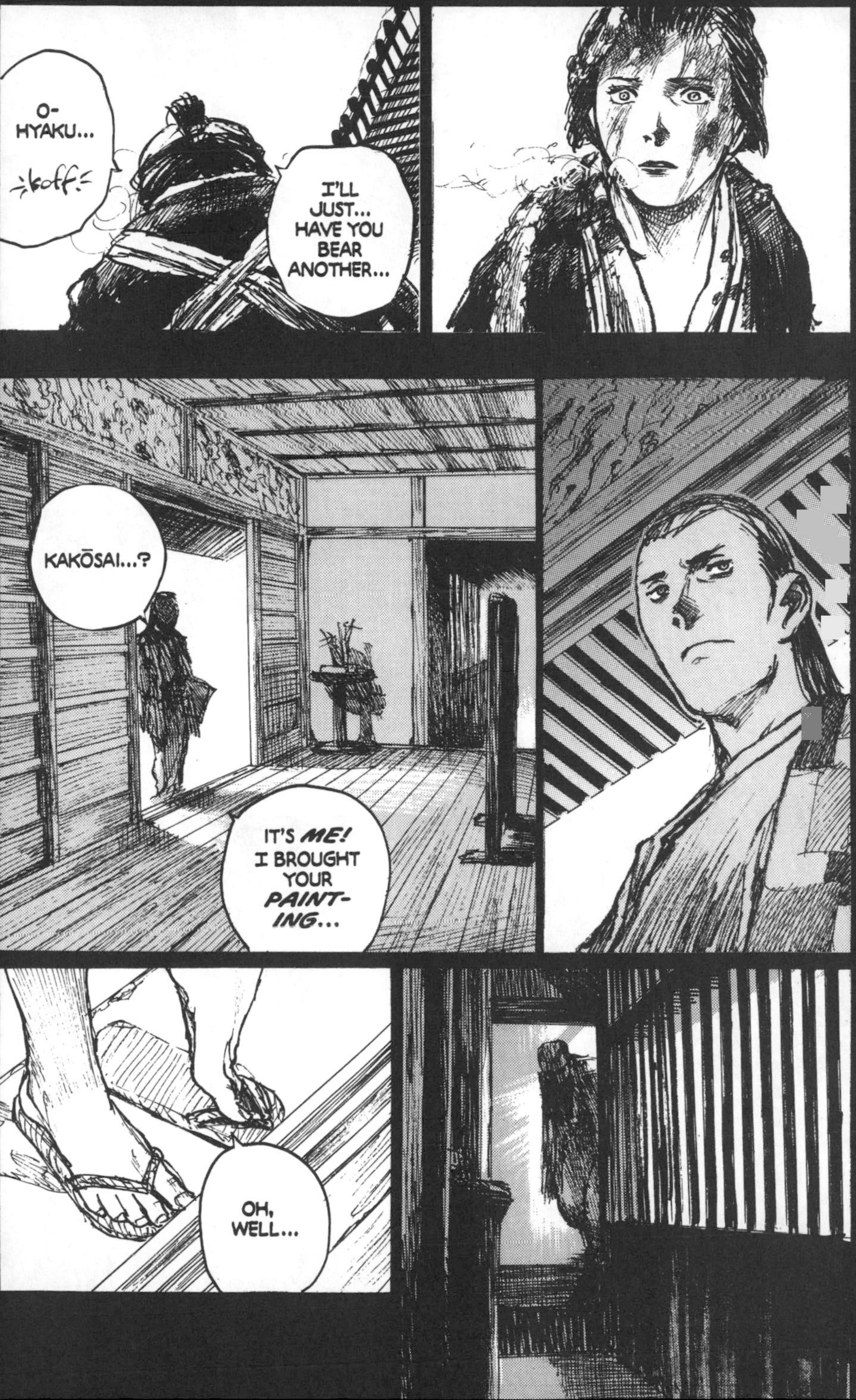
O-HYAKU...
koff
I'LL JUST... HAVE YOU BEAR ANOTHER...
KAKŌSAI...?
IT'S *ME!* I BROUGHT YOUR *PAINTING...*
OH, WELL...

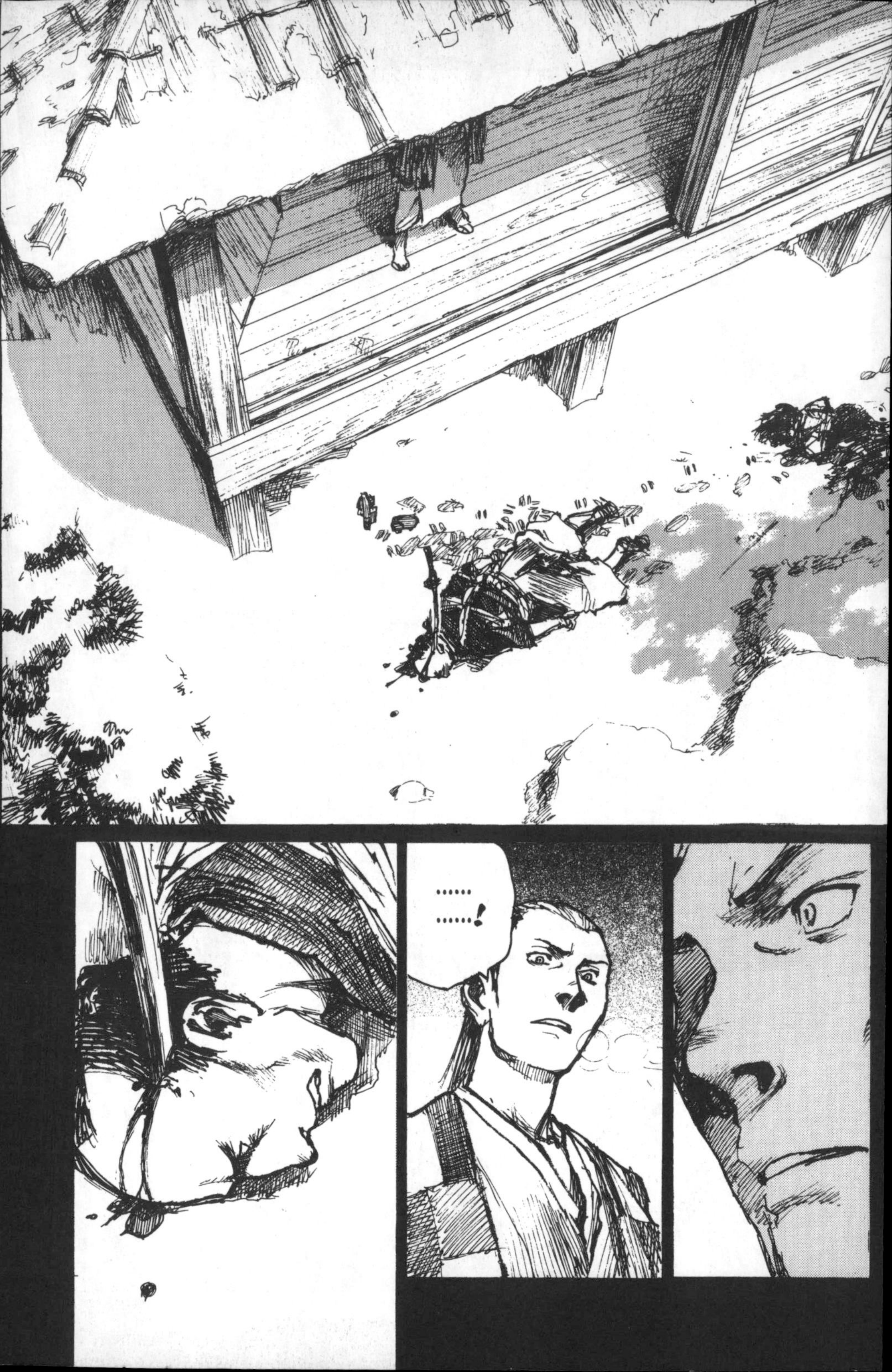
……
……!

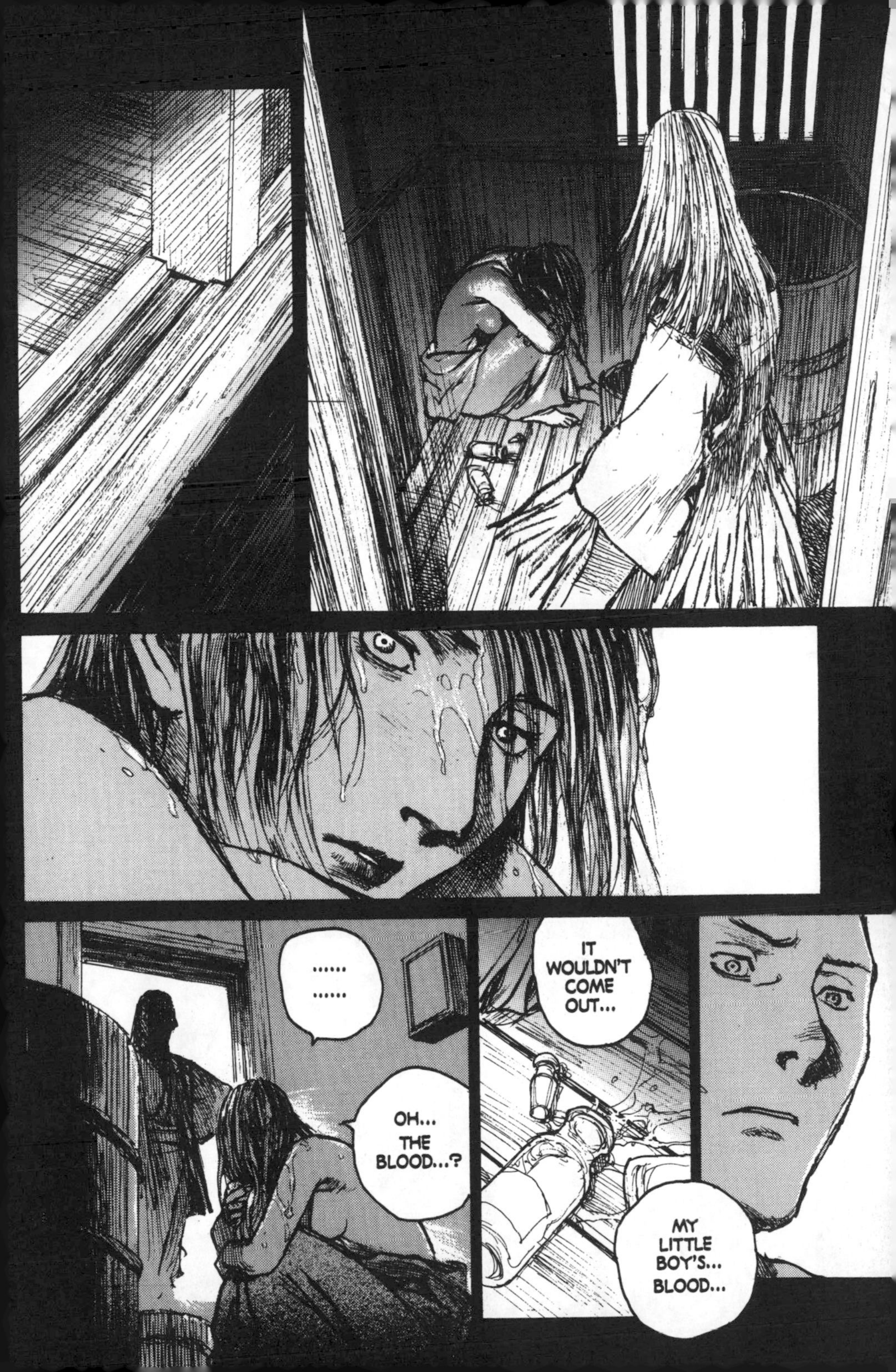
......
......
OH... THE BLOOD...?
IT WOULDN'T COME OUT...
MY LITTLE BOY'S... BLOOD...

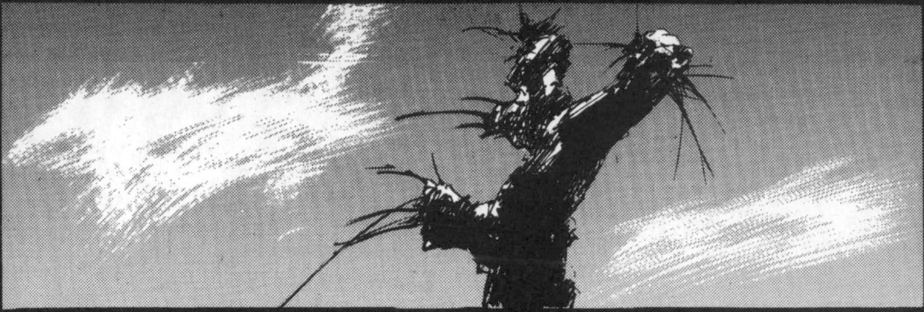

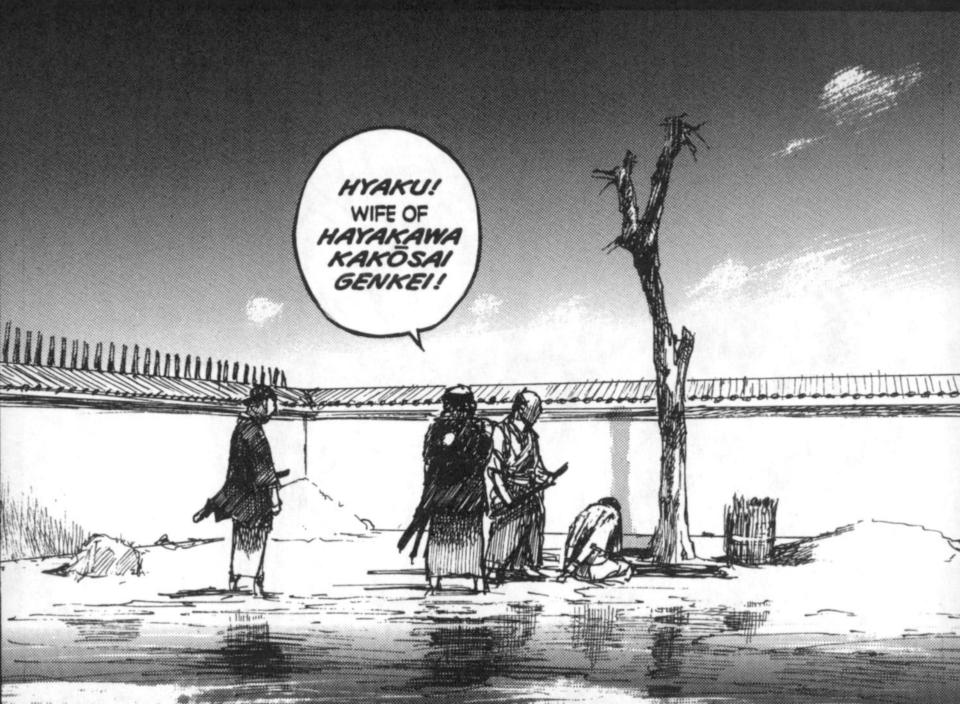
HYAKU! WIFE OF HAYAKAWA KAKŌSAI GENKEI!

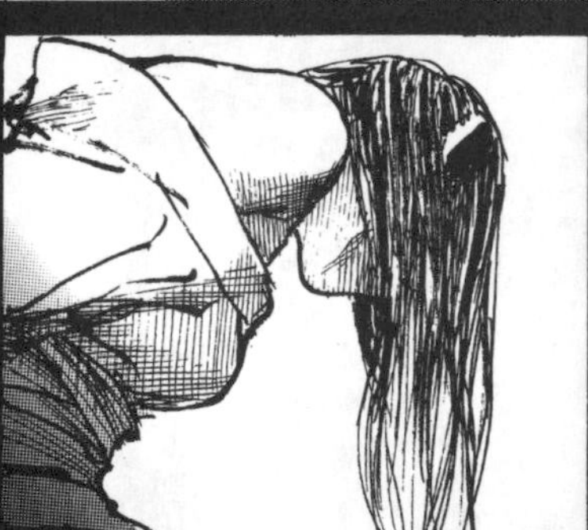

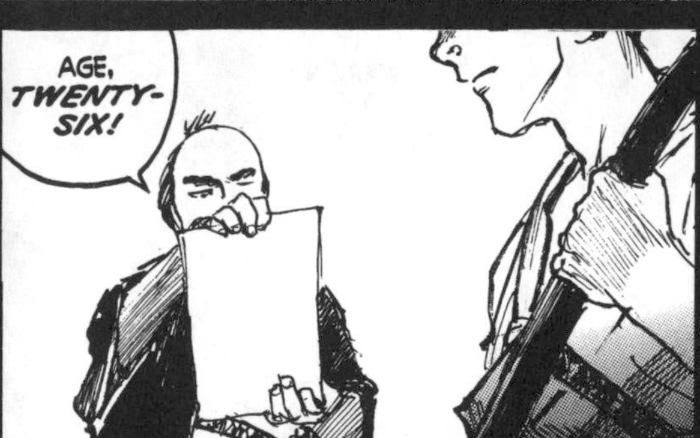
AGE, TWENTY-SIX!

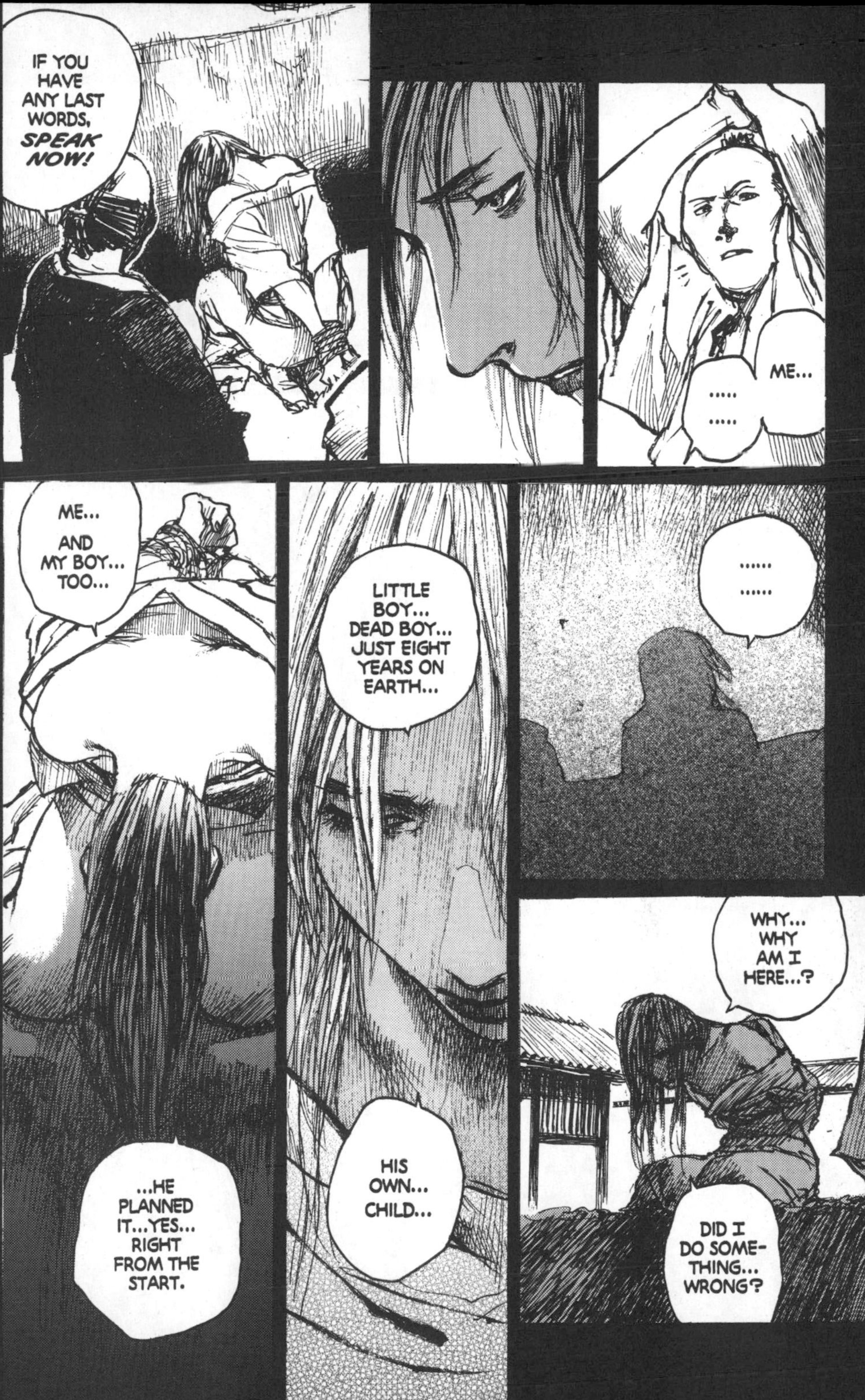
IF YOU HAVE ANY LAST WORDS, SPEAK NOW!
......
......
ME...
ME...
AND MY BOY... TOO...
...HE PLANNED IT...YES... RIGHT FROM THE START.
LITTLE BOY... DEAD BOY... JUST EIGHT YEARS ON EARTH...
HIS OWN... CHILD...
......
......
WHY... WHY AM I HERE...?
DID I DO SOME-THING... WRONG?

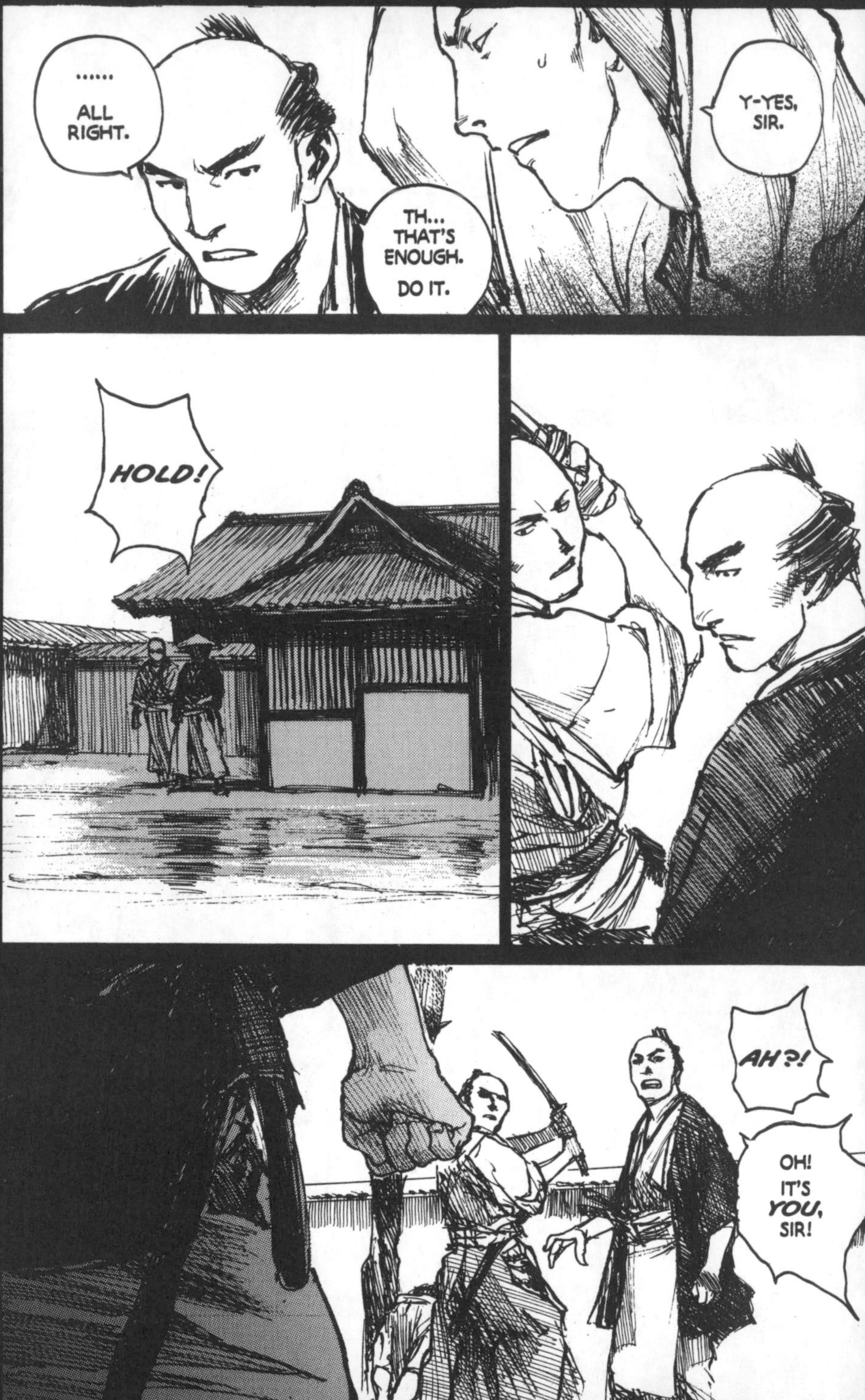
...... ALL RIGHT.
TH... THAT'S ENOUGH. DO IT.
Y-YES, SIR.
HOLD!
AH?!
OH! IT'S YOU, SIR!

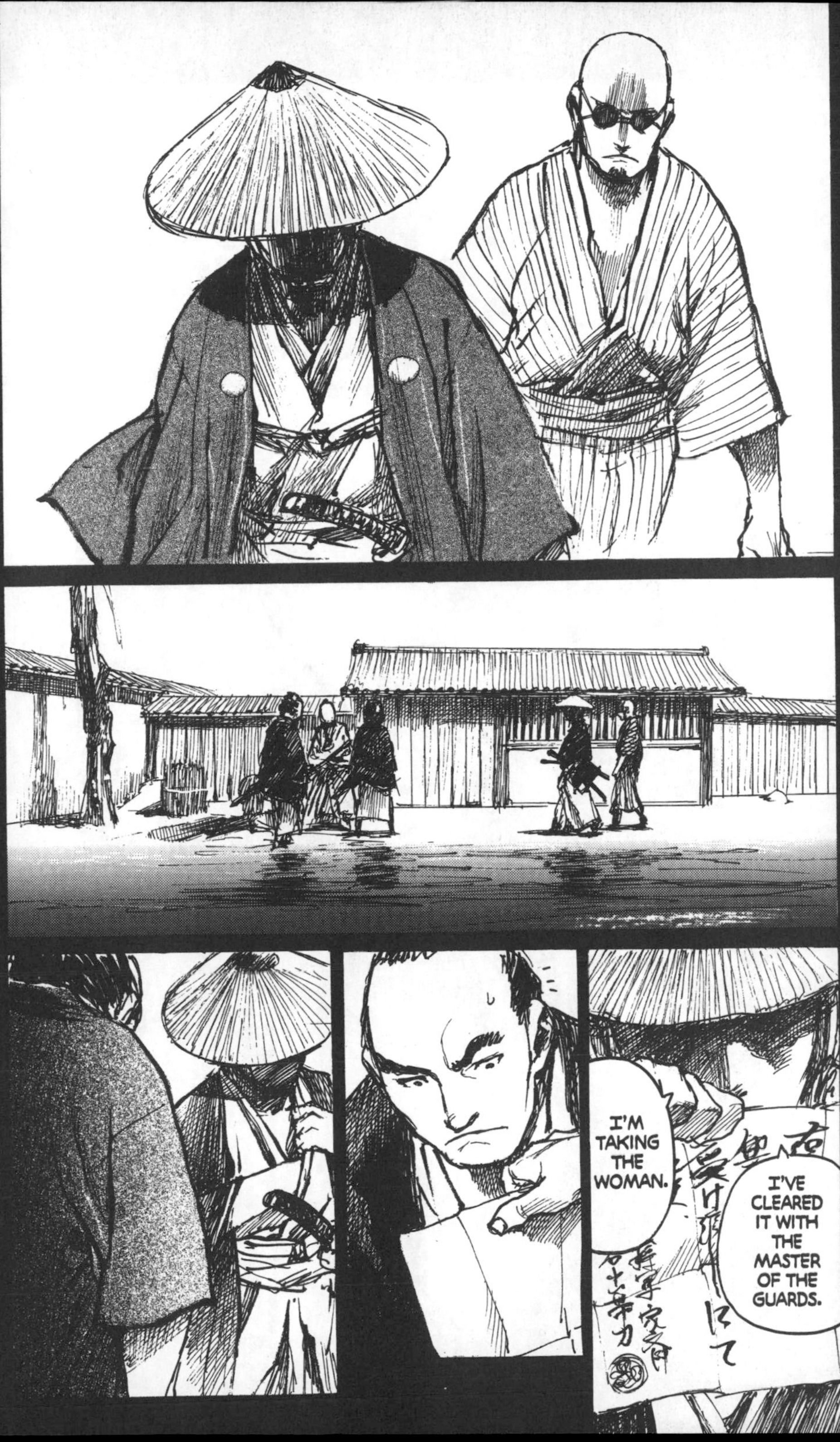
I'M TAKING THE WOMAN.
I'VE CLEARED IT WITH THE MASTER OF THE GUARDS.

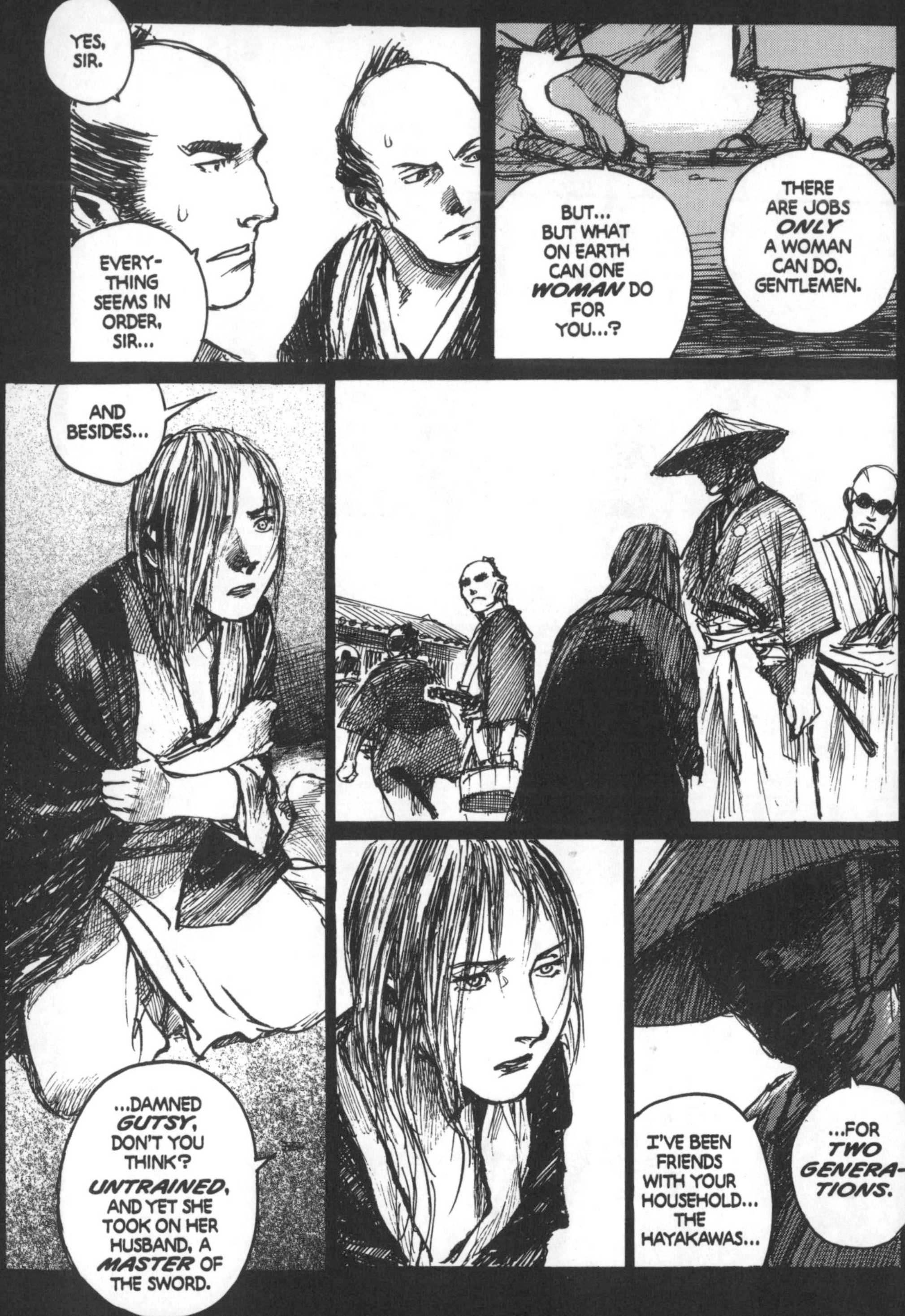
YES, SIR.
EVERY-THING SEEMS IN ORDER, SIR...
BUT... BUT WHAT ON EARTH CAN ONE *WOMAN* DO FOR YOU...?
THERE ARE JOBS *ONLY* A WOMAN CAN DO, GENTLEMEN.
AND BESIDES...
...DAMNED *GUTSY*, DON'T YOU THINK? *UNTRAINED*, AND YET SHE TOOK ON HER HUSBAND, A *MASTER* OF THE SWORD.
I'VE BEEN FRIENDS WITH YOUR HOUSEHOLD... THE HAYAKAWAS...
...FOR *TWO GENERATIONS*.

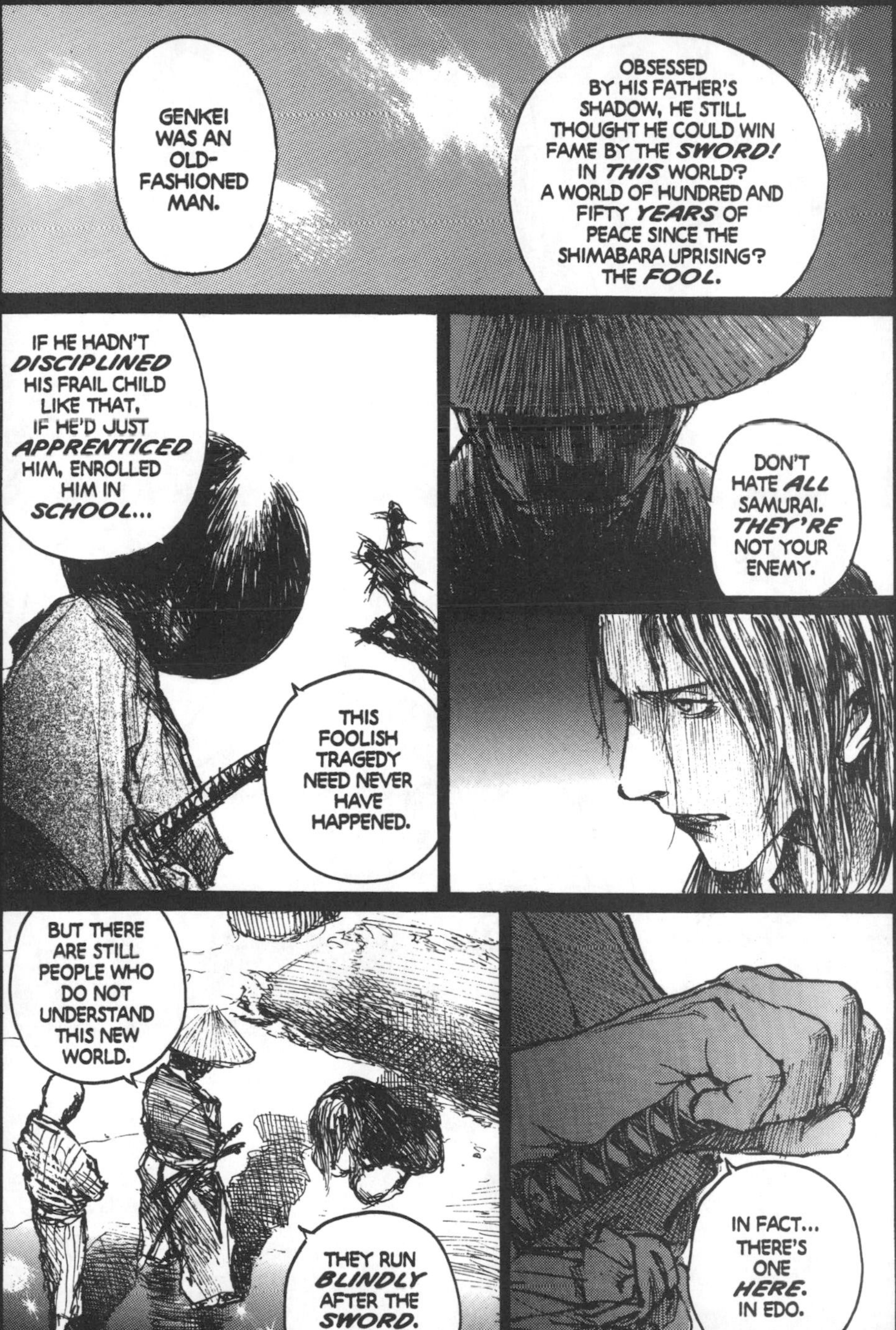
GENKEI WAS AN OLD-FASHIONED MAN.
OBSESSED BY HIS FATHER'S SHADOW, HE STILL THOUGHT HE COULD WIN FAME BY THE *SWORD!* IN *THIS* WORLD? A WORLD OF HUNDRED AND FIFTY *YEARS* OF PEACE SINCE THE SHIMABARA UPRISING? THE *FOOL*.
IF HE HADN'T *DISCIPLINED* HIS FRAIL CHILD LIKE THAT, IF HE'D JUST *APPRENTICED* HIM, ENROLLED HIM IN *SCHOOL*...
THIS FOOLISH TRAGEDY NEED NEVER HAVE HAPPENED.
DON'T HATE *ALL* SAMURAI. *THEY'RE* NOT YOUR ENEMY.
BUT THERE ARE STILL PEOPLE WHO DO NOT UNDERSTAND THIS NEW WORLD.
THEY RUN *BLINDLY* AFTER THE *SWORD*. INEXPLIC-ABLE.
IN FACT... THERE'S ONE *HERE*. IN EDO.

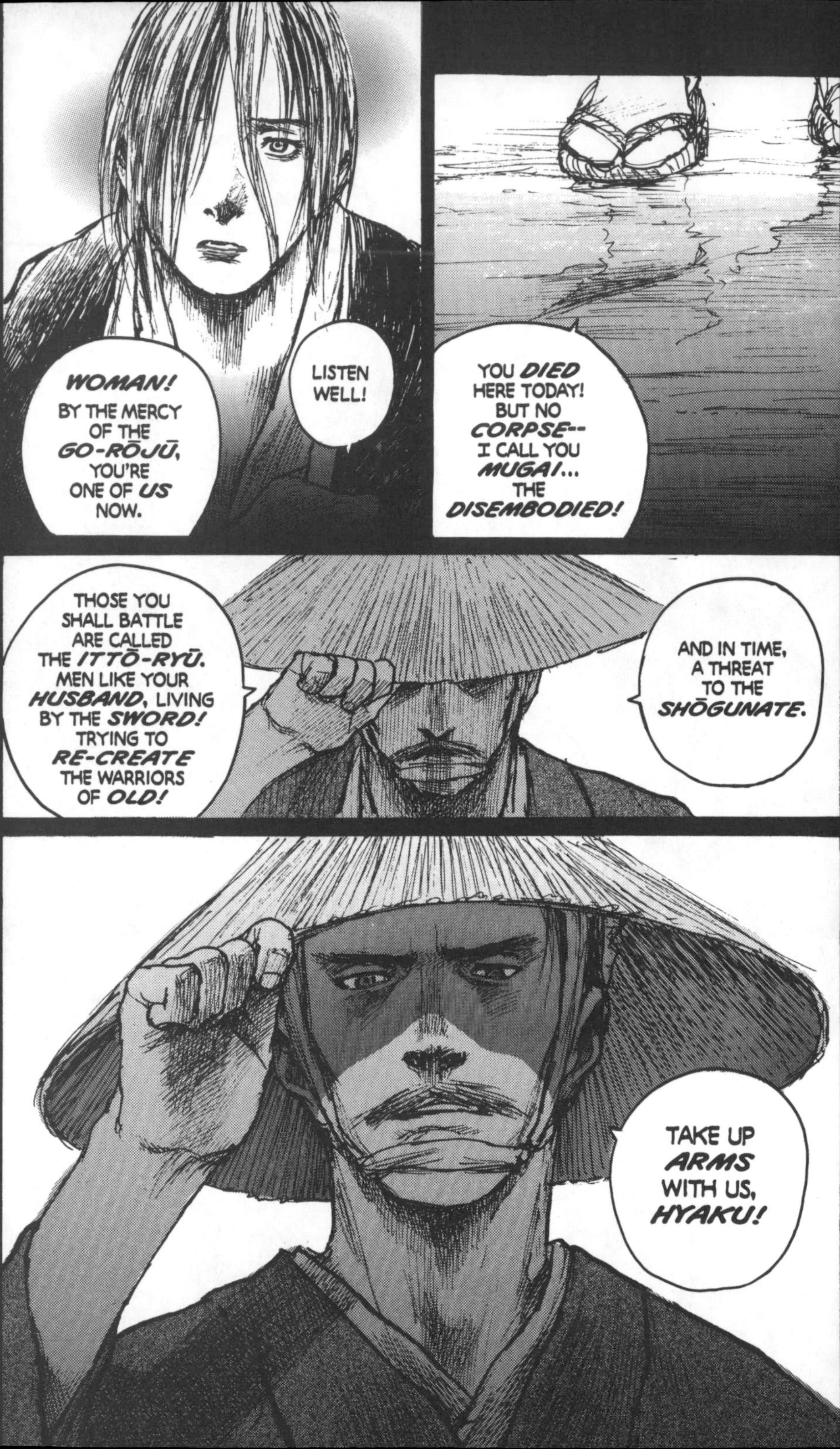
WOMAN! BY THE MERCY OF THE GO-RŌJŪ, YOU'RE ONE OF US NOW.
LISTEN WELL!
YOU DIED HERE TODAY! BUT NO CORPSE-- I CALL YOU MUGAI... THE DISEMBODIED!
THOSE YOU SHALL BATTLE ARE CALLED THE ITTŌ-RYŪ. MEN LIKE YOUR HUSBAND, LIVING BY THE SWORD! TRYING TO RE-CREATE THE WARRIORS OF OLD!
AND IN TIME, A THREAT TO THE SHŌGUNATE.
TAKE UP ARMS WITH US, HYAKU!

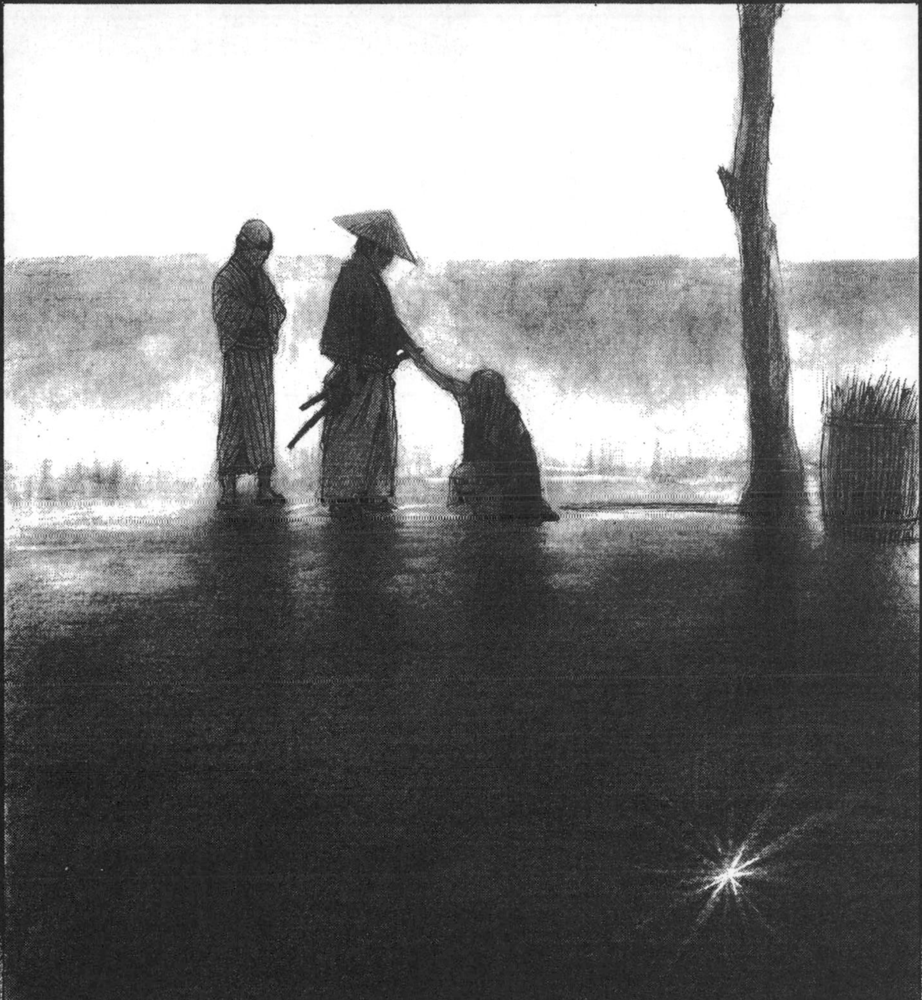
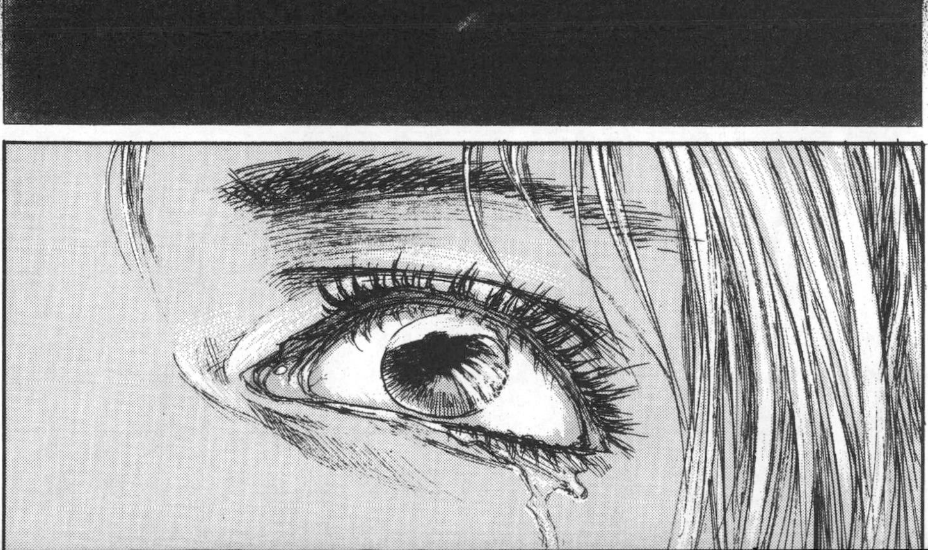

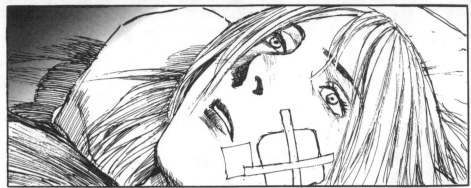

YOU'RE
BACK
WITH
US...?

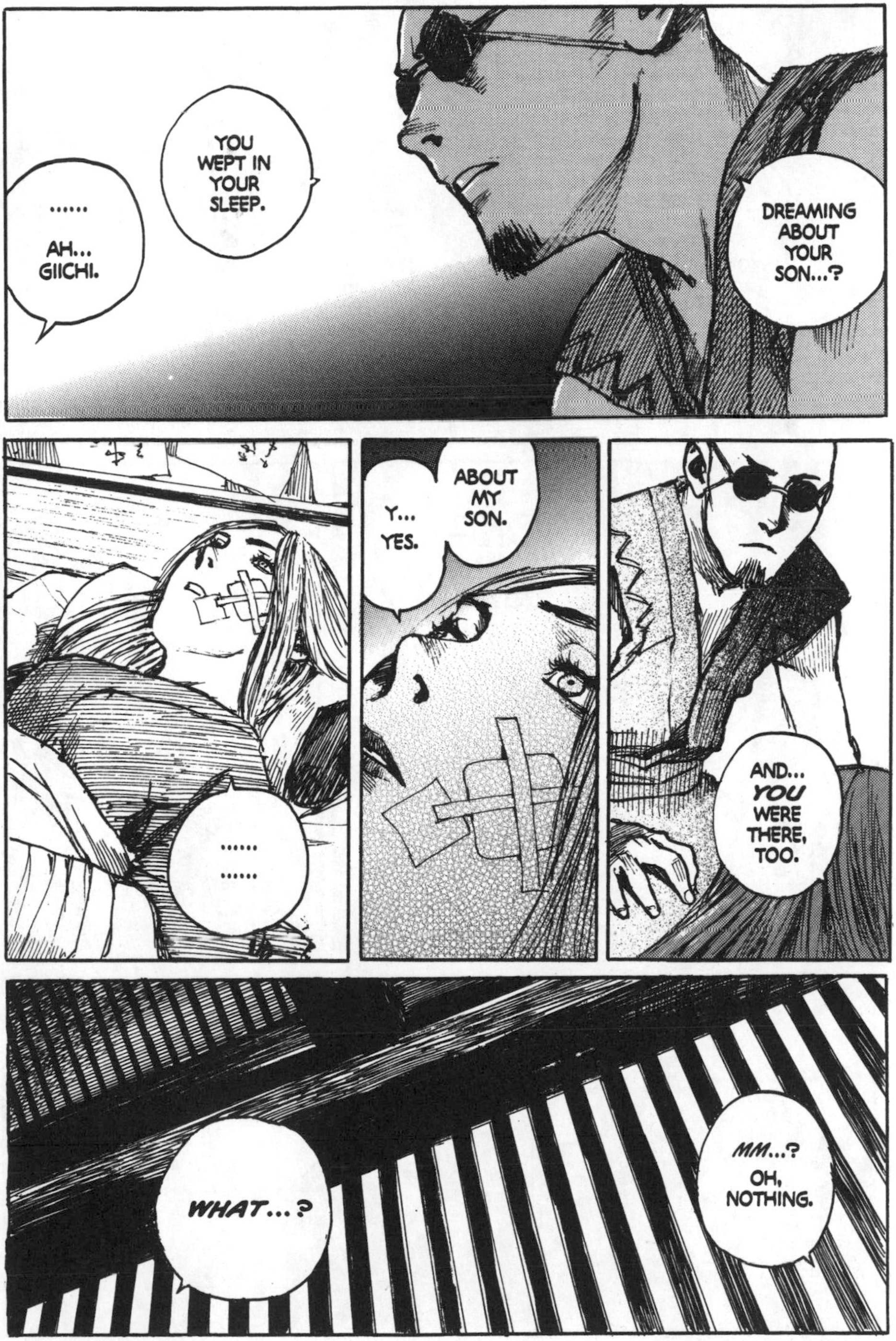

...... AH... GIICHI.
YOU WEPT IN YOUR SLEEP.
DREAMING ABOUT YOUR SON...?
......
......
Y... YES.
ABOUT MY SON.
AND... *YOU* WERE THERE, TOO.
WHAT...?
MM...? OH, NOTHING.

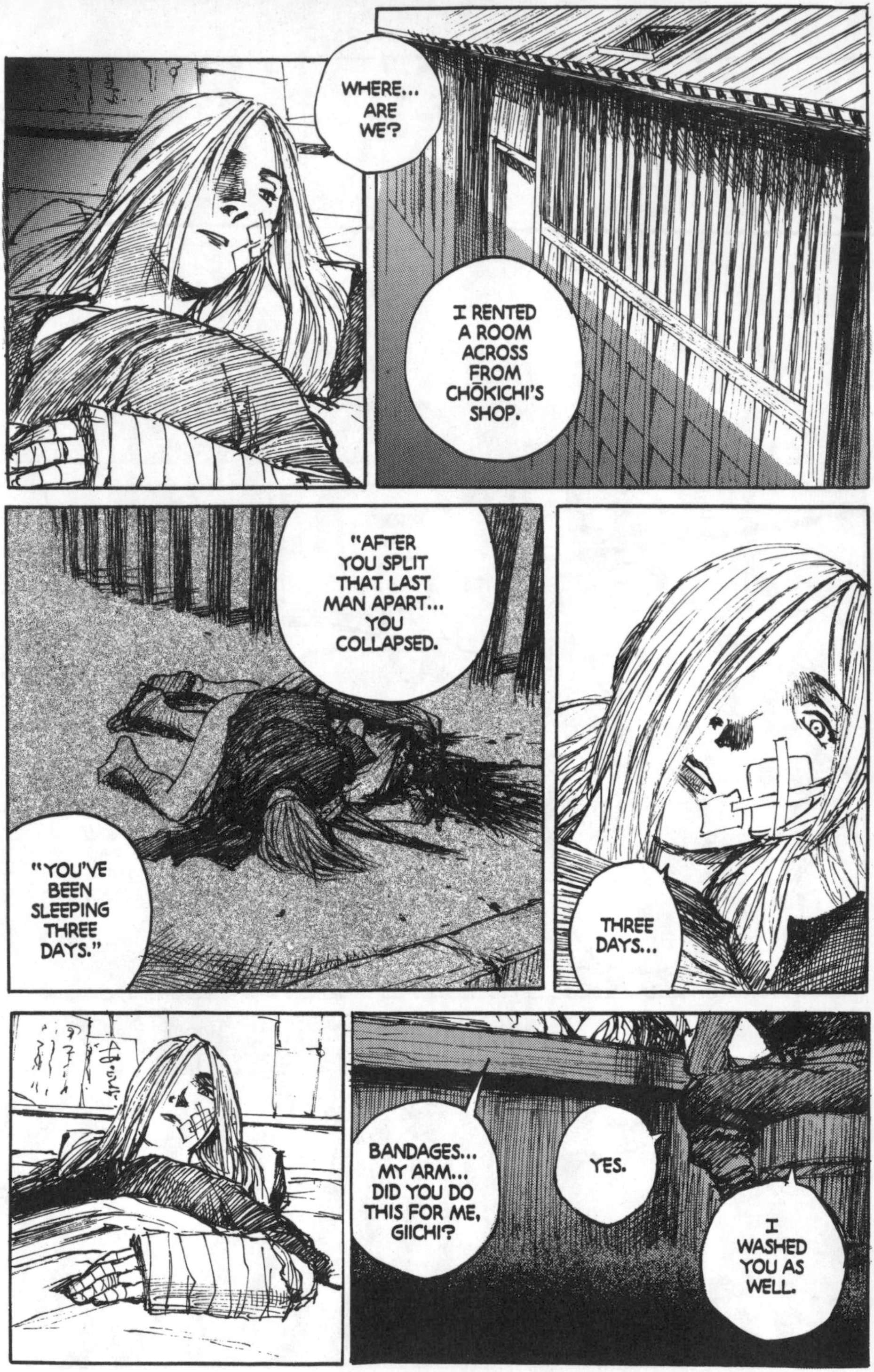
WHERE... ARE WE?
I RENTED A ROOM ACROSS FROM CHŌKICHI'S SHOP.
"AFTER YOU SPLIT THAT LAST MAN APART... YOU COLLAPSED.
"YOU'VE BEEN SLEEPING THREE DAYS."
THREE DAYS...
BANDAGES... MY ARM... DID YOU DO THIS FOR ME, GIICHI?
YES.
I WASHED YOU AS WELL.

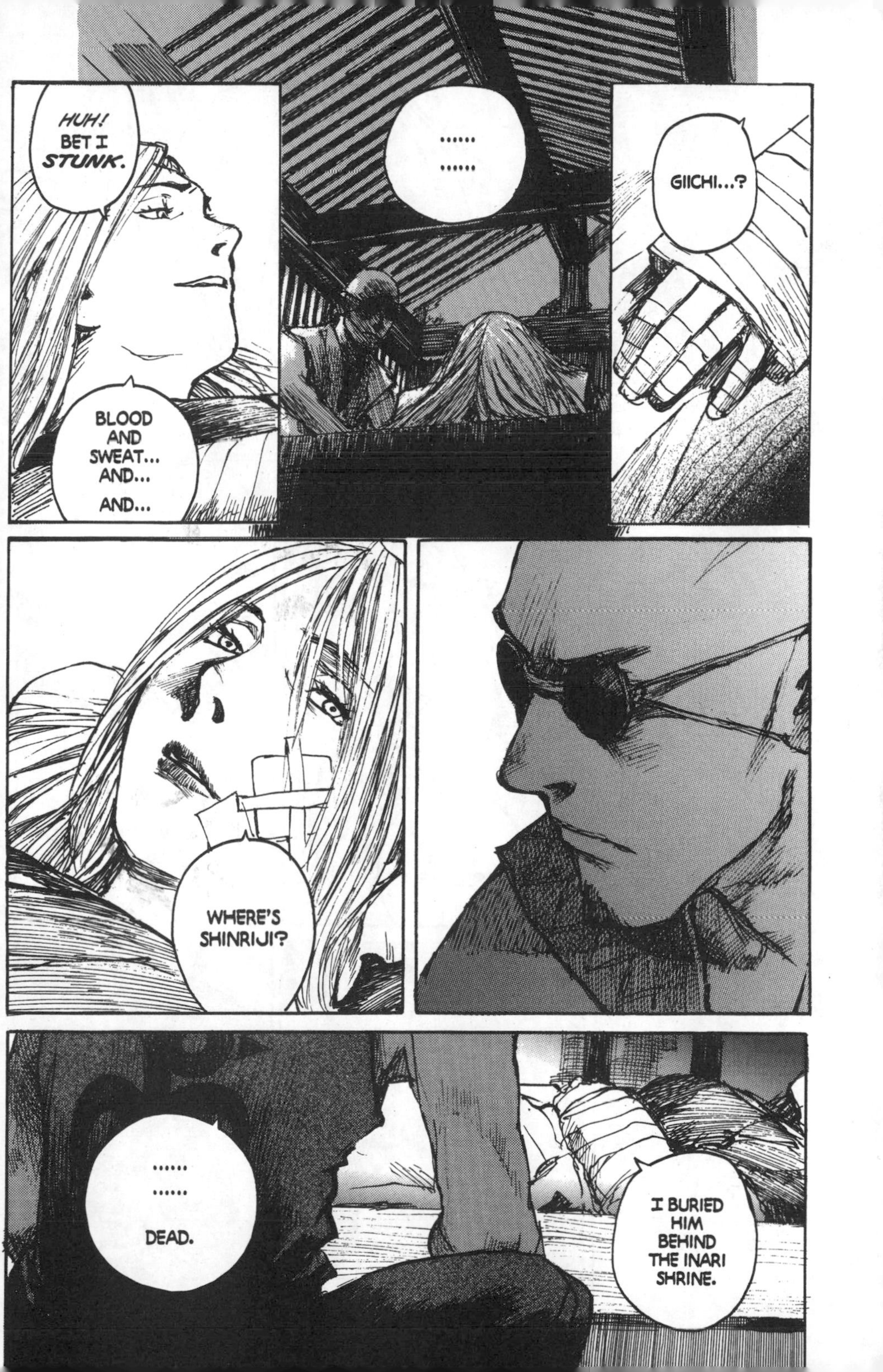
HUH! BET I STUNK.
BLOOD AND SWEAT... AND... AND...
......
......
GIICHI...?
WHERE'S SHINRIJI?
......
......
DEAD.
I BURIED HIM BEHIND THE INARI SHRINE.

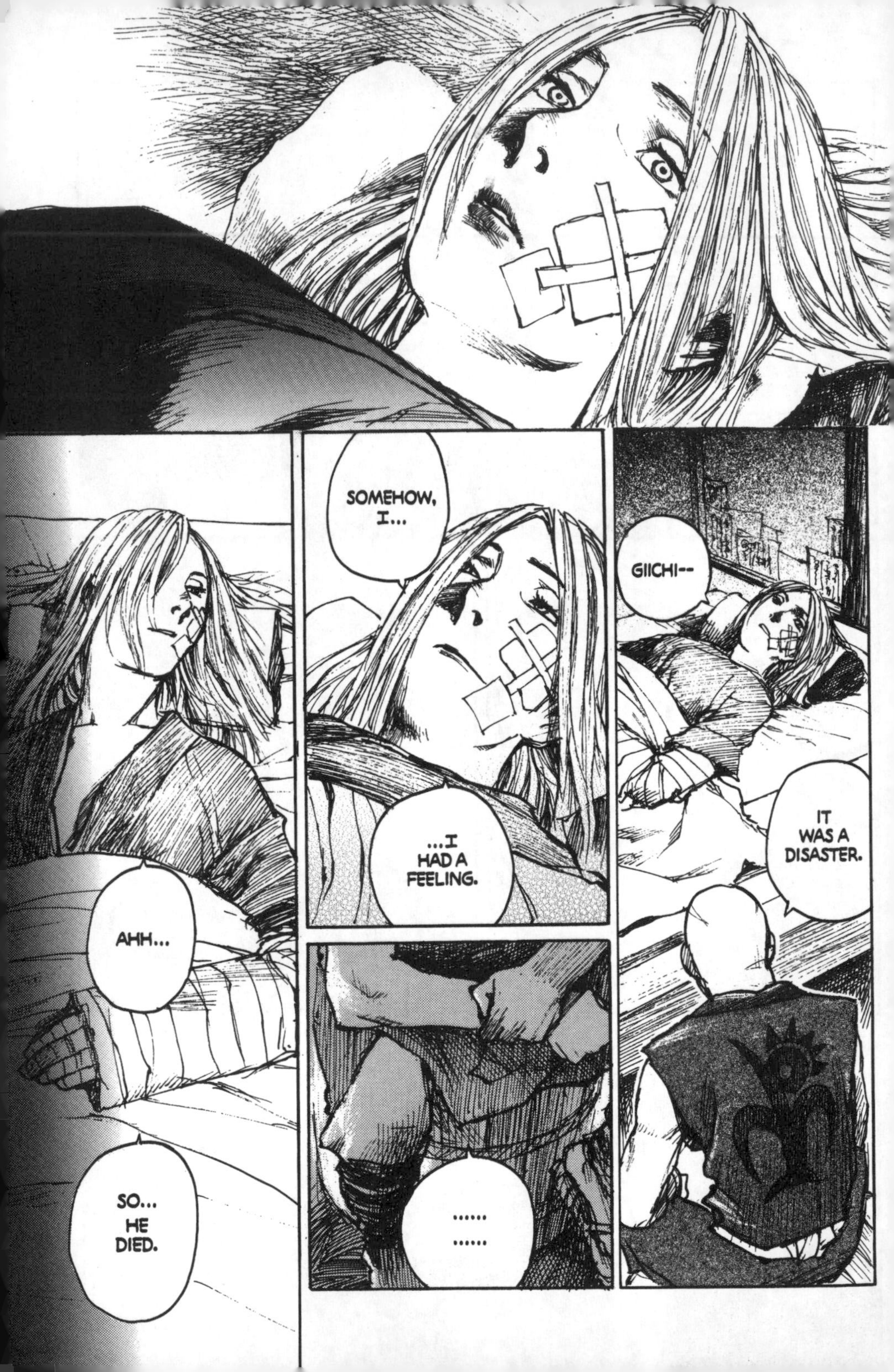
GIICHI--
IT WAS A DISASTER.
SOMEHOW, I...
...I HAD A FEELING.
....
AHH...
SO... HE DIED.

NO... I WOULDN'T CALL IT A *DISASTER*.

WE JUST GOT A LITTLE...

...*CARE-LESS*.

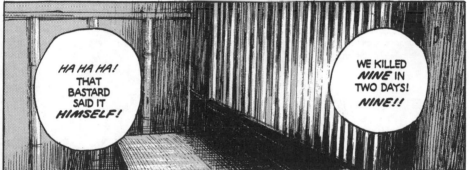

HA HA HA! THAT BASTARD SAID IT *HIMSELF!*

WE KILLED *NINE* IN TWO DAYS! *NINE!!*

AND ALL *WE* LOST WAS...

...WAS *SHINRIJI*. ONE LIFE AND... A BROKEN ARM.

NOT A BAD *TRADE*... WOULDN'T YOU SAY?

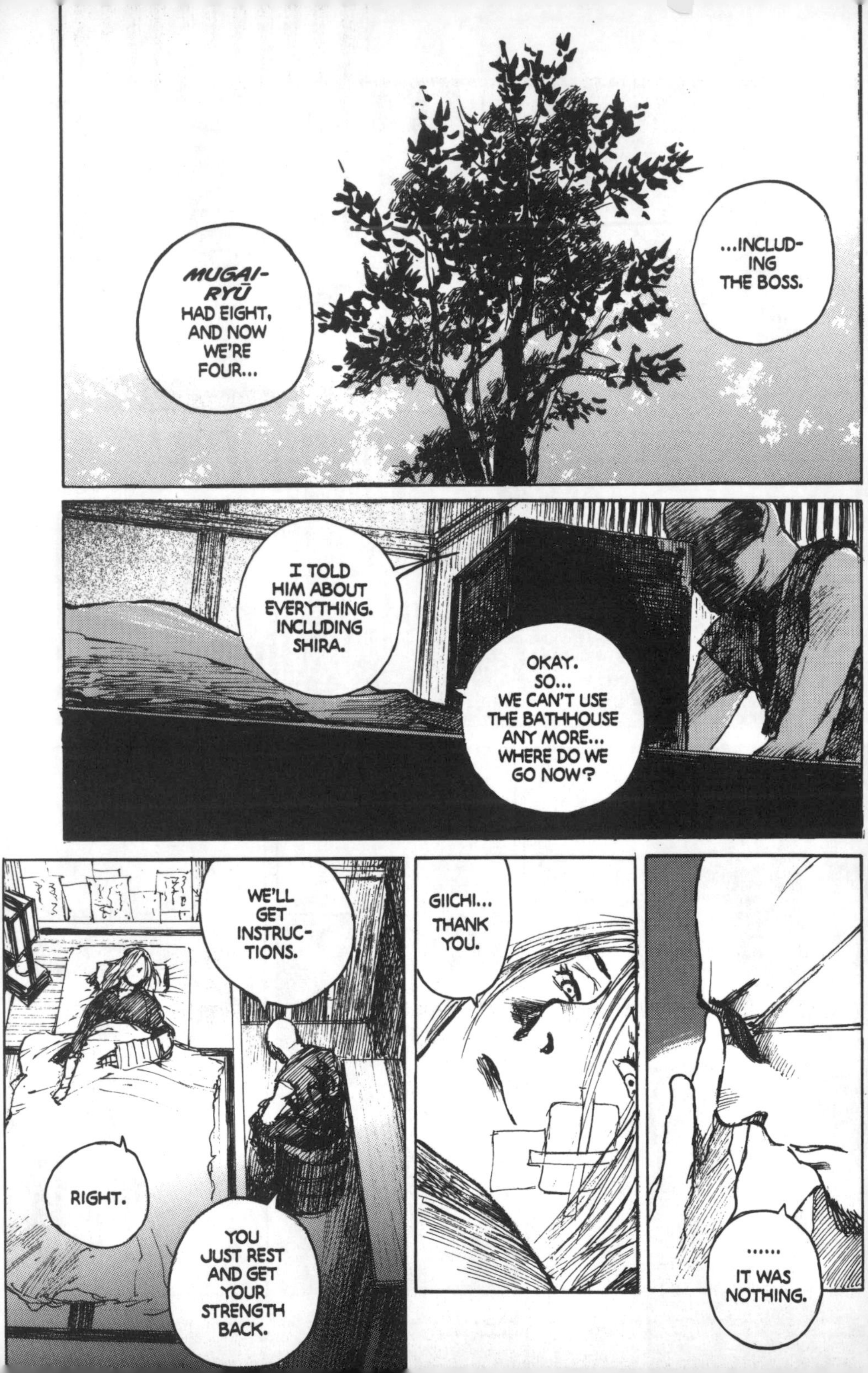

MUGAI-RYŪ HAD EIGHT, AND NOW WE'RE FOUR...
...INCLUDING THE BOSS.
I TOLD HIM ABOUT EVERYTHING. INCLUDING SHIRA.
OKAY. SO... WE CAN'T USE THE BATHHOUSE ANY MORE... WHERE DO WE GO NOW?
WE'LL GET INSTRUCTIONS.
RIGHT.
YOU JUST REST AND GET YOUR STRENGTH BACK.
GIICHI... THANK YOU.
......
IT WAS NOTHING.

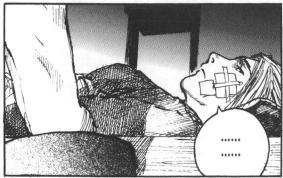

......
......

UM...
......
......

I'M A
LITTLE
HUNGRY.

CHŌKICHI'S
STILL IN
THE
SHOP.

SHALL I
HAVE HIM
MAKE YOU
SOME-
THING...?

MAYBE
SOME
RICE
GRUEL?

SURE...
ANY-
THING.

SORRY.

IT'S
NOTHING.

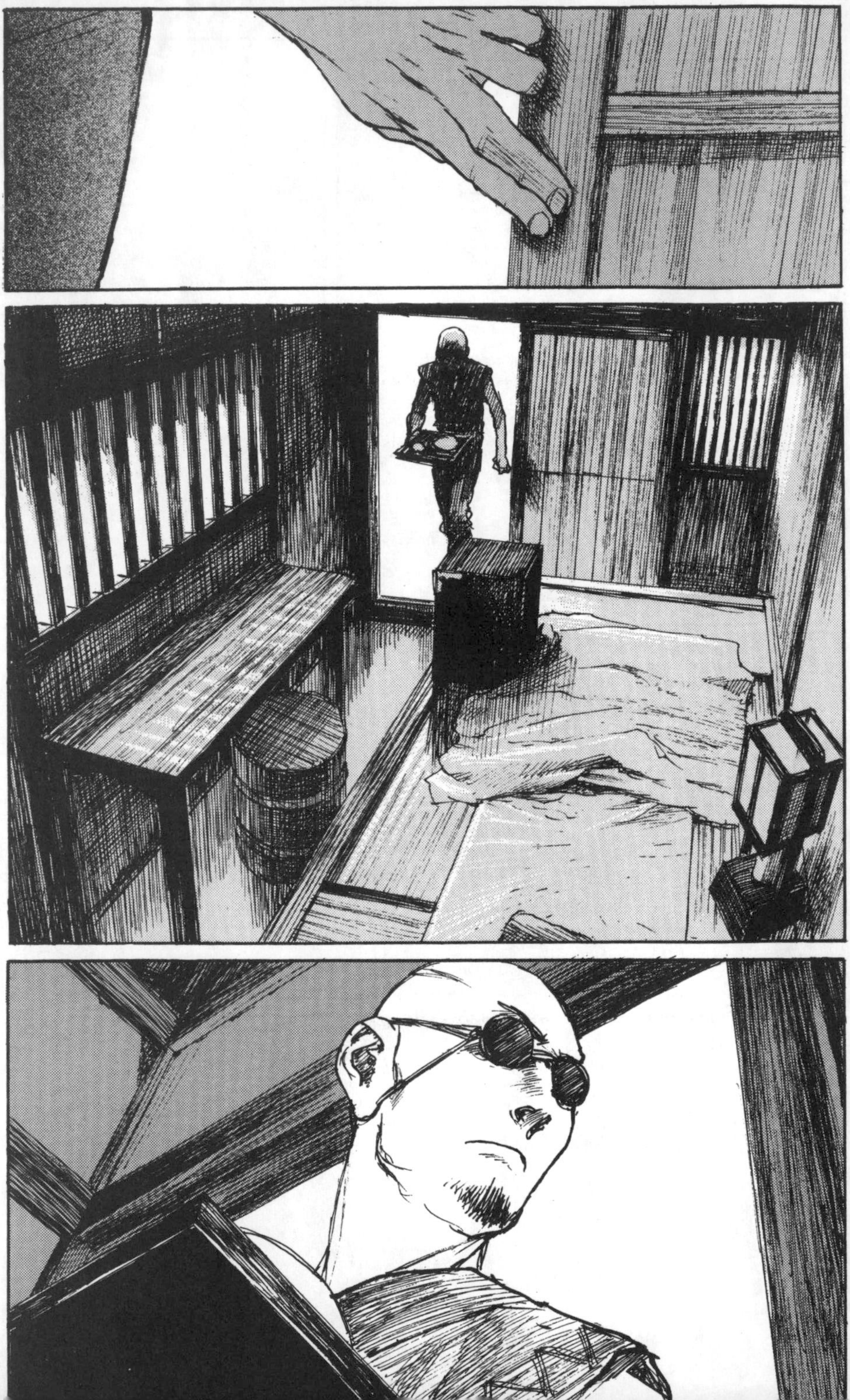

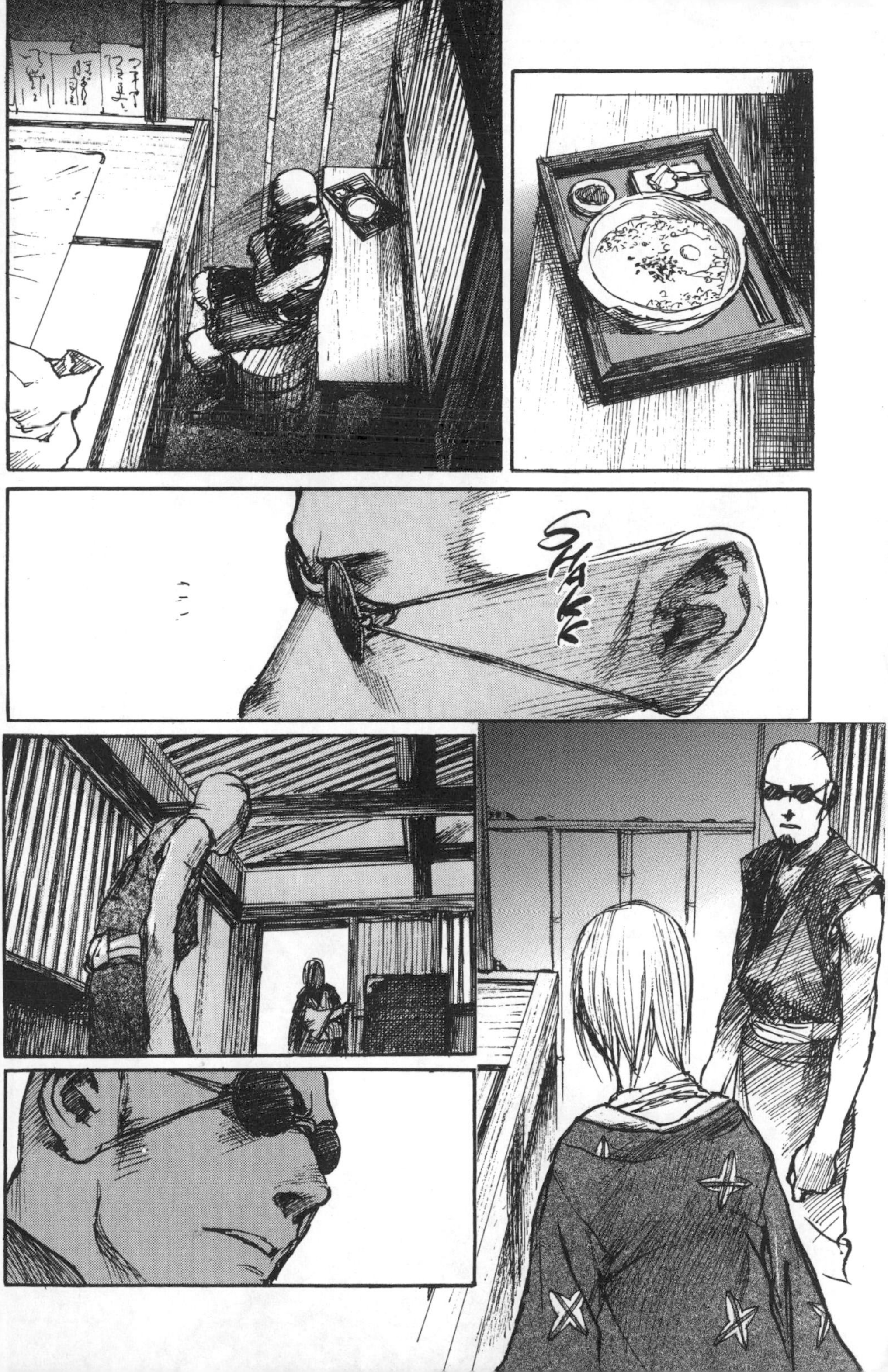
SHAKK

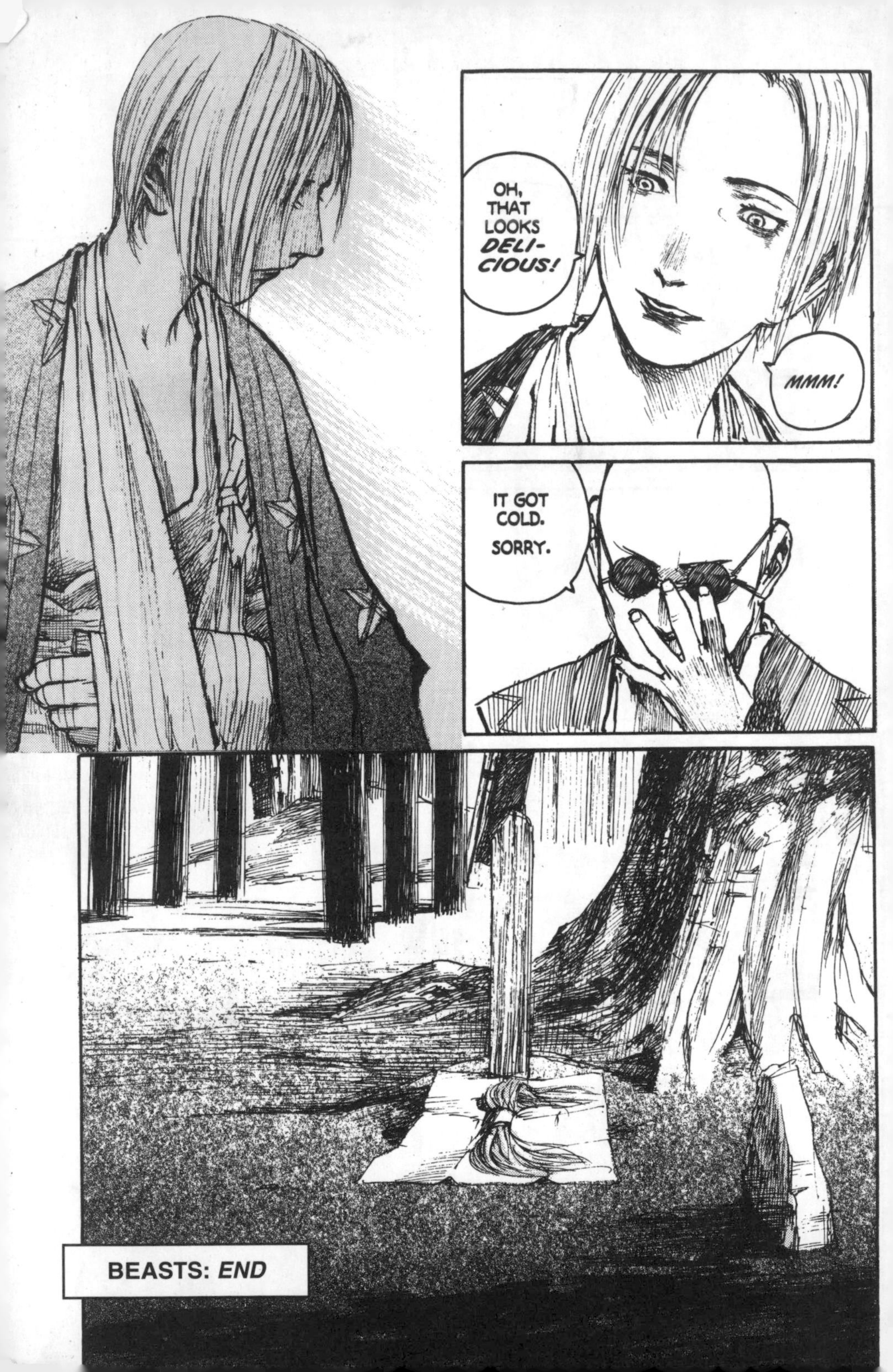
OH, THAT LOOKS DELICIOUS!
MMM!
IT GOT COLD. SORRY.
BEASTS: END